Infocommunication Skills as a Rehabilitation and Social Reintegration Tool for Inmates

Lídia Oliveira
University of Aveiro, Portugal

Daniela Graça
University of Aveiro, Portugal

A volume in the Advances in Religious and Cultural Studies (ARCS) Book Series

IGI Global
DISSEMINATOR OF KNOWLEDGE

Published in the United States of America by
IGI Global
Information Science Reference (an imprint of IGI Global)
701 E. Chocolate Avenue
Hershey PA, USA 17033
Tel: 717-533-8845
Fax: 717-533-8661
E-mail: cust@igi-global.com
Web site: http://www.igi-global.com

Library of Congress Cataloging-in-Publication Data

Names: Oliveira, Lidia, 1968- editor. | Graca, Daniela, 1980- editor.
Title: Infocommunication skills as a rehabilitation and social reintegration tool for inmates / Lidia Oliveira and Daniela Graca, editors.
Description: Hershey : Information Science Reference, [2018] | Includes bibliographical references.
Identifiers: LCCN 2017060871| ISBN 9781522559757 (hardcover) | ISBN 9781522559764 (ebook)
Subjects: LCSH: Criminals--Rehabilitation. | Mass media and criminal justice. | Computer literacy.
Classification: LCC HV9275 .I54 2018 | DDC 365/.661--dc23 LC record available at https://lccn.loc.gov/2017060871

This book is published in the IGI Global book series Advances in Religious and Cultural Studies (ARCS) (ISSN: 2475-675X; eISSN: 2475-6768)

British Cataloguing in Publication Data
A Cataloguing in Publication record for this book is available from the British Library.

For electronic access to this publication, please contact: eresources@igi-global.com.

Advances in Religious and Cultural Studies (ARCS) Book Series

ISSN:2475-675X
EISSN:2475-6768

Editor-in-Chief: Nancy Erbe, California State University-Dominguez Hills, USA

MISSION

In the era of globalization, the diversity of the world and various cultures becomes apparent as cross-cultural interactions turn into a daily occurrence for individuals in all professions. Understanding these differences is necessary in order to promote effective partnerships and interactions between those from different religious and cultural backgrounds.

The **Advances in Religious and Cultural Studies (ARCS)** book series brings together a collection of scholarly publications on topics pertaining to religious beliefs, culture, population studies, and sociology. Books published within this series are ideal for professionals, theorists, researchers, and students seeking the latest research on collective human behavior in terms of religion, social structure, and cultural identity and practice.

COVERAGE

- Sociology
- Cultural Identity
- Globalization and Culture
- Group Behavior
- Gender
- Human Rights and Ethics
- Cross-Cultural Interaction
- Social Stratification and Classes
- Impact of Religion on Society
- Cults and Religious Movements

IGI Global is currently accepting manuscripts for publication within this series. To submit a proposal for a volume in this series, please contact our Acquisition Editors at Acquisitions@igi-global.com or visit: http://www.igi-global.com/publish/.

The Advances in Religious and Cultural Studies (ARCS) Book Series (ISSN 2475-675X) is published by IGI Global, 701 E. Chocolate Avenue, Hershey, PA 17033-1240, USA, www.igi-global.com. This series is composed of titles available for purchase individually; each title is edited to be contextually exclusive from any other title within the series. For pricing and ordering information please visit http://www.igi-global.com/book-series/advances-religious-cultural-studies/84269. Postmaster: Send all address changes to above address.

Titles in this Series

For a list of additional titles in this series, please visit:
https://www.igi-global.com/book-series/advances-religious-cultural-studies/84269

Handbook of Research on Heritage Management and Preservation
Patrick Ngulube (University of South Africa, South Africa)
Information Science Reference • ©2018 • 508pp • H/C (ISBN: 9781522531371) • US $265.00

Redefining Translation and Interpretation in Cultural Evolution
Olaf Immanuel Seel (Ionian University of Corfu, Greece)
Information Science Reference • ©2018 • 310pp • H/C (ISBN: 9781522528326) • US $195.00

Educational Development and Infrastructure for Immigrants and Refugees
Şefika Şule Erçetin (Lancaster University, UK & Hacettepe University, Turkey)
Information Science Reference • ©2018 • 375pp • H/C (ISBN: 9781522533252) • US $195.00

Social Considerations of Migration Movements and Immigration Policies
Şefika Şule Erçetin (Lancaster University, UK & Hacettepe University, Turkey)
Information Science Reference • ©2018 • 283pp • H/C (ISBN: 9781522533221) • US $195.00

Global Ideologies Surrounding Children's Rights and Social Justice
Icarbord Tshabangu (Leeds Trinity University, UK)
Information Science Reference • ©2018 • 296pp • H/C (ISBN: 9781522525783) • US $195.00

Interpretation of Visual Arts Across Societies and Political Culture Emerging Research ...
Mika Markus Merviö (Kibi International University, Japan)
Information Science Reference • ©2017 • 110pp • H/C (ISBN: 9781522525547) • US $115.00

Family Dynamics and Romantic Relationships in a Changing Society
Nava R. Silton (Marymount Manhattan College, USA)
Information Science Reference • ©2017 • 439pp • H/C (ISBN: 9781522524045) • US $215.00

Creating a Sustainable Vision of Nonviolence in Schools and Society
Swaranjit Singh (California State University, USA) and Nancy D. Erbe (California State Education Vendor, USA)
Information Science Reference • ©2017 • 322pp • H/C (ISBN: 9781522522096) • US $195.00

For an entire list of titles in this series, please visit:
https://www.igi-global.com/book-series/advances-religious-cultural-studies/84269

IGI Global
DISSEMINATOR OF KNOWLEDGE

701 East Chocolate Avenue, Hershey, PA 17033, USA
Tel: 717-533-8845 x100 • Fax: 717-533-8661
E-Mail: cust@igi-global.com • www.igi-global.com

Editorial Advisory Board

Table of Contents

Detailed Table of Contents

This chapter focuses on the relevance of information and communication technologies (hereinafter, ICTs) as an essential part of the day-to-day life of all societies nowadays. Nevertheless, a means that continue to be behind this reality is the penitentiary area regarding inmates' rights. Introducing ICTs within prison could improve the social reinsertion of persons serving a prison sentence. Deprivation of liberty entails normal contact with the prison subculture and the harmful effects of it, causing in cases of long-term sentences the so-called phenomenon of "prisonization." This negative effect of imprisonment could be reduced if ICTs were used inside prisons in the different areas where they can have an impact, and which are treated in this research, as (1) access to information and culture, (2) basic and advanced training, (3) employment, (4) communication with the outside world, (5) treatment, or (6) leisure and entertainment. The value that new technologies would add to these areas in prison constitutes a way of humanization of prisons in the twenty-first century.

The development of information and communications technology (ICT) over the past few decades has been positively surprising. Prison development has also been surprising, in a negative way. Hardline policy positions towards crime and the expansion in the consumption of ICT products are contemporaneous. They are co-occurrences. What makes sense of this apparent contradiction is the way societies experience distinct dispositions depending on the issues they have to face. The same people are able to be optimistic, in relation to the positive use of computers, and pessimistic as to the possibility of the criminal-penal system being able to combat crime. Is it possible for society to experience a disposition in which punitiveness regarding prisoners is replaced by the hope of reintegration for those convicted of crime? The answer is: there can be a shift of the dominant disposition, but for that we must reshape the whole of this society into another.

ICT have an important role in various areas of Portuguese society. Social reintegration is a key theme in the Portuguese penal system and its legislation. This dichotomy led to question if the existence of internet access in the school prison has been a reintegration key point. Literature reveals that education is a pivotal factor in the preparation of the inmate to reintegrate society and in the prevention and reduction of recidivism. The present schooling guidelines reinforce the importance of technology base knowledge in the curriculum of any individual. Thus, the acquisition of such competences is of extreme importance, and cannot be ignored in the education that is offered to all those that sit in the margin of society. Two case studies consisting in the implementation of short courses on infocomunicational skills in two prisons allowed to explore the relation between the concepts inmate, internet, and education. The results contribute with a proposal of a curriculum and training model on infocomunicational competences acquisition to apply in prison context.

Information literacy in prisons is still an incipient issue for the scientific community, as evidenced by the absence of studies on information literacy activities in prisons. There are hardly any specific training programs for the acquisition of informational competences in Spanish prisons. They are presented results of research that have been aimed at creating a theoretical-application model of training in informational and digital skills for people in prison. The project had a methodological approach based on action research. The digital divide makes it difficult to integrate people into the labor market, leading them to social exclusion. In the case of female prisoners, this gap is even more accentuated and integration difficulties increase, so the project has adopted a gender perspective. In order to meet the objectives, a training program aimed at social and labor inclusion was created with the aim of improving the living and working conditions of women prisoners and increasing their participation as active citizens in the information society.

In Spain, there are a few projects that link communication with social intervention in prisons. These projects have remained invisible to society, and similar initiatives taking place in other prisons were even unknown amongst themselves. It is not common to find radio, programs of digital literacy, magazines, or even television and cinema in prisons. These are activities that remain within the walls and come about from the restlessness of the educators who voluntarily produce them. The work presented comes about the doctoral research work that for 4 years explored these initiatives. Through qualitative methodology, based on the use of in-depth interviews, the authors give voice to 20 prisoners and educators that participate in these projects in Spanish jails. Without claiming to be representative, the results show that these activities can become a powerful tool for social-educative integration and personal transformation.

The development of information and communication technologies (ICT), especially the internet, means that not all the population has the same opportunities of access and use of these technologies or the training necessary to use them effectively. These technologies are producing socio-economic transformations. They also bring about important changes in the way they work, communicate, behave, and socialize. All these changes constitute a factor of social exclusion and have led to the emergence of the so-called digital divide (BD). This BD has accentuated the social gap and has contributed to the fact that certain population groups, such as female inmates, are considered to be "socially excluded" or "excluded digital," and in the case of

heinous crimes to serve their sentences. Media materials that can nurture the mind such as poems, songs, bookmarks, jingles, letters, etc. for instance that bear words and thoughts of endearment can build a positive attitude and look forward to an accepting society.

In recent years, political instability has resulted in the rising wave of unemployment, poverty rate, and insecurity, all which have attendant effect on the crime rate across Nigeria. Presently, the prison population is 68,259: a number which has soared from 44,450 in year 2000. Several reports on the activities of the Nigerian prisons services widely indicate that there is a disturbing crime rate. Going by these statistics, the focus of this chapter is on the use of communication technologies skills for rehabilitation and reintegration of inmates into society. Since communication technologies provide a unified learning process for knowledge sharing, prisoners need to have access to these new forms of information exchange. This clearly implies that inmates need info-communication skills to prevent recidivism. Using the backdrop of the Nigeria's prison terrain, the chapter recommends an overhaul of the prisons with a reliable information and communication framework.

We live in a period of new literacies development, specifically the technological ones. Contact with new media or changes in more traditional ones leads to a need for different social, intellectual, and educational tools. As a consequence of the new demands of the twenty-first century, teaching had to be updated and monitored in order to foster the inclusion of individuals at school, work, socially, and digitally. The learning of technological tools should not marginalize individuals for their geographic, economic, and/or social characteristics, and should happen in an equitable way regardless of the teaching context. Media education is a factor that can favorably contribute to the process of the inmate inclusion in "free society" and to reduce recidivism. The chapter intends to reflect on the integration of the new media in the Portuguese education system in general, and later to analyze it in micro contexts, by comparative observation of the "citizen-inmate."

Foreword

In his most recent book, *The Strange Order of Things*, the world acclaimed neuroscientist Antonio Damasio discusses the power of homeostasis as the imperative force that ensures that "life is regulated within a range that is not just compatible with survival but also conducive to flourishing, to a projection of life into the future of an organism or a species". According to Damasio's perspective, homeostasis is based on the complementary power of persistence, the imperative force aiming at assuring survival, and prevalence, the imperative force related to the projection of a future flourishment.

The inmate condition is one of the most difficult and demanding experiences a human being may face. The deprivation of liberty, the suspension of self-determination, is a major challenge to the real power of homeostasis to keep alive the senses of survival and of projection of life into the future.

The fast rate of evolution of the digital technologies, spreading the digital transformation in every single human activity, should be a concern of the entities in charge of the preparation of inmates for their future reintegration in society and communities. Initiatives such as the Onlife Manifesto or the Digital Competences Framework (DigComp) provide a clear view of the need for a huge effort in developing digital competences as they are a key asset for individual development and social integration in a hyper connected world. This is, of course, especially relevant for inmates whose specific living conditions limit the direct access to the advances in digital technologies and its applications.

This book, *Infocommunication Skills as a Rehabilitation and Social Reintegration Tool for Inmates*, is a very valuable contribution to the understanding of how developing digital competences may foster the rehabilitation and integration of inmates. Joining contributions by scholars from very diverse geographies and socioeconomic contexts such as Germany, Nigeria, Philippines, Portugal, and Spain, the 12 chapters of this book offer a fresh approach to the conceptual, operational, and technological aspects relevant to an updated view of the state of the art on the field. Evidences from several case studies reported are specially interesting and inspiring as they provide results from real experiences deserving to be analyzed and discussed attentively.

It is very clear to me that this book is unavoidable as a scientific reference to professionals and academics but also to anyone, including students, looking forward to a comprehensive and up-to-date introduction to the field. My sincere congratulations to the authors, organizers and publisher for their excellent contributions. I'm pretty sure that inmates all over the world will also join me on these congratulations.

Fernando Ramos
University of Aveiro, Portugal

Preface

In the last decades, information and communication technologies, and in particular the Internet, have been disseminated and became fundamental elements of the daily life of individuals and organizations. The different sectors of activity have been incorporating new dynamics of interaction, production, generation of knowledge, social mobilization, etc. This new scenario was called Network Society (Castells, 2010). The network society is characterized by generating a context of hyper connection that promotes the erosion of the spatial and temporal constraints, thus giving birth to a space for flows.

We live in confusing times, as is often the case in periods of historical transition between different forms of society. This is because the intellectual categories that we use to understand what happens around us have been coined in different circumstances and can hardly grasp what is new by referring to the past. I contend that around the end of the second millennium of the common era a number of major social, technological, economic, and cultural transformations came together to give rise to a new form of society, the network society. (Castells, 2010, p. xvii)

This new form of society, the networked society, is consolidated through new social, cultural and economic dynamics supported by the infocommunicational infrastructure that the Internet provides. In the contemporary context it is impossible to promote socioeconomic and personal development outside the communicational sphere provided by the Internet and the new media.

In this new techno-social scenario, it is necessary to take into account the physical component of access to information and communication technologies and Internet access, but also the operational, cognitive and social skills to know how to use the technologies and their services, as well as having level of informational behavior - knowing how to identify information needs, knowing how to identify and evaluating information sources, analytically and critically selecting the available information and producing new knowledge from that information. There is also a need to develop communication skills in order to benefit from online services and social interaction platforms in order to increase the level of social capital and the benefits it can bring to the individual.

However, these infocommunication skills in digital environments are not innate skills. Therefore, there is a need for specific training for the use of new media and the usufruct of the digital society, that is, the need to promote media literacy, as recognized in the European Union discourse quoted in the article "Info-communication skills in digital environments" (Borges & Oliveira, 2011):

Media literacy is the ability to access the media, to understand and to critically evaluate different aspects of the media and media contents and to create communications in a variety of contexts. Media literacy relates to all media, including television and film, radio and recorded music, print media, the Internet and all other new digital communication technologies. It is a fundamental competence not only for the young generation but also for adults and elderly people, for parents, teachers and media professionals. The Commission considers media literacy as an important factor for active citizenship in today's information society. (Borges & Oliveira, 2011, p. 299)

Education systems have already recognized this need and include in their programs and training plans the development of the media literacy of the new generations. It is possible to question and analyze if this training should not be more extensive and more in-depth, even if it is present in the training objectives from pre-school to the end of schooling.

However, there is a group of people who, because of their status as prisoners, do not have access to the dynamics of networked society. Nevertheless, in order to promote the social integration of these people after the period of imprisonment, it is essential to know what has been done within prisons in the use of media to promote media literacy so that inmates, when return to society outside the prison walls, have the infocommunication skills essential to exercise their citizenship, to be able to find work and enjoy digital services for their daily routines, training and social reintegration.

THE CHALLENGES

It is clearly a challenge at international level to define a training strategy for the acquisition of infocommunication skills for people in prison. Prisons are spaces of repression (Fassin, 2017), but should aim to create conditions for these people to have access to training in order to requalify not only ethically and morally, but also on a personal and professional level.

The challenge of understanding the formative scenario in prisons, namely how media use can contribute to generating new training opportunities for prisoners, is complex. However, it is of paramount importance that after imprisonment these individuals have the skills to integrate and benefit from the information society in which they are inserted.

To analyze the possibility of implementing internet access scenarios in the prison context (Rocha, 2010, 2016) allows us to understand which critical factors may or may not block this possibility, whether technical factors related to the security levels that these computers / servers have to have up to the level of teachers / trainers who accompany prisoners in activities in which access to the internet could be justified, such as training scenarios, maintaining social ties with family and friends (list of authorized contacts) and of mothers or fathers with their children, etc. As well as uses that are intended to keep you informed, to be able to correspond with the respective lawyer, consult the employment center or the bank account.

The use of ICT depends upon not only the possibility to have access to technology but also the existence of knowledge on how to best make technology work for one's own success and advantage. That is, the user as to have a set of skills which are not acquire simply by connecting, literally. Those are Infocommunication Skills. Literature reveals that education is a pivotal factor in the preparation of the inmate for his return and integration in the society as well as in the prevention and reduction of recidivism. Therefore, the acquisition of Infocommunication Skills is of extreme importance and cannot be ignored in the education that is offered to all those that sit in the margin of society.

SEARCHING FOR A SOLUTION

Conducting a survey of media use experiences in a prison setting contributes to the identification of consistent media training and use proposals in order to give inmates the opportunity to acquire skills that are fundamental to their post-seclusion life. This is the challenge for which this book intends to contribute with a set of texts that present either theoretical frameworks or examples of media use and the respective contributions to the formative dynamics of the prison contexts in which they were performed. In the investigations presented here, it is evident that with appropriate policies it is possible to introduce information and communication technologies, such as access to the Internet, in prisons.

It is important to underline the role of the school and the library in prison as structures in which access to ICTs and the Internet is gaining a formative meaning that will enable prisoners to improve their level of education, as well as access to the culture and social interaction that promotes the reintegration. As provided in the Guidelines for Library Services to Prisoners of the International Federation of Library Associations (IFLA): "Where prison security permits, prisoners shall be provided with access to education and treatment purposes, as well as pre-release planning." (Lehmann & Locke, 2005, p.9).

The chapters in this book highlight the usefulness of new technologies in the prison context with a view to the social and professional reintegration of prisoners, once they return to their status as citizenship in freedom.

ORGANIZATION OF THE BOOK

The book is organized into 12 chapters. A brief description of each of the chapters follows:

Chapter 1, "Internet Behind Bars: Reality or Utopia?" focuses on the importance of information and communication technologies in the everyday life of contemporary society and how they should be considered as an inmate's right in order to contribute to social reinsertion. The possibility of accessing the Internet in prison is presented as an opportunity for inmates to have access to a set of services that contribute to minimize the phenomenon of "prisonization". The author identifies a set of areas to which inmates would have access through the Internet: (1) access to information and culture, (2) basic and advanced training, (3) employment, (4) communication with the outside world, (5) treatment or (6) leisure and entertainment. Emphasizing how this possibility is a way to humanize the prison context in the 21st century. And although society tends to think that Internet access for inmates is a privilege they should not have, in fact it should be borne in mind that the purpose of the prison sentence is for that person to undergo a process of resocialization, for which access to Internet services makes an important contribution. The chapter presents an analysis of the situation in Spain.

Chapter 2, "The Role of Information and Communications Technology in the Social Reintegration of Ex-Prisoners," focuses on the difficulty of moving from a punishment-based view to a view focused on the social reintegration of prisoners. This difficulty makes the same people who defend the importance of the use of information and communication technologies in social dynamics, then do not recognize their importance in the prison context as a way of promoting competences conducive to the social insertion of prisoners. The chapter aims to answer a set of questions: Can the introduction of ICT in prison transform it? What does this experience tell us? What is the dominant disposition in the prison sector? How can the evolution of societies, or any possible revolutions that might come to take place in the future, change the structural place of prison in society? The author emphasizes that the introduction of information and communication technologies in prisons is not enough, but that it is necessary to check whether these technologies are used in a way that is useful for the very transformation of prisons as organizations. Thus, a puncture-centered vision is abandoned for a vision centered on the possibility of prisoners developing their cognitive skills and decision-making skills. As the author emphasizes the use of ICT in prison is dependent on the sociopolitical view: "The role of ICT in the social reintegration of ex-prisoners depends on the dominant social disposition in relation to the political and social place of punishment."

Chapter 3, "Curriculum and Training Model for Infocommunicational Competences Acquisition in Prison: A Case Study in Two Portuguese Prisons," proposes to answer two research questions: "How Internet access by prisoners in Portuguese prisons in a training context can be a reality?" and "What curricular structure should a training program in Internet usage adopt in the specific context of the Portuguese Prison System?". In this sense, it is proposed a training model and a curriculum for the development of infocommunicational skills for the prison population. A curriculum and a training model elaborated from the analysis of the Portuguese Ministry of Education guiding documents and the review of the literature for training in digital skills were applied in two prisons in Portugal (a male prison and a female prison). This application enabled through participant research with the prisoners to generate knowledge that were used in improving the curriculum and the training model now presented. The chapter contributes to demonstrate the feasibility of introducing access to information and communication technologies and Internet use in establishments with a curriculum model of training in infocommunication competence in digital environments.

Chapter 4, "Research on Information Literacy and Social Inclusion of Female Inmates," focuses on the study of information literacy activities in prisons, specifically on informational literacy training programs for the social inclusion of women prisoners in the jails of the Community of Madrid). The authors propose the theoretical-application model of training in informational and digital skills for people in prison, focusing on the case of female prisoners, with the aim of promoting social and labor inclusion, with the purpose of improving the living and working conditions of women prisoners and increasing their participation as active citizens in the information society. The training proposal called CIDIS (Informational and digital competences for social inclusion) proposed at the end of each topic a practical activity to reinforce the theory learned. These activities are grouped in three blocks: Digital Competence, Information Competence and, Digital Competency Activities and Information Competence. The training in information skills increase the knowledge of inmates and prepare their entry into labor market and exercise their citizenship.

Chapter 5, "Communication Media in Digital Literacy as Intervention Tools in Prisons: The Case in Spain," focused on presenting a set of projects that have been taking place in prisons in Spain and which clearly prove to be the powerful tool for social-educative integration and personal transformation for prisoners. The chapter has as its background the central idea of deepening the understanding how education and communication, focused on social change, can be a powerful tool in the field of prisons. In this way, the objective was to carry out a survey of experiences carried out in Spanish prisons and to verify if the performance of communication media workshops in prisons are relevant and useful for the prisoners and educators and also if the participation of prisoners in the media communication in prison context gives prisoners positive expectations about their future. In the scope of this investigation, interviews with prisoners and educators were carried out. In summary, this investigation allowed to realize a map, which until now was totally non-existent, of all the educational-communicative practices that are carried out in prisons in Spain and evidence the media as a therapeutic tool for the transformation of the person and the prison context, as well as to promote change in their vision of society.

Chapter 6, "Policies on Literacy, Equality, and Gender: The Case of Spanish Prisons," based on the importance of digital technologies in the daily lives of individuals and in social dynamics, analyzes policies, projects and programs that are carried out both in Europe and in Spain in the field of informational and digital literacy for social and labor inclusion, as well as equality and gender policies, in the prison context. Emphasizing that people who do not have access to the acquisition of information literacy are in a situation of digital exclusion, which favors social exclusion. These exclusion mechanisms tend to be larger for the female population, which also occurs in the female gender prison population. The author emphasizes the relationship between information literacy and lifelong learning and the importance of information literacy for social, economic and cultural development. The author also stresses the importance of the policies of information and digital literacy and gender policies for social inclusion, focusing on the European situation and Spain. The author concludes that promoting information literacy policies in the penitentiary system is the way to provide opportunities for equality and social and labor reintegration.

Chapter 7, "Prison Blogs, a Place of Freedom Behind Bars: Notes From a Workshop at the Barcelona Youth Detention Center," focuses on the analysis of the possibility through Cultural Workshop, where blogs were created, encourage prisoners to read and write more. It emphasizes the role that the prison library can play as a mean to give the opportunity to inmates to develop themselves intellectually, socially and culturally. In this way, it is evidenced that the Internet and prison library are two important resources for the personal development of prisoners and, therefore, enhancers of their social and professional reinsertion. The author points out that the prison context has a lack of technological infrastructure and that the library does not always have the necessary resources due to lack of investment, however, the library should be considered as a fundamental resource associated with which access to information and communication technologies should be made available communication and access to the Internet, which will combat the digital divide and several illiteracies that the prison population has.

Chapter 8, "Inmate Communication as a Conscientization Approach to Societal Mainstreaming," underlines the importance of strengthening the emotional and mental stability of inmates through activities that allow them to prepare a new life when they are released from prison. In this process of supporting the personal development of prisoners, it is essential to use adequate communication processes, especially with the use of new media, which are an important resource for distance learning. In addition to the acquisition of knowledge and skills, it is important to develop processes of awareness and reflection that promote psychological and emotional well-being, which will reflect positively on the lives of prisoners and society as a whole. Improvements are therefore recommended at the level of the Justice System and Correctional System in the Philippines in order to progressively improve the conditions offered to prisoners and the communication system that promotes opportunities.

Chapter 9, "Communication Technologies for Social Integration of Inmates in Nigeria," underscores the significant increase in prison population in Nigeria and the importance of the use of communication technologies skills for rehabilitation and reintegration of inmates into society. The main focus is social and the role of communication technologies in improving the quality of life of prison inmates to reintegrate them into their communities. In this process it is emphasized the role of social values and skills learned promoted through the use of communication technologies that assume a role of instruments of socialization and education. It is highlighted that in Nigeria the latest common rehabilitation strategy of inmates is vocational skills acquisition as well as adult schooling. The chapter also discusses the possibility of introducing a private prison system in Nigeria. In essence, the idea of recommending the use of information and communication technologies in prisons in Nigeria is reinforced in order to promote conditions of education, acquisition of skills and employability of prisoners to promote social reintegration.

Chapter 10, "New Media Usage and the Impact on Inmates' Technological Profiles and Their Infocommunicational Skills," reflects on the integration of the new media in the Portuguese education system in general, and later to analyze it in micro contexts, by comparative observation of the "citizen-inmate". The authors present the evolution of the introduction of information and communication technologies in Portugal and specifically in the educational context as background for the presentation of a model of use of information and communication technologies in the Portuguese prison system, based on the results of two studies of a case in a female prison and a male prison in Portugal. The results allow to highlight the importance of the acquisition of information-communicational skills by prisoners as a crucial means of increasing the skills and knowledge and motivation to learn, but also increase in the self-image and self-esteem of the participants. Then it is clear that these contributions are undoubtedly an added value for the future of these people.

Chapter 11, "Restricted Communication: Social Relationships and the Media Use of Prisoners," aims to understand what the patterns of media use of an inmate before the incarceration and the communication habits and the restraint of the use of media during imprisonment. How do the prisoners deal with this situation and how do they adopt the most traditional means (letters and phone calls) to maintain their contacts with the family or other social contacts. The study was conducted in a female prison in Germany. These are the research questions guiding the study: (1) How are the patterns of media use of an individual changing in the case of imprisonment? (2) How does the change affect the social relationships of a female prisoner? (3) What role does the lack of social media play in the shift of the communicative figurations? It is clear that it is a difficult balance between punishment and resocialization, and the difficulty of promoting the social health of inmates in order to promote their social reintegration.

Chapter 12, "Prison and Social Reintegration: The Voice of a Formerly Deprived Individual," focuses on the analysis of a case study to understand how prison years affect the lives of prisoners in a systemic way. The author stresses that despite all the initiatives the conditions in prisons, focusing on the reality in Venezuela, are still rather precarious by empowering violence and prison subculture where human rights are not always respected. In the chapter are shown the inhuman conditions in Venezuelan prisons, in which the prison violence is not only physical but also psychological, a scenario that shows that they are still far from reaching a promoting context of re-socialization as foreseen in the country's constitution.

The reading of these 12 chapters gives a broad overview of the prison reality in several countries underlining a common brand of recognition of the creation of socio-educational and communication conditions in prison that promote the personal and professional development of prisoners and bring them to social reintegration. It presents a very interesting set of projects and experiences in a prison context that aimed to introduce or increase the use of information and communication technologies and the Internet in prisons in order to develop infocommunication skills, as well as information and media literacy in prisoners and promote their social-affective linkage with their personal social network to support their social reintegration. Although the difficulties, shortcomings and specificities of the prison context have not been ignored.

We hope for a fruitful reading that will contribute to a more egalitarian future.

Lídia Oliveira
University of Aveiro, Portugal

Daniela Graça
University of Aveiro, Portugal

REFERENCES

Borges, J., & Oliveira, L. (2011). Competências infocomunicacionais em ambientes digitais. *Observatorio (OBS*), 5*(4).

Castells, M. (2010). *The Rise of Network Society*. Oxford, UK: Blackwell Publishers.

Fassin, D. (2017). *Prison worlds: An ethnography of the carceral condition*. Cambridge, UK: Polity Press. Retrieved from https://www.google.com/books?hl=pt-PT&lr=&id=qZFNDwAAQBAJ&oi=fnd&pg=PR3&dq=Prison+Worlds+an+Ethnography+of+the+Carceral+&ots=1ba538Uv7H&sig=tXWSErGMJ-kRDfEI2GGPvUsUuNg

Lehmann, V., & Locke, J. (2005). *Guidelines for library services to prisoners*. The Hague, The Netherlands: IFLA Headquarters.

Rocha, D. G. S. (2010). *Utilização da Internet nos Estabelecimentos Prisionais Portugueses. Realidade ou Utopia?* Aveiro: Departamento de Comunicação e Arte da Universidade de Aveiro.

Rocha, D. G. S. (2016). *Desenvolvimento de Competências Infocomunicacionais em Contexto Prisional: Proposta de um Modelo de Formação para a Utilização da Internet no Contexto Prisional Português*. Universidade de Aveiro-Portugal.

Acknowledgment

The editors of this book acknowledge the precious contribution of all the people involved in this project. Without their support this book would not be in your hands now.

Therefore, we thank each of the chapters authors who contributed with their time and expertise to this book, and the reviewers who helped improve the quality, coherence, and content presentation of each chapters.

Lídia Oliveira
University of Aveiro, Portugal

Daniela Graça
University of Aveiro, Portugal

Chapter 1
Internet Behind Bars:
Reality or Utopia?

Carmen-Rocio Fernandez-Diaz
University of Malaga, Spain

ABSTRACT

This chapter focuses on the relevance of information and communication technologies (hereinafter, ICTs) as an essential part of the day-to-day life of all societies nowadays. Nevertheless, a means that continue to be behind this reality is the penitentiary area regarding inmates' rights. Introducing ICTs within prison could improve the social reinsertion of persons serving a prison sentence. Deprivation of liberty entails normal contact with the prison subculture and the harmful effects of it, causing in cases of long-term sentences the so-called phenomenon of "prisonization." This negative effect of imprisonment could be reduced if ICTs were used inside prisons in the different areas where they can have an impact, and which are treated in this research, as (1) access to information and culture, (2) basic and advanced training, (3) employment, (4) communication with the outside world, (5) treatment, or (6) leisure and entertainment. The value that new technologies would add to these areas in prison constitutes a way of humanization of prisons in the twenty-first century.

INTRODUCTION

Information and communication technologies (hereinafter, ICTs) are currently an essential part of the everyday life of all societies, as they offer the stage where a huge number of behaviors that used to take place in the physical world are carried out. Thus, interpersonal communication, the purchase of any object or service, the performance of various leisure, work or training activities, take place in the virtual space.

DOI: 10.4018/978-1-5225-5975-7.ch001

In this context, areas of reality that have remained outside the so-called "information society" are hardly imaginable. The immediacy and comfort that ICTs offer for the realization of any activity that can be carried out through them, position them in a privileged place in front of the traditional ways. Thus, in relation to the world of crime, ICTs have been applied not only in the area of penalties, with the introduction of probation period and electronic monitoring (Mata y Martín, 2014), but also, within the prison environment, technical mechanisms have been already used in one of its two pillars, the penitentiary system, such as, for example, body search, X-rays or the intervention of communications (De Marcos Madruga, 2014, pp. 235-237; Weinrath, 2016, p. 171).

However, it is possible to identify a means that keeps its back to this reality in the penitentiary environment, and it is in relation to the prisoner's rights and treatment. If we take a look, for example, to written communications system in prison, it can easily be seen how this is generally based, in the reality of Spanish prisons in which focuses this work, on the sending of letters and telegrams. This is established by the Spanish prison regulations in *Real Decreto 190/1996*, of 9 February, which approves the *Reglamento Penitenciario* (Prison Regulations) of 1996 (hereinafter, RP). This last text is the one that develops the content of the *Ley Orgánica 1/1979*, of September 26, *General Penitenciaria* (General Penitentiary Law) of 1979 (hereinafter, LOGP), whose articles 51 to 53 establish general rules on communications and visits in prison. The mere fact that the Spanish regulation of this aspect dates from years, and its lack of subsequent modification, already presages a great obsolescence in this area.

The idea of introducing the Internet in prison generates stupefaction in society, as it usually generates the inmate's enjoyment of leisure activities considered "privileges", because in this context normally operate the idea put forward by Garland (2003), in virtue of which "...any show of compassion for offenders, any invocation of their rights, any effort to humanize their punishments, can easily be represented as an insult to victims and their families" (p. 143). This idea, as Jewkes (2009) points out regarding the United Kingdom and that can be extrapolated to other national realities, is consolidated by the mainstream press, that generally report prisons as 'holidays camps' in which inmates enjoy luxuries they do not 'deserve', which serves to "further stigmatise a population which is already at the margins and which rarely has a right of reply" (pp. 171-172).

An example of this is the presence of swimming pools in prisons (Daunis, 2016, p. 161; El Confidencial Digital, 24/08/2013), exit permits when they were introduced (Tocino, 2014, p. 29) or televisions in the cells (Knight, 2016, pp. 96-97). However, in the field of new technologies, social rejection may be even greater, since, as the latter author points out in another work, unlike "to the one-way nature of television", internet in the context of the prison supposes "that the prisoner can 'reach' outside world and the world can also reach them" (Knight, 2015, p. 3).

At a time when the trend is overpopulation of prisons, these aspects, which would be part of the rights of the prisoner during his stay in prison, uses to be considered a luxury and the prevailing idea is that, as Pollock (2004) says, "prisons, once built, rarely are the subject of news reports, and <<success>> is still defined as when the prison stays off the front page…" (p. 8). In a similar sense, says Jewkes (2009), that "fed a diet of media stories about notorious offenders, violent assaults and security breaches, little thought may be given to the things that normalize prison regimes such as access to education, decent healthcare, or providing a means of communication between inmates and their families" (p. 180).

However, certain penitentiary realities of the Western world that have given way to technological development in the context of prison can already be identified. A good example of this is Belgium, where prison services have provided a whole package of digital capabilities and opportunities for prisoners (Knight, 2015, p. 4), as getting judicial advice, accessing their own judicial files or applying for jobs inside and outside prison (Knight, 2015, p. 8). The Belgian penitentiary system is so advanced in this sense that there is in-cell digital provision, through which prisoners can enjoy digital access to their prison accounts via their in-cell televisions. In the UK in mostly private prisons kiosks, handheld devices, interactive televisions and in-cell telephones are becoming a feature of prison life for some prisoners (Knight, 2015, p. 8).

The present work focuses specifically on the Spanish penitentiary reality and the possibility of introducing new technologies in its prisons, although this aspect, the experiences in this sense in other countries will also be mentioned.

SOCIAL REINSERTION AS A GUIDING PURPOSE OF CUSTODIAL SENTENCES

The Spanish Constitution establishes in Article 25.2 that prison sentences and security measures will be oriented towards re-education and social reinsertion. Rivers of ink have been written about this section, especially in relation to a debate that has been nourished as much by the doctrinal discussion of constitutionalists as by the jurisprudence of the Spanish Constitutional Court itself. In this sense, a sector of the doctrine defends that this precept lodges a right of the person, consisting in the provision by the State of the necessary conditions for the reincorporation to the society in satisfactory conditions, with the constitutional requirements of respect to the human dignity and freedom (Cobo del Rosal & Boix Reig, 1982, p. 222). On the contrary, the Spanish Constitutional Court has argued that re-education and social reinsertion are a command of the Constitution lawmaker to the legislator to guide criminal and penitentiary policy, a command from which no subjective rights derive (Auto from the Constitutional Court 15/1984, of January 11).

Leaving aside this debate, the truth is that whatever it is, prison sentences must pursue that end. However, what is meant by "resocialization" is one of the most discussed aspects, if not the most, of the execution of prison sentences (Manzanos Bilbao, 1994, p. 121). Thus, one of the most recognized authors in this field in Spain, Ríos Martín, has pointed out that the aforementioned constitutional command requires that people sentenced to custodial sentences are not eliminated from society, but must continue to be an active part of the social community (Ríos Martín & Cabrera Cabrera, 1998, p. 134), which is also evidenced by the LOGP in its Recital of Motives.

In line with this statement, it is worth asking whether the concept of social reinsertion implies the existence of a prior exclusion and if such exclusion could lead to the loss of the quality of citizen. In this sense, as pointed Easton (2011), modern concepts of citizenship have rooted this notion "in terms of the social contract, with an assumption that the person who benefits from the protection and advantages of society is also obliged to obey its rules and, by definition, the prisoner is the outsider, who seeks the benefits without the corresponding burdens" (pp. 15-16). Therefore, what the author suggests is the adoption of a concept of citizenship most favorable to the notion of prisoners' rights, "which sees citizenship as an instrument of social inclusion rather than exclusion, and which incorporates social rights" (p. 18).

However, although it is clear that the issues initially raised must have an answer in the sense of not considering the inmate a social outsider in terms of loss of citizenship, the question that now arises is whether this is fully carried out or not.

If check the Dictionary of the Royal Academy of the Spanish Language, we note that the second meaning of the term "reinsert" (*reinsertar*) means inserting again a criminally or marginally convicted subject into society. However, if the society to which the subject returns is governed in an immense number of areas by ICTs, the question that immediately arises is the following: how can the reinsertion of a subject into a society in constant technological evolution, be encouraged without offering during the period of exclusion from this any tool that allows he or she to evolve to him or her also in parallel? To get an idea, imagine long sentences of more than five years in which the only means of communication are letters and telegrams, education is limited by the texts that the penitentiary offers or the only way of working is physics or intellectual always intramural. It seems clear that, without attending to the particularities of the society in which the inmate will reinsert, it is difficult for this enterprise to succeed and that a prison treatment which is far from the reality of our society could mean opting for an effective exclusion of it of the individuals deprived of freedom.

In this sense, it is interesting the opinion of Tocino (2014), who points out that, without the opportunity to advance in the technological changes during the life in prison, this becomes a fossilized reality, a situation of paralysis that does not correspond with the conditions of the future life in freedom and that, therefore, prevents to reach the goal of the penitentiary system: the social and labor rehabilitation of the prisoners (p. 34). And, as he finally concludes, without minimal digital skills he or she will be considered illiterate and with a very low probability of finding a place in a hard labor market like the present one (p. 40). In this line, some authors speak of a redefinition of the notion of literacy, since new technologies have posed great challenges to education (Burgos, García & Tomás, 2014, p. 102). Other authors, such as Jewkes (2009), claim that "in the twenty-first century, the denial of access to the internet constitutes a distinctive pain of imprisonment" (p. 171).

In fact, the Report of the Special Rapporteur on the promotion and protection of the right to freedom of opinion and expression, Frank La Rue, published by the Human Rights Council of the General Assembly of the United Nations on its seventeenth session that took place in May 2011, recognizes the access to Internet as a fundamental human right, emphasizing that there should be as little restriction as possible to the flow of information via the Internet, except in few, exceptional, and limited circumstances prescribed by international human rights law.

For all the reasons said above, the changes that take place in reality in freedom, should be taken into account in prison reality, which not only has to do with the constant evolution of new technologies, but also with other areas. Thus, as stated by Benito Rangel, Espartero Martínez, García Marijuán, Garrido Martínez & López-Araujo (2002), it can´t be programmed, for example, the development of skills for adaptation to a fixed job when, even for those who work most of the time, the change of work, the change of company, the eventuality, seems to be the most common pattern in the labor market (p. 4).

Considering the above, the idea of social reinsertion, following the theories of resocialization for legality or minimal re-socialization programs, should aim at the subject adapting its external behavior to the norms that regulate social coexistence, complying with the criminal law when its sentence will ends and, with this, that he or she does not return to commit a crime (Daunis, 2016, p. 18). To this end, life in prison must be oriented as much as possible to the search for that aim, for which any activity that moves away the inmate from criminal behavior will promote the achievement of that end. In fact, following the opinion of Díez Ripollés (2011), a certain level of social inclusion of suspects, offenders and ex-offenders is one of the most effective strategies for the prevention of delinquency, while the promotion or deepening of social exclusion of these subjects by the criminal control institutions generates greater delinquency in the medium and long term (p. 9).

In this sense, a work occupation, participation in training activities or communication with the socio-affective environment, are possible prosocial activities or routines that constitute an investment of time in favor of a life in freedom within the law and that can prevent in the future the new commission of crimes. As Easton (2011) points out, prison conditions, provision for work, training and education are crucial activities "in terms of making prison life tolerable and providing prisoners with key skills to assist their reintegration in society" (p. 85). Definitively, according to European Prison Rule 103.4, sentenced prisoners sentence plans shall as far as is practicable include work, education, other activities and preparation for release.

From this point of view, new technologies bring an infinite range of possibilities to prosocial activities that may favor the social reinsertion of the subject deprived of freedom. Nowadays it is difficult to find inmates who have not had any contact with the new technologies. However, for example, sentences of 15 or 10 years place the prisoner out of prison in the early or mid-2000s. At that time the new technologies were not as sophisticated as they are today. Even so, the increasingly advanced pace of technological development means that sentences of only one year, already imply a significant out-of-date with respect to it. As Tocino (2014) affirms, as time progresses, the digital gap will become greater, and each time, it will inevitably be harder to close (p. 41). This gap could generate a double exclusion, social and technological, since audiovisual media and new technologies constitute new forms of communication and participation, and help to understand our environment and to transform it (Burgos et al., 2014, p. 102). To the double social and digital exclusion have already referred some authors as offline and online exclusion, respectively (Helsper, 2012), and the relationship between both finds its clearest example in the penitentiary field (Novo-Corti & Barreiro-Gen, 2014).

For this reason, the social reinsertion that is intended to be achieved during the inmate's prison life must also include the idea of inclusion in a technological or digital sense, in order to take advantage of all the possibilities that ICTs offer to favor a successful re-socialization.

AREAS OF APPLICATION OF THE NEW INFORMATION AND COMMUNICATION TECHNOLOGIES IN PRISON AND REASONS FOR THEIR INTRODUCTION

In order to achieve a better social reinsertion of persons deprived of freedom, activities should be strengthened in certain areas in which ICTs play a fundamental role, to the point that many of them are nowadays inconceivable without their intervention. Their presence would undoubtedly reduce the phenomenon of prisonization by supposing less criminogenic contagion, since it would imply less contact with the prison subculture and greater contact with the world in freedom. These areas are those listed below.

Access to Information and Culture

The information nowadays flows through digital channels at an astonishing speed. The possibility of having access to an updated information means being up to date and acquiring culture immediately and without barriers. This aspect is restricted if the form of access to information is limited to traditional media such as newspapers. However, it must be said that this field is not the most adversely affected one in the absence of ICTs in the prison environment, since there was allowed the presence of television. It was a breakthrough, which at the time produced social rejection, and which has subsequently been normalized (Jewkes, 2009, p. 177).

Socio-cultural activities related to new technologies would also open a new socializing and re-socializing path within the prison. Thus, the publication of magazines, newsletters, blogs or web pages in prison would allow a form of expression of the inmate that could favor by some manner the social reinsertion, reducing in turn the criminogenic effects of the prison. An experience in this sense occurred in the year 2007 in the penitentiary of Teixeiro (A Coruña, Galicia) with the project *Chicass10* that brought Internet to the center, taking the magazine that was produced, with great success, to digital support. The participants did not have direct access to the Internet, so they had to write the entries in advance, however, this process lead to the creation of a space of freedom and communication for the inmates (Tocino, 2014, p. 31). Nevertheless, similar experiences took place before. Thus, in 2006 the library of the youth penitentiary in Barcelona launched a blog publishing workshop to stimulate reading and writing among inmates in order to improve their information skills and to promote their digital literacy (Burgos et al., 2007, p. 102).

The blog activity in prisons and the freedom of expression that is defended with it, meets an inescapable obstacle, which is the one related to when details of the crimes committed are included, which may suppose a detriment of the rights of the victims. Therefore, in these cases, the doctrine has been clear to point out that "the prisoner's right to freedom of expression may be limited in the case of criminal autobiographies, but not if the prisoner is making serious representations relating to his conviction or sentence, or on the processes of justice" (Easton, 2011, p. 156).

Basic and Advanced Training

Education is the cornerstone of resocialization and all that it entails. Thus, it is pointed out by the doctrine, who defends that "…education can help to make the inmate's time in prison productive and improve his or her life upon release" (Pollock, 2004, p. 133). Without offering a basic training, it will be difficult for the penitentiary system to promote the re-education and social reinsertion of persons deprived of their liberty. For this reason, this issue is no longer debated in the doctrine, since all prisons tend to provide their inmates with primary, secondary, high school, university and vocational training programs, thus meeting the different needs that may arise in the prison to each one of them. However, it is well known that the educational system can no longer be conceived without the practical application of new technologies, not only for distance studies, but also to deepen them, to do research or to access to various electronic bibliographic sources, currently of daily use for any student and that those sentenced to a custodial sentence cannot take advantage, thus limiting their studies.

In fact, the Spanish press has recently echoed a case in which this limitation even prevents the inmates from pursuing high school studies, because they do not have an Internet connection in prison, as in the Alcolea penitentiary, in Córdoba (20 minutos, 15/04/2017).

The LOGP foresees in Article 56.2 that in order for inmates to access the public service of university education it will be necessary for the Penitentiary Administration to sign the appropriate agreements with public universities. Said agreements -the precept continues-, will guarantee that education is taught under the conditions and with the rigor and quality inherent to the type of studies, adapting when it will be necessary, the pedagogical methodology to the special circumstances that concur in the penitentiary area.

With this being foreseen by the LOGP, an open path in this sense is given by Article 129.1 RP, according to which the inmate may be authorized to have a personal computer when reasons of an educational or cultural nature make it necessary or advisable for the development of the corresponding training programs. In these cases, the inmate will be obliged to present a report justifying the need endorsed by the teacher or tutor, and will be required to make good use of it, which will be presumed provided that the inmate is willing to show the totality of the files thereof, upon request of the Governing board (article 129.3).

This article shows that if there is an area in which the use of new technologies is accepted in the penitentiary environment, it is the one of education. Proof of this is that the use of ICTs in prison has been admitted in several countries for this purpose, because, as Elvira-Valdés (2014) points out, these can be considered as a tool for social inclusion that contributes to the process of humanization of prisons

(p. 90). This author highlights precisely the case that in this sense was experienced in Venezuela with the *Proyecto Infomovil*, which developed a technological literacy plan for people deprived of their liberty. In the United Kingdom, the online learning organisation *Learndirect* had installed PCs in 20 prisons in 2009, which were used to deliver courses in literacy and numeracy and to impart skills of employment (Jewkes, 2009, p. 172). However, pioneers in this field are the Nordic countries, where, since the early 2000s, access to the internet for training in the penitentiary is a reality. Thus, in Denmark, since the year 2000 some prisoners of open prisons have Internet access in their own rooms to complete assignments and study, not only in the classroom (Nordic Council of Ministers, 2005, pp. 38-39). In Norway, since the year 2003 all the prison schools reported that they had integrated use of ICT into subject teaching or as a teaching tool and in the same year the Ministry of Justice already authorized use of the Internet and e-mail in prison education under strictly regulated conditions (Nordic Council of Ministers, 2005, pp. 83-84).

In Spain, an experience in this sense was the one carried out in Catalan prisons with the *Òmnia* project, which sought to anticipate the processes of social reinsertion through the access and use of ICTs in prison, actively involving inmates in their own process of learning, giving them the tools for their later use in freedom (Bobes, 2010).

The results of these projects are important because today technologies are also a tool for training and for supporting the learning process. Thus, the aforementioned project, which launched in 2006 the library of the youth penitentiary center in Barcelona in which a blog publishing workshop was promoted, also fostered the acquisition by the inmates of various skills, such as the identification and selection of information sources, the use of the word processor and its function of spell checker, the use of design programs for retouching images, the consultation of various dictionaries or the learning of writing techniques for the web environment (Bueno et al., 2014, p. 106).

The teaching of self-learning is undoubtedly a key aspect of resocialization, since it encourages inmates to learn to take care of themselves and to take control of their lives. In this sense, new technologies provide innumerable instruments so that anyone can go to the resources they need in each case and can advance their training and, without them, can hardly reach training levels such as those given in freedom. This means, as Vogel (2009) points out, that "without digital skills and tools there can be no expectation of succeeding in today's world" (p. 165).

Employment

The implementation of new technologies in prison could also improve one of the major failures of prison systems in relation to resocialization, such as the job-related areas. The economic crisis that Spain suffered in recent years and which has created an unemployment rate of 16.38% as of September 2017 (Instituto Nacional de Estadística –National Statistics Institute-, 2017), has undoubtedly had repercussions in the penitentiary area, where external companies create job offers for the inmates through previous collaboration agreements. The possibility of having access to exclusively remote employment offers, that is, that could be carried out from prison without having to travel, would open a window to the outside world of work, relieving in some way the limitations imposed by face-to-face work.

Training for employment could also increase its offer with the implementation of ICTs in the penitentiary environment. Suffice with pointing simply, as Daunis (2016) affirms, the low number of professional training courses offered in 2015: only 8,410 places for the 56,968 inmates who were in Spanish prisons, equivalent to one training course for every seven inmates (p. 158).

On the other hand, experiences in this sense can be found in the United Kingdom, where 25 prisoners of HMP Wolds, a prison located in Yorkshire, have completed a full training programme in order to work producing websites and online marketing services to companies doing business on the web (Jewkes, 2009, p. 172). Apart from this, as this author points out, "access to computers, e-mail and the internet would allow users in prison to interact with potential employers" (Jewkes, 2009, p. 184).

The application of ICTs in these cases would be especially useful for inmates preparing for release, who could this way find offers prior to their release.

Communication With the Outside World

Another aspect of greater importance to achieve resocialization is given by the fact that inmates can maintain contact with their closest socio-emotional environment (Fernández Díaz, 2015). This idea finds support in Hirschi's theory of social bonding, the central assumption of which is that "the main element that holds young people from engaging in criminal activities is their emotional attachment to socially integrated people" (Redondo Illescas & Garrido Genovés, 2013, p. 297), with the links or elements of connection with conventional society, according to Hirschi (1969), four: attachment, commitment, involvement and belief (pp. 16-26). Applying the theoretical idea of this author to the person deprived of freedom, it can be concluded that a greater contact with the social-affective environment of the inmate has in some way a positive impact on his or her future resocialization.

The connection to the Internet for this purpose would allow a greater contact between the inmate and his or her environment and would allow unthinkable situations with the current communication channels and which are expressly forbidden in cases in which the inmate has a personal computer for educational or cultural purposes, as established in Article 129.2 RP.

However, the use of new technologies in this field is especially important because of its instantaneous and interactive nature, in contrast to traditional forms of communication. On the one hand, *email* is one of the ways that would speed up the communication of the inmate with his or her surroundings outside the walls and experiences have already been given in this regard (Knight, 2015, pp. 4-5). First of all, since 2006, the United Kingdom offers the *emailaprisoner* service, in which the prisoners are allowed to receive printed versions of emails from an authorised sender instead of a letter, which are downloaded by officers (http://www.emailaprisoner.com/). Since 2010, the prisoner has also the possibility to answer, however, this version is not so widespread. Secondly, since 2007, in the prisons of the United States there is *TRULINCS* (Trust Fund Limited Inmated Computer System), a program that does offer a complete electronic service to inmates who pay fees to send and read emails (https://www.bop.gov/inmates/trulincs.jsp). Thirdly, Belgium's experience with the introduction of new technologies in prison is also noteworthy, since through the *PrisonCloud* service it is offered a "flexible IT platform designed for the secure distribution of content and services to inmates" (https://www.ebo-enterprises.com/prisoncloud).

On the other hand, those inmates who are serving sentences in prisons away from their place of residence could contact their relatives through *videoconferencing* without obliging them to move every time they want to visit the inmate in question. This option is not intended to replace traditional visits, which could continue to occur, but, as Knight (2015) points out, is supposed to enhance the quality of those interactions (p. 7). The possibility of communication by videoconference exists in Spain, not in the penitentiary regulations *per se*, but through Instruction 2/2007 of the General Directorate of Penitentiary Institutions, regarding the implementation of the videoconference system. According to this Instruction, there are three types of videoconferences allowed in the penitentiary environment: the first type is for judicial actions; the second one is for communications between inmates and family members; and the third one is for medical consultations.

Instruction 2/2007 is an example of progress in the penitentiary environment because, as stated in its introduction, "it is necessary to take advantage of all the resources offered by the incorporation of new technologies in the field of telecommunications, which undoubtedly, will allow an adequate updating and modernization of the penitentiary system". However, in the opinion of the author of this research, this advance does not fully meet the communicative needs of a large number of inmates, especially the ones related to relatives and next of kin, so, although positively considered, it still presents two important limitations. The first one is created by the Instructions, as it requires the videoconference to be carried out between prisons, and the closest prison to the family residence, where relatives or next of kin will have to move to, to have these systems (Instruction 2/2007, III.2.b.).

The second limitation is given by some of the requirements needed for this type of communication to take place, for instance, that the inmate must not have made any communication in the last four months or the one that establishes that the duration of the video conference must last only fifteen minutes (Instruction 2/2007, III.2.2.2).

These two limitations affect certain groups of inmates. Thus, on the one hand, there are many inmates that are against their children to visit them in prison, because of the shock that it may mean for them to see their parents through a glass and in an environment where shouting predominates (Fernández Díaz, 2015, pp. 18-19). This leads to affirm, as Easton (2011) pointed out, that "the social exclusion of prisoners is shared by their families" (p. 144). On the other hand, this problem has a special incidence in the case of foreigners, as their families not only cannot visit them regularly, but also face difficulties with any other type of communication. Thus, in the Spanish penitentiary system, telephone communications take place in a very limited way, allowing Instruction 4/2005, from the General Directorate of Penitentiary Institutions, to update Instruction 24/96, of December 16 regarding communications and visits, in its seventh paragraph, first letter a), a maximum of five calls per week, each lasting five minutes. In addition to the above, the calls that can be made depend on the balance that the inmate has available, being the calls abroad especially expensive. It is important to emphasize here that the rate of foreign inmate population in Spain was almost 30% in August 2017, according to data from the General Secretariat of Penitentiary Institutions, belonging to the Ministry of Home Affairs. Therefore, the introduction of new technologies in this area would encourage the maintenance of family ties in a large number of cases that, otherwise, would be very difficult to maintain, leading to a possible desocialization of the inmate.

In fact, several international texts consider the possibility of introducing new technologies in communications that take place between prisons and the outside. Thus, on the one hand, the European Prison Rules published in 2006 by the Council of Europe, in rule 24.1, states that "Prisoners shall be allowed to communicate as often as possible by letter, telephone or *other forms of communication* with their families, other persons and representatives of outside organisations and to receive visits from these persons". On the other hand, the United Nations Standard Minimum Rules for the Treatment of Prisoners, approved by Resolution of the General Assembly on December 17, 2015, known as "Nelson Mandela Rules", and which follow the previous ones of 1955, foresee expressly article 58, as a novelty, that the periodic communication to which inmates are authorized with family and friends, can be carried out "...by means of telecommunications, electronic, digital or of other kinds that are available...". This way we can see how this text echoes current reality, including new technologies as a possible form of communication.

However, it is regrettable that the greatest advances in the introduction of new technologies in prison are focused almost exclusively on the field of education, because, although it is also one of the most important for the re-socialization of the subject deprived of freedom, this means partially recognizing the use of ICTs for this purpose and, as Knight (2015) points out, paying little attention to their social and emotional uses (p. 4).

Prison Treatment

Another aspect in which the introduction of ICTs in prison could have a very positive impact is the one of improving prison treatment. It includes the issues that have already been mentioned, such as education or work, among others. However, ICTs could also improve aspects of treatment that address certain individual problems of the offender and that give rise to the so-called specialized treatment programs in the Spanish penitentiary system (Daunis, 2016, pp. 166-179).

In this sense, psychosocial intervention programs are those that can benefit the most from the introduction of ICTs in prison. Thus, they can considerably improve treatment programs for drug addicts, the programs addressed to sex offenders or those, who committed crimes against road safety. Other programs that promote personal growth or that related to teaching of life skills are also a possible prosocial use of time.

New technologies offer many more alternatives to create treatments adapted to the needs of each inmate. Thus, depending on his or her characteristics, criminal typology, etc., a program adapted to him or her can be elaborated. This would avoid creating typical programs applicable to any inmate, since, as Pollock (2004) points out, "there is a tendency to offer a one-size-fits-all treatment program to all inmates and, because inmates are different, this approach is bound to fail" (p. 132).

In addition to the above statement, new technologies were introduced in the Spanish penitentiary through Instruction 2/2007, which enabled videoconferences in case of medical consultations that may take place between prisons and health centers of the public network, private health centers or between other prisons (III.3.). The Instruction requires the centers between which the videoconference is to be carried out to have compatible systems, to guarantee the confidentiality of the communication during the whole health consultation and the inmate to state his express wish of having the consultation that way. In addition, the Instruction indicates that the purpose of introducing this possibility is to facilitate and improve the health care of inmates, making it more accessible to them, with prior authorization of the General Subdirectorate of Health.

As the Australian newspaper *Government News* points out, online therapy means continuity, as prisoners could keep the same therapist, even if they were transferred or released (28/01/2015).

Leisure and Entertainment

One of the areas in which new technologies have a special impact is undoubtedly leisure. Any activity in which the inmate invests his or her time in order to entertain himself or herself, will not only make his or her stay in prison more bearable, as time is the greatest obstacle, but will also help him or her to free himself or herself from tensions that deprivation of liberty generates. Proof of this is the study of Ribbens and Malliet (2015), in which they show how "digital games provide inmates with an additional tool to manage time, interact with fellow inmates, escape the prison walls, experience aesthetic emotions and regain the feeling of being in control of a situation" (p. 1).

Besides, it has already been mentioned that the Belgian penitentiary system is particularly advanced in terms of the presence of new technologies in prison. A good example of it is the prison of Antwerp, in which the welfare of the inmates prevails, allowing them to make calls from their cells, to play computer games and to download music and films, including adult ones (BBC News, 22/04/2016).

Judicial Proceedings

As already pointed out, when talking about the field of interpersonal communications and medical consultations, Instruction 2/2007 also allows videoconferences to carry out legal actions, that is, for the holding of trials and proceedings, at the request of judicial bodies (III.1.). This is also expressly foreseen in article 229.3 of the *Ley Orgánica del Poder Judicial* (Law of the Judiciary) and in article 325 of the *Ley de Enjuiciamiento Criminal* (Criminal Procedure Law). This means great advantages for the Administration, by allowing it to dispense with the transfer of the inmates in certain cases (De Marcos Madruga, 2014, pp. 239-240), which also favors the agility of the procedures, avoids custody and travel expenses and reduces risks of escape (Martín Moral, 2014, p. 48).

However, it seems that this videoconferencing system has not been fully implemented in Spain. In fact, a recent newspaper article states that the penitentiary and juvenile justice centers of Catalonia will begin to install these systems that will connect them with the bar associations. This installation, which is expected to be completed by 2018, could halve the 37,000 face-to-face visits that are made each year between lawyers and inmates, saving time and costs (La Vanguardia, 23/03/2017).

RISKS OF THE EXISTENCE OF INTERNET IN PRISON

Once seen the areas of the introduction of new technologies in the prison environment and the positive aspects that entails, it is necessary to allude to the obvious risks that may arise from such implementation.

In Spain, Instruction 3/2010, of the General Secretariat of Penitentiary Institutions, of security enforcement protocol, indicates that the absence of ICTs in prison is due to security reasons and establishes the adoption of a series of measures of control to prevent the introduction into prisons of classic forbidden objects, as well as more sophisticated electronic elements, among which are means of communication with the outside, such as mobile phones.

The reason used to reject the presence of such devices is based mainly on the fact that, as the Instruction says in its second subsection third paragraph, its use as a means of communication with the outside world, provides inmates with the opportunity to bypass both the mandatory control and the registration of their communications, as the intervention of the same when agreed, allowing them on the other hand, to maintain uncontrolled contact with their criminal environment, continue their criminal activity and even organize from within the facility the commission of new crimes.

Indeed, new technologies not only offer advantages, but have created also new risks before the appearance of criminal behaviors that can be committed exclusively through those and whose sophistication allows its effects to have a more immediate, accurate, unpredictable and uncontrollable nature than with the traditional attack techniques. Hence, Criminal law has not been alien to this reality and has adapted its contents to new behaviors that are carried out entirely in cyberspace (Picotti, 2007, p. 113), and that require a highly specialized and precise criminalization, which is in constant transformation and evolution (González Cussac, 2013, p. 225).

In fact, bearing in mind that such risks could also occur especially in the penitentiary environment, as evidenced by the aforementioned Instruction, the last reasons that this argument are considered by the author superfluous, to the extent that they can also be used to deter promotion of communication even with the existing media. It seems rather that what is mainly intended, in line with the argument used by the Instruction, is to avoid the uncontrolled use of these new means of communication, without, if necessary, being able to exercise control over the content of the same, as it is possible to do it in the current forms of communication.

Therefore, with the aforementioned Instruction, the main risk that seeks to be avoided has to do with the security of the facility and the possible harmful consequences that could occur due to the uncontrolled use of new technologies in prison. These consequences, fundamentally, would come from the possible perpetration of new crimes committed through their use. Thus, as De Marcos (2014) points out, the exchange of information that would take place using personal computers could endanger the security of the facility itself, in addition to encouraging in many cases criminal practices (think of drug trafficking, economic delinquency...), when not the address of the same from the prison itself (p. 242). As Pollock (2004) points out, in general terms, and with respect to the protection of the right to freedom of expression of the individual foreseen in the First Amendment of the U.S. Constitution, First Amendment of the U.S. Constitution, "the prisoner´s right to receive mail and publications is balanced against the prison´s right to protect safety and security" (p. 159).

However, as other authors have pointed out, fears regarding security "have previously been rehearsed in relation to other communication technologies, but have been either successfully managed or dismissed" (Jewkes, 2009, p. 177) and that "the consequences of not allowing prisoners access to online education, information and entertainment are considerably greater than the potential security threats posed by any individual inmate" (Jewkes, 2009, p. 185).

In short, the misuse that can occur in this context on the part of the subjects deprived of liberty is an indisputable risk, as it is also in the telephone communications, in the visits of relatives and friends or in the exits to the outside when they enjoy of release. However, in the opinion of the author of this work, to make the prison sentence useful and reach one of the purposes pursued, it seems appropriate to assume this risk, maintaining the balance between the rights of the inmate and the security of the facility, without sacrificing any of the two sides of the scales. For this, it is necessary to confront a control of the risks that may arise from the inclusion of new technologies in the penitentiary environment, subjecting them to certain restrictions and establishing a series of security measures, as will be explained below.

PROPOSAL FOR THE INTRODUCTION OF NEW TECHNOLOGIES IN PRISON

Based on the considerations made so far, it seems appropriate to consider, at least, the possibility of introducing ICTs in different areas of daily life in prisons.

The majority of those mentioned, such as education, employment or communications, would allow a better resocialization of the prisoner, as it is pointed out by the 2011 ODA report on penitentiary reality and policy carried out by experts from the *Instituto Andaluz Interuniversitario de Criminología* (Andalusian Interuniversity Institute of Criminology), in its Section of Málaga, based on a broad notion of "treatment" and locating the origin of crime in social deficiencies, it is considered that investments in welfare within prison favor reinsertion (García España & Díez Ripollés, 2011, pp. 240-241).

Therefore, to implement it realistically, it is necessary to consider, in the opinion of the author, two fundamental aspects: on the one hand, the establishment of certain security limitations, referred to the form of access and, on the other hand, certain limitations as for the inmates who can access new technologies in the penitentiary environment.

In the first place, regarding security limitations, the implementation of ICTs in the penitentiary environment could be materialized through the installation within each prison of a computer room monitored by a main computer, from which certain restrictions could be established in each place with a user profile for each inmate. In this way, each inmate would have a username and a password with which he or she would access the terminal, with any action he or she made on the network being registered. Thus, as pointed out by Elvira-Valdés (2014), a regulated and standardized use of ICTs in jail would allow to have detailed records in terms of equipment and serials" and if crimes were committed through them, "this strategy would result in more effective to carry out the location and point out those responsible (p. 94).

The regulation of these restrictions could start with those that already exist in the Spanish penitentiary legislation. Thus, regarding communications, the inmate could have personal e-mail and an account to make video calls, which could be governed by similar guidelines to those currently in force for written communications, that is, always establishing previously the sender's name and surnames (Article 46.2° RP) and registering the messages sent or received by inmates (Article 46.2° and 4° PR), always respecting to the maximum the conditions of privacy and may be intervened for the same reasons as oral communications (Article 46.1° PR), i.e. for reasons of security, interest of the treatment and good order of the establishment (Article 51 LOGP and Article 43 RP); Or some of the legal provisions established for telephone calls could be adopted analogously, such as that the mails can be stored, as currently established in *Instrucción 4/2005* in its seventh comma paragraph first letter c) regarding telephone calls, which will be archived monthly in electronic format; Or archiving a copy of the authorized email addresses, in addition to the familiar, friendship or professional relationship of the persons with whom it is desired to maintain this type of communications (seventh comma paragraph first letter e) of *Instrucción 4/2005*).

A good example that a safe implementation is possible, is Instruction 2/2007, which introduced the possibility to celebrate videoconferences in prison for judicial actions, medical consultations and communications, with certain personal (II.2.b) and technical (II .2 C) security means.

Secondly, in relation to the limitations regarding inmates who could make use of new technologies in prison, this possibility should not be offered to the entire prison population. Thus, on the one hand, inmates classified in the first penitentiary degree (also called grade 1) would be clearly excluded from said option, ruling for them certain restrictions even with regard to the dimensions of the radio and television sets they have in their cells (Carou, 2017, pp. 212 y 231). On the other hand, it should not be applicable to all inmates classified in the second degree or in the ordinary regime (also called grade 2). Thus, accepting that new technologies can pose a risk to the security of the facility and the future commission of new crimes, but that in turn constitute a very positive tool for reinsertion, the inmates who should be able to access those are the ones who find near the enjoyment of exit permits. This proposal would make the return to life in freedom more progressive, favoring a greater prior contact of the inmate with the outside world.

In the Spanish penitentiary system, inmates who can enjoy ordinary exit permits, as established in article 47.2 LOGP, are those who have extinguished a quarter of the total sentence and who have good behavior. In these cases, the prison supervision judge may authorize the ordinary exit permits, previously requested by the prisoner.

In similar terms, to access new technologies in the penitentiary area, it could be established as a requirement that the inmate has completed one sixth of the sentence, that he has good behavior and, in the opinion of the author, it would also be necessary to include a third requirement, at least to afford its incipient introduction in prisons, and is to consider the type of crime committed. Thus, those inmates whose criminal activity has been closely related to new technologies, would not have access to these in prison. This applies for cases in which the crime was committed entirely using the Internet, such as computer fraud, child grooming or hacking, among many others. An alternative in these cases, in which Internet access could be allowed to these inmates, would be the restriction of access to certain websites, as in Antwerp prison (Belgium) where inmates can Access the internet, but only certain sites and where Facebook, for example, is not allowed (BBC News, 22/04/2016).

An interesting experience for the proposal is that of The Guardian, in its newspaper of October 3, 2016, in which it explains that in the United States there are some companies that are exclusively dedicated to providing technological devices with Internet connection in a good number of prisons. Companies as Edovo, JPay or American Prison Data System have distributed over the last years basic tablet computers to thousands of inmates, offering educational and entertainment content. This practice is a good example to be followed in Spanish prisons, because its features could be applicable to any penitentiary system. Some of those features applied in different prisons in the UK are the following: first, tablets are limited to 15 minutes, which could be extended as a reward for good behavior; second, they are connected to a secure private network, are monitored remotely 24/7 and can be immediately shut down at the request of prison officials; and third, inmates earn points by taking educational and rehabilitative courses, which can be spent later on games, music or videos (The Guardian, 03/10/2016).

Experiences like this and those revised throughout the whole research make it possible to draw a future in which prison sentences do not remain anchored in another decade and seize on new technologies and the possibilities they offer for persons deprived of liberty.

CONCLUSION

In Spain, the presence of new technologies in the penitentiary sphere is not a novelty in terms of the security of the facility. Neither is it within the scope of the penalty system. Therefore, its introduction in relation to the rights of the inmates and in order to promote their social reinsertion should not take long to come.

There are many experiences that can be found at the international level, which show that the usefulness of new technologies in prison has a very positive effect on the resocialization of the inmate population, allowing them to have greater contact with the world in freedom and less with the prison subculture, which gives rise to the phenomenon of 'prisonization'.

Therefore, its introduction in realistic terms means that the inmate can have access to new technologies prior to the enjoyment of exit permits, for a progressive adaptation to life in freedom aimed at resocialization, understood in terms of returning to the law, with the sole purpose that the person who has been deprived of liberty dedicate his or her time to prosocial activities that take him or her away from the new crime commission.

As Knight (2015) points out "…the enriching benefits of prisoners taking control of their own lives, however small can nourish the social and emotional responses to modern imprisonment. Exploring and evaluating these kinds of impacts are necessary in order to fully understand the psychosocial dimensions on the experience of incarceration and marry the aims of imprisonment with resettlement and desistance" (p. 9).

To conclude, reforming prisons in this sense is considered by the author of this paper an opportunity to offer inmates a progressive resettlement to life in freedom. The value that new technologies would add to education, employment, communications or treatment to a person deprived of liberty constitutes a way of humanization of prisons in the 21st century.

REFERENCES

Benito Rangel, F., Espartero Martínez, P., García Marijuán, J. A., Garrido Martínez, A., & López-Araujo, J. F. (2002). La Ciencia y Práctica Penitenciaria en una Sociedad en Cambio: Apuntes para una Reflexión de Futuro. *Revista Electrónica de Ciencia Penal y Criminología*, *4*(1).

Bobes, M., & García, A. (2010). El Uso de las TIC como Herramienta Educativa y Terapéutica en el Contexto Penitenciario. El Proyecto Òmnia en las Prisiones Catalanas. *Revista de Educación Social*. Retrieved from http://www.eduso.net/res/?b=14&c=131&n=3

Burgos Oliván, L., García Villar, A., & Tomás Humbert, C. (2007). El Blog desde la Prisión: Un Instrumento de Inclusión Social. *Educación y Biblioteca*, *158*, 102–109.

Carou García, S. (2017). *Primer grado penitenciario y estado de derecho: El estatus jurídico de los reclusos en régimen de máxima seguridad*. Barcelona: Bosch.

Cobo del Rosal, M., & Boig Reig, J. (1982). Derechos fundamentales del condenado. Reeducación y reinserción social. Comentarios a la Legislación penal, 217-227.

Daunis Rodríguez, A. (2016). *Ejecución de Penas en España*. Editorial Comares.

De Marcos Madruga, F. (2014). Las nuevas tecnologías en los centros penitenciarios y sus implicaciones jurídicas. In *Sistema penitenciario y nuevas tecnologías* (pp. 225–249). Valladolid: Lex Artis.

Díez Ripollés, J. L. (2011). La Dimensión Inclusión/Exclusión Social como Guía de la Política Criminal Comparada. *Revista Electrónica de Ciencia Penal y Criminología (RECPC)*, *13-12*, 1-36.

Easton, S. (2011). *Prisoners' Rights. Principles and practice*. London: Routledge.

El Confidencial. (2013, August 24). ¿Viven bien los presos en las cárceles españolas? *El Confidencial Digital*. Retrieved from http://www.elconfidencialdigital.com/te_lo_aclaro/Viven-bien-presos-carceles-espanolas_0_2113588622.html

Elvira-Valdés, M. A. (2014). Presos 2.0: Comunicación y TIC's en Contextos de Encarcelamiento. *Perspectivas de la Comunicación*, *7*(1), 84–96.

Europa Press. (2017, April 15). El Gobierno confirma que los internos de la prisión "no tienen conexión a Internet para estudiar", según Cs. *20 minutos*. Retrieved from http://www.20minutos.es/noticia/3012115/0/gobierno-confirma-que-internos-prision-no-tienen-conexion-internet-para-estudiar-segun-cs/

Europa Press. (2017, March 23). Las cárceles catalanas empiezan a conectar por videoconferencia a presos y abogados. *La Vanguardia*. Retrieved from http://www.lavanguardia.com/vida/20170323/421130274867/los-carceles-catalanas-empiezan-a-conectar-por-videoconferencia-a-presos-y-abogados.html

Fernández Díaz, C. R. (2015). Las Relaciones del Interno con el Mundo Exterior y su Importancia para la Reeducación y Reinserción Social. *Revista Electrónica de Ciencia Penal y Criminología (RECPC)*, *17*(7), 1-26.

García España, E., & Díez Ripollés, J. L. (2011). *Realidad y Política Penitenciarias*. Valencia: Tirant lo Blanch.

Garland, D. (2003). *The Culture of Control. Crime and Social Order in Contemporary Society*. Oxford, UK: Oxford University Press.

González Cussac, J. L. (2013). Tecnocrimen. In *Nuevas amenazas a la seguridad nacional. Terrorismo, criminalidad organizada y tecnologías de la información y la comunicación*. Valencia: Tirant lo Blanch.

Helsper, E. (2012). A Corresponding Fields Model for the Links between Social and Digital Exclusion. *Communication Theory*, *22*(4), 403–426.

Hirschi, T. (1969). *Causes of Delinquency*. Berkeley, CA: University of California Press.

Instituto Nacional de Estadística. (2017, September). *Unemployment rate in Spain*. Retrieved from http://www.ine.es/dyngs/INEbase/es/operacion.htm?c=Estadistica_C&cid=1254736176918&menu=ultiDatos&idp=1254735976595

Jewkes, Y. (2009). The role of the Internet in the twenty-first-century prison. Insecure technologies in secure spaces. In *Technologies of Insecurity. The surveillance of everyday life* (pp. 171–188). Routledge-Cavendish.

Knight, V. (2015, July). Some Observations on the Digital Landscape of Prisons Today. *Prison Service Journal*, *220*, 3–9.

Knight, V. (2016). *Remote Control. Television in prison*. London: Palgrave Macmillan.

Martín Moral, M. F. (2014). La utilización del sistema de videoconferencia en el marco de las instituciones penitenciarias. In *Sistema penitenciario y nuevas tecnologías* (pp. 45–60). Valladolid: Lex Artis.

Mata y Martín, R. M. (2014). Sistema penitenciario y nuevas tecnologías. In *Sistema penitenciario y nuevas tecnologías* (pp. 9–25). Valladolid: Lex Artis.

Nordic Council of Ministers. (2005). *Nordic Prison Education. A lifelong learning perspective*. Copenhaghen: Temanord.

Novo-Corti, I., & Barreiro-Gen, M. (2014). Barreras Físicas y Barreras Virtuales: Delito y Pena en la Era Digital. Nuevas Políticas Públicas para la Reinserción. RiHum So - Revista de Investigación del Departamento de Humanidades y Ciencias Sociales Universidad Nacional de La Matanza, 2(5), 85-104.

Picotti, L. (2007). Intercettazioni "Illegali" tra Nuove Tecnologie e Vecchi Strumenti Penali. *Diritto dell'Internet, 2*.

Pollock, J. M. (2004). *Prisons and prison life. Cost and consequences*. Los Angeles, CA: Roxbury Publishing Company.

Redondo Illescas, S., & Garrido Genovés, V. (2013). *Principios de Criminología* (4th ed.). Valencia: Tirant lo Blanch.

Ribbens, W., & Malliet, S. (2015). Exploring the Appeal of Digital Games to Male Prisoners. *Poetics*, *48*, 1–20.

Ríos Martín, J. C., & Cabrera Cabrera, P. J. (1998). *Mil voces presas*. Madrid: Universidad Pontificia de Comillas.

Sansom, M. (2015, January 28). A digital future for prisons. *GovernmentNews*. Retrieved from https://governmentnews.com.au/2015/01/a-digital-future-for-prisons/

Tighe, S. (2016, April 22). Prisoners allowed access to adult films and internet. *BBC News*. Retrieved from http://www.bbc.com/news/world-europe-36067653

Tocino Hernández, C. M. (2014). Internet en la cárcel. In *Sistema penitenciario y nuevas tecnologías* (pp. 29–43). Valladolid: Lex Artis.

Tynan, D. (2016, October 3). Online behind bars: if internet access is a human right, should prisoners have it? *The Guardian*. Retrieved from https://www.theguardian.com/us-news/2016/oct/03/prison-internet-access-tablets-edovo-jpay

United Nations General Assembly. (2011). *Report of the Special Rapporteur on the promotion and protection of the right to freedom of opinion and expression*. Human Rights Council of the General Assembly of the United Nations. Retrieved from http://www2.ohchr.org/english/bodies/hrcouncil/docs/17session/A.HRC.17.27_en.pdf

Vogel, B. (2009). *The Prison Library Primer. A Program for the Twenty-First Century*. London: The Scarecrow Press.

Weinrath, M. (2016). *Behind the walls. Inmates and Correctional Officers on the State of Canadian Prisons*. Vancouver: UBC Press.

KEY TERMS AND DEFINITIONS

Information and Communication Technologies: Different ways of telecommunications normally used to access, send, or store information and to communicate through them.

Inmate: A person who is serving an imprisonment sentence in prison, deprived of his or her liberty.

Internet: A form of information and communication technology that can access, send or store data or communicate with others through different devices, such as cell phones or computers.

Prison: A facility where a person, who is sentenced to imprisonment after committing a crime, serves his or her sentence, deprived of liberty.

Prisonization: The adaptation and acceptance of the life and culture within prison.

Recidivism: To commit a new crime after having served an imprisonment sentence.

Resocialization: The process of going back to life in freedom after serving an imprisonment sentence.

Chapter 2
The Role of Information and Communications Technology in the Social Reintegration of Ex-Prisoners

António Pedro Dores
University Institute of Lisbon, Portugal

ABSTRACT

The development of information and communications technology (ICT) over the past few decades has been positively surprising. Prison development has also been surprising, in a negative way. Hardline policy positions towards crime and the expansion in the consumption of ICT products are contemporaneous. They are co-occurrences. What makes sense of this apparent contradiction is the way societies experience distinct dispositions depending on the issues they have to face. The same people are able to be optimistic, in relation to the positive use of computers, and pessimistic as to the possibility of the criminal-penal system being able to combat crime. Is it possible for society to experience a disposition in which punitiveness regarding prisoners is replaced by the hope of reintegration for those convicted of crime? The answer is: there can be a shift of the dominant disposition, but for that we must reshape the whole of this society into another.

DOI: 10.4018/978-1-5225-5975-7.ch002

INTRODUCTION

(...) technical feasibility alone is not enough - political motivation is also essential.
Patricia Fara (2009) Science: 421.

The development of information and communications technology (ICT) over the past few decades has been surprising. It has decidedly altered our daily lives. And, is always the case with such phenomena, there are enthusiasts, techno-optimists, and conservatives, techno-pessimists. The latter, concerned with the growth of unemployment caused by automation and with the ecological consequences of industrialization for the survival of the human species.

Prison development has also been surprising (Wacquant 2016). The exponential increase in the number of prisoners and the growth of international institutions for the prevention of torture were not part of the imagination of those who, in the 1970s, anticipated the year 2000 as symbolizing the realization of the Western civilizational ideal. Also surprising in light of what was that ideal is the complicit popular indifference in relation to torture which has taken hold since.

In the modern imagination, ICT represents a revival of a joyful sense of progress that has been lost in other fields, such as energy and the economy. On the other hand, the prison situation elicits a depressive apprehension, even among defenders of the criminal-penal system.

Societies experience distinct dispositions depending on the issues they have to face. The same people are able to be optimistic, in relation to the positive use of computers, and pessimistic as to the possibility of the criminal-penal system being able to combat crime, without it compromising their intellectual or moral coherence and constancy

We do not need the results of a survey in order to know that, in recent decades, despite the evidence on climate change, modernism is the dominant disposition. Nor do we need special deductive powers to know that the target audience of this book seeks the answer to the question: is it possible for society to experience a disposition in which punitiveness regarding prisoners is replaced by the hope of reintegration for those convicted of crime?

Table 1. Dispositions elicited by ICT and prisons

ICT **Prisons**	**Techno-optimism**	**Techno-scepticism**
Tough on crime	Modernism	Reactionary
Hope of resocialisation	This book's target audience	New Wave

The answer is: there can be a shift of the dominant disposition, but for that we must reshape the whole of this society into another.

By the 80's the digital revolution was impacting every sphere of social life, and ICT in particular was generating great enthusiasm. As symbol of late modernity, ICT became the focus of those energies that, in the 60's, had been applied to social revolution. During that same period, prisons turned from places where people were isolated from society for relatively short periods of time in order to be prepared for positive opportunities upon release, into warehouses where people are expected to do little other than what they can to survive longer and longer sentences in increasingly dehumanizing, overcrowded conditions.

Society and individuals are like that: of an unstable disposition. At one moment they blame the criminals, and at another the state which incarcerates them. Hence, for long periods of time the bulk of the blame was emphatically placed upon the state. Then the dominant disposition changed. This would lead us to believe it can change again in the future, even if things must get worse before they get better.

This chapter briefly discusses the resistance within organizations to the introduction of ICT, the type of organization built by the penal system over the last decades and the paradoxical ambiguity of the incarceration mandate pursued by the state and society. Social analysis will not be useful to clarify what is going on if it does not attend to the analysis of social dispositions: the previously mentioned macro dispositions and the micro dispositions which separate the uses of ICTs by the lower class (games) and the middle class (learning). Would the prison system accept becoming a school for its inmates as its objective? Experience shows that the introduction of ICTs into the prisons is very slow and often clandestine, driven by the efforts of the prisoners, not the teachers. For now, the dominant disposition does not support the use of ICTs for education in prison, except in isolated pilot studies – as modernist propaganda capable of masking the violations of human rights and the organizational consequences of the reactionary impulse which drives the hard-line policy positions towards crime.

BACKGROUND

This is a reply taken from Durkheim's theory (1960), which posited the existence and study of the spirit of mechanical solidarity (existing in rural and simpler societies) and the spirit of organic solidarity (existing in urban societies). The author also proposed the study of sectoral solidarities in complex societies, such as the one that Garland (2001) described among the professionals in UK and USA prisons, which was in effect after the 1980s: the place of interventions aiming at social reintegration had been severely discredited.

Experience shows that societies transform themselves. Medieval times transformed into capitalistic times and, for Socialists, there is hope that this structural transformation will continue to develop. Be it as a result of technological development or moral evolution, societies change. They also change due to wars and class struggles. They experience periods of nostalgia or hope in the future. Conservatism or progressivism succeed or fail. Guessing the future is not for us, but we cannot ignore the fact that the future will be different from the present – as can be easily established by anyone with more than 20 years of memory.

In terms of incarceration, conservatism and punitiveness remain dominant since the 80s. Compared by contrast with the enthusiasm in relation to technological progress. New technological utopias compared with the return of torture and mass incarceration.

MAIN FOCUS OF THE CHAPTER

Can the introduction of ICT in prison transform it? What does past experience tell us? What is the dominant disposition in the prison sector? How can the evolution of societies, or any possible revolutions that might come to take place in the future, change the structural place of prison in society? This chapter will consider some answers to these questions.

Issues, Controversies, Problems

The Introduction of ICT in the Prison

In the 1980s, there was hope that ICT could solve the challenge of making the schools for the masses able to meet the individual needs of each student, with nothing more than technological investment. Already then it was, to some, clear that it would be impossible to achieve that goal. But the enthusiasm for pursuing it was great. There were those who wanted to end schools (Illich 1971), those who wanted to save on the educational budget by reducing the number of teachers, those in favour of new teaching methods, tailored to the particular needs of each student. More importantly, there was drive for the idea from both sides of those most directly involved with the practical aspects of the issue: on the teachers' side by those involved in computer-in-school programmes, and on the parents' side, by those anxious to offer their children the skills with which to tackle the future (Dores 1996).

By contrast, there is no such enthusiasm for social reintegration as an objective in today's prisons, not even at the departmental level (Firouzi et al., 2016). But there are experiments in some French prisons with using ICT to combat digital-exclusion and illiteracy, and the installation of a university centre in an Italian prison, the operation of which makes computers and the Internet indispensable (Crétenot 2014). This same source also noted the existence of therapeutic prisons in Britain where individuals, on entry, were surprised to be treated as persons rather than prisoners. In Spain, in recent years, there was a attempt to generalize access to therapeutic prisons (Ministerio del Interior, 2018). However, before there was time to evaluate the impact of the shift, there was a reversal in those policies.

As it happened with schools, the resistance to modernization observed in prisons, in relation to new conditions arising from social changes, ends up generating spontaneous phenomena. In schools, with the evolution of the market for personal computers and mobile phones, the question has now become the ban on the use of laptops and mobile phones in classrooms. IPads subvert the logic of teaching, in particular to the extent that they constitute extensions of human memory and give access to the solutions to all the problems already solved.

The pedagogical notion of re-creating in each child and youth the cognitive history of humanity is very quickly becoming obsolete. Youngsters and even children are often able to teach teachers how to use ICT. Some basic schools and pedagogical thinkers imposing, as they can, throwback rules to recreate the ideal conditions for traditional teaching/learning, without ICT.

In prisons, besides the introduction of radios, televisions, CD players, Gameboys, sometimes admitted as perks and privileges, in the perspective of the effort to humanize prison services, there is also the illicit trafficking in mobile phones, with or without access to the internet. For prisoners with the resources to make these purchases, and for their friends, there is the possibility of overcoming the limitations imposed by the prisons on telephone contact with family and friends. At the same time there is the possibility of prisoners intervening in social networks. Arguing security concerns, prison services ineffectively prohibit the use of ICT in prison. In the process the space for a new market is created; one in which mobile phones and IPads found during security searches are resold to prisoners at exorbitant prices.

There is also the possibility of prisoners creating (authorized or not) newspapers and (forbidden) blogs. In one case or another, especially when there is a guarantee that such writing opportunities will not be used to reveal the intimacies of prison life, there is authorization for available ICT to be put to such uses, under the direct control of staff, of course. Yet, in practice there are no cases of continuity of such projects, especially since the temptation by the prisoners to claim freedom of expression – which theoretically is within their rights – is simply resolved by the authorities with the termination of the project.

The Dominant Disposition in the Prison Sector

At the moment, the punitiveness of criminal sentences is only discussed in politics in terms of making them more severe. The discovery of sex crimes (Wacquant n.d.), the fear of migrant workers (Palidda & Garcia 2010) and terrorism, leave the public confused and governments struggling with security hard line pressures coming also from progressives groups (Karam, 1996; Paladines, 2013). Although the situation may change at any moment, for we live unstable times, both sides, governments and oppositions, are impervious, at least publicly, to any notion of mercy. Political party platforms too are silent as to the problem of how to overcome the chronic situations of torture identified, in all countries, by the international bodies responsible for that work.

In continental Europe, the independence and autonomy of the judiciary have been used to exempt politicians and the legislature from taking any sort of position on what happens in the prisons. The Portuguese case, although particular, shows how it is possible for legislation to be completely and radically unrelated to actual penal practices. Despite the Portuguese situation comparing badly, in the sense of it being disproportionately harsh, with other European penal systems, and of its social reintegration services – created in 1982, to copy the institutions of the countries of the then EEC, which Portugal was preparing to join – having never, in practice, fulfilled the functions of providing effective support to ex-prisoners, the Penal Code of 2009 considers the social reintegration of the individual as the sole purpose of sentencing.

At the same time as the legislature enacts more judicial protections for prisoners and a singular, absolute priority for social reintegration, the penal system continues to function as if those laws did not exist or could be interpreted against themselves, at the whim of its officials. Officials immersed in a punitive culture of arbitrariness and impunity, which they apply to prisoners and is also applied to them. Generating what is called the prison secret, the fear of witnessing (Cordeiro, 2018). The separation between penal policy (officially shown as residing in legal texts and best political intentions) and penal practices (hidden from the public, professionals, prisoners and inspectors, with the collaboration of all parties, with the exception of the rare, largely ignored, whistle-blower).

The UK and USA systems' alternative is not the most favourable. There, they looked at the studies that revealed the virtually insurmountable difficulties of rehabilitating prisoners (Martinson 1974) as a basis for abandoning the efforts of the previous decades (after the Second World War) to reverse recidivism rates through specialized social work. Instead they have given priority to what they call prevention, that is, the incapacitation of the convicted. Namely, by resuming the broad use of the death penalty, or keeping individuals in prison for life and as isolated as possible, such as in solitary confinement that can last for years.

The frankness with which the Bush administration studied the legality of torture in US prisons hides the secret prisons of the CIA and what goes on in Guantanamo. All of it taking place under cover of public favour, which was surprised by Abu Grahib's photos and strives to ignore that such practices were exported from the United States' own prisons (Perkinson in press).

How can the enthusiasm and hope created by ICT, the modernist spirit, infect the disposition of the criminal-penal system and the opportunities for ex-prisoners to reconstruct their lives? Despite the punitive focus of the penal system, does it make sense to be hopeful, regardless of current sentencing practices?

If you adopt the theory of dispositions, the answer is yes: two radically distinct dispositions can coexist and be experienced by the same people (although at different times). Then the question becomes another: what are the opportune times for the hope associated with ICT to enter the life of the prisoners?

The Structural Place of the Prisons, in Society

We do not need the results of a study to state, with confidence, that 'though on crime', as a precept, occupies the social, individual, institutional and professional mind in such a way that the hope of reintegration is satisfied (or not) at the margin of the political and institutional representation of those who contribute to the successful return of prisoners to society. In fact, family members and friends the ones who are quietly charged with working for the reintegration of the prisoners. The success rates are slim, indicted by high rates of recidivism and the reproduction of detention dynamics within the family. Those sentenced to prison are much more likely to end up in prison again. The children of parents who have been incarcerated are much more likely themselves to end up in prison. Abandoned children, cared for by the state or philanthropic organizations, are also much more likely to end up in prison.

There is a recognized effectiveness problem with the organizations and professionals theoretically charged with the prevention of crime and social opportunity inequalities among abandoned children. As previously stated, the diagnosis of this situation did not lead to questioning the functionality of establishing social-assistance-criminal-penal circuits. By the contrary, it originated a disconnection of social assistance from the criminal-penal system, in the UK and USA, and a disassociation between legislative prescriptions and penal practices, of which the Portuguese case is a clear example. Other European countries, in their own way, suffer from the same problem: despite the obligation to comply with Council of Europe requirements and recommendations on prison management, to meet the statute of European Union countries, none of the eight prison systems studied by the European Prison Observatory takes them into account (Maculan et al., 2014).

The practical responsibility for the reintegration of prisoners lies with the part of the society most affected by the problems arising from the identified institutional, organizational and professional difficulties. To that end, that part of society, generally impoverished by the arrest of those who, lawfully or unlawfully, provided it with income, has to endure and overcome the hostility of organizations and professionals, at the margin of what is established to support said reintegration. This is very visible and evident in the arrogance and intimidation with which visitors (the future possible reintegrators) are received and treated in prisons.

This distance between relatives and friends of prisoners and the state is reinforced by the dominant disposition, characterized by the increasingly more evident distance between voters and their representatives (Oborne 2008). After the era of affirmation of human rights regimes, following the Second World War, effected by the anti-colonial and civic movements of the sixties, a gap developed between what politics and politicians can discuss (both in countries emerging from colonization and in the colonizing countries) and the realities of everyday life. There is an increasing distaste for politics, as conducted by the states and the media, and sense of alienation from decisions made within complex organizational networks (Castells 2004). At the same time, there is an imagining of alternatives in affinity networks (Castells 2012), at the margins of the states.

The theory of class struggle is not up to the task of explaining the function of prisons, given that the experiences of 'real socialism' have not been edifying in this respect. Nor, for that matter, are there among opposition parties, however fringe, any known political intentions to reform existing social-criminal-penal institutions. Sociological studies in this area use mainly the functionalist paradigm, through the concepts of anomie and social control, to explain the social-criminal-penal system in light of the theory of state reaction to contain the populations' sense of insecurity (Ferreira 1997).

Social control theory does not, however, explain the fact that it is often the state, and the media, who provoke and use the people's feelings of insecurity for their own ends (Roberts & Hough 2002). Neither does it explain the lack of reaction on the part of the state and public opinion to the inefficient crime prevention achieved by the professional practices of the social-criminal-penal system. Nor the absence of political and public scandal when collusion between state organizations and organized crime becomes evident (Woodiwiss 2001; Rabbit 2016).

Current social theory limits itself to working within its own self-imposed (national) constructions (Kuhn 2016). Following Durkheim's classic recommendation, it explains social facts through social facts. It has developed anti-biological and anti-ideological prejudices and feelings. It has, in fact, isolated itself from the natural sciences and abandoned the ambition to, one day, be able to compare to them from the point of view of cognitive rigor. It also isolated itself from doctrinal knowledge, relegating the relations between social theory and law or theology (as it does with science) to subspecialties. It refuses to mix methods and concepts with these other disciplines, although doing so is its tradition: there are social scientists working at the same time in two or more of these fields. But there is no epistemic place where such areas of knowledge can mix and influence each other.

The circumstances here briefly presented lead sociologists to predominantly adopt juridical narratives to describe what they witness in and around prisons. All at once, they distort reality, so that it conforms to such preconceptions, and subvert the declared principles of ideological neutrality, in the name of which they conform to the dominant doctrines.

Prisoners, for example, serve as criminal case studies, just because they were convicted. Without any attention being given to the widely known fact of the high level of criminal impunity shown by the comparison of victimization survey data and conviction rates (certainly less than 10% of the crimes declared by victims). And without taking into account instances of miscarriage of justice, whose numbers may be important, if, for example, we take into account reports of judicial error in death-penalty cases in the USA. There is no social theory on how to identify a criminal among the members of a society. Instead, there is a characterization of the penal population and, accordingly, the elaboration of a statistical profile of the average prisoner – young, poor, with little schooling, raised in an unstructured family, keeper of bad company – as bases for elegant but false justifications of how poverty explains the criminal mind (Merton 1970): the number of all living Portuguese who have been incarcerated should be no more than 150,000. Unfortunately, there are at least 2.5 million poor in the country. Therefore it must be that a logic which only affects an ultra-minority is being confused with an ideological problem of stigma contamination.

Objectively, the phenomenon of the revolving door, the high rates of recidivism, is used against a minority of the population, much more specific than the poor. A minority that is yet to be sociologically described. A minority that endure such a though and disturbing life experience that its results are deeper and stronger than the best intentions of reintegration into society, as recidivism shows.

Social theory has obvious difficulties when it comes to addressing certain realities considered marginal. Its focus is the study of power dynamics (Lahire 2012: 125; Therborn 2006: 3). It disregards all that happens through, within and among social support networks (care). Using Mouzelis's (1995) diagnosis, current social theory reduces social reality (to the study of power) and reifies the descriptions of society. It recreates what has been reduced according to the prejudices of testimonies that use common sense to confirm, through questionnaires and interviews, the ideology of the authority of the day. It does so in favour of the nation state (Kuhn 2016), using ideal types fabricated to match prevailing ideologies, and continues to deny the existence of realities stemming from the practice of promoting social inequalities (Bhambra 2014: 146-150).

The role of the prisons is, possibly, structural and structuring (Foucault 1975; Wacquant 2000). But the precise characterization of that role has not been found.

Dispositions

Information and communication technologies and prisons are consigned to mental and moral sub-paradigms. Although they share the same culture, like Rousseau and Hobbes, Kant and Machiavelli, technologies are assigned angelic references (techno-optimism) and prisons demonic references (Zimbardo 2007).

Positive and negative modernism are both human experiences known to us all. Some of us, few, have the opportunity to live immersed in the hope of ICT; but no one to the same level as Bill Gates or Steve Jobs. Others, also few, experience the hopelessness of prisons; but no one like those who are forced to live in isolation, for life. Many more live the hopelessness of being abandoned by fortune, like those who live in famine (Caparrós 2014) or are subjected to genocide. Although all can understand each other, because they are all human, the loss of contact between them produces isolation, alienation, forgetfulness, abandonment. There is a spontaneous inability to validate the behaviours that result from different living conditions, given that human attention is limited and focused on each individual's own survival – be it physical survival, in the cases of those who cannot assume to have access to basic resources from day to day; or the survival of identity, even for those who can take their day-to-day security for granted.

Social theory has enshrined the conceptual distinction between social structures. The social positions that impose on each person a repugnance for certain dispositions. Be it as an assimilated way of avoiding social risks, or as sympathy for other dispositions, generally those recommended by those who are in a similar or dominant social position. As Elias (1990) has noted, historically, people tend to imitate dominant cultural practices. Civilization can be described, to a large extent, as the development of the opportunity to democratize the life of the Versailles aristocrats, in their capacity to control violence and in their cultural rituals, at the table or in the management of the home, for example. Or, as Foucault pointed out (2004), by learning to take care of the self, as the patricians in the classical era did, as a way of mystically representing social interests through self-presentation.

The stability of power is sociologically explained by the capacity of social structures for the violent, but above all empathic, rational and calculated, imposition of positive dispositions: according to Nietzsche (1997), the morality of the rulers. Negative dispositions express themselves discreetly (Scott 2013).

In the origins of social studies, this was not the dominant theory. Karl Marx, for example, described industrial conditions in the second half of the nineteenth century as favourable to the re-creation of the revolutionary spirit (Hobsbawn 1997). Engels (1975) described the repugnance provoked by bourgeois and aristocratic social insensitivity to the living conditions of the workers. At the turn of the nineteenth to the twentieth century, Max Weber, in a Protestant version (Weber 2005), countered the Marxist theses with the hegemonic presence of the capitalist spirit. Novak (2001) added a Catholic version, Sennet (2006) a political version, Boltansky and Chiapello (1999) an intellectual version. In the 21st century, the American tycoon Warren Buffett confirmed Max Weber's version: referring to the class struggle, he said "the rich have won!" That is, hegemonic positive and negative feelings are the most experienced by those who are in a position to accumulate wealth and are, generally, shared by societies. Although with reserves, shifts, fracas, riots and revolutions.

Although Emile Durkheim noted how each individual's social position, according to age, marital status, religious belief, sex, etc. affects emotional state and the vulnerability of life (Durkheim 1973), and how human culture, as a means of facing the challenges of survival, evolves starting from simple models of solidarity (Durkheim 2002), Barbelet (2001) noted that current social theories fail to consider emotions, dispositions and the associated instability, in the study of social structures.

When we propose to anticipate what the encounter between ICT and prisons might be, we need to reconsider the essential dilemmas of modern understandings and feelings. ICT is an instruments of socialization suited to the higher classes. They have been democratized, but only in how they are offered, as consumer products. Rare are those who intervene in the industrial objectives of ICT, in the way electronic equipment and services are produced. Electronic equipment and services the functionalities of which are left to the private decision of the large international companies and, to a lesser extent, of the states. Conversely, prisons are forms of repression used primarily against the lower classes, although most of the poor have no problems with justice.

Understanding and being able to impact the developments of and surrounding ICT, or understanding and living in prison, or in sympathy with prisoners, are rare conditions. The importance of each, in its own way, stems from its ability to spread a particular disposition (of disgust or empathy) to the whole of society: trust in progress, confidence in the state security services to protect society.

We must guard against over-interpretations of the potential for diffusion of such dispositions. For example, although younger generations are more likely to use the new ICT tools, the hypothesis that such familiarity has negative cognitive effects in the younger generations cannot be dismissed (Desmurget 2012). Likewise, the preventive value of criminal sentences depends on their appropriateness, reasonableness, regularity and speed. Of course, the war on drugs, with its violations of procedural rules, such as the presumption of innocence (Maia and Costa 2003), did not prevent trafficking or consumption (LEAP 2016) and created difficult situations in the prisons, in the police itself (Machado in press) and in society (Woodiwiss 1988).

ICT can expand the empathy of the ruling classes to the prison, by making instruments of high moral, social and cognitive value (with their prestige) available. They may also stimulate the irreverence of the enthusiasm that machines and mathematics carry in modern societies – at least since Newton, modern culture likens those instruments and principles to God (Fara 2009: 264-272). As such, ICT will be well received by prisoners; as they are by the societies in general. But it also necessary to take into account the fact that most prisoners have experienced scholastic rejection and thus developed a distaste for social learning dynamics. The fear of not being able to learn can, and does inhibit learning.

As it happens with all that is proposed to those in prison, with attraction of having someone whose hand to hold and with whom to share an opportunity to socialize comes the fear of new betrayals, abandonments, frustrations, adverse criticism, which are the result of the social repugnance that guides, structurally, the relationship of the majority of the prisoners with society, since having memory of (not) being people.

It is possible to find people who are predisposed and interested in using ICT inside the prisons. In particular, people interested in occupying their time and keeping in touch with family, friends and others on the outside. There are those who want to take computer courses so they can become professionals. These activities require the creation of a sufficiently broad space for socialization to include the freedom of virtual travel on computer networks. The sentence of restricting ambulatory freedom to a prison does not, in itself, conflict with the freedom to use computer networks. What prevents the widespread use of ICT in prisons is the anthropological value of rituals associated with security and the priority given to them, even when contradictory to the fulfilment of the purpose of sentences: social reintegration and crime prevention.

Recursivity

Prisons produce depressive situations and feelings. ICT produces expansive situations and feelings. History shows how it is practically impossible for contemporaries of a great discovery, such as writing or the press, to anticipate the social transformations that will follow over time. It is natural that today too it is impossible for us to see the current and future impact of the use and development of ICT.

Will the use of ICT in prison be what will help prisons become more capable of facilitating social reintegration, rather than being another way of incapacitating prisoners and their families? Will that process of prison transformation be political; one of dawning social awareness and construction of new institutional practices? Or, by the contrary, one whereby, gradually, prisons, open to various initiatives, including the introduction of computers into institutional daily life, adapt and recognize the advantages of giving priority to the expansion of existential opportunities for prisoners, as ways to facilitate reintegration?

Our personal desires, including those of legislators, as we have seen above, are not enough to transform reality. However, history shows how, through the prevailing disposition of the time, collective desires – what Durkheim called collective consciousness, a synonym for society and solidarity in his work – daily practices and institutional priorities change. What at a certain moment in history seems impossible, becomes banal after a short time. Something which happens without anything more than the individual or professional will to update behaviour to the disposition of the time.

For example, cheap full-time communication, even when people are not at home near a landline, are now a given. The idea of a woman requiring a man's authorization to travel, or to need to prove her marital relationship with a man accompanying her to spend the night in a hotel, is ridiculous and does not enter anyone's mind. In Portugal, 50 years ago, mobile phones and the liberation of women were unthinkable.

ICT, more than the invention of writing and of the press, have the potential to rapidly change societies. What direction will such change take? Or better, in what direction will they be used, by whom and for what purposes?

They have been used to make networks, as noted by Manuel Castells (op. cit.). Networks capable of making the global financial system a reality. A system which then failed a few years after its implementation. That is, ICT, the global structures of production, storage, and diffusion of information and accessibility to that data, works by becoming meshed in society, to serve the interests of its users. And they can be misused, not only in the moral sense – for example, in war, as denounced by the US soldier Manning – but in the economic sense – through corrupt practices – and in the political sense – as in the use of Big Data to incite antagonism toward foreigners, in the Brexit and Trump campaigns.

ICT is used in prisons. The question is whether they have been used in relevant and useful ways. And how new ICT initiatives in prisons can transform them into better organizations.

For the purpose of planning such actions it is, therefore, necessary to define what is meant by better functioning prisons. There are those who understand it as the more effective incapacitation of prisoners as to future criminal behaviour, and those who understand it as prisons serving only to reintegrate people with deviant behaviour, and to do so more efficiently. In practice, the incapacitation of people is a virtually impossible task. Even for the USA which has the capacity to invest lots of money into it. In fact, both in the USA and Europe, as positive results from such weighty investment become harder to come by, policies of reducing the number of prisoners are being implemented. Social reintegration is not done in prisons, in isolation. As the name of the process indicates, social reintegration takes place in society, when people, after the punitive imposition of isolation as punishment for the crimes of which they have been convicted, have the possibility to try to once more live with the people they choose and that accept them.

The confusion of purposes and interpretations of the law, which make prisons "separate societies", does not help to rationally determine what might be a good intervention strategy for volunteers or reformers. Social theory's inability to produce theories independently of doctrinal preconceptions about how and why prisons function stems from the difficulty in establishing the recognition that prison systems do not serve their legally prescribed purposes such as crime prevention, respect for the dignity of prisoners, protection and betterment of society.

Legislative and legal practice, on the other hand, tends to be so unrealistic that it serves as much to cover up and inhibit discussions about what goes on in the prisons as to help society take notice and responsibility, so as to participate in the penal system, what is in fact the social-criminal-penal system.

The practice of states, and also prisons, being open to civil initiatives is characterized by these being conducted in the form of projects. Periodically, for a given period of time, a year, for example, a group of people is allowed to practice their intervention in a prison. If things prove to be functional, authorization may be given for the group to grow and for the same intervention to be extended to other establishments. Throughout, such projects remain contingent on authorization and financing, circumscribers of the freedom of evaluation and self-evaluation of results and, particularly, the possibility of studying the expansion of best practices in a generalized way.

Therapeutic prisons, university satellite campuses inside prisons, the use of internet-based computers to combat illiteracy and digital-exclusion, are examples of consistent projects that may, or may not, transform prisons. We need only a social and political environment, a dominant type of solidarity, to use Durkheim's concept, prone to the generalization of such programmes, so that they may become structural rather than marginal (Dores et al., 2016).

What purpose, what justification, what justice, what law, could cover such a generalization?

Given the lack of legal definition for the purpose of sentencing, or, what amounts to the same, the unrealistic legal definition of the purpose of sentences, what can the purpose of the introduction of ICT in prisons be?

Positive psychology offers a justification: to combat the depression created by prison life, ICT may contribute to opening horizons, the possibility of progress, the opportunity for literacy, motivate toward education, and generally expand the sphere of activity of those with access to such instruments. Alberoni (1989) observes that from all depression, individual and social, comes an incipient state, where new opportunities to transform how we live are opened. Hulsman (1993), an author oriented by the abolitionist ideology dominant prior to the 1980s, urges his readers to not lose sight of the yet utopian horizon of one day society refusing inhumane practices, such as retaliation through the social-criminal-penal system. He notes that, locally, there are people and groups of people capable and more or less competent to feel the moral and humane repulsion that penal practices elicit and act accordingly. Even within the currently dominant punitive disposition, most professionals, at all levels of the state and social hierarchy, cannot help but act as abolitionists. That is, most human beings will attempt to prevent or hinder practices that they feel are inhumane. What they do not feel it is the existence of conditions to do it in a systematic way and to demand from others morally appropriate behaviour. They know that they will not be protected, by the contrary, by their superiors.

ICTs are instruments whose progressive social prestige, as well as renown for openness and capacity to transform people and the world, can bring into the prisons (depressive) spaces of freedom capable of minimizing damage and increasing opportunities for the transformation of those prisons, in favour of the better civilizational values: the containment and prevention of violence and harm doing. But the larger struggle, which will at the same time define the possibilities for the transformation of prisons and societies, is organized around the decision to maintain the hegemony of the punitive disposition, which seeks whom to blame for collective and individual insecurities, or to have the courage and lucidity to face the problems, to solve them; problems as serious and different as the education of abandoned children, the reduction of harm caused by sexism, corruption, and xenophobia.

SOLUTIONS AND RECOMMENDATIONS

It is desirable that prisoners take the time to improve their cognitive and decision-making skills. Nelson Mandela is an example of someone who, at least, did not lose determination and a sense of life well lived. But this is not the case with most prisoners.

For those who want to promote ways to counteract the hardening, dulling effect that prison tends to have on the individual, ICT is a useful tool. Electronic games, TVs, and access to music are, clearly, ways to make life in prison more bearable. It suffices to see how they are used to punish, and force compliance through confiscation or denial of access. In order to go further, that is to say, in order for sentences to cease being susceptible to being connected with torture, it is necessary to understand the reasons why torture persists in prisons, despite all the international agreements and commitments by states seeking to prevent this from happening. Including the way repression against prison inmates that try to follow sociability trends technologically driven is (or not) ill treatment.

The role of ICT in the social reintegration of ex-prisoners depends upon the dominant social disposition in relation to the political and social place of punishment. When punishment is used to reinforce social stigma, breaking the morale of individuals who already face difficulties in integrating society, good will cannot do much for them. When the time comes for society and the state to adopt a disposition of hope for the resocialisation of everyone, the ICTs, inside and outside of the prison system, will be able to cooperate to educate prisoners and reorganise the penal system in accordance with the applicable international norms, presently violated everywhere.

FUTURE RESEARCH DIRECTIONS

Dispositions inside a library, regarding a book, depends on the discipline of the library. It also depends on the discipline surrounding the library and the discipline that relates the library to other libraries, around the world.

Books and libraries are symbols of knowledge, wisdom and pacification, meditation and silence. Looking for compared discipline and dispositions on libraries, inside and outside prisons, and the way ICT uses relate to those, would be clarifying on the issues regarding the uses of technology inside prison system.

CONCLUSION

Technologies are produced to serve specific purposes, including mass consumption. But also pleasure and pain. Information and communication technologies can be used to think more intelligently about how to solve problems through mathematical calculations that cannot be done on paper. They serve to present ideas that facilitate the transmission of knowledge in universities and businesses. Artificial intelligence optimizes the effort of thinking and can also take thought to another level of questioning.

Information and communication technologies specifically designed for prisons already exist: they are surveillance and security technologies. There are no emancipating technologies in prison. Prison establishments serve security purposes, and only metaphorically, idealistically, do they serve other purposes, such as reintegration or professional training, with all the practical limitations that recidivism rates reveal.

In regard of torture issues, prison video monitoring systems have proved to be insufficient. The idea that open violence is the dominant mode of interaction between people, even criminals, does not fit with what we know about human nature (Collins 2008). According to Collins, few are those who, trained to exercise violence in a conscious and planned manner, can do so. Those who do, use a variety of self-perception manipulation techniques so as to be able to perform violent acts as if they were not that, at least at that moment. There are those who develop the ability to turn off spontaneous empathy, and to reinforce this process, focus on other things, such as the techniques of exerting violence – the use of clubs, Taser guns, techniques for hitting without leaving marks etc. Violence, in these terms, becomes an experiment. It serves to test the effects produced by well-planned and well-defined causes, such as a particular technique. As a young prison guard declared publically in relation to an incident that lead to a criminal conviction, when the guards used a Taser on a defenceless prisoner in an effort to force him to comply, they had already tried a whole range of manual persuasion techniques, as it were, and they had not worked. With the Taser, he assured his audience, the prisoner's behaviour had changed. Thus proving the effectiveness of the action. Sufficient justification for its professional application.

In prison, the tensions created by the antisocial character of the environment, are regularly discharged in orgies of violence: repression or riots. The stupefying boredom of routines, explodes into action, from time to time, only to immediately return to the routine. When someone plans an act of violence, as it happens regularly in prisons, they sometimes do so in such a way as to permit the self-serving use of image and sound recording. In the case of the guards, for example, the images can serve to show how hard their work is and their operational capacity to maintain security. Sometimes they lose the ability to judge how their actions can be perceived by those who live outside the prison, as in the case of the recording of the use of the Taser that ended up in court. Other times, aware that certain acts are unlawful, they use spaces not covered by surveillance equipment, to act out their plans.

The ICT that we refer to in this chapter are those that may have re-socializing uses, not security ICT. Prison services and professionals, as a rule, resist the possibility of using the former, to improve the lives of the prisoners, and learn to use the latter, as professionals keeping up to date.

Technologies seduce people as consumer products. And they are boycotted in those aspects of life where their presence is inconvenient. For example, when they serve, in fact or allegedly, to reduce employment, they can be destroyed, as in the case of the Luddites. Technologies, they say, are neutral: their impact depends on who uses them. But firearms and canon (with all their modern derivatives), for example, while depending on who uses them, have shifted global equilibrium in favour of the West, which developed them and continues to produce them on a scale unmatched by any other civilization. ICT has a very different and equally transformative connotation: the knowledge society, which began to be established with the discovery of the press in the 15th century. At the same time that the Inquisition took hold in the Iberian Peninsula and the Age of Exploration launched Europe into the world. Technologies are part of the world and are at the same time used for the best and the worst that societies can offer.

There are libraries in prison. But their use is clearly different from the use of the same instrument in universities. Access to digital documents and books is the state of the art in the best libraries. In prison, differences in the use of libraries are to be expected. Both for security reasons – knowledge is an important part of the monopoly on violence – and the particular limitations that such institutions place on the organization of discussions conducive to the development of cognitive skills. Investment, always scarce, is directed to meet security problems.

ICT is transforming the world. That is, people and societies are using and experimenting with ways of interacting through the use of ever more flexible and miniaturized technologies. In innovative ways. In prisons, for example, the prohibited mobile phone business is, along with illicit drugs, practically unstoppable. They are used by prisoners to communicate with families and friends. And they can serve organizational purposes. However, there are no known instances of disputes about the way prisons function being organized.

The coevolution of societies and technologies will, undoubtedly, continue to characterize the future. In what way, is not known. But we do know that the uses of ICT will depend on the dispositions adopted by societies in each historical period, as it happens with fashion. In the 19th century, the enthusiasm for the penitentiary as a way to replace transportation (exile) and even more degrading sentences, such as public corporal punishment, came with the enthusiasm for modern machines, such as the automobile and airplane, for example. After WWII, in the West, enthusiasm for progress and substantial improvement in the living conditions of workers in the richer societies was accompanied by a reduction in the use of prisons, to the point where there was a widespread belief that prisons would be obsolete by the end of the century. Starting in the 1980s, however, the disposition in the most influential Western nations changed, hardened. They lost their faith in progress. Prisons have become institutions central to the, symbolic, imposition of an inconsequential moralism, like that of the War on Drugs, which, to the present, has not ceased to be increasingly influential. Could the introduction of more ICT in the prisons help reverse the current security hard line trend?

In fact, the security hard line trend and the expansion in the consumption of ICT products are contemporaneous. They are co-occurrences. There is no record of friction between the two.

REFERENCES

Alberoni, F. (1989). *Génese*. Lisboa: Bertrand.

Barbelet, J. (2001). *Emotion, Social Theory and Social Structure - a macrosociological approach*. Cambridge, UK: Cambridge University Press.

Bhambra, G. K. (2014). Connected Sociologies. London: Bloomsbury.

Boltansky, L., & Chiapello, È. (1999). *Le Nouvel Esprit du Capitalisme*. Paris: Gallimard.

Caparrós, M. (2014). *A Fome*. Lisboa: Círculo de Leitores.

Castells, M. (2004). *A Galáxia Internet – Reflexões sobre a Internet, Negócios e Sociedade*. Lisboa: Fundação Calouste Gulbenkian.

Castells, M. (2012). *Redes de Indignación y Esperanza*. Madrid: Alianza.

Collins, R. (2008). *Violence: A Micro-sociological Theory*. Princeton, NJ: Princeton University Press.

Cordeiro, A. D. (2018, March 3). Activista acusado pela sexta vez por denunciar condições nas cadeias. *Público*. Retrieved from https://www.publico.pt/2018/03/03/sociedade/noticia/academico-enfrenta-tribunais-pela-sexta-vez-por-denunciar-situacao-das-prisoes-portuguesas-1805085

Crétenot, M. (2014). *From national practices to European guidelines: interesting initiatives in prisons management*. Rome: European Prison Observatory.

Desmurget, M. (2012, January). *TV Lobotomie : La vérité scientifique sur les effets de la télévision*. Paper presented at Forum Social Local du Morbihan.

Dores, A. P. (1996). *O Movimento Informático nas Escolas Portuguesas: Análise Sociológica do Caso do Projecto Minerva*. Lisboa: ISCTE.

Dores, A. P., Pontes, N., & Loureiro, R. (2016). *Manifesto for a new penal culture*. Rome: European Observatory of Prisons.

Durkheim, É. (1960). *De la division de travail social*. Paris: PUF.

Durkheim, É. (1973). *O suicídio: estudo de sociologia*. Lisboa: Editorial Presença.

Durkheim, É. (2002). *As Formas Elementares da Vida Religiosa*. Oeiras: Celta.

Engels, F. (1975). *A situação da classe trabalhadora na Inglaterra*. Lisboa: Editorial Presença.

Fara, P. (2009). *Science: a Four Thousand Years History*. Oxford, UK: Oxford University Press.

Ferreira, E. V. (1997). *Crime e Insegurança em Portugal: Padrões e Tendências (1985-1996)*. Oeiras: Celta.

Firouzi, O. (2016). *Reducing the prison population in Europe: does community justice work?* Rome: European Observatory of Prisons.

Foucault, M. (1975). *Surveiller et punir: naissance de la prison*. Paris: Gallimard.

Foucault, M. (2004). *A Hermenêutica do Sujeito*. São Paulo: Martins Fontes.

Garland, D. (2001). *The Culture of Control – Crime and Social Order in Contemporary Society*. Oxford, UK: Oxford University Press.

Hobsbawn, E.J. (1997). *A era das revoluções*. Rio de Janeiro: Paz e Terra.

Hulsman, L. (1993). El enfoque abolicionista: Políticas criminales alternativas. El Poder punitivo del Estado. Criminologia critica y controlo social. *NeoPanopticum - Derecho, criminologia y ciencias sociales*, 75–104.

Illich, I. (1971). *Deschooling Society*. Preservenet.

Karam, M. L. (1996). A Esquerda Punitiva. *Discursos Sediciosos – Crime, Direito E Sociedade*, (1). Retrieved from http://emporiododireito.com.br/a-esquerda-punitiva-por-maria-lucia-karam/

Kuhn, M. (2016). *How the Social Sciences Think about the World's Social - Outline of a Critique*. Stuttgard: Ibidem.

Lahire, B. (2012). *Monde pluriel. Penser l'unité des sciences sociales*. Paris: Seuil.

LEAP. (2016). Law Enforcement Against Prohibition. *LEAP*. Retrieved March 26, 2016, from: http://www.leap.cc

Machado, H. (in press). Cabo esconde fortuna da droga a chefe da PJ. *Correio da Manhã*. Available at: http://www.cmjornal.pt/portugal/detalhe/gnr_esconde_fortuna_da_droga_a_chefe_da_pj

Maculan, A., Ronco, D., & Vianello, F. (2014). *Prisons in Europe: overview and trends*. Rome: European Observatory of Prisons.

Maia e Costa, E. (2003). Prisões: a lei escrita e a lei na prática em Portugal. In A. P. Dores (Ed.), *Prisões na Europa - um debate que apenas começa - European prisons – starting a debate* (pp. 93–102). Oeiras: Celta.

Martinson, R. (1974). What works? Questions and answers about prison reform. *The Public Interest*, (35): 22–54.

Merton, R. K. (1970). Estrutura social e Anomia. In Sociologia - Teoria e Estrutura. S. Paulo: Mestre Jou.

Ministerio del Interior. (2018). *Módulos terapêuticos*. Retrieved from http://institucionpenitenciaria.es/Reeducacion/ProgramasEspecificos/modulosTerapeuticos.html#c2

Mouzelis, N. (1995). *Sociological Theory: What Went Wrong? – diagnosis and remedies*. London: Routledge.

Nietzsche. (1997). *A Genealogia da Moral*. Lisboa: Guimarães.

Novak, M. (2001). *A Etica Católica e o Espírito do Capitalismo*. S.João do Estoril: Principia.

Oborne, P. (2008). *The Triumph of the Political Class*. London: Pocket Books.

Paladines, J. V. (2013). Feminismo Punitivo, cuando el género se redujo al castigo. *Defensa Y Justicia, Revista Institucional de La Defensoría Pública Del Ecuador*, (5). Retrieved from http://www.rebelion.org/docs/174609.pdf

Palidda, S., & Garcia, J. Á. B. (Eds.). (2010). *Criminalización racista de los migrantes en Europa*. Comares Editorial.

Perkinson, R. (in press). Some US prisons as bad as Abu Ghraib. *Straits Times Interactive*.

Roberts, J. V., & Hough, M. (Eds.). (2002). *Changing Attitudes to Punishment - public opinion, crime and justice*. Devon: Willan Publishing.

Scott, J. C. (2013). *A Dominação e a Arte da Resistência – discursos ocultos*. Lisboa: Letra Livre.

Sennett, R. (2006). *The New Culture of Capitalism*. New Haven, CT: Yale University Press.

Therborn, G. (2006). Meaning, Mechanisms, Patterns and Forces: an Introduction. In G. Therborn (Ed.), *Inequalities of the World – New Theoretical Frameworks, Multiple empirical approaches* (pp. 1–58). London: Verso.

Wacquant, L. (2000). *As Prisões da Miséria*. Oeiras: Celta.

Wacquant, L. (2001). Moralisme et panoptisme punitif - La chasse aux délinquants sexuels aux États-Unis. *Sociologie et Sociétés*, *33*, 139–157.

Wacquant, L. (2016, October). *The puzzling return of prisons in the 21st Century*. Paper presented at the meeting of Ordem dos Advogados, Lisboa, Portugal.

Weber, M. (2005). *Protestant Ethic and the Spirit of Capitalism*. London: Routledge.

Woodiwiss, M. (1988). *Crime, Crusades and Corruption - Prohibitions in the United States, 1900-1987*. London: Piter Publisher.

Woodiwiss, M. (2001). *Organized Crime and American Power: A History*. Toronto: University of Toronto Press.

Zimbardo, P. (2007). *The Lucifer Effect: understanding how good people turn evil*. Random House.

KEY TERMS AND DEFINITIONS

Development: Is a quantitative way of evaluating and describing change in time.

Disposition: Is a pattern of incorporated way of receiving and reacting into and to the environment.

Dominant Disposition: Is the pattern of incorporated way of receiving and reacting into and to the environment which used in priority in a determined epoch and society.

Evolution: Is a qualitative way of evaluating and describing change in time.

ICT: Devices and use of devices based of microelectronic processing of information and communication.

Recursivity: Human kind biological condition that imposes to people´s mind to live in the past and in the future, to alternate dark and high concerns and prospects about self and humanity, rather than to live without reflexive references.

Social Reintegration: The process of personal change when someone experience freedom from prison.

Prison: Penitentiary system establishment.

Punitiveness: Disposition that uses scapegoats as main strategy in order to really or symbolically solve problems.

Chapter 3
Curriculum and Training Model Proposal for Infocomunicational Competences Acquisition in Prison:
A Case Study in Two Portuguese Prisons

Daniela Graça
University of Aveiro, Portugal

Lídia Oliveira
University of Aveiro, Portugal

ABSTRACT

ICT have an important role in various areas of Portuguese society. Social reintegration is a key theme in the Portuguese penal system and its legislation. This dichotomy led to question if the existence of internet access in the school prison has been a reintegration key point. Literature reveals that education is a pivotal factor in the preparation of the inmate to reintegrate society and in the prevention and reduction of recidivism. The present schooling guidelines reinforce the importance of technology base knowledge in the curriculum of any individual. Thus, the acquisition of such competences is of extreme importance, and cannot be ignored in the education that is offered to all those that sit in the margin of society. Two case studies consisting in the implementation of short courses on infocomunicational skills in two prisons allowed to explore the relation between the concepts inmate, internet, and education. The results contribute with a proposal of a curriculum and training model on infocomunicational competences acquisition to apply in prison context.

DOI: 10.4018/978-1-5225-5975-7.ch003

INTRODUCTION

In the current Portuguese social context in which new technologies, and especially the Internet, have played an indispensable role in the daily lives of individuals and in human relations, and in which post-seclusion social reintegration is a key issue in legislation concerning the Portuguese Prison System, the availability of Internet access emerges as a potential factor for the rehabilitation and social reintegration of prisoners. The existing literature reveals that re-education is a determining factor in the process of preparing the prisoner for a return to the "free society" and reducing post-seclusion criminal recidivism. Considering that current education cannot ignore (and doesn´t ignore) the need to include technology in the individual's personal and professional life, the learning of technological tools should not be censored in the more specific teaching contexts of society.

In a country and a world in which the Internet and Information and Communication Technologies are considered crucial instruments for the integration of citizens and the development of a functional and competitive knowledge society, it cannot be ignored that in Portugal there are more than fourteen thousand individuals in detention, and that more than half of the prison population does not have compulsory education completed. In fact, 58.4% of the population is distributed between the level of education equivalent to the 2nd cycle of basic education (6th year) or below it (Figure 1) - Literary Qualifications of the Recluse Population by Gender and Nationality (2nd quarter of 2016), and of these, 3.4% do not know how to read or write and the rest of them can only read and write. These values are dramatic and confirm the weight of education in the course of individuals. If the period of imprisonment is not channeled to change this reality, if the inmate population is not allowed to improve their educational qualifications and if it is not done in a comprehensive way, including all educational aspects, these individuals will have zero infocommunication literacy, distorted and/or basic to survive in the contemporary world when the respective periods of imprisonment end.

It is in this context marked by the digital exclusion that the proposal of a training model in the area of Information and Communication Technologies (ICT) in network, directed to the reclusive population, is presented, making possible the acquisition of infocommunicational competences that are considered elements of socio-professional integration in the post-seclusion period. In this sense, we try to understand the possibility of using the Internet, in the teaching-learning context of the Portuguese Prison Institutions.

This chapter presents the training model for the acquisition and/or development of infocommunicational skills (operational/instrumental, information, communication and security) by individuals. This model includes several strands that are operationalized in a training program: curriculum, objectives and competencies to be

Figure 1. Literary qualifications of the recluse population by gender and nationality (2nd quarter of 2016)

Source: Prison Statistics (2nd quarter of 2016), Directorate General for Reinsertion and Prison Services, page 5, with graphical additions from the authors.

Literary Qualifications	Men						Women						TOTAL	
	Portuguese		Foreign		Total		Portuguese		Foreign		Total			
	#	%	#	%	#	%	#	%	#	%	#	%	#	%
Can not read or write	369	3,3	48	2,2	**417**	3,1	60	9,3	5	2,3	**65**	7,5	**482**	3,4
Can read and write	318	2,8	90	4,1	**408**	3,0	44	6,8	26	11,9	**70**	8,	**478**	3,4
With education attendance	10380	92,8	2035	92,8	**12415**	92,8	524	81,0	172	78,5	**696**	80,4	**13111**	92,0
1st cycle of Basic Education (1st, 2nd, 3rd and 4th years)	3255	29,1	322	14,	**3577**	26,7	193	29,8	34	15,	**227**	26,	**3804**	26,7
2nd cycle of Basic Education (5ht and 6th years)	3069	27,4	359	16,	**3428**	25,6	99	15,3	16	7,	**115**	13,	**3543**	24,9
3rd cycle of Basic Education (7th, 8th and 9th	2937	26,2	654	29,	**3591**	26,8	131	20,2	51	23,	**182**	21,	**3773**	26,5
Secondary Education (10th, 11th and 12th years)	908	8,1	563	25,	**1471**	11,0	79	12,2	38	17,	**117**	13,	**1588**	11,1
Higher Education	197	1,8	132	6,	**329**	2,5	22	3,4	30	13,	**52**	6,	**381**	2,7
Other	14	0,1	5	0,2	**19**	0,1		0,0	3	1,4	**3**	0,3	**22**	0,2
Unavailable Information	123	1,1	21	1,0	**144**	1,1	19	2,9	16	7,3	**35**	4,0	**179**	1,3
TOTAL	**11190**	**100**	**2194**	**100**	**13384**	**100**	**647**	**100**	**219**	**100**	**866**	**100**	**14250**	**100**

achieved, duration and strategies. This program was applied in two prisons and from these case studies results were obtained regarding the changes in the self-perception of the participants in the training regarding their capacity to use the Internet and its impact on their lives (pre- and post-seclusion).

There were three research questions that served as a beacon for the investigation: (QI01) In what way Internet access by prisoners in Portuguese Prisons in a training context could be a reality?, whose objective was to understand how access to the Internet in the context of teaching and learning in Portuguese Prisons can occur in both technical and conceptual terms; (QI02) Which program structure should adopt a training course in Internet use in the specific context of the Portuguese Prison System?, which reflects the idea that training in the context of the Portuguese Prison System should be delineated taking into account the particular characteristics that characterize (e.g. safety issues) and the target profile of the training (individuals who have had a tortuous life path and unhappy contact with the school); and (QI03) What impact would the training in Internet use have on the prisoner's perception of their cognitive and technical abilities and, consequently, their employability? Why perceive the real impact that Internet use training has on reinsertion and to what extent this impact depends on the individual's perception of himself and his abilities can be decisive for assessing learning and indicating programmatic and/or structural corrections to be made in future formations.

BACKGROUND

Teaching in Reclusion: Rehabilitation, Recidivism and Employability

The role of teaching in the context of imprisonment should focus on preparing the individual for a period of rehabilitation that will allow him to give more present and future solutions upon his release. Education is a tool and methodology for preparing for life and for the labor market, playing a crucial role in achieving this goal.

Education has as its main objective the formation of individuals, broadening their understanding of the world, encouraging their creative and cognitive development and their evolution as a person (Onofre, 2009). The condition of seclusion results, among other things, from a failure on that route which was expected to be continuous and devoid of abuse. According to Onofre in "School Education in Prison in the Teachers' View - A Hiatus between the Proposed and the Lived" (2009), seclusion education must consider the ontological essence of the individual and the context in which it is embedded. That is to say, education should be oriented towards the encouragement of the individual, and teachers and/or trainers (and all participants in the individual's experience of seclusion) can help the individual redirect the focus of learning to their own needs, preferences and requirements, helping them acquire the knowledge necessary for professional integration, for self-fulfillment, and for self-motivation in order to overcome the ways of being and living that have led one to seclusion (Batra, Jasso, & Stevens, 2012). Education should therefore contribute to the "humanization, awareness and training" (Onofre, 2009, p.10) of the inmate, based on a multidisciplinary and educational program where all the professionals involved in the educational process are integrated (Rogers, Hurry, Simonot, & Wilson, 2014) and where the teacher/trainer takes on a role not only as mentor but also as tutor and example (Baskas, 2016).

In "The Path to Successful Reentry: The Relationship Between Correctional Education, Employment and Recidivism" Jake Cronin (2011) begins by saying that the vast majority of prisoners in the state of Missouri, where the study was conducted, will leave prison but a lot will return there. This is supported by "The influence of GED obtainment on inmate release outcome" (Zgoba, Haugebrook, & Jenkins, 2008), where it is verified that 67% of the inmates will re-offend and, consequently, return to prison. The author explains that in order to counteract this trend, educational programs were implemented to help inmates reintegrate successfully into free society. The study evaluates the impact of educational programs in the post-seclusion period of the individual using as indicators the values of employability and recidivism. The results show that individuals who have progressed in the respective educational path are more likely to get a full-time job and that those who have a full-time job are less likely to relapse.

In the same vein, the Manifesto for a New Criminal Culture argues that "it is necessary to value the idea of condemnation to mean an obligation to seek new guidelines for their life from the public and private services that may support." and that "the crime university must be replaced by lifelong learning." (Dores, Pontes, & Loureiro, 2016, p.4)

Lochner & Moretti (2004) investigated the relationship between schooling and crime through three sources of information - information about the individual, information on reclusions, and crime information - and found that school attendance significantly reduced criminal activity. Also, Steurer, Smith & Tracy (2001), in a study analyzing the educational participation in seclusion of about 3600 individuals in the post-seclusion period, indicate that mere attendance reduces the probability of returning to prison by 29%. In this study the authors analyze recidivism through three practical synonyms of the concept: re-arrest, re-conviction, re-incarceration; and the results are, for each indicator, enlightening. The difference in re-arrest between individuals who attended school and those who did not attend is 13%, for re-conviction indicator of 21%, and for re-incarceration of 29%.

While it is obvious that the educational pathway can have a determining influence on the individual's journey, it is imperative to rethink education when these individuals become prisoners. It is in this sense that several governmental entities seek to guide their work regarding the full return to free society by the inmates. Indeed, education or learning is, or ought to be, a method of rehabilitation and of preparation of the individual for post-seclusion life as he seeks to counteract two possible causes of crime: lack of academic qualifications and lack of professional qualifications (Sedgley, Scott, Williams, & Derrick, 2010).

The educational gap between the general population and the reclusive population is evident if one analyzes the profile of the prisoner, transversal to the societies, and determinant as to the transference to the crime.

In the general population, the percentage of individuals with upper secondary education aged 18 or under was eighteen (Harlow, 2003). In the population identified as having been sentenced as a young person, only one in five had completed secondary or equivalent education, and only one in ten had attended or even obtained a higher education diploma. These data may lead to the conclusion that individuals with a lower level of formal learning have a higher propensity for criminality when still young, as opposed to those who have a longer and more stable educational pathway (Harlow, 2003).

In the United States in 1997, about 41% of prisoners in Federal Prisons and Local Prisons had not completed secondary or equivalent education. Still on the US inmate population, Weissman et al (2008) indicate that 68% of inmates dropped out of secondary school and that 40% had some cognitive trait that made learning difficult.

In order to understand the relationship between education, employability and recidivism, Cronin (2011) evaluated three interrelated hypotheses: (i) incarcerated education increases the probability of finding a full-time job; (ii) education in seclusion reduces the likelihood of recurrence; and (iii) having a job reduces the likelihood of recurrence. Associated with the first hypothesis presented is the idea that the relation between the education degree completed and the professional level achieved is interrelated. That is to say, that the increase of the degree of education causes the extension and improvement of the professional options, just as the inverse. According to the documentary analysis carried out by Tyler & Kling (2002), this interrelationship happens in one of three ways: (i) the acquired qualifications and the gain of knowledge through education make the individual more employable, (ii) the credentials of education work as factors of interest to potential employers, and (iii) education results as an incentive for individuals to succeed in work and future learning.

However, while it is empirically and statistically confirmed that education and the increase and development of qualifications are fundamental to professional success, regardless of the individual, the criminal record continues to be a barrier to the full reintegration into the labor market in the post-seclusion period and, consequently, in the free society.

Indeed, according to Devah Pager (2003), mere contact with the criminal justice system automatically and severely limits the individual's professional future, even making the odds of being employed between one-half and one-third less than the individual without a criminal record. A good example of the truth of this situation is the policy adopted by Finland in respect of learning certificates granted in confinement which, following current legislation, omit the place of obtaining an academic degree in order to normalize the position of individuals and to promote the fight against professional discrimination (Newman, 2011).

According to Jo Hawley, the impact of obtaining second-level qualifications in seclusion on the success of employability is not, according to the studies, markedly significant. However, although the acquisition of skills may not be an entry card for the labor market, non-acquisition is certainly a hindrance (Hawley, 2011) and brings greater distance between the individual and a greater professional success either in terms of labor market options, or in the economic result that may result (Tyler & Kling, 2002). In agreement, Cronin (2011) argues that obtaining a high school diploma can put the inmate at the same level of employability as if he had reached that academic level before the seclusion.

Sedgley et al (2010), in a study that analysis the impact of education and of two employability programs on the degree of recidivism of 4515 inmates in the state of Ohio over a ten-year period, state that there is an inverse proportionality relationship between propensity for crime and the level of human capital developed. Cronin (2011) also concludes that education during incarceration reduces the likelihood of a return to prison, in this case 8%.

Still, the same author (Cronin, 2011) describes the process that begins with incarceration education as follows: the individual obtains the secondary level academic degree, which increases the chances of finding a full-time job and reduces the likelihood of a return to prison, and finally, having a full-time job significantly decreases the likelihood of recurrence. This process between employability and recidivism really becomes a vicious circle in the prisoner's life whether in the positive or negative sense. That way, in the negative sense, the non-evolution of the individual in his academic qualifications and professional capacities does not contribute to the obtaining of a job, and non-employability contributes to the recidivism; in the positive sense, there is the opposite, personal and professional valuation of the individual increases the odds and widens the range of possibilities of obtaining a job, and the resulting stability contributes to the maintenance of a life away from crime. Cronin's (2011) study demonstrates that there is indeed a very strong relationship between employability and recidivism by stating that "Those who have a full-time job are much less likely to return to prison than similar inmates who are unemployed." (P. 4) and adds that the percentage of recidivism of prisoners with a full-time job has decreased by half compared to the number of unemployed prisoners.

In post-secondary education, in Education Behind Bars: Lowering Recidivism Through Post-Secondary Education in Correctional Facilities, an article that analyzed the school scene in the prison system in New York, USA, reveals that access to post-secondary education is indicated as one of the four key ways of increasing the success of post-seclusion re-integration and reducing recidivism, suggesting that individuals with less school attendance are more likely to become prisoners. The article concludes that the frequency of post-secondary education, combined with preparation for change, enables the inmate to create and maintain a stable life after incarceration (Schirmer, 2008).

An analysis of the educational interventions in juvenile correctional settings in the USA between 1970 and 2012 by Wexler, Pyle, Flower, Williams, & Cole, concludes that the application of explicit and objective teaching methodologies that have had previous success with adolescents in the regular school context give greater guarantees of success in a prison context (Wexler, Pyle, Flower, Williams, & Cole, 2013).

Information and Communication Technologies in Seclusion Education

Considering that one of the objectives of prisons should be to provide individuals with educational instruments that favor their social reintegration, access to the Internet from the establishment of incarceration is a demandable right. Indeed, in the current context of a multicultural society, literacy must be multiple, in order to mitigate the division between prison and society, now not only social but also digital.

The article "Digital literacy in prison: an experience with young inmates" (Franganillo, Burgos, García, & Tomàs, 2006) analyzes the work carried out with a group of individuals in the Centro Penitenciario de Jóvenes de Barcelona, since 2006, in the areas of digital literacy and cultural dynamism, whose focus is the creation and publication of blogs. The objectives of the work are to promote education and increase its level of information, encourage reading and writing, increase contact with the outside world, awaken or enhance information capacities and stimulate digital literacy. Being a collaborative project between the organization Òmnia21, the library of the Centro Penitenciario de Jóvenes de Barcelona and the Facultad de Biblioteconomía y Documentación de la Universidad de Barcelona, led to a double reflection: Internet access in seclusion is a demandable right that can favor the reintegration of the individual into society; and, the prison library can be an instrument that influences future social and labor integration of prisoners.

Prisoners should be able to learn about and assimilate the technological and social changes that will enable them to readapt successfully in the future. From the point of view of Burgos Oliván (Burgos, Oliván Lola, García, Villar Aída and Tomás Humbert, 2007), it is necessary to develop technological and informational capacities integrated in a broad literacy, in which the informative, personal and social dimensions do not dissociate.

In Educational Opportunities Within Correctional Institutions (O'Neill, MacKenzie, & Bierie, 2007) the authors analyze the differences in teaching in two distinct contexts of seclusion: Boot Camp and traditional prison establishment. The main conclusion is that there are large differences in opportunities in both contexts of teaching, and that in Boot Camp inmates have easy access to teaching. Another conclusion obtained is that when equivalent groups are compared by access control, Boot Camp inmates have a higher ability to obtain a diploma (O'Neill et al., 2007).

In fact, new technologies alone do not make individuals wiser or freer. They simply give them the learning tools and tools for possible progress as an individual. It seems, therefore, to be crucial that digital literacy be integrated into a broader and more inclusive evolutionary process (Oliván, 2007).

In Blended Learning, Facilitating Education in Prisons (Fong, 2008), as a consequence of the idea that traditional teaching is not the most appropriate for teaching in the context of imprisonment, the author defends teaching in blended learning as an appropriate alternative, the greater flexibility, the greater number of options and learning pathways.

In Portugal, a distance learning project was started at the beginning of 2011, applying the elearning method in prisons and with inmates. This is a teaching-learning method that requires greater autonomy, motivation and responsibility on the part of the student. But that, alternatively, offers a response to a variety of obstacles in the education process.

The non-governmental organization Justice Action, in the "Computers in Cells" report (Justice Action, 2011), proposes to place computers in all cells based on the idea that the prison system should follow the change verified by the passage of the profile merely punitive for a reclusive aspect of rehabilitation. In this document it is recognized that security issues and public opinion cannot be forgotten, but it is also argued that in the case of security there are solutions to this scenario that result from technological advances.

The proposal of this organization includes access to e-mail for communication with the social support network and with teachers, information on legislation, and programs to support learning. It also suggests access to a previously verified and approved list of Internet sites at a later stage in this change process. Indeed, in Computers in Cells it is stated that the formulation of an effective rehabilitation program should treat education as a priority and provide individual computers. It is also argued that, to become real, this scenario will not only reduce recidivism, but also exalt the post-seclusion social reintegration of individuals, by providing them with good employment prospects (Action, 2011).

The article "Educating in Prisons: New Challenges for Social Education in Correctional Institutions" (Caride Gómez & Gradaílle Pernas, 2013) critically examines conservative and progressive educational practices, identifying conservatives as having efficacy-based educational programs and profitability, with a purely administrative function, sufficient to meet the expectations of prisoners while in confinement, and leaving to their choice the increase or not of competences and qualifications; and progressives as practices that project their action through models of integration and reintegration, education being understood as an opportunity for the integral development of the individual, promoting social rehabilitation with a realistic attitude, not understating the potential social discrepancies that have (educational, professional, affective, relational, economic, cultural, etc.).

While it is considered that all alternatives should be part of the range of options available to provide a context of successful seclusion and can thus adapt and apply the most appropriate method to the various existing situations, it should also be considered that teaching in this specific context will serve as a form of socialization, of contact with the outside, and of learning to know and be present (Rocha & Oliveira, 2014). For individuals whose motivation is low or zero, and/or whose experience with the school was traumatic, prior to incarceration, it is crucial to provide a stimulating teaching practice that allows the individual to identify and relate in a healthy way to the school, now in seclusion (Hurry, Brazier, Snapes, & Wilson, 2005). The context and format of teaching are indeed determinants of successful learning. A direct interaction with learning, a regular relationship with the study, with teachers, trainers or tutors, with the tasks and objectives to be achieved, allows the individual-inmate to feel integrated into a social group outside the prison in the school community, which results in positive, pro-social, normal-life and self-identity (Pike, 2014).

The study "Derribando el autoestigma: medios de comunicación en prisiones como aliados de la inclusión social" (Contreras-Pulido, Martín-Pena, & Aguaded, 2015) analyzes 39 experiences of media use - 14 publications in magazine format, three experiences of television and/or cinema, one experience of photography, six experiences of ICT and 15 of radio - that took place in Spanish prisons with three objectives: (i) to improve the socio-educational conditions of inmates, (ii), and (iii) overturning stigmas that came from themselves or the society. One of the main conclusions obtained from this analysis is the improvement of self-esteem and personal appreciation of own abilities. In addition it registers itself the development of the capacity of working in team, the sense of a group and utility for the common good. All these factors also contribute to increase hope for a better future, to improving self-perception, interpersonal relationships, and the capacity of communicating and expressing themselves.

A study based on the analysis of data obtained from a sample composed by 2875 inmates from a population of 4823 in 12 prisons with functional libraries in Nigeria, concludes that there are significant relationships between information needs, accessibility to the information resources of the library, and utilization of library information resources and the psychological well-being of prisoners. (Emasealu & Popoola, 2016)

The same idea is shared by Farley & Pike (2016) in Engaging prisoners in education: Reducing risk and recidivism, which demonstrates that the existence of a school course can promote the stability of the environment in the prison establishment by keeping the individual occupied, oriented objective which will subsequently contribute to reducing the risk of recurrence. It also explains that if school attendance of prisoners had a greater incentive on the part of the institutions, the prison system, and that if education of individuals was considered as a potential method of reducing security risks and instability in establishments, many of the system would be reduced. (Farley & Pike, 2016)

In a study based on data from three UK prisons, in order to understand how the lack of access to the Internet affects prisoners, whether and how inmates experience (re)learning of digital skills during rehabilitation and reintegration, if inmates feel greater disadvantages on release, and what are the benefits and risks of enabling inmates to access the Internet, Bianca C. Reisdorf & Yvonne Jewkes concluded that individuals show a great deal of curiosity and enthusiasm, as well as fear and reservation over the Internet. The authors suggest that the system should seek to balance the paradox between security issues inherent in the prison context and the possibility for individuals to have a normal life in seclusion and to be able to acquire the basic digital skills in order to enhance the success of rehabilitation, a post-liberation job, and generally reintegrate into society. (Reisdorf & Jewkes, 2016)

In general, in the United Kingdom and Australia inmates are not allowed to use the Internet even if it is to learn in a school context. Formal education and training in prisons in these two countries is done through non-digital means usually through content provided on paper. In both countries, in order to balance the asymmetry between the educational preparation that inmates acquire and the world they will encounter after seclusion, where digital literacy requirements are increasing, there are some elearning-based education projects which provide digital skills education for students in seclusion even without access to the Internet. (Farley & Pike, 2016)

In the case of the United Kingdom, there is a secure and restricted Internet network called Virtual Campus which allows inmates to communicate with university education tutors via a messaging service or to access Open University courses through Walled Garden22 in a secure manner, accessing educational resources and being restricted from accessing any other websites. (Pike & Adams, 2012)

In Australia the Making the Connection project of the University of Southern Queensland consists of the introduction of a server with a version of the e-learning management system and portable computers that work in interconnection from four states of the country. (Farley, Pike, Hopkins, & Byrne, 2015)

The Spanish situation with regard to the use of the Internet in the context of imprisonment is defined in its general features:

- Access to the Internet is restricted to use in an educational context, under supervision and only authorized if well justified and approved by the teacher/trainer and if accepted by the institution of incarceration;
- It is regulated at national level by policies of control of bandwidth and security measures that distinguish three types of users;
- The uses made are reported in monthly reports. (Pulido, 2010)

In Portugal, access to the Internet in a prison context happens, as in Spain, in the school context and only in the context of subjects related to the theme of information and communication technologies. There are some exceptions where access does not only occur within these disciplines as in the case of individuals attending specific projects (EPris) or university education. In these cases there is always monitoring and supervision of a technician of the establishment who has the responsibility to guide the use of the Internet.

One of the projects carried out in Portugal is the EPris project of the Piaget Institute of Gaia (Vila Nova de Gaia), which was developed from January 2014 to April 2016, in a partnership between the Ministry of Justice and the Santa Casa da Misericórdia do Porto, which aimed to "promote social reintegration of prisoners in society, work and employment through education." EPris created multimedia prototypes for elearning training for inmates of the Estabelecimento Prisional de Santa Cruz do Bispo Feminino, thus using ICT as an instrument of social inclusion and bet on the development of personal, social and professional skills (International Telecommunication Union, World Summit on the Information Society, & WSIS Stocktaking Process, 2015, pp. 123).

Some good examples of access to technology by inmates are Metropolitan Remand Center (Australia, Vitoria), Alexander Maconochie Centre25 and Halden26. In the Metropolitan Remand Center (Australia, Vitoria) it is possible for inmates to have personal computers, if this need is justifiable, for three types of situation: preparation for a court case/situation, participation in an educational/training program, and special needs. The rule is "Prisoners who can demonstrate a need to make an application to purchase a computer, be able to pay for the purchase of an approved computer and software, and abide by the rules." (Justice Action, 2011, p.3). At the Alexander Maconochie Centre25 (Australia, Canberra), since March 2009, there are computers with Cybersource PrisonPC software in most cells (Justice Action, 2011, pp. 3-4). In the high-security prison Halden26 (Norway, Halden) inmates have access to computers at school and in the cells and access to the Internet - limited by the firewall in order to ensure the necessary security - and educational resources. This re-education and rehabilitation approach will be part of what contributes to a low rate of recidivism, 20%, far below 50% in the UK and 60% in the USA (Justice Action, 2011, p.4).

Use of the Internet by the Prisoners in the Portuguese Prison System

Information obtained from the Direcção-Geral dos Serviços Prisionais (DGSP) in November 2008 indicates that only prisoners attending computer courses or similar have access to the Internet, always under surveillance and with limited access. Also, in this period, after collecting and analyzing the data available on the DGSP website, it was possible to perceive that of the 49 prisons in the Portuguese prison system, only nine taught the aforementioned computer course, and that of the 12,294 inmates, only 209 date of data collection and analysis, the respective course (see Table 1 - Internet use by prisoners (2009).

However, from the experience with the prisons participating in this investigation and from the contact with the DGRSP, it can be said that, to the extent that the characteristics of the context allow, inmates attending some school year have access to technology learning since the purpose of the DGRSP, the EPs and the schools is that the learning that inmates receive is as similar as possible to any other student in this country.

Table 1. Use of the Internet by Inmates (2009)

Central Prison Establishments
Alcoentre Prison Establishment
Professional training and labor activity Course: Computing initiation. Participants: 1
Funchal Prison Establishment
Education and Teaching Course: extracurricular activity in computing. Participants: 84
Lisboa Prison Establishment
Professional training and labor activity Course: computing – basic knowledge. Participants: 21
Monsanto Prison Establishment
Education and Teaching Course: extracurricular activity in computing. Participants: 32 Note: taught by Maria Amália Vaz de Carvalho Secondary Education School teachers
Sintra Prison Establishment
Professional training and labor activity Course: Computing in User Optics (TIC) Participants: 12 Course: Computing – Basic Skills Participants: 15
Vale de Judeus Prison Establishment
Professional training and labor activity Course: Computing Operator. Participants: 12, 7 approved Course: Computing – Office Software. Participants: 12, 8 approved Course: Computing – Office Software. Participants: 12
Special Prison Establishment
Santa Cruz do Bispo Special Prison Establishment
Education and Teaching Course: Adults Education and Training 3rd cycle Basic Education on Computing. Participants: 8 Note: course with two years of duration Professional training and labor activity Course: Computing Participants: no data Note: ministered by João Gonçalves Zarco Secondary Education School

However, since the difference in context cannot be ignored and the existing technological infrastructures in prisons are clearly different from those of schools, that is, in relation to them, it cannot be said that, despite all the efforts and the commitment of the professionals of the prison system and of the school system working in prisons, individuals in seclusion have access to a similar learning experience on infocommunication competences comparing to the students who receive them in a school context.

This leads us to perceive and conclude that the expectation regarding the development of competencies cannot, in fact, be the same when it comes to a student in school and to a student in the school in detention not only because of the personal baggage of each one, but also by the context in which the individual is, and by the way that learning reaches the individual.

TWO CASE STUDIES

Estabelecimento Prisional de Santa Cruz do Bispo Feminino

Estabelecimento Prisional de Santa Cruz do Bispo Feminino (EPSCBF) is a partnership project between the Portuguese State, specifically between the Ministry of Justice, and Santa Casa da Misericórdia do Porto. In this joint project, except for the safety and execution of sentences, Santa Casa guarantees all activities in support of penitentiary treatment: health, support for penitentiary treatment, nursery, canteen, maintenance and conservation of facilities and equipment, assistance religious and spiritual education, vocational education and training.

In fact, it is the goal of Misericórdia do Porto to contribute to a greater humanization and capacity to respond to the needs of the prison population, so that one day, returned to free life, it can be worthy of social respect and able to reach full integration in the community to which it returns and belongs.

As regards the EPSCBF participants in the case study of the nine who initiated the training program six concluded it. Two participants withdrew from the training because they started work; the third withdrawal was due to the exit of the prison establishment. In the analysis of the sessions only eight participants were considered due to the fact that one of the initial participants (who gave up starting work) participated only in the first session.

Demographic analysis results from data obtained from the completion of a questionnaire survey. The sample is made up of people born between 1963 and 1982, thus having, at the date of data collection, ages between 52 and 33 years. In fact, there is a 52-year-old, four-year-old 46, one 42, one 38, and one 33 years old (Figure 2 - Age (EPSCBF)).

Figure 2. Age (EPSCBF)

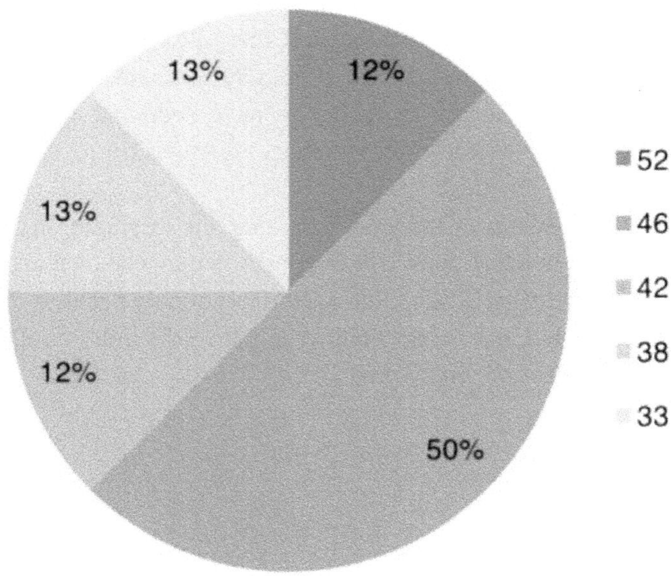

Regarding marital status, in the sample of eight people there are two single women, two married, one in union, one divorced and two widows. These data show that the majority of the sample does not have a relation, the total number of unmarried, divorced or widowed persons corresponding to 63% (Figure 3 - Civil Status (EPSCBF)).

As far as the academic level is concerned, data collected indicates that one person has completed the second cycle of basic education, four have completed secondary education, two have attended other courses - professional courses - and one has completed a bachelor's degree. Considering the degree "other courses" as professional courses equivalent to secondary education, we have a percentage of 75 corresponding to people with secondary education completed (Figure 4 - Academic Qualification (EPSCBF)).

Regarding the professional status prior to imprisonment, as shown in Figure 5 - Occupation at the time of confinement (EPSCBF), 87% of the sample was in the labor market. In fact, only one of the sampled persons was unemployed at the time of confinement (13%).

Figure 6 - Internet use before confinement (EPSCBF) shows that 87% of respondents used the Internet prior to seclusion, which corresponds to seven of the eight participants in the training program (only participant 3 indicated that they did not use the Internet prior to confinement).

Figure 3. Civil Status (EPSCBF)

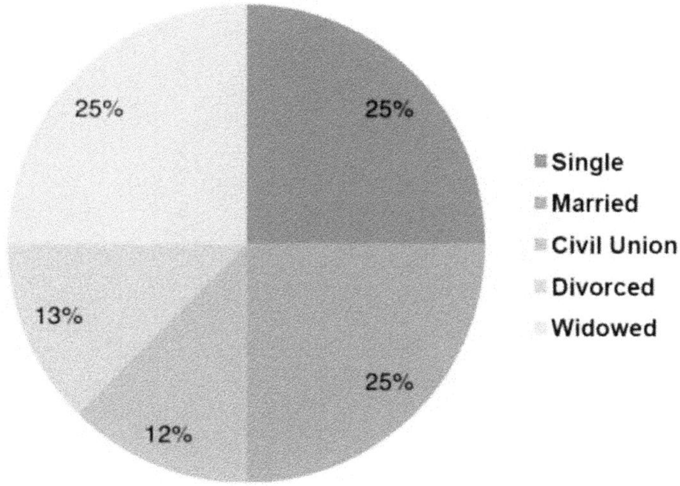

Figure 4. Academic Qualification (EPSCBF)

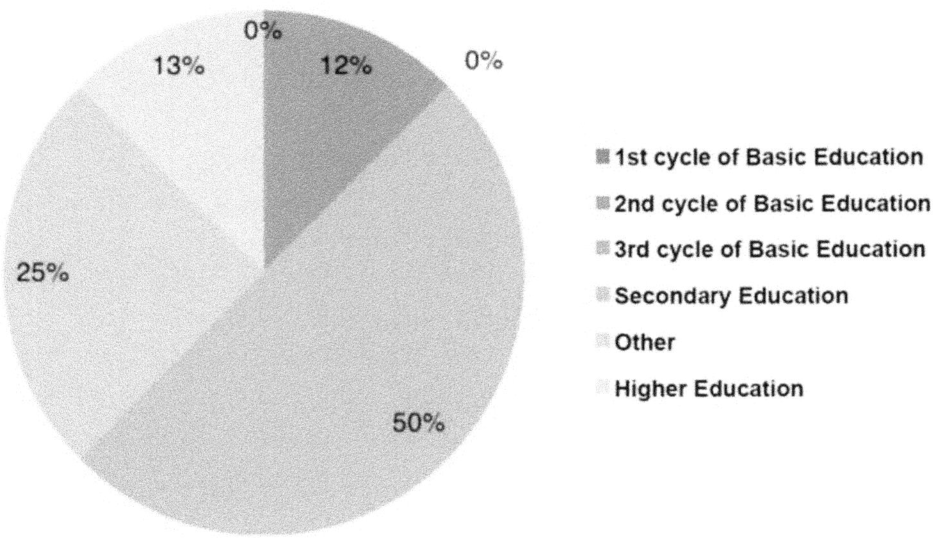

In response to the question "C.02 How did you find out what the Internet is? (Select only one of the options presented.) ", Despite the indication given, some participants responded with more than one option, which resulted in a higher-than-expected number of data. In fact, responses were obtained from seven participants (participant 3 did not respond), and a total of twelve data. It may be speculated that

Figure 5. Occupation in confinement (EPSCBF)

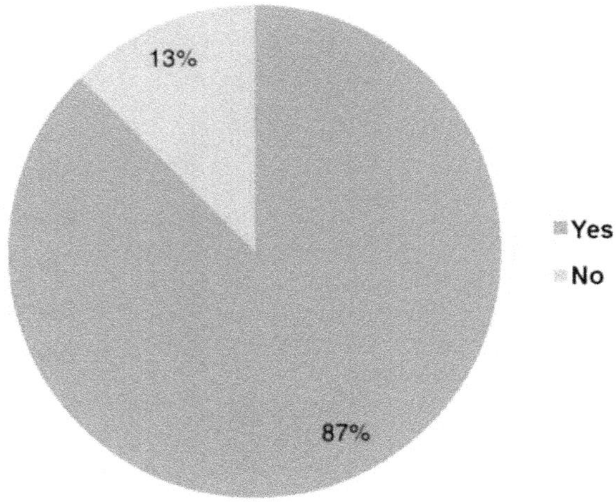

Figure 6. Internet use before confinement (EPSCBF)

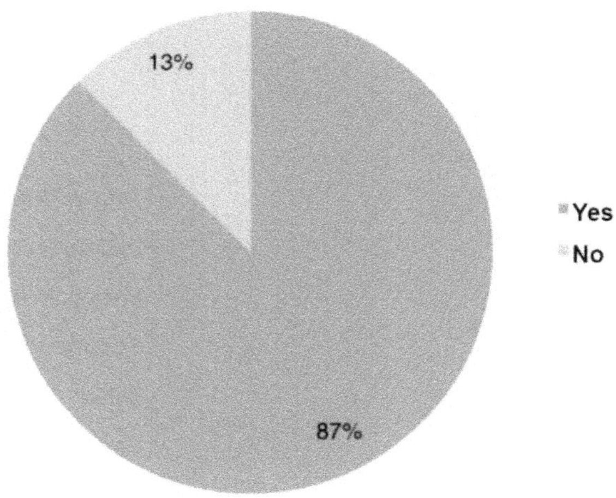

this circumstance reveals that the Internet's form of knowledge happened gradually in more than one context and with more than one transmitter of knowledge. And, as with the training provided in the present research, the participants had some knowledge of the technology, variable in quality and quantity among them, and not necessary for further improvement and/or depth.

As you can see in Figure 7 - How did you find out about the Internet (EPSCBF), the answers were distributed among the options "In training/in class", selected by

Figure 7. How did you find out about the Internet (EPSCBF)

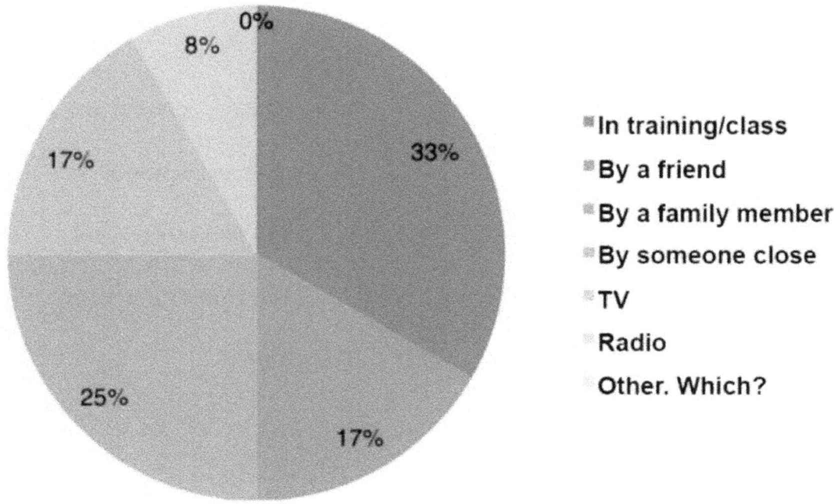

four respondents (33%); "By a friend", selected by two respondents (17%); "For a relative", selected by three respondents (25%); "By an acquaintance", selected by two respondents (17%); and, "By the television", selected by a respondent (8%). The "By radio" and "By other means. Which one? ", Were not selected by any of the respondents.

It is important to point out that the main form of Internet knowledge indicated by the participants is related to the social network of support, either with the closest, friends and family (42%) or the most distant, known (17%). In fact, this form of knowledge of the Internet corresponds to 59% of the answers given. This characteristic of the process of knowledge of the Internet technology is of greater importance when it is attentive to the fact that this is a form of informal learning and, consequently, does not leave to the one who receives the knowledge of the subject in a sustained and consistent way. In terms of regular use of the Internet, Figure 8 - How many times did you use (EPSCBF), 43% of the participants (participants 4, 6 and 8) used the technology every day and several times a day, 28% used between five and once a week (participants 1 and 2), and that 29% used the Internet only very rarely (participants 5 and 7).

Question E.01: "Do you attend or have you attended any school year/course/ training in seclusion?" answers were obtained from all participants in the training program, eight of which were six and six were negative, as in Figure 9 Frequency of Course in Reclusion (EPSCBF).

Figure 8. How many times did you use (EPSCBF)

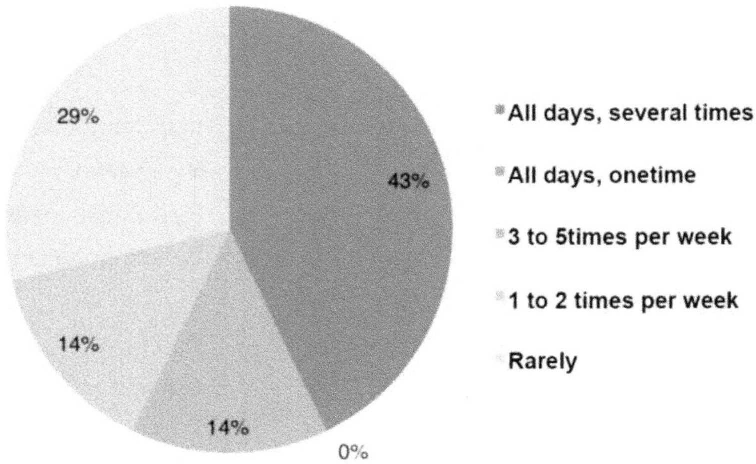

Figure 9. Course frequency in seclusion (EPSCBF)

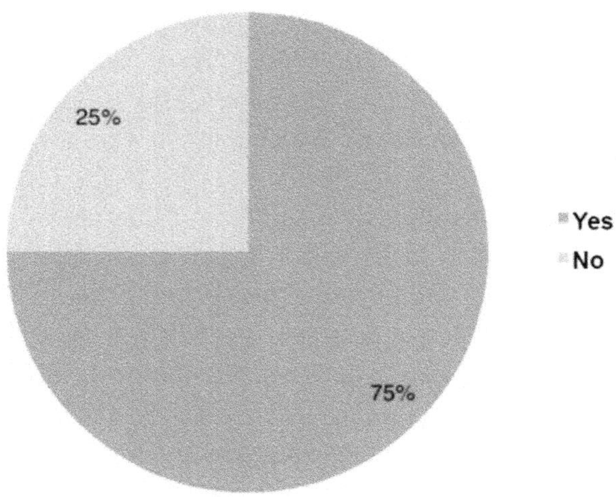

Curricular Program for Training Program

The contents of the training program, systematized in Table 2, served as basis for the dynamics of the case study in the female prison.

In a conclusive analysis of the participants' contributions in the twelve initial modules of the training program, a few key points that allow a categorization of the sample of participants and the reflections of the training program in it can be pointed out:

Table 2. Theoretical index of trainee manual, EPSCBF, version 03/Final

Themes Distribution per training session		
Session/ Module	**Theme**	**Subtheme**
01	Technology	History History of Technology Chronology Computer Information and Communication Technologies
02	Hardware	Definition Input Devices Output Devices Storage Devices
03	Software	Definition Operating system Software Execution programs Communication programs
04	Internet	Definition Users Utility
05	World Wide Web	Url Hypertext World wide web Website
06	Search Engine	Definition Users Utility Types Search
07	Surf the Internet	Relive a visit Actual Visits versus Virtual Visits
08	Email	Definition Password Examples of websites for email creation
09	Security	Privacy OLX Ikea La Redoute Social Security System Fiscal National System
10	Internet job search	Active job search IEFP Netemprego Egor Careerjet Trabalho Certo Sapoemprego

continued on following page

Table 2. Continued

Themes Distribution per training session		
Session/ Module	**Theme**	**Subtheme**
11	Create a blog	Key words Challenge: create a blog Challenge: Customize a blog Challenge: Write and publish a text on a blog
12	Synchronous Communication	Chat Skype
13	Evaluation of Training program	Challenge: to design a proposal to use the Internet in the prison establishment Evaluation of Training program

- The participants feel the need to learn in general, as a result of the lack of knowledge;
- The participants show a desire to obtain more knowledge, to receive it by stimulating means, namely by demonstration, and by experiment;
- There are differences in the assimilation of knowledge between participants - some are clarified in a first teaching moment, others feel a need to review the contents - that became visible in Module 02;
- The participants consider the curious facts taught in the session as points of greatest interest;
- Exploring the Internet by researching or experimenting with new things brings participants good sensations, such as increased sense of normalcy and freedom;
- Any online activity that allows participants to think outside their current condition bequeathed them emotional well-being even if that activity is related to the reality in which they live;
- It is uncomfortable for participants to think about what their post-seclusion life will be like;
- Although participants generally like to participate orally, to some question-answer activities they prefer to respond in writing, which seems to result from the need for individuality and participation without observation and/or criticism from colleagues;
- The moments of sharing and conversation during the lessons reinforce the normal sense of life, of freedom;
- Sharing without constraints, as they would in freedom, brings emotional security to the participants;

- The taste for participation is a determining factor in the success not only of the presence and, consequently, oral participation, but also of the teaching-learning process;
- Happy participants contribute greatly to the success of the training program;
- Participants anticipate that their knowledge will enable them in the future to perform tasks such as searching for and finding information on subjects that interest them, whether for personal, utilitarian and/or civic purposes;
- Participants consider that the obtained knowledge on online job search will be useful for reasons of convenience, broad-based provision and clarification;
- The training program emphasized or reinforced participants' willingness to move forward in learning and to apply it;
- Approaching the end of the prison sentence puts the participants in a position of questioning about their place in society, that is, what place they may occupy in the future;
- The participants' interest in gaining knowledge and experimenting with synchronous communication is unanimous;
- All participants indicate that the main advantage of knowledge about synchronous communication is the possibility of contacting their social support network;
- Participants demonstrate high learning expectations and do not consider another scenario if not to continue learning.

The design of the proposal for Internet use in the EPSCBF was developed in conversation and with the participation of all the participants. There were some minor disagreements during the discussion about some conditions of Internet use that with the sharing of opinions and the questioning of the options have dissipated. The final proposal was therefore the consensus of all participants.

The analysis highlights the following results:

- Main problems identified: security, financial and management.
- Who could use: inmates who go to school and/or who work (it is due to the merit of keeping the active life in seclusion).
- Authorization criteria for use: lack of academic habilitation obliges to attend a training program (short as the one applied) and those who do not go to school or work have to complete the training program regardless of their skills.
- What you could use: communicate with family and friends (the same phone contacts, ten are allowed to have) through email and chat tools; access information justified by work or school; access daily news information; job search; perform personal services (finance, social security) and communicate with lawyers.

- How would it be possible at the level of the structure: a room with ten computers, which already exists, with a guard to monitor (similar to what happens with the school library that has a responsible guard).
- Access format: 30 minutes per prisoner per day; three hours in the morning (9 a.m.-12 p.m.); (14h-17h) and Monday to Friday (this allows 120 inmates to use the service on the same day and after three days it has been possible for all prisoners in the EP to have used their 30 minutes).

The trainees participated actively in the exercise, giving their opinion, considering the context for which the proposal is thought.

The observation made during the discussion showed that five of the six participants have a clear and realistic perception of their status as prisoners and therefore respect the prison establishment and the DGRSP as regulators of their current life span. In the ideas given, the participants sought to have a flexible thinking in order to create a proposal that respected all the rules and constraints of the establishment and the prison system were related to infrastructure, resource management or security.

Participants unanimously consider that content, in terms of themes, language clarity, audiovisual media, demonstrations and exercises, is appropriate. Most participants consider the duration of the adjusted training program. As a suggestion of improved training, it should be noted that there should be more time for experimentation, specifically job search on the Internet, and that the training program should be longer. As subjects to be pointed out were the participants named the email and the blog. The participants' satisfaction with the training program is unanimously positive.

Analyzing participants' general satisfaction, which can be seen from the answers given throughout the case study, it is considered that the training program had a very positive impact not only on the infocommunicational knowledge of the trainees, but also on their relation with learning and also in their self-image and self-esteem.

Two relevant factors have been identified, one in Module 06 and one in Module 09. The first has to do with the evaluation format of the training session which is concluded to be advantageous for the organization of session time, to be written by each participant. The second is about freedom for oral participation, which has shown to be a motivator for participation in the training program: "Allow participants to share without conditioning, just as they would in any training session in their life outside the EP, what they think, what they have lived or what they feel, it leaves them with peace and emotional well-being and security. "

Estabelecimento Prisional de Santa Cruz do Bispo Masculino

Estabelecimento Prisional de Santa Cruz do Bispo Masculino (EPSCBM) is intended for citizens sentenced to prison time on a day off basis, prisoners sentenced to serve a common prison sentence, in an open regime in the interior, in an open regime abroad, unenforceable to comply with security measures in the Clinic of Psychiatry and Mental Health, attributable to serving sentence in an establishment destined to unmanageable.

The training program that integrated the case study began with 16 participants serving time at the Free Drug Unit (ULD). Of these 16, two individuals participated only in the beginning of the action - one individual was transferred from the unit to the main building of the EP, thus leaving to be able to attend the training program, another left in precarious and did not present itself back to continuation of the two individuals attended almost all of the training - left the ULD and the EP due to fulfillment of two-thirds of the sentence or completion of the same. In the course of the training, the ULD received a new prisoner who showed interest in this sense and integrated it. Thus, a total of 17 individuals attended the training course, of which only 13 completed. From now on, participants will be identified as "Participant 1", "Participant 2", (...), "Participant 13", whenever necessary.

Since ULD is an autonomous unit of the rest of the establishment, where inmates live while they are serving their sentence, the daily dynamics are concentrated in a single space and the whole group spends time together, lives together and organizes the days as a family. For example, the task of preparing lunch for all is distributed by two or three members, on a rotating basis. This task means that some of the participants can not be present in one or another session of the training program and, in a way, in some cases, this conditioning functioned as escape from the session. In other words, on one hand, inmates are encouraged to take part in the action because it happens in their space and because it is an agenda activity that the prison establishment has determined, on the other hand the participants have the possibility to take a break integrating into the task lunch preparation, if they prefer to do so.

As regards the demographic characterization, as can be seen, the group participating in the training program applied in EPSCBM is composed of people born between 1973 and 1995, thus being individuals between the ages of 43 and 21. In Figure 10 - Age (EPSCBM), it is possible to visualize the age distribution of participants per decade and to confirm that the majority of individuals are between 30 and 39 years old. It is also found that individuals under the age of 30 or over 40 are approximately equal in number. The total age relationship with the number of participants is shown in Table 3 - Ages (EPSCBM), revealing that although it is possible to indicate a larger group in a given age group, the distribution of individuals by the different ages presented is quite variable but within a reduced margin. That is, the age group corresponds to a wide range between the oldest and the youngest participant, however, there is no age that is the same for more than two (2) participants.

Regarding marital status, the analysis of the data is quite simple: 82% (14 individuals) indicate to be single (see Figure 11 - Marital Status (EPSCBM)), one

Figure 10. Age (EPSCBM)

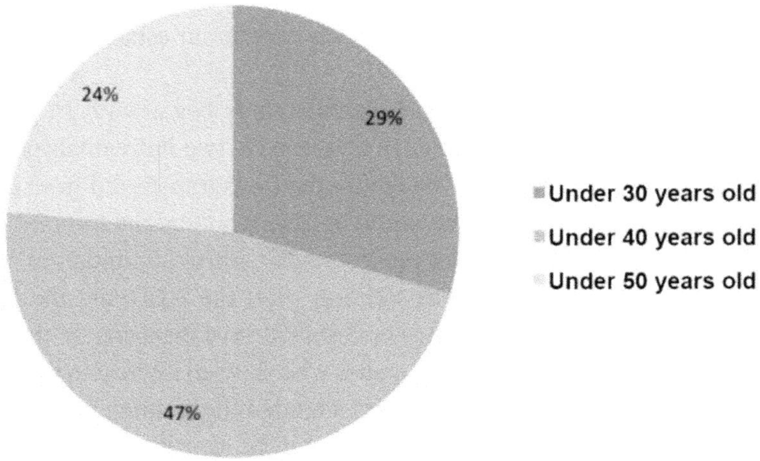

Table 3. Ages (EPSCBM)

Relação do número de participantes com as idades dos mesmos											
21	23	27	30	31	32	35	37	38	40	42	43
1	2	2	1	2	1	2	1	1	1	2	1

Figure 11. Marital status (EPSCBM)

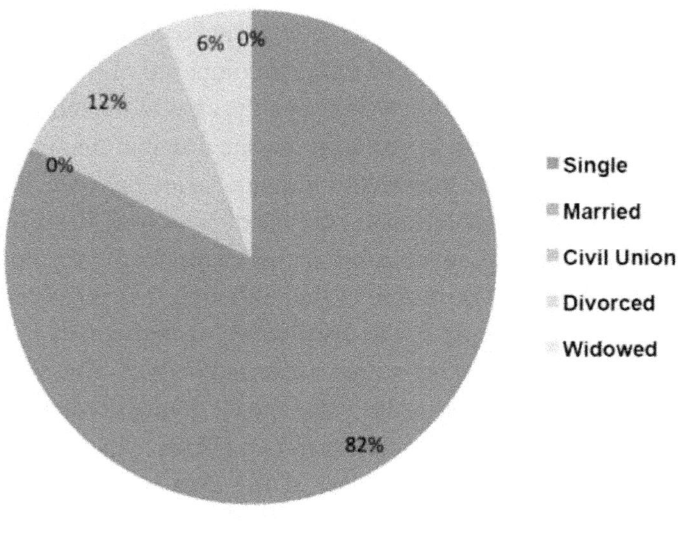

(1) participant indicates to be divorced, and two (2) indicate that they live in a situation of union of fact. There is, therefore, no married or widowed participant.

Regarding school qualifications, a large part of the participants - 47% referring to eight (8) - indicate that they have completed the 3rd cycle of elementary school, that is, the 9th year of schooling. The same number of participants indicated that they had a lower level of education, specifically: two (2) participants who completed 1st cycle (4th or 4th grade) - 12% - and four (4) participants who completed the 2nd cycle - 35%. Of the seventeen participants (17) only one indicates that they have completed secondary education (6%).

Statistics from the Direcção-Geral de Reinserção e Serviços Prisionais on portuguese literacy indicate that 79.1% of the male population attended and/or completed basic education, and that only 13.5% attended and/or completed secondary education or higher (see Figure 12 - Literary Qualifications of the Recluse Population by Sex and Nationality (1st Quarter 2016) (EPSCBM)). Despite the fact that the percentage of male prisoners who completed basic education is high, only 26.6% of them reached the last stage of this level of education, and a large percentage reached only the first cycle of basic education: 26.9% (corresponding to 3,603 individuals).

Concerning the professional situation of the participants in the pre-confinement training, as can be seen in Figure 13 - Occupation at the time of confinement

Figure 12. Literary qualifications of the recluse population by sex and nationality (1st Quarter 2016) (EPSCBM)

Source: Directorate-General for Reinsertion and Prison Services, Directorate for Organization, Planning and External Relations Services, "PRISON STATISTICS (1st Quarter 2016)", p. 5, taken from http://www.dgsp.mj.pt, on August 4, 2016, with graphic additions from the authors.

Literary Qualifications	Men						Women						TOTAL	
	Portuguese		Foreign		Total		Portuguese		Foreign		Total			
	#	%	#	%	#	%	#	%	#	%	#	%	#	%
Can not read or write	369	3,3	53	2,4	**422**	3,2	56	8,8	9	4,1	**65**	7,6	**487**	3,4
Can read and write	323	2,9	94	4,2	**417**	3,1	42	6,6	23	10,4	**65**	7,6	**482**	3,4
With education attendance	10324	92,7	2080	92,4	12404	92,6	517	81,5	176	79,3	693	81,0	13097	91,9
1st cycle of Basic Education (1st, 2nd, 3rd and 4th years)	3277	29,4	326	14,5	**3603**	26,9	189	29,8	36	16,2	**225**	26,3	**3828**	26,9
2nd cycle of Basic Education (5ht and 6th years)	3060	27,5	369	16,4	**3429**	25,6	93	14,7	17	7,7	**110**	12,9	**3539**	24,8
3rd cycle of Basic Education (7th, 8th and 9th	2893	26,0	669	29,7	**3562**	26,6	132	20,8	54	24,3	**186**	21,7	**3748**	26,3
Secondary Education (10th, 11th and 12th years)	885	7,9	569	25,3	**1454**	10,9	83	13,1	39	17,6	**122**	14,3	**1576**	11,1
Higher Education	195	1,8	141	6,3	**336**	2,5	20	3,2	27	12,2	**47**	5,5	**383**	2,7
Other	14	0,1	6	0,3	**20**	0,1		0,0	3	1,4	**3**	0,4	**23**	0,2
Unavailable Information	123	1,1	23	1,0	**146**	1,1	19	3,0	14	6,3	**33**	3,9	**179**	1,3
TOTAL	**11139**	**100**	**2250**	**100**	**13389**	**100**	**634**	**100**	**222**	**100**	**856**	**100**	**14245**	**100**

Figure 13. Occupation in confinement (EPSCBM)

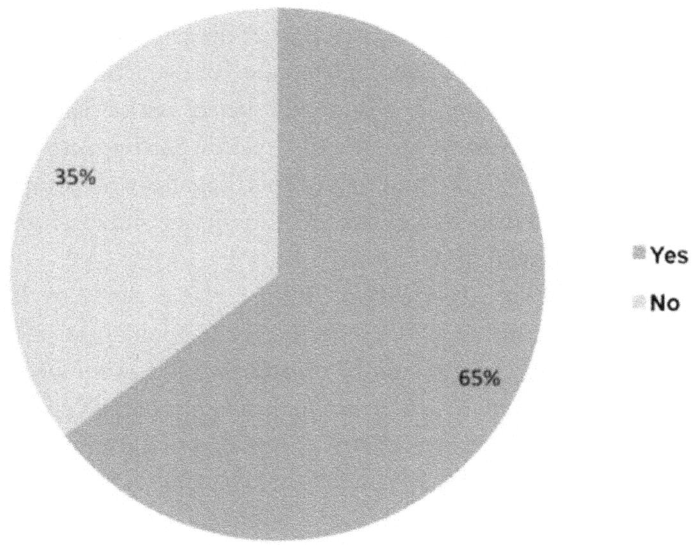

(EPSCBM), 65% were employed, which corresponds to 11 individuals. Thus, out of 17 people, only six (6) indicate that they were unemployed at the time of their incarceration (35%).

Figure 14 shows that 82% of respondents (14 participants) used the Internet prior to seclusion, and that three did not use it (18%).

To the question "C.02 How did you find out what the Internet is? (Select only one of the options presented.) "38 replies were obtained (one participant did not respond). As in the case of the EPSCBF, most of them did not respect the indication that they should select only one of the respondent response options. Analyzing all the data obtained it is concluded that the main form of knowledge about what the Internet is indicated is "For a relative" with 26%, which corresponds to the responses of ten of the participants. Second is the option "In training/in classes" with 24% corresponding to nine answers; and 19% of the response options (seven individuals) include the "For a friend" option (see Figure 15 - How You Met the Internet (EPSCBM)).

Two of the main response options reveal that, as in the case of female participants, the social support network played a significant role in the first contact with the Internet since it has 45% of the response options. This becomes more definite if you add the value relative to the "For an acquaintance" option. In fact, the three values added give a total of 53% of the response options.

Figure 14. Internet use before confinement (EPSCBM)

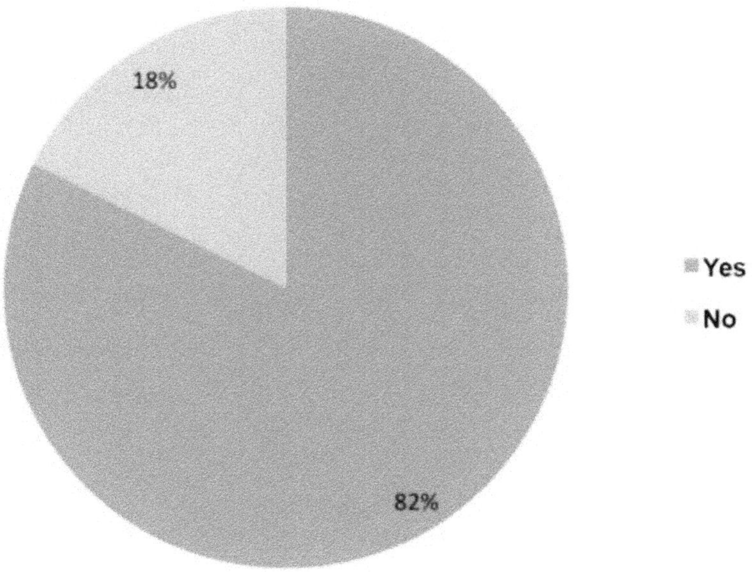

Figure 15. How did you know the internet (EPSCBM)

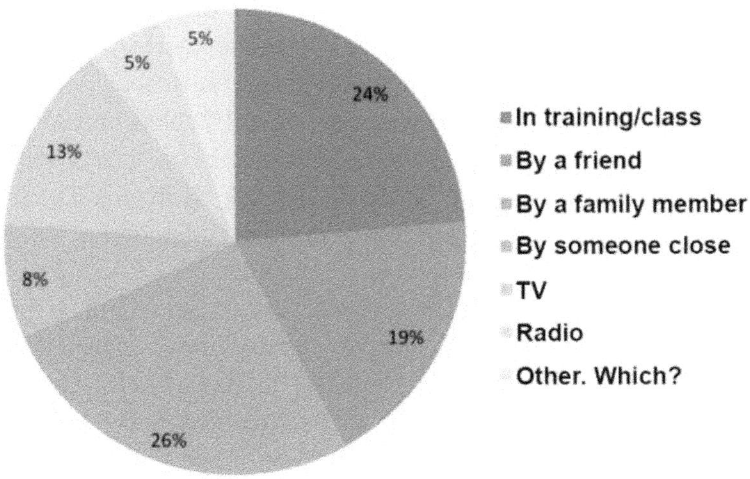

Of the 17 participants in the training course 15, they answered the question of how often the Internet was used prior to incarceration. As shown in Figure 16 - How many times did you use (EPSCBM) 67% of the respondents (10 participants) indicated having Internet use daily and several times a day; no respondent indicated

Figure 16. How often did you use the internet (EPSCBM)

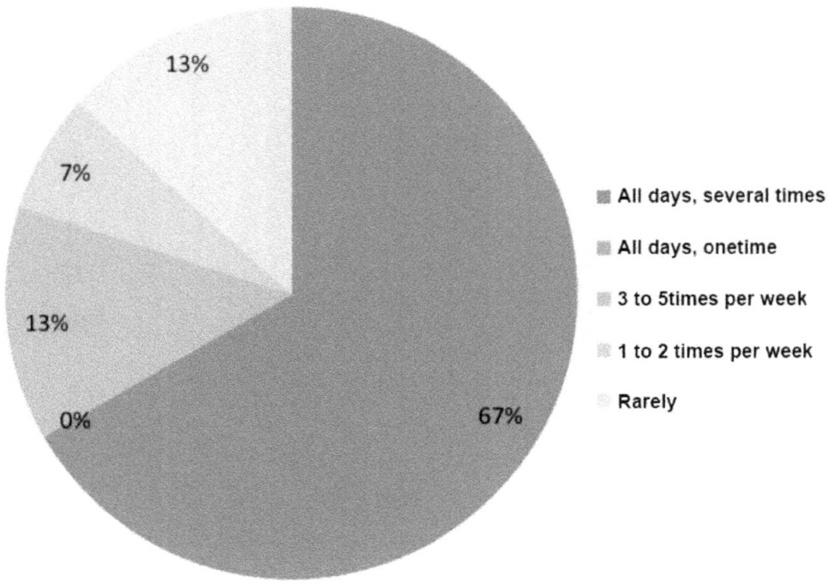

using the Internet every day only once a day; 13% (two participants) indicated to use three to five times a week; 7% (one participant) indicated to use once or twice a week; and 13% (two participants) reported using the Internet very rarely.

Regarding the curriculum for the training program, the thematic structure applied in the EPSCBM was drawn from that applied to in Estabelecimento Prisional de Santa Cruz do Bispo Feminino (see Table 2 - Thematic Index of the Trainee Manual, EPSCBF, Version 03/Final). In the Table 4 – Trainee Handbook Thematic Index, EPSCBM sees the definitive organization of the curriculum of the applied training program. This curriculum is organized in ten modules.

In contrast to what happened in the EPSCBF experience, for the training course at EPSCBM a more compact and objective curriculum was developed, reducing the number of modules by excluding themes ("Creating a blog") and reorganizing them. For example, some were joined such as "Internet" and "World Wide Web (WWW)" (module 04), and "Search" and "Browse" (module 05) have been added.

In a conclusive analysis of participants' contributions in the first nine modules of the training program, a number of key points can be identified that allow a categorization of the sample of participants and the reflexes of the training program in it:

- The participants feel that the learning obtained in the training program will help them in the future in the day-to-day life;
- Prior knowledge about the topics covered in the training program is reduced;

Table 4. Trainee handbook thematic index, EPSCBM

Themes Distribution per training session		
Session/Module	**Theme**	**Subtheme**
01	Technology	History History of Technology Chronology Computer Information and Communication Technologies
02	Hardware	Definition Input Devices Output Devices Storage Devices
03	Software	Definition Operating system Software Execution programs Communication programs
04	Internet	Definition Users Utility
05	Search and Browse	Browsers Search Engine Search To browse
06	Email	Definition User Password Examples of websites for email creation
07	Create Online Accounts	Privacy OLX Ikea La Redoute Social Security System Fiscal National System
08	Internet job search	Active job search IEFP Netemprego Egor Careerjet Trabalho Certo Sapoemprego
09	Synchronous Communication	Skype Chat
10	Evaluation of Training program	Challenge: to design a proposal to use the Internet in the prison establishment Evaluation of Training program

- There are differences of knowledge between participants in the same group, which became obvious in Module 03 of the training program;
- The contents addressed in the training program are assimilated at least superficially;
- Participants feel they need to use the computer in order to cement learning;
- Participants generally feel that all issues need to be deepened;
- In general, trainees are motivated to learn, have an interest in the training program and like the way the contents are transmitted to them and how the training program is organized;
- The experience of new activities using the Internet, even in a demonstrative format, encourages participants curiosity and interest, culminating in an increase of motivation for learning.

Design of Internet Use Proposal in the Prison

The design of the Internet use proposal in the Prison was developed in conversation and with the participation of all the participants. There was some disagreement regarding the organization of the use of the Internet that was solved with the clarification of some questions. The final proposal was therefore the consensus of all participants.

The main problem identified was security (connection to the street, business continuation they had out there) and the solution presented was the limitation of access. Although they have expressed the idea that everyone should have access to the Internet without exception.

- **For What One Could Use:** Search; Study and learn; Talk to family; Access bank accounts (transfer money to own accounts) and be informed (three newspapers).
- **In What Context:** Leisure (emotional support); Teaching (learning) and Personnel (financial management).
- **When:** In the hours of the phone calls and in the free part of the day (11h30-12h15 + 13h-13h50 + 17h50-18h45; 9h-12h15 + 13h-17h30; Monday morning, Wednesday afternoon).
- **For How Long:** 30 minutes.
- **Where:** Room (aquarium).
- **How:** With supervision of the remote guard (counter); Three computers; and Training.
- **In What Way:** With confidence; anyone who misused would be punished, would cease to use; With tutoring for new elements and prior registration with indication of the type of use to be made.
- **What One Could Use:** Skype, chat, email, contact control.

The trainees had a participative attitude in the exercise, gave their opinion, and considered the context for which the proposal is thought.

Compared with the research group EPSCBF, this group seemed much less concerned with the obvious issues that need to be considered when proposing, as in this case, a proposal for such an unusual and decontextualized change in the prison setting. Indeed, the idea of 'trust' put forward by participants as a viability mechanism seems to be more of what they think the system owes them than what they need to prove.

Despite this more demanding and reactionary position, the probabilities that the participants attribute to the possibility of a proposal such as this being accepted by the management of the prison establishment and subsequently by the Direcção-geral de Reinserção e Serviços Prisionais are rather small. Indeed, when questioned about what percentage of acceptance they believe the proposal will have, the participants mostly respond 'zero'. And even those who believe that there is a reduced chance that the proposal will be accepted are quite cautious in predictions not indicating values above 25%.

As can be seen in Figure 17 - Participants' opinion on the possibility of accepting the proposed Internet use (EPSCBM), only participants 7, 12 and 15 have some hope in a scenario of Internet use in ULD indicating, respectively, 25%, 20% and 10%.

Participants 10 and 16, like most of the sample, answered 'zero', stating that at the time they did not believe in the possibility of the designed scenario becoming a reality. However, they said that considering that other conditions may change, this situation may change. Thus, the participant 10 said "From this moment to 5 years, 25%.". That is, the trainee believes that in 2021 the probability of being possible to have a scenario of Internet use in ULD will have a percentage of 25.

The participant 16 presented a very interesting suggestion that consists in the creation of a pilot project that, using the rules designed by the group, was implemented during a period of time to be determined. To this scenario of application of the proposal of use of the Internet designed by the trainees the participant attributed a possibility percentage of 70.

As for the assertiveness and clarity of the content, the media used (audiovisual) and the exercises applied, and the added value of the demonstrations, the participants consider that the training program is well structured and well implemented. Regarding the duration of the training program some participants point out that it is appropriate, others consider that it should be longer. Most participants argue that there should be more time for technology experimentation. The training program was a positive experience which brought participants information and knowledge and increased their willingness to learn and their self-esteem.

An analysis of the responses obtained at all stages of the training activity shows that, apart from some organizational and structural issues, the training program is

Figure 17. Participants' opinion on the possibility of accepting the proposed Internet use (EPSCBM)

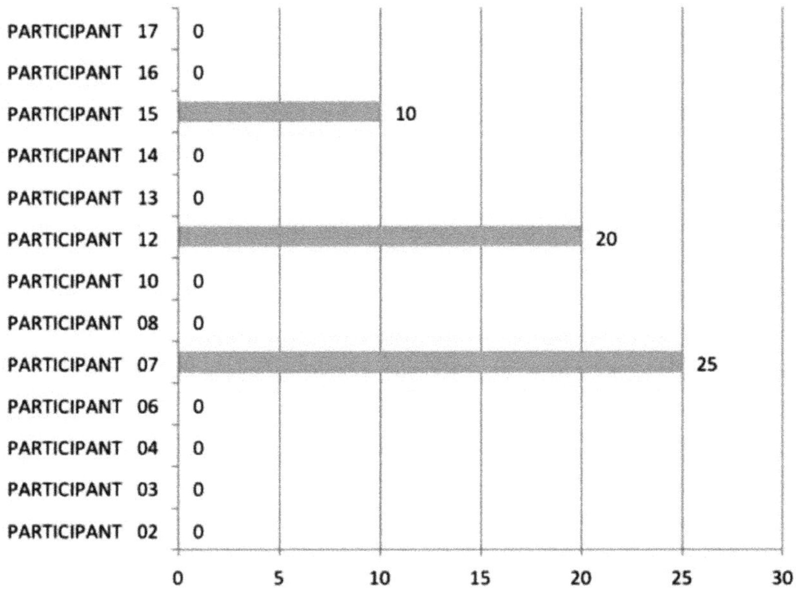

to the liking of all participants. In fact, participants are satisfied with the obtained knowledge, and possibly more relevant, they have acquired the motivation to learn and the will to acquire more knowledge.

Thus, it is possible to state that there are no doubts regarding the added value in providing similar training programs in prison context and for target audiences such as those presented here.

FUTURE RESEARCH DIRECTIONS

As a suggestion for future work it is recommended to apply the training model proposed here in several prisons so that it can contribute to the enrichment of learning scenarios and so that those can contribute to the improvement of the own curricular and training model.

From the experience of the two case studies presented here it is recommended that the teaching strategy allows the existence of ludic moments in each lesson, such as asking a trainee to choose something they would like to share with the group, be it a song, a video, news, etc. Thus, as a closing moment of the lesson, a trainee researches what they want to share, with supervision of the teacher, and displays it to the group, allowing the possibility for a moment of discussion about the choice made.

On the other hand, although innovation and creativity are not exclusive competences of digital infocommunication scenarios, they should be considered as crucial in the contemporary context of digital content production and consumption (on and offline). In this sense, we challenge researchers to design and implement a research project in prison context that aims to develop innovation and creativity skills using digital tools as a way to broaden inmates aesthetic and professional horizons.

By doing differently in the prison context, as in any context, different results can be expected.

CONCLUSION

The research work developed and presented here fits the problem of the development of infocommunication skills in the context of digital tools usage, online, in the context of imprisonment. Its main goal is to contribute with a proposal for a Training Model in Infocommunication Skills in the context of Internet usage, able to be adopted as a reference by DGRSP, and encourage its application in the teaching curriculum in prisons.

The first and second research questions, "How Internet access by prisoners in Portuguese prisons in a training context can be a reality?" and "Which curricular structure should a training program in Internet usage adopt in the specific context of the Portuguese Prison System?", were answered and the results obtained contribute to the construction and development of any work implemented in prison in the field of information and communication technologies, specifically in the development of infocommunication competencies of individuals in detention.

Although it cannot be said that the third research question — What impact would learn how to use the Internet have on prisoner's perception of his/her cognitive and technical abilities and, consequently, their employability? — made a clear contribution, one cannot say that it did not brought answers. In fact, some of the results identified with the two case studies are representative of the consequences that learning with the goal to develop infocommunicational competencies have on the individual, on his/her ideas, perspectives and ambitions, on the way he/she sees and foresees his future.

The design of the training model that it is presented here as the result of the research work benefits from and incorporates information and reflection from various sources, namely the literature reviewed, the ICT training framework proposed by the Portuguese Ministry of Education for Basic Education and, the empirical data collected in the two case studies. The final result, in particular with regard to the themes, can be seen in Table 5 - Thematic Model for Training Program.

Table 5. Thematic model for training program

Themes Distribution per training session		
Session/Module	**Theme**	**Subtheme**
01	Technology	History History of Technology Chronology Computer Information and Communication Technologies
02	Hardware	Definition Input Devices Output Devices Storage Devices
03	Software	Definition Operating system Software Execution programs Communication programs
04	Internet and the World Wide Web (WWW)	Internet World wide web Web site Users Utility
05	Search and Browse	Browsers Search Engine Search To browse
06	Email	Definition User Password Examples of websites for email creation
07	Create Online Accounts	Privacy Business pages (OLX, IKEA, etc.) Social Security System Fiscal National System
08	Internet job search	Active job search IEFP Pages of Job search pages and human resources (Netemprego, Egor, Careerjet, Trabalho Certo, Sapoemprego)
09	Synchronous Communication	Skype Chat

Specifically on the use of the Internet for learning purposes, both experiences have shown that, within the conditions appropriate to the prison context, this possibility exists and is practiced albeit in very restricted and conditioned ways.

Thus, it is concluded that in a one-to-one relationship, in which the organics and dynamics of the prison are maintained and not disturbed, and when there is justification and authorization for use, Internet access may exist in a school and/or training context for the purpose of learning.

Indeed, before a population with a low level of academic education it is verified that any learning is added value in the increase of competencies and knowledge, and even in the construction of the person as a citizen and professional. Regarding this research, specifically the attempt to provide basic infocommunication skills to the individual, the advantages become more obvious not only because individuals who already use technologies do so in a non-effective and non-efficient way with respect to the positive return in professional success, but also because the learning they eventually receive post-seclusion will more likely be informal and, therefore, not geared to an effective and efficient use of information and communication technologies in order to achieve a place of success in the future society, but oriented towards trivial use.

The results obtained with both case studies applied in prisons participating in this research show that there was a very positive impact not only on the infocommunication knowledge of the individuals, but also on the relationship acquired with learning. The gain of knowledge and skills brought, in turn, a positive increase in the self-image and self-esteem of the participants. In fact, the satisfaction of the participants with the obtained learning increases the motivation to learn and the will to acquire more knowledge.

In view of all the difficulties they face following their detention, this contribution is considered to be an asset for the future of these people. And it is argued that training programs such as those applied in this research should be a constant in Portuguese prisons, always with necessary adaptation to the structures and dynamics of each one, and to the profiles of the individuals involved.

REFERENCES

Baskas, R. S. (2016). Creating a Curriculum and Accommodating Teaching Methods at a Federal Prison's Special Housing Unit. *ERIC*, 1–14.

Batra, R., Jasso, T., & Stevens, Y. (2012). Learning behind bars: Exploring prison educators' facilitation of inmates' self-directed learning through Garrison's model. *11th Annual College of Education & GSN Research Conference*, 2–9.

Burgos, García, & Humbert. (2007). El blog desde la prisión: un instrumento de inclusión social. *Educacion Y Bibliotecas, 19*(158), 102–109.

Caride Gómez, J. A., & Gradaílle Pernas, R. (2013). Educar en las cárceles: Nuevos desafíos para la educación social en las instituciones penitenciarias. *Review of Education*, (360): 36–47. doi:10.4438/1988-592X-RE-2013-360-219

Contreras-Pulido, P., Martín-Pena, D., & Aguaded, I. (2015). Derribando el autoestigma: medios de comunicación en prisiones como aliados de la inclusión social. *Cuadernos.Info, 36*(36), 15–26. 10.7764/cdi.36.708

Cronin, J. (2011). *The path to successful reentry: The relationship between correctional education, employment and recidivism.* University of Missouri, Institute of Public Policy.

Dores, A. P., Pontes, N., & Loureiro, R. (2016). *Manifesto para uma nova cultural penal.* Academic Press.

Emasealu, H. U., & Popoola, S. O. (2016). Information Needs, Accessibility and utilization of Library Information Resources as Determinants of Psychological Well-being of prison Inmates in Nigeria. *Brazilian Journal of Information Science, 2*(2010), 29–46.

Farley, H., & Pike, A. (2016). Engaging prisoners in education: Reducing risk and recidivism. *Journal of the International Corrections and Prison Association, 1*(1), 65–73.

Farley, H., Pike, A., Hopkins, S., & Byrne, C. (2015). Bringing digital literacies to students in prison: challenges and opportunities. In *Proceedings of the 15th EPEA Training Conference (EPEA 2015)* (pp. 1–1). University of Southern Queensland.

Fong, J. (2008). Facilitating education in prisons. In E. W. C. Leung, F. L. Wang, L. Miao, J. Zhao, & J. He (Eds.), Advances in Blended Learning (Vol. 5328, pp. 1–15). Berlin: Springer. doi:10.1007/978-3-540-89962-4_1

Franganillo, J., Burgos, L., García, A., & Tomàs, C. (2006). Alfabetización digital en la prisión: una experiencia con jóvenes internos. In *Alfabetización digital en la prisión: una experiencia con jóvenes internos* (pp. 102–118). Badajoz: II Congreso Internacional de Alfabetización Tecnológica. Retrieved from http://www.franganillo.net/franganillo2006.pdf

Harlow, C. W. (2003). *Education and Correctional Populations. Bureau of Justice Statistics Special Report.* U.S. Department of Justice, Office of Justice Programs Revised. Retrieved from https://www.bjs.gov/content/pub/pdf/ecp.pdf

Hawley, J. (2011). *Prison Education and Training in Europe: A Review and Commentary of Existing Literature, Analysis and Evaluation. Education And Training*. Retrieved from http://ec.europa.eu/justice/news/consulting_public/0012/Fullreport_en.pdf

Hurry, J., Brazier, L., Snapes, K., & Wilson, A. (2005). *Improving the literacy and numeracy of disaffected young people in custody and in the community*. Retrieved from http://www.nrdc.org.uk/publications_details.asp?ID=28#

Justice Action. (2011). Computers in Cells: Maintaining Community Ties and Reducing Recidivism. *Justice Action*. Retrieved from http://search.proquest.com/docview/1033447378?accountid=13042%5Cnhttp://oxfordsfx.hosted.exlibrisgroup.com/oxford?url_ver=Z39.88-2004&rft_val_fmt=info:ofi/fmt:kev:mtx:journal&genre=article&sid=ProQ:ProQ:ncjrs&atitle=Computers+in+Cells:+Maintaining+Commun

Lochner, L., & Moretti, E. (2004). The Effect of Education on Crime: Evidence from Prison Inmates, Arrest, and Self-Reports. *The American Economic Review*, *94*(1), 155–189. doi:10.1257/000282804322970751

Newman, G. R. (2011). Crime and Punishment around the World. Santa Barbara, CA: Abc-clio.

O'Neill, L., MacKenzie, D. L., & Bierie, D. M. (2007). Educational Opportunities Within Correctional Institutions: Does Facility Type Matter? *The Prison Journal*, *87*(3), 311–327. doi:10.1177/0032885507304351

Onofre, E. M. C. (2009). Educação Escolar na Prisão na Visão dos Professores: um hiato entre o proposto e o vivido. *Reflexão E Ação*, *17*(1), 227–244.

Pager, D. (2003). The mark of a criminal record. *American Journal of Sociology*, *108*(5), 937–975. doi:10.1086/374403

Pike, A. (2014). *Prison-based transformative learning and its role in life after release*. The Open University.

Pike, A., & Adams, A. (2012). Digital exclusion or learning exclusion? An ethnographic study of adult male distance learners in English prisons. *Research in Learning Technology*, *20*(4), 363–376. doi:10.3402/rlt.v20i0.18620

Pulido, M. P. (2010). Programs promoting reading in Spanish prisons. *IFLA Journal*, *36*(2), 131–137. doi:10.1177/0340035210369875

Reisdorf, B. C., & Jewkes, Y. (2016). (B)Locked sites: Cases of Internet use in three British prisons. *Information Communication and Society*, *19*(6), 771–786. doi:10.1080/1369118X.2016.1153124

Rocha, D. G. S., & Oliveira, L. (2014). Informação e comunicação em plataformas digitais: novos desafios para o sistema prisional português. In A. M. da Silva, B. Passarelli, & F. Ramos (Eds.), *e-Infocomunicação - Estratégias e aplicações* (pp. 169–200). São Paulo: Senac; doi:10.13140/RG.2.1.3628.4329

Rogers, L., Hurry, J., Simonot, M., & Wilson, A. (2014). The aspirations and realities of prison education for under-25s in the London area. *London Review of Education, 12*(2), 184–196. doi:10.18546/LRE.12.2.04

Schirmer, S. L. (2008). Education Behind Bars. *Current, 11*(2), 1–128.

Sedgley, N. H., Scott, C. E., Williams, N. A., & Derrick, F. W. (2010). Prison's Dilemma: Do education and jobs programmes affect recidivism? *Economica, 77*(307), 497–517. doi:10.1111/j.1468-0335.2008.00751.x

Steurer, S. J., Smith, L., & Tracy, A. (2001). *OCE/CEA Three State Recidivism Study*. Retrieved from http://www.ceanational.org/PDFs/3StateFinal.pdf

Tyler, J. H., & Kling, J. R. (2002). *What is the Value of a Prison GED?* Unpublished, Brown University. Retrieved from http://users.nber.org/~kling/PrisonGED.pdf

Weissman, M., Cregor, M., Gainsborough, J., Kief, N., Leone, P., & Sullivan, E. (2008). *The right to education in the juvenile and criminal justice systems in the United States. Dignity in Schools Campaign*. Retrieved from https://www.aclu.org/files/images/asset_upload_file164_38663.pdf

Wexler, J., Pyle, N., Flower, A., Williams, J. L., & Cole, H. (2014). A Synthesis of Academic Interventions for Incarcerated Adolescents. *Review of Educational Research, 84*(1), 3–46. doi:10.3102/0034654313499410

Zgoba, K. M., Haugebrook, S., & Jenkins, K. (2008). The influence of GED obtainment on inmate release outcome. *Criminal Justice and Behavior, 35*(3), 375–387. doi:10.1177/0093854807311853

KEY TERMS AND DEFINITIONS

Education: Process that allows the individual to develop their cognitive and social skills. Education involves the acquisition of knowledge, skills and metacognitive processes. By this process the individual becomes more apt to understand the world, to understand himself and to act in an informed, conscious, and critical way.

Infocommunicational Skills: A set of competences of a diverse but complementary nature, encompassing operational capacities to know how to use computer and telecommunications equipment, to install/configure software; (identify a need for training, choose the source and strategy to find the information needed, select information and use it analytically and critically), communication skills (ability to select interlocutors, argumentation and respect) and ethical competences (respect for standards, in particular intellectual property).

Inmate: Person who for having disregarded/failed to comply with the rules established with the society is deprived of his freedom.

Prison: Physical and normative space in which inmates must remain with the objective of reviewing their behavior against the law/social norms and enjoy this period to acquire new competences that allow them a better social insertion.

Chapter 4
Research on Information Literacy and Social Inclusion of Female Inmates

Aurora Cuevas-Cerveró
Universidad Complutense de Madrid, Spain

María Antonia Agúndez Soriano
Colegio Universitario de Estudios Financieros (CUNEF), Spain

ABSTRACT

Information literacy in prisons is still an incipient issue for the scientific community, as evidenced by the absence of studies on information literacy activities in prisons. There are hardly any specific training programs for the acquisition of informational competences in Spanish prisons. They are presented results of research that have been aimed at creating a theoretical-application model of training in informational and digital skills for people in prison. The project had a methodological approach based on action research. The digital divide makes it difficult to integrate people into the labor market, leading them to social exclusion. In the case of female prisoners, this gap is even more accentuated and integration difficulties increase, so the project has adopted a gender perspective. In order to meet the objectives, a training program aimed at social and labor inclusion was created with the aim of improving the living and working conditions of women prisoners and increasing their participation as active citizens in the information society.

DOI: 10.4018/978-1-5225-5975-7.ch004

INTRODUCTION

The research we present is a response to the lack of informational literacy training programs for the social inclusion of women prisoners in the jails of the Community of Madrid (Spain). The economic and gender gap hinders the integration of these women in the labour market and leads them to social exclusion. If we add to this the informational and digital gap, we are facing a serious case of social exclusion. That is why the objective of this research has been to develop a formative proposal of information literacy for social inclusion, with the aim of allowing inmates to acquire the necessary information and digital skills for their social and educational development from the perspective of social and labour inclusion, thus improving their living and working conditions and increasing their participation as active citizens in contemporary society.

First of all, in order to achieve our objective, an analysis of the general and specific environment has been carried out, which has allowed us to define the context for the implementation of our training proposal. The review of the literature and the experiences found related to our object of study has allowed us to determine the need to produce a training program for the acquisition of informational and digital competences in the female prison context.

In addition, in order to elaborate our proposal, we have relied on the theoretical framework of information literacy for social inclusion and the collection of data through a user study conducted directly to the inmates in our case study. The analysis of the collected data reflected relevant facts, which showed that the inmates had a very low level of computer and informational knowledge. This study has allowed us to develop a training proposal according to the specific needs of our study group. Our proposal includes training in informational and digital competencies for the social inclusion of women inmates of the "Jaime Garralda" Mothers Unit in Madrid, a prison in which women who have just been mothers living with their children remain for up to three years.

With our work we intend to contribute to diminish the informational and gender gap suffered by these women, facilitating their integration into society and allowing them to take advantage of all available resources, so that they can relate, work, communicate, entertain, produce, and access administrative procedures. It is also intended to facilitate that woman prisoners are more autonomous, economically independent, more critical and more reflective, that is, in short, more socially and professionally integrated.

This work that we present here emanates from the doctoral thesis carried out by Agúndez-Soriano and directed by Cuevas-Cerveró in 2015 in response to the lack of information literacy training programs for the social inclusion of women prisoners. Information Literacy whose acronym is ALFIN, is a translation of Information

Literacy and alludes to the ability to determine what information is needed and when, how to find it, evaluate it, recover it and communicate it, in an autonomous way and making an ethical and responsible use of it. In the mid-90s there began to be a connection between the concept of information literacy and education. Authors such as Johnston and Webber (1999) cited in Bawden (2002), argue that information literacy should be treated as an academic discipline and that is how it should be taught. In this way, there begins to be a close relationship between permanent learning and information literacy, which points to continued learning for the acquisition of informational knowledge with a view to informational literacy of people. One of the most cited definitions at the international level is the American Library Association (ALA) defines the literate person informationally saying: To be competent about the information an individual must recognize when it is necessary, and have the ability to locate, evaluate and use effectively the information that is required ... People prepared in this aspect is, finally, the one that has learned to learn. They know how to learn because they know how information is organized, how to find it, and how to use it so that others can learn from them. They are people prepared for lifelong learning because they are always able to get the information they need for any task or decision that comes their way. (ALA, 1989). For its part, the European Union (2006), again relates information literacy with continuing education, in its "Action Program in the field of lifelong learning" 7 where it points out that new technologies are a tool that can lead to inclusion and that, therefore, people who do not use them are excluded from a society that is increasingly digitalized.

The authors define information literacy in the following way: "Information literacy comprises a set of competencies that lead to an adequate, reflective, critical and responsible use of information and contribute to the social inclusion of citizens." (Agúndez-Soriano, 2015, p. 60). For his part, Cuevas (2007) believes that this concept is linked to the historical, economic, cultural and social context, and points out that a person will be informationally literate when he or she is able to decode the relevant information and codify a new message to communicate.

Information literacy (ALFIN) in prisons is still a very incipient topic for the scientific community. After an exhaustive bibliographic review to know the best evidences in informational literacy research in prisons for social inclusion, we have not found evidence of previous studies on informative literacy training programs for women prisoners, we have only found previous studies that deal with the inequality between the programs taught to prisoners and those taught to inmates, the latter being sexist programs (cleaning, cooking, hairdressing) (Burgdorf, 2012; Imel, 1990; Jensen, 1976; Sobel, 1982). Other studies have been carried out to highlight and demonstrate the importance of the training courses so that the inmates do not reoffend, carried out comparative studies between groups that have been given training courses and groups that they do not (Ely, 2012; Flamer, 2012; Fine et.al,

2001; Elvira-Valdés, 2014). Other studies are aimed at manifesting the need for social and digital inclusion to be carried out through information literacy for disadvantaged groups, thus encouraging them to be part of society, involving public libraries so that they can also develop from there programs oriented to this end (Aranda, 2005; Bernsmann and Croll, 2013; Berrio, 2012; Cuhman and Mclean, 2008; Hendry, 2000; Lombarte, 2005; Oguz and Kurbanoglu, 2013).

Other authors make an approach to the Spanish penitentiary reality from a gender perspective. Furthermore to analyzing the types of centers and the impact of prison life on the inmates, they analyze the set of socio-educational and socio-labor programs that make up the panorama of the female prison centers with the purpose of knowing the impact that these programs can have in social and labour reintegration (Añaños, 2013, p. 91, Añaños, Fernández, and Llopis, 2013, p. 15, Del Pozo, Jiménez, and Turdi, 2013, p. 57, Fernández, 2011). Castillo-Algarra and Ruiz-García 2007). Contreras, Martín Pena and Aguadez (2015) carry out a study on media literacy in Spanish prisons for the social inclusion of prisoners.

In relation to the search of activities carried out in Spanish prisons on information literacy, we have only found seven activities oriented to digital literacy, which do not have any element linked to information literacy, three of which are taught in prisons of Catalonia, one in Pontevedra, one in Granada, another is taught throughout Spain and another in a penitentiary center in Madrid, being this last experience limited to prisoners with functional diversity. In this sense, we have to say that the General Secretariat of Penitentiary Institutions (in charge of managing penitentiary centers in Spain), did not provide us with any information about the training programs currently taught in these centers. We have based on information found on official pages, different types of publications of the Secretariat's document collection and on the Web.

Methodology

The project has had a methodological approach based on action-research. It is a qualitative research approach that provides the means to carry out systematic actions that collaborate in solving problems. It proposes the collaboration between researcher and researched, in this way the probability of the action is increased, but it also favors the access to information that the Researchers as external agents do not have. The chosen method to carry out the development of this research is the case study and was developed in the "Jaime Garralda" Mothers Unit in Madrid, based on the need to build a contextualized training proposal aimed at our study group.

Our case study was conducted on a sample of 10 women prisoners, aged between 24 and 38 years serving a sentence in this mothers Unit.

For all inmates, this was the first time they entered prison and at the time of this study they all had a final sentence. Two of the inmates were classified in third grade and the rest in second grade, but with third grade privileges, allowing them to leave the prison temporally.

We consider the case study the optimal method to reach our objectives, since it allows us to obtain results from the practice carried out with the inmates in real situation, in the sense pointed out by Walker (1983) when he says that the case study it is the examination of an example in action. The study of specific incidents and events and the selective collection of information of a biographical nature, of personality, intentions and values, allows the person to capture and reflect the elements of a situation that give it meaning (Walker, 1983, p. 45).

Although our research was qualitative, we considered quantitative elements to support certain aspects of our work. For this reason, we have applied the survey as a method and the questionnaire as a quantitative technique. Through this technique we have met the training and information needs of our study group and we were able to design a training proposal tailored to their needs. Two questionnaires were designed, one diagnostic as a user study, carried out before the training, and another to verify results, post-training. The second questionnaire allowed us to evaluate the computer and documentary knowledge acquired by the inmates in the training and also to know their opinion about the training received, facilitating the evaluation of the impact.

We have applied the technique of open, participant and structured observation to record the most relevant events that have taken place during our study.

During the implementation of the training program, all relevant facts were recorded, in order to be able to assess whether the defined strategies and the content of the program arrived correctly to the inmates.

Observation indicators that were used during the implementation of the training program were:

Respect to the Training Process

- Interest in the subject exposed
- Appropriate behavior
- Motivation
- Communication with classmates
- Participation in conversation
- Attention in class
- No class attendance
- Difficulties due to language
- Difficulties due to their educational level

- Reading with ease
- Reading comprehension what she reads
- Understanding concepts and vocabulary

Regarding the Activities Carried Out

- Realization of the proposed activities
- Active participation in them
- Know how to work in a group
- Interest in activities
- Preparation of activities correctly

These indicators were applied both in the training process and in the activities.

The triangulation of the methods and techniques allowed us to better understand our study group, since each of them provided specific data that helped reach the proposed objectives.

Our proposal is based on the application of methodological principles of information and evidence-based documentation (EBLIP: Evidence-Based Library and Information Practice), a process that consists of searching and selecting the best evidences in informational literacy research (studies, experiences) in relation to our question or research problem to make decisions about the orientation of the training proposal.

To design the training program according to the characteristics of the group of women prisoners of the "Jaime Garralda" Mothers Unit in Madrid, we propose, according to Sackett (2004) and Civallero (2007), to combine the best evidence in research in information literacy with the evidences derived from a study and analysis of the needs of inmates. Once the training program has been designed and implemented, it is proposed that it can be carried out to other Spanish prisons.

For the search and selection of the best evidence in research in information literacy, we rely on the evidence-based practice process proposed by Booth and Brice (2004) and Connor (2007):

1. Define the research question or problem

It is about posing a specific question according to the information needs that exist. These questions have to be related to the research problem and you have to help us find the best evidence to answer the question asked. In our study, we believe in the need to train inmates in information literacy so that they acquire informational and digital skills, as this contributes to these women have better access to the labour market and a higher level of income, being able to integrate and participate more actively in society.

For all these reasons, the research question that we propose and that will serve us to carry out the design of the training proposal is the following:

What characteristics and orientation should a formative proposal present that has the purpose of acquiring informational and digital skills on the part of inmates for their social and labour reintegration in Penitentiary Centers of the Community of Madrid?

2. Search and select the best evidence to answer our question:
    a. Based on a systematic review of the specialized literature
    b. From obtaining other additional evidence, through the application of research techniques (in our case, the survey and the observation technique):
        i. Initially, carrying out a diagnosis to determine the formative and informative needs of inmates in order to define objectives and strategies for inmates to develop basic digital skills and information skills related to the search, retrieval, evaluation and use of information according to their needs, thus contributing to their social and labor reintegration.
        ii. During the implementation of the training proposal, recording all the facts that may be relevant in order to assess whether the strategies defined and the content of the training proposal are reaching the inmates appropriately.
        iii. And finally, assessing the impact of the training proposal based on the objectives initially defined, evaluating the results obtained from the implementation of the proposal and reformulating, if necessary, the orientation of the training proposal.
3. Analyze and evaluate the validity and relevance of the evidence obtained.
4. Apply the results of the evidence in the decision making process. In our case, the training proposal for the acquisition of informational and digital skills by inmates in Penitentiary Centers of the Community of Madrid, based on our case study in the "Jaime Garralda" Mothers Unit in Madrid.
5. Evaluate the effectiveness of the results obtained from the implementation of the training proposal based on the evidence found.

Our research study has ethical implications that are evident, while working with women in difficult situations deprived of freedom, which requires a great sensitivity to understand them and the ability to exercise a respectful and kind treatment. We follow the legislation that regulates ethical conduct in research, reflected in the Code of Good Scientific Practices of the Spanish National Research Council (CSIC 2010).

The permission for the publication of this research was obtained two years after its completion, 2013-2014.

Formative Proposal: Results and Evaluation

From the analysis of the user study carried out to the inmates before starting the training, it shows that they have a very low level, both in computer knowledge and in documentary knowledge. In relation to the latter, neither they recognize the information needs nor knew how to differentiate between the relevant and irrelevant information, they demonstrated that they did not know how to search, analyze or evaluate the information, with 50% of the inmates having many problems when recognizing a website, to use dictionaries or digital encyclopedias or catalogs. A lack of reading-writing habits was also detected, with a very low level of reading comprehension. In terms of computer skills we realized that the level was very low. The few knowledge they showed had been acquired by themselves and limited to the use of email and chat. Some of the inmates had some knowledge of Word acquired in some of the courses taught by ONG's in prison. As a result of these detected deficiencies, it was decided that our formative proposal should also include both digital competences and informational competences. Once the formative and informative needs of the participating inmates were detected, the next step was the formulation of the training program, the execution of the training and the evaluation of the project. With this training program what is intended, based on the two main concepts of the Information Society - ICT and information literacy - is to train the group of women prisoners to acquire the necessary information and digital skills to contribute to their social inclusion and labour specifically we pursue with this proposal:

- To provide the inmates with a formative program in informational competences in order to have an impact on their social and labor inclusion and increase their possibilities of development as people.
- Reduce the economic-social-labor differences of this group.
- Develop the autonomy and personal initiative of the inmates.
- Produce a growth in the living standards of the inmates improving their cultural life.
- Develop critical thinking and social responsibility of these women.

Our training project is called CIDIS (Informational and digital competences for social inclusion) and has been designed taking into account the characteristics of the participating inmates. The distribution of hours for the implementation of the CIDIS training program was as follows:

- **Total Duration of the Course (in Weeks):** 29 weeks
- **Hours per Week:** 2 hours (including theoretical and practical hours)
- **Total Counting of Tutorials:** 16 hours
- **Course Total (in Hours):** 74 hours

The entire training program is accompanied by a tutorial made through a PowerPoint and a printed guide book for an optimal follow-up of the course. The book-guide that was provided to the inmates was carried out with a simple and easy-to-read vocabulary so that they could understand all the concepts that were being explained, in order to capture the attention of the inmates. The slides to support the theory were made in a way that was entertaining and easy to understand. The same procedure was followed when preparing the activities. In this case study we find inmates of different nationalities and languages as well as different levels of studies. Another aspect to take into account was the difficulty of many of the inmates with reading and writing so activities were carried out aimed at solving these deficiencies. The lack of Internet connection in the computers was one of the most important problems we had. We solve it through the tutorial with captures of each one of the screens of each one of the subjects and with connection to Internet through the mobile of the professor in one of the computers.

To guide this research, we have used informational and digital inclusion indicators extracted from the IDEIAS model (Digital inclusion and informational education for health) (Cuevas-Cerveró & García-Moreno, 2010; Cuevas-Cerveró, 2009).

To carry out the CIDIS training proposal, various topics and didactic activities have been developed grouped into three blocks. At the end of each topic, a practical activity is proposed to reinforce the theory learned. These activities are grouped in block three.

1. **Block I:** Digital Competence
2. **Block II:** Information Competence
3. **Block III:** Digital Competency Activities and Information Competence

Block I: Digital Competence

This block focuses on the digital competences derived from ICT literacy. The objectives are:

- Develop skills to work with a computer.
- Use the Windows operating system, word processor and spreadsheet.
- Prepare presentations.
- Acquire skills to use a browser.

- Use email, social networks.
- Create a blog.
- Use electronic services.
- Use an image editor.

Block II: Information Competence

This second block focuses on informational competences derived from information literacy. The main objectives are:

- Develop skills related to access, use, evaluation and presentation of information.
- Recognize the need for information.
- Develop search strategies.
- Acquire skills to select and evaluate information.
- Analyze and synthesize contents.
- Organize the information.
- Communicate the information.
- Quote and reference.
- Use information in an ethical and responsible manner.
- Train inmates to use dictionaries, encyclopedias and digital catalogs.

Block III: Digital Competency Activities and Information Competence

This last block focuses on the practical part of the CIDIS training proposal. The objective is that through the completion of activities included at the end of each topic, inmates can consolidate the theory learned in blocks I and II and thus acquire informational and digital skills.

The development of the different sections will consist of:

- Explaining to the inmates each one of the sections of each topic, so that once the theoretical part is finished they can, on their own, complete and answer the questions of the practical part of this topic.
- Throughout the explanation they will be asked questions to check that they are following the agenda well.
- After the practice, it will be corrected in class and the different answers given by the participants will be discussed.
- If necessary, the contents will be reviewed, with new explanations, clarifications and examples.

Block I was performed in 41 hours (including block III activities), block II was performed in 33 hours (including block III activities). In total there were 74 hours, including 16 hours of tutoring.

For the evaluation of the training program, once the training was completed, a final questionnaire was passed to the participating inmates, which allowed us, after analyzing the results obtained, to make a comparison between the knowledge of the inmates before and after carrying out the training. The inmates had to rate from 1 to 5 the computer and documentary knowledge acquired, as well as the evaluation of the received training proposal, where 1 has a value of nothing and 5 of a lot. In the analysis of the data we see that the scores are, in general, of 4 and 5. When considering these two scores jointly, 100% of the answers in several items are reached. Specifically, it should be noted that this is the case for the two items directly related to the job search (the preparation of a curriculum vitae and the search for online employment). This data shows that the learning carried out by the inmates in these two aspects is highly significant for them, which is fundamental when evaluating the training received by the inmates, focused on the reintegration of this group of women at risk of work exclusion.

Regarding the documentary knowledge acquired, it should be noted that most of the items in this part of the questionnaire refer to activities where not only technological knowledge of a procedural nature (for example, the search for information using search engines available on the Internet) come into play.), but also skills linked to the treatment and use of information (for example, organizing, analyzing, selecting and summarizing the information found). This shows the extent of the training course given to inmates, which invokes different types of knowledge that facilitate the inclusion of inmates in a complex work world that demands this variety of learning. It is important to note from the questionnaire that inmates value this diversity of contents and competences demanded in the training program received positively.

Eventually, in terms of the assessment made by the inmates of the course, 80% assess it with the highest score of 5, being the same valued with a 4 for the remaining 20%. The great acceptance of the course on the part of the inmates refers both to the activities carried out and to the method followed to impart it. It is interesting to note the highly positive assessment that the inmates make of both the knowledge acquired and its practical application in the future. We consider this data as highly important, since the practical application of the knowledge acquired is a key factor in the interest and motivation to participate in this type of training aimed at incorporating into the labour market people excluded or at risk of exclusion.

In view of the data reflected in the final questionnaire and those obtained thanks to the observation technique, we can draw three general conclusions. Firstly, the inmates value the program very positively, both in its theoretical aspect and in its practical application, and consider it important that, in the future, other inmates may benefit from similar training that will help them integrate into the world of work. and social at the end of his sentence. Secondly, the inmates are motivated to participate in this type of training courses even if this motivation is lower at the moment of starting the program. Thirdly, the inmates consider that both the methodology and the contents and activities proposed during the training are very appropriate for them, which translates into an active participation of the inmates in the proposed activities, manifested in aspects such as assistance to class, attention and positive attitude. Therefore, in the analysis of the data obtained, we observed how the gaps and informational needs that they presented initially had been significantly reduced. As a result of the results of this research, we support the need to implement the training program in female penitentiary centers of the Community of Madrid.

FINAL THOUGHTS

After presenting the CIDIS training proposal and its evaluation, we propose some reflections as a conclusion based on the initial objectives set out in this research.

1. An important limitation that we have found in approaching this study has been the lack of previous research to support our work. We have to say that there are very few investigations related to prisons and particularly those related to the training in informational competences carried out in the specific context of our research, the female penitentiary centers of the Community of Madrid.
2. After an intensive search to determine the training in information literacy that prisoners receive focused on the knowledge of experiences or evidence related to our object of study, we observed that, in Spanish prisons, there are no experiences that address the acquisition of competences. Informational Hence the need to implement training programs to train inmates to acquire the necessary information skills to access an increasingly digital society.
3. Considering that the educative level that prisoners have is low, the access to work is limited, so the formative programs of information literacy will serve them to be able to adapt to the current demands of society.
4. To ensure the effectiveness of these training programs for female inmates, free access to the Internet in the computer room of currently prohibited penitentiary centers should be ensured, taking the necessary security and surveillance measures.
5. Training in prisons should be the same for men and women, all of whom can access it on an equal footing, since the training of female inmates is a key element so that they can overcome the social exclusion in which they are immersed even before his entry into prison. In this way, it would help to eliminate the

inequality that exists between inmates and inmates in the educational and labour fields, as indicated in article three of the General Penitentiary Organic Law. Most of the training programs taught in women's prisons reinforce the traditional role of women in society. They are usually training programs for cooking, hairdressing, auxiliary geriatrics, aesthetics, sewing and crafts. In this sense, it is contradictory that training programs be offered in prisons as a means to reintegrate inmates and that training in information skills, essential to integrate them into society today, is not taken into account.

6. If the main objective for the reinsertion of female inmates is to train them for this purpose, the best tool is training and, more specifically, training in information skills. That is why our research is aimed at promoting information literacy for women prisoners and their promotion in Spanish prisons. In this way, we will also be avoiding that your stay there is not a waste of time. This training would serve to increase the knowledge of inmates and to prepare their entry into the labour market once their freedom has been obtained.
7. An important prerequisite to determine the specific training objectives of the group and the fulfillment of these, is to detect the level of prior knowledge and training needs of each group to which our training proposal can be addressed. In this way, the initial diagnosis presented in this thesis can allow the adjustment of the training proposal to the specific needs of other groups. As a result of the deficiencies detected after the analysis of the data obtained in the initial questionnaire, it is recommended that the training proposal should include informational and digital competencies.
8. The initial diagnosis helped us to find out that the inmates had a very low level of computer and documentary knowledge. In relation to the latter, they did not recognize the information needs or knew how to differentiate between relevant and irrelevant information. In addition, through the questionnaire it was demonstrated that they did not know how to search, analyze or evaluate information and that they presented many problems when recognizing a web page, as well as using dictionaries or digital encyclopedias or catalogs. All this allowed us to focus our training proposal to achieve these objectives.
9. Likewise, a lack of reading habits was detected in the inmates, with a very low level of reading comprehension, which led us to include activities aimed at improving this aspect. In terms of computer skills, we realized that the few knowledge they showed, had been acquired by themselves and were limited to the use of email and chat. A proposal of structured training and guided by a specialist, as in the case of this research, allows us to correct errors in which people who learn by themselves frequently fall, as well as to make contact with knowledge that, in another way, results in very difficult or impossible to access. In addition, group learning facilitates learning, as we have seen.

10. At the same time that we gave the CIDIS training proposal, changes were made based on the difficulties expressed by the inmates to follow certain topics, such as the topic dedicated to electronic services, Excel, and search and use of information. When checking the greater motivation shown by the inmates when dealing with subjects with less theoretical load and more practical content we decided to adjust these three subjects reducing the theory and expanding the practical part.
11. When detecting the difficulties of the inmates with reading and writing, we decided to incorporate spelling and reading exercises as part of the program. Another change that was introduced, also motivated by deficiencies detected in the training process, was to add group activities to improve the level of communication between them and encourage teamwork.
12. The final work of the course has allowed the inmates participating in the case study to put into practice the skills, abilities and knowledge acquired during the execution of the training proposal. They have learned to work collaboratively, establishing more respectful relationships among the members of the groups. They have organized the work correctly by planning tasks and have managed to convey in a clear manner the knowledge learned.
13. The implementation of the training proposal has shown us the importance of adjusting to the reality and the needs of the population to which it is addressed. However, in line with this implementation, we have also verified that it is crucial to include challenges and challenges in the proposal. Addressing and overcoming them contributes effectively to the increase in female prisoners' self-esteem, which significantly improves their learning and contributes to the improvement of their literacy levels. As a result, it contributes to overcoming the informational and gender gap currently experienced by women prisoners and other socially marginalized groups.
14. In the final questionnaire, it was possible to detect that the new knowledge acquired after the implementation of the CIDIS training proposal had been highly valued by the participating inmates.
15. After the execution of the CIDIS training program and due to the deficiencies already detected in both reading and writing, we think that, in the future, it will be important to add a new topic dedicated to the promotion of reading and reading comprehension. The purpose of this new content is that the inmates acquire fluency in reading promoting the reading habit and developing reading comprehension. They must also learn to express themselves properly in writing and without spelling errors. We understand that both reading and writing is a necessary prerequisite to enter the different stages of information literacy. This new topic may be adapted according to the context of each group.

16. Once the execution of the training program was finished, we wanted to monitor the inmates who participated in the study to know the impact of the program once the freedom was obtained. However, we find ourselves with a reality that we had not foreseen in the beginning: once the inmates obtain their freedom, their social or labour reintegration is not followed up by the penitentiary institutions.
17. The fact that it has not been possible to monitor the inmates participating in this investigation after their release from prison has made it impossible to verify the relationship between the training received and their integration into the workplace and society once in freedom. It would be interesting to be able to carry out research in this direction in the future.
18. Information professionals can provide knowledge and experience in terms of information and digital skills. From our practical experience in the framework of this research, we can also point out the following personal competences as necessary: communicative capacity, listening capacity, ability to organize teamwork, capacity to create an environment of mutual respect and trust, ability to plan, capacity to favor permanent adult education, ability to recognize the value of working with people at risk of exclusion. The competences indicated in the previous point should be included in the training plans of the trainers who will teach the information literacy courses, which is an important prerequisite for the good achievement of the objectives pursued in the training of female inmates. Or other groups at risk of exclusion.

REFERENCES

Agúndez-Soriano, M. A. (2015). *Alfabetización informacional para la inclusión social de las mujeres reclusas de la Comunidad de Madrid: un estudio de caso* (Unpublished doctoral dissertation). Universidad Complutense.

Añaños, F. (2013). Formación educativa previa ante las discriminaciones: Las mujeres reclusas en España. *Review of Education*, (360), 91–118. Retrieved from http://www.mecd.gob.es/dctm/revista-deeducacion/articulosre360/re36006.pdf?documentId=0901e72b814a77e6

Añaños, F., Fernández, M. P. & Llopis, J. J. (2013). Aproximación a los contextos en prisión. Una perspectiva socioeducativa. *Pedagogía social. Revista interuniversitaria*, (22), 13-28.

Aranda, M. J. (2005). *Reeducación y reinserción social: Tratamiento penitenciario: análisis teórico y aproximación práctica* (Unpublished doctoral dissertation). Universidad Nacional de Educación a Distancia.

Bernsmann, S., & Croll, J. (2013). Lowering the threshold to libraries with social media: The approach of Digital Literacy 2.0, a project funded in the EU Lifelong Learning Programme. *Library Review*, *62*(1-2), 53–58. doi:10.1108/00242531311328168

Berrio, C. (2012). Entre la alfabetización informacional y la brecha digital: Reflexiones para una reconceptualización de los fenómenos de exclusión digital. *Revista Interam. Bibliot.*, *35*(1), 39–53.

Booth, A. (2002). Evidence-based librarianship: One small step. *Health Information and Libraries Journal*, *19*(2), 116–119. doi:10.1046/j.1471-1842.2002.00373.x PMID:12389610

Burgdorf, A. M. (2012). *Women in Prison: Planning the Getaway Vocational Education in a Southern Women's Correctional Institution* (Unpublished doctoral dissertation). The University of Memphis.

Castillo-Algarra, J., & Ruiz-García, M. (2007). Un reto educativo en el siglo XXI: La educación de los delincuentes en el sistema penitenciario. Una perspectiva de género. *Review of Education*, *9*, 301–315.

Civallero, E. (2007). Aplicación de la metodología de investigación-acción en prácticas bibliotecológicas basadas en la evidencia. *73rd IFLA General Conference and Council. World Library an Information Congress.*

Comité de Ética, C. S. I. C. (2011). *Código de Buenas Prácticas Científicas del CSIC/Code of Good Scientific Practices of CSIC.* Madrid: Consejo Superior de Investigaciones Científicas (CSIC). Retrieved January 7, 2018, from https://www.cnb.csic.es/documents/CBP_CSIC.pdf

Connor, E. (Ed.). (2007). *Evidence-based librarianship: case studies and active learning exercises*. Oxford, UK: Chandos Publishing. doi:10.1533/9781780631080

Contreras Pulido, P., Martín-Pena, D., & Aguaded, I. (2015). Derribando el autoestigma: Medios de Comunicación en Prisiones Como aliados de la Inclusión Social. *Cuadernos.Info*, *36*, 15–26. doi:10.7764/cdi.36.708

Cuevas-Cerveró, A. (2007). *La promoción de la lectura como modelo de alfabetización en información en bibliotecas escolares* (Unpublished doctoral dissertation). Universidad Carlos III.

Cuevas-Cerveró, A. (coord.). (2009). IDEIAS, Inclusión digital y educación informacional para salud. Madrid: Universidad Complutense.

Cuevas-Cerveró, A., & García, M. A. (2010). IDEIAS. Un modelo de evaluación para inclusión digital y alfabetización informacional orientado a salud. *El Profesional de la Información*, *19*(3), 240–245. doi:10.3145/epi.2010.may.03

Cushman, M., & Mclean, R. (2008). Exclusion, Inclusion and Changing the Face of Information Systems Research. *Information Technology & People*, *21*(3), 213–221. doi:10.1108/09593840810895993

Del Pozo, F. J., Jiménez, F., & Turbi, A. (2013). El tratamiento con mujeres: Actuación socioeducativa y sociolaboral en prisiones. *Pedagogía Social. Revista Interuniversitaria*, (22), 57-72. Retrieved January 12, 2018, from http://www.redalyc.org/html/1350/135031394005/

Elvira-Valdés, M. A., & Durán-Aponte, E. (2014). Estudiar en mayúsculas: La educación formal en instituciones penitenciarias venezolanas. *Sophia*, *10*(1), 64–73. Retrieved from http://www.scielo.org.co/pdf/sph/v10n1/v10n1a06.pdf

Ely, J. W. (2012). *Effects of Occupational Education Programs Offered by the Oklahoma Department of Career and Technology Education, Skills Centers Division, on the Recidivism Rate of Selected Groups of Released Offenders in Oklahoma* (Unpublished doctoral dissertation). Oklahoma State University.

Fernández, R. (2011). *Exclusión social de mujeres presas: Análisis de necesidades y su percepcion del proceso de rehabilitacion en el centro penitenciario de Villabona* (Unpublished doctoral dissertation). Universidad de Oviedo, Departamento de Psicología.

Fine, M. (2001). *Changing Minds: The Impact of College in a Maximum-Security Prison. Effects on Women in Prison, the Prison Environment, Reincarceration Rates and Post-Release Outcomes*. Academic Press.

Flamer, E. (2012). *Recidivism, Disciplinary History, and Institutional Adjustment: A Quantitative Study Examining Correctional Education Programs* (Unpublished doctoral dissertation). University of Phoenix.

Hendry, J. D. (2000). Social inclusion and the information. *Library Review*, *49*(7), 331–336. doi:10.1108/00242530010344192

Imel, S. (1990). *Vocational Education in Corrections. Trends and Issues Alerts*. Columbus: ERIC.

Jensen, G.F., & Jones, D. (1976). Perspectives on Inmate Culture: A Study of Women in Prison. *Social Problems*, *54*(3), 590–603.

Lombarte, S., & García, I. (2005). Estudio de un caso sobre el uso de las tecnologías de la información y la comunicación para la inclusión social. *Teoría de la educación: Educación y cultura en la Sociedad de la Información, 6*(1). Retrieved January 12, 2018, from http://www.redalyc.org/articulo.oa?id=201021059007

Oguz, E.S. & Kurbanoglu, S. (2013). Strengthening Social Inclusion in Multicultural Societies Through Information Literacy. *Bilgi Dunyasi = Information World, 14*(2), 270- 290.

Sackett, D. L. (2004). *Evidence Based medicine: How to practice and teach EBM.* London: Churchill Livingstone.

Sobel, S. B. (1982). Difficulties Experienced by Women in Prison. *Psychology of Women Quarterly*, *7*(2), 107–118. doi:10.1111/j.1471-6402.1983.tb00823.x

Walker, R. (1983). La realización de estudios de casos en Educación. Ética, teoría y procedimientos. In W. Dockrell & D. Hamilton (Eds.), *Nuevas reflexiones sobre la investigación educativa* (pp. 48–82). Madrid: Narcea.

KEY TERMS AND DEFINITIONS

Action Research: Is a disciplined process of inquiry conducted by and for those taking the action. The primary reason for engaging in action research is to assist the "actor" in improving and/or refining his or her actions. It is an empowering experience. Action research has this positive effect for many reasons. The most important is that action research is always relevant to the participants. Relevance is guaranteed because the focus of each research project is determined by the researchers, who are also the primary consumers of the findings.

Female Inmates: They are women deprived of freedom, generally in prisons, for having committed some type of crime.

Information Literacy: Crucial skill in the pursuit of knowledge. It involves recognizing when information is needed and being able to efficiently locate, accurately evaluate, effectively use, and clearly communicate information in various formats. Increasingly, information is available in unfiltered formats, raising questions about its authenticity, validity, and reliability. This abundance of information is of little help to those who have not learned how to use it effectively.

Prisons: A prison, also known as a correctional facility, jail, gaol, penitentiary detention center or remand center is a facility in which inmates are forcibly confined and denied a variety of freedoms under the authority of the State.

Social Inclusion: Is the act of making all groups of people within a society feel valued and important. The provision of certain rights to all individuals and groups in society, such as employment, adequate housing, healthcare, education and training, etc.

Chapter 5
Communication Media and Digital Literacy as Intervention Tools in Prisons:
The Case in Spain

Paloma Contreras-Pulido
University of Huelva, Spain

Ignacio Aguaded
University of Huelva, Spain

ABSTRACT

In Spain, there are a few projects that link communication with social intervention in prisons. These projects have remained invisible to society, and similar initiatives taking place in other prisons were even unknown amongst themselves. It is not common to find radio, programs of digital literacy, magazines, or even television and cinema in prisons. These are activities that remain within the walls and come about from the restlessness of the educators who voluntarily produce them. The work presented comes about the doctoral research work that for 4 years explored these initiatives. Through qualitative methodology, based on the use of in-depth interviews, the authors give voice to 20 prisoners and educators that participate in these projects in Spanish jails. Without claiming to be representative, the results show that these activities can become a powerful tool for social-educative integration and personal transformation.

DOI: 10.4018/978-1-5225-5975-7.ch005

INTRODUCTION

After the adoption of the Spanish Constitution in 1978, society in the country took a bold step towards its evolution, with an important change also produced in the legal framework and the penitentiary system. Since then, the physiognomy, the prisoner's routine, and the way of life of the incarcerated has substantially changed. With a philosophy what that is based on re-socialization and re-education took its first steps what is now the Spanish penitentiary system.

The fundamental law that governs the prisoner's way of life in Spain is the Organic Law 1/1979, from September 26th. The first article of the preamble of the General Penitentiary Law (LOGP) states that:

Penal institutions covered by this Act have as their main goal the re-education and social reintegration of those sentenced to custodial sentences and measures, and the retention and custody of detainees, prisoners and convicts. They are also responsible for the welfare of those released. (LOGP, 1/1979)

Also, the LOGP (1/1979) has in its preamble, a primordial aspect that gives foundation to this research work:

When upholding the re-socialization purpose of the punishment, the Law seeks to denote that the punished is not a being that is eliminated from society, but a person that continues to be part of it, and although subject to a particular regiment, is an active member, motivated by his previous antisocial behavior and aiming to prepare his return to freedom in the best conditions to socially exercise his freedom. (LOGP, 1/1979, Preamble)

In the legal context that the Spanish prisons find themselves immersed in, we see the emergence of communication experiments that are based on the production of content in different formats (radio, journals, blogs, etc.). These are created by people that are deprived of liberty, but accompanied by one or various educators, give voice to the day to day events in the prisons. These productions in many cases "escape" the confines of the walls to reach the general population, but with little or no visibility.

On the other hand, once the Spanish legal context has been explained, in the following chapter we will try to make progress on whether the use of the media in prisons, rather than considering themselves from a professional media production point of view, is in some way a therapeutic tool that helps these people to improve their way of seeing and seeing themselves in the world. In short, to elucidate whether this activity can break the self-stigma of the person in the face of society (Goffman, 1989; Contreras-Pulido et. al, 2015).

This has a lot to do with the educational function that the media can also have, that is to say, with the so-called "educommunication" and media literacy, something to which any person would be entitled, prey or not, as Gil-Cantero (2013) states: "The right to education and teaching is automatically identified with a right of access to the cultural assets of society, to literacy, to virtual literacy, to formal levels of education, to professional studies, etc." (p. 54). But in this specific case we will focus on the so-called "educommunication for social change" (Barranquero, 2007), which is closely linked to projects that seek collective transformation in a context of development or exclusion.

With all of the above, in this chapter we intend to learn, through the research carried out, what it means for prisoners and educators who carry out some type of activity related to communication in five Spanish prisons. In addition, for the first time a census of the media that exist in this context in Spain is provided.

BACKGROUND

This research is mainly based on the analysis of a series of activities linked to the media and media literacy that come from the Title V of the Penitentiary Treatment of the Roya Decree 190/1996 from February 9th, thanks to which, the Penitentiary Regulation was approved. In this section, it states:

The contact of the intern with the outside will be fostered and facilitated, counting with, whenever possible, the community resources as fundamental instruments in the re-insertion work (…). The collaboration and participation of the citizens and public and private institutions or associations will be facilitated (Title V of the Penitentiary Regulation 1890/1996).

On the other hand, and related to this aspect, a preliminary study was performed in the year 2010: "Social perception through the locked gaze: the discourse of Huelva prisoners through UniRadio", whose results were published in various scientific journals. This type of activities is relevant to imprisoned individuals, and modifies their perception as people who are lacking freedom.

Thanks to this previous qualitative research, performed on a group of prisoners from a Huelva prison (Spain), who created a weekly radio program, we could confirm that the studied population who "were exposed as prisoners to the society at large, at least in a radio program manner, changed their own perception as such. Contrary to what it seemed, our broadcasters do not flee from this condition, do not hide, but instead demand to be taken into account by those 'outside'" (Contreras-Pulido & Aguaded, 2013).

Being a prisoner is a powerful social label and, therefore, a stigma that will pursue the person even if he complies with his sentence and with the society. Howard Becker (1963) held in his work that "the deviant is one to whom that label has successfully been applied" (p. 35), which will undoubtedly have repercussions in its family life, its affective life, its labor and social integration. But it will also be the same person who internalizes the stigma, in a process that will take her to believe that her identity is as "the others" see it.

Goffman (1989) adds this persons also have the need to definitively refuse to see themselves as excluded without turning back: "His deepest feelings about what he is may be his sense of being a 'normal person' a human being like anyone else, a person, therefore, who deserves a fair chance and a fair break" (p. 24).

Specifically, the production of media that have eco outside the prison and, thus, the development of a media literacy (including the digital) inside their walls could be of great help against stigma and self-stigmas. This is how Cabrera (2005) indicates that "to develop projects for the social inclusion of excluded groups will mean to help them familiarize with the tools, processes and environments that accompany the unstoppable expansion of information and communication technologies" (p. 17)

On the other hand, for the socio-educational work with prisoners it is necessary to "convert the inmates in active, participatory citizens committed to initiatives that facilitate their re-education and social reintegration" (Caride & Gradaílle, 2013, p. 41).

We could add here that without a doubt, today, where more than ever we are media citizens (Gozálvez-Perez, 2014; Pérez-Tornero and Varis, 2010) and therefore citizenship must be empowered through education and media literacy (Gozálvez-Perez and Contreras-Pulido, 2014). Nowadays, the need of media-literate citizens (which includes both traditional media and information and communication technologies) is pressing. Organizations such as UNESCO, the European Commission and the UN have promoted various statements and documents to defend such literacy and alert States to carry out media literacy programs both in formal environments (schools) such as non-formal (family, civic centers, etc).

However, taking into account the context in which we are focusing, we can attend to a concrete perspective of education and communication from the point of view of the so-called social change. In these matters, Barranquero (2007, p. 17) provides a number of premises related to educommunication for social change, which should also mark the intentionality of projects such as the creation of media in prisons. Among them, he highlights that the important part of the experience is not the final product, but the path undertaken to achieve it, where huge potential for development of skills and abilities, construction and improvement converge, which can be planned transversely along the process. This is important, but also important is the fact that it is the community that needs those changes that is making such activity. Thus, it favors their true empowerment through participation.

This would therefore be our theoretical framework within which the research presented below would be framed and which emerges from the interest in deepening the understanding of how education and communication, focused on social change, can be a powerful tool in the field of prisons.

MAIN FOCUS OF THE CHAPTER

Issues, Controversies, Problems

Step 1: In the present work, our objectives are, on the one hand, to outline the media experiments that are currently present in Spanish penitentiary centers, as well as to discover if the communication media workshops in prisons are relevant and useful for the prisoners and educators. Lastly, we will try to see verify if the participation in communication media that are developed in the context of the prison, gives prisoners positive expectations about their future.

Step 2: The nature of this study is completely conditioned by its research context. Prisons are not precisely the most welcoming place for engaging in this type of work. But, taking into account that what is being done in this research work is to arrive at conclusions through the voices of those imprisoned and their educators as sample objects, we opted for the use of qualitative methodology.

We believe that this type of methodology, in this context, favors not only the gathering of data, but of becoming close, in first-person basis, to a reality that would be difficult to tell about in any other way, and therefore, it would also be more complicated to fulfill the specific objectives of this investigation, which, as previously mentioned, do not try to gather quantitative data. This will allow us to count on observations and results that were not originally expected. As Strauss and Corbin (2002) assert, the motive for choosing qualitative methods should be:

The nature of the problem that is investigated. For example, research that tries to understand the meaning or nature of the experience of people that have problems such as chronic illness, addiction and divorce, and the act of 'uncovering' lends itself to field work to find out what people do and think (Strauss & Corbin, 2002: 20)

We based our research work on different methods of qualitative research, also taking into account that these start with participative action that we have turned into research. For seven years, an intervention was done in the Penitentiary Center of Huelva, where radio shows were created with interns from this prison. Therefore, our methodology starts, in first place, through participatory-action research (PAR).

For Flores and others (1999), what is interesting in this type of design is to understand the study problems from the perspective of the minorities, favoring plurality, the equal distribution of knowledge, and as a consequence, the empowerment of said social groups and communities. The instruments of production of data that are counted on are participatory observation, the field diary/notes, the interviews, the discussion groups, the strategic planning, the logical framework and the Strengths, Weaknesses, Opportunities and Threats (SWOT) analysis.

Lastly, and once the general research framework has been set, we will make use of the semi-structured interview for performing the investigation.

Interview Process

After soliciting the necessary permits for performing the interviews, they were recorded in audio format, which were then transcribed. The transcription process was lengthy, taking into account the difficulties that were experienced in the recording of a few of the cases, especially due to the space that was used for the interviews of the interns and educators. In some of the instances, the interviews were inaudible due to the structure of the room itself, having metallic doors or fences, where large amounts of noise were heard from the hallway racket in the buildings. Due to this, a noise reduction process and improvement of the audio file was performed, for the faithful transcribing of the conversation.

Afterwards, the transcriptions were organized in a Word file, transferred to the qualitative analysis program Nvivo v.10 for the posterior categorization and codification process.

Next, we show the characteristics of the semi-structured interviews that were performed on the prisoners as well as the educators. With this interview we tried to give answers to the objectives that were set out in our investigation. For example, to verify if this type of activity was relevant and useful for the prisoners and educators and if these projects gave the prisoners positive expectations about their future.

This interview was designed to ask a number of identical questions to the prisoners as well as the educators, and on the other hand, various specific questions to each collective. We show the differences in the table 1.

Table 1. Interview to the prisoners

1. What kind of medium (communication analog or digital), radio, TV, blog, etc., do you think is more efficient for its producing in prisons?
2. Why do you think it's important for this type of project to be found in prisons?
3. What does taking part in this type of project give you? What changes have been produced since you started?
4. What do you think it can provide you with for your life outside of jail?
5. Do you think the people in charge of directing them (educators, in this case) are sufficiently prepared/ trained?
6. What would you improve?
Interview to the educators
1. What kind of medium (communication analog or digital), radio, TV, blog, etc., do you think is more efficient for its producing in prisons?
2. Why do you think it's important for this type of project to be found in prisons?
3. What changes do you observe in the prisoners once the they participate in the Project?
4. What do you think it will provide them with for their life outside of jail?
5. Do you think you have the necessary preparation/training?
6. What would you improve?

Sample:

In this research work, we have opted for selecting a sample that is not probabilistic. Meaning, we used a directed and intentionally chosen sample, due to the characteristics of the studied population, and the context where they were found. Non-probabilistic samples, although considered non-rigorous and lacking a theoretical base, are frequently used. There are even a few cases where their use is more convenient, for example, when a case study is to be done, when using heterogeneous populations, or in studies that are directed toward specific populations and groups where a careful and controlled selection of subjects having determined characteristics is important (Scharager & Armijo, 2011).

Therefore, we are not looking a for representative sample, due to, as previously mentioned, the people that are currently involved in some activity that is linked to the production of some type of communication media in Spanish jails is almost impossible to quantify due to many factors:

1. There is no official registration of this type of activities that are currently done in Spanish prisons. In fact, as previously mentioned in the reasoning for this research study, this has led to mayor research difficulties.

2. The number of participants in any of the voluntary workshops in the prisons varies by day, week, or month, due to the penitentiary population's own mobility, and to their specific restrictions on participation used as a punishment, etc.
3. In the case of the educators, we will observe that the number of interviewees was smaller, due to the fact that these activities are done by at most by two people, who, in some cases, do it voluntarily, which is an extra effort in their daily life. This is why they were added to the study, even though they comprised a small and non-representative group.

To present the specific sample in our study, we will begin by describing the context in which the people interviewed interact and participate. We chose five penitentiary centers because they stand out in the type of activities the interns took part of with communication media. The description of each of them has been given by the educators that were part of the study themselves.

Radio Encadenados (Chained Radio): 25 years of radio in the Penitentiary Center (P.C.) (Santoña-Cantabria)

This radio station was born in 1988, and currently counts with two programs that are broadcasted in two stations in the area. The dynamics consists of the recording of the programs in the humble studies of the prison, with the educator being the one responsible for sending the audio file to the radio stations. At the same time, they are shared in a blog that the educator has for the diffusion of the program, which has the same name as the Penitentiary Center (http://eldueso.blogspot.pt/). This penitentiary center was selected as a sample for this research work for being one of the ones with the greatest experience in the domain of the utilization of communication as an intervention tool in prisons. This was besides its fortitude for being one of the pioneering center of other, similar activities that bring the interns closer to the street, such as the of Social Commitment Program.

La Voz del Mako (Mako's Voice): Magazine and blog from the P.C. of Albolote (Granada)

The Mako's Voice Magazine, as defined by its own interns, is "a magazine created by interns for interns". This publication emerges from the educator's own initiative first, and then from the interns, who, sometimes with enormous difficulties, from material resources, such as the impossibility of printing the magazine due to the lack of a printer or paper, do everything possible to keep the activity in progress.

It is comprised of about eight interns (the number varies as a function of their availability, and the present resources the program counts on at the moment), and is mainly supervised by an educator.

This magazine has gone through diverse phases. Its format is on paper, and is distributed in the Penitentiary Center of Albolote (Granada, Spain), but thanks to the collaboration of external collectives, they have also had the chance to present it and bring it to light outside the prison walls. Through the blog http://lavozdelmako.wordpress.com/, their articles receive opinions from readers in the outside.

For its diffusion through the blog and for its creation as a professionally formatted magazine, they have counted with the collaboration of media experts who have taught various courses in journalism to the interns.

D' Magazine Universo Cultural from P.C. Quatre Camins (Barcelona): This project was born in 2002 under the umbrella of the Directorate General of Justice, which created a program named "Internet, program of coexistence". At the start, it was a paper-format magazine, which had its biggest momentum with the creation of the denominated Community of social educators of Cataluña in 2007.

The podcasts are usually stored in a blog (https://espaitic.wordpress.com/dmagazines/). One of the important landmarks for the team of people that participated in the workshop was the possibility of accessing the Internet, thanks to the location of a Punto Òmnia (a project that was pushed forward by the Generalitat de Cataluña, with the objective of training and teaching to avoid the social exclusion in the scope of the new technologies, managed with the collaboration of NGOs and other associations) in prison.

El Zapato Roto (The Broken Shoe): From the year 2007, the University of Huelva's radio, UniRadio, and the Penitentiary Center of Huelva have maintained a close relationship in creating activities with the interns from the Socio-cultural Centers in the prison. More specifically, the participation of prisoners and educators in the broadcaster's morning magazine program where they participated in a half-hour space every week was put into place. But this radio experimenting the prison has been developing in a progressive manner until reaching a level of self-sufficiency. At the start of the 2011/2012 season of the station, a proposal was put forward to the Center's management, the interns and the educators, so that they should have their own space, taking over an entire hour each week.

The current team of the "El Zapato Roto" is composed of a total of eight interns that count with the support of an educator. Of the eight interns, seven are dedicated to the work of presenters, and one of them to the technical control. The program is edited and post-produced by the own interns, and is posteriorly sent to the broadcaster. "El Zapato Roto" is broadcasted every Thursday via FM radio in Huelva (103.6 FM) and through the Internet for the rest of the world (http://goo.gl6UFX8B).

Onda Cerebral (Brain Wave). Seville P.C. Psychiatric Hospital: In Spain, there are only two Psychiatric Penitentiary Hospitals: Seville and Alicante. In Seville, there are 185 interns with severe mental disorders or other psychological alterations, who have committed a crime that is found in the Penal Code. They are considered to be immune to prosecution, meaning that they are not subject to criminal liability. More specifically, the object of our study is Onda Cerebral. This broadcasting station is run entirely by the center's interns, under the coordination of its educator. It broadcasts on 107.8 FM in Seville, with a reach of only three kilometers. In total, there are six hours per week of programming, which include interviews, sports, humor and music. The radio broadcasts from a small studio that is set up in a room located in one of the psychiatric penitentiary's yards.

For the sample, a total of 29 interviews were performed: 23 to prisoners and 6 to educators. The quantity varies as the number of educators per workshop tends to be between one and two. This was not an impediment for the investigation, as the study was not done to compare both collectives, only to present their visions.

Step 3:
Result One: To draw up a map showing the existing experiences in Spain of media and ICT in prisons.

We present, in first place, the results found after the search of experiments with communication media in Spanish jails. Let's not forget that this search was performed without the help of the Institution that supervises this type of activities, as a specific census on them was not available. A total of 39 experiments in Spain were found, distributed in the following manner: 14 magazines/journals; 3 television stations or experiments with cinema; 1 of photography; 6 experiments with ICT (Information and Communications Technologies); 15 with radio. Very isolated activities in Spain. Especially digital literacy, which is only done in Cataluña. The census of these activities is not recorded. Difficulties due to the lack of information from the Directorate General of Penitentiary Institutions. Little by little, glimmers of change with media such the radio, which in some cases counts with 25 years of history. This type of project is maintained thanks to the volunteer work of the educators. Next, we show a map (Figure 1) that was designed ad hoc, which gathers all of these activities:

Result Two: If the communication media workshops in prisons are relevant and useful for the prisoners and educators

As for the question of what communication media do you consider to be more efficient for achieving in prison? Most prisoners think that the radio is the best, because it is a type of media that achieves the preservation of anonymity, and in second place, projects that include the use of the Internet. For the educators, the Internet should be one of the most urgent projects that should be included in prisons.

For the incarcerated, these types of projects have great importance, also due to the connection with the exterior world and their families.

- **P20H:** First, it is the only contact with the outside that many people have. Because really, my family comes to visit me, but in reality, to many people, it is the only contact they have with the outside. Second, because the people inside that listen to it feel important, because not only can 5 or 6 people make the programs, but the people that are in their cell, who have transmitted their message, and has been heard. Or, look, this is coming out on the radio, but far from Huelva, or my family is listening to it, and my family is listening to me.
- **P13A:** Because it makes you evade the place where you're at. Besides the fact that you are psyched up, this moment in time, you are not a prisoner. For

Figure 1. Map of communication media in Spanish jails
Source: Author generated (Contreras-Pulido et al., 2015)

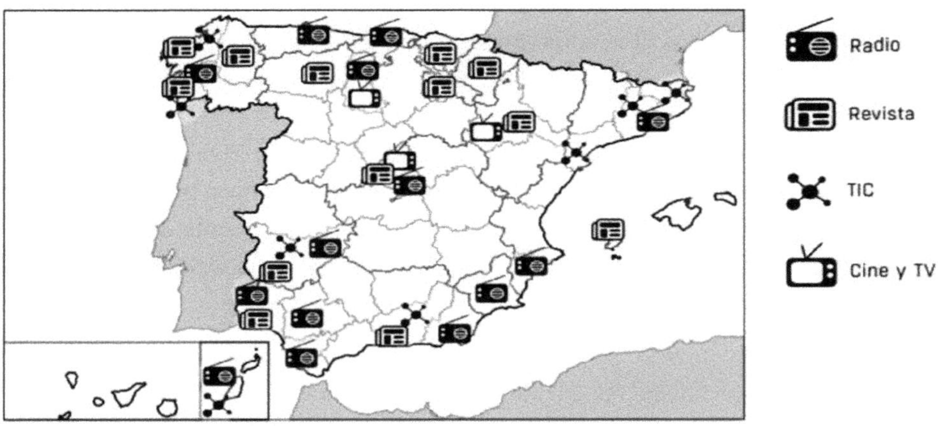

the people on the street too. In the street, you can express yourself. Even if you want to tell your family you are ok, that this is not as harsh as they tell you, the family doesn't believe it, besides the fact that you don't tell them everything that happens here.

They also placed great value in displacing the stereotypes that society has towards the imprisoned:

- **P10A:** It's very nice, because it reaches all the prisoners and the street, the people see us differently. The people on the street don't know how we feel. The people think that jail is Oohhh! and you see that we mobilize...the people don't think that there are people in here from all the social spheres...
- **P23H:** For me, even though I'm in a therapeutical module, is also therapeutical. I stop being in the yard, I stop having the habits that I used to have, and now I associate with other types of people, and truthfully, my stay in prison is easier, and at the same time, I'm contributing, right?, giving the people on the outside a different vision, maybe this is the most important thing.. maybe it is...the thing that most gratifies me, on the personal level.

In the case of the educators, they talk about the importance that these types of media also have for society at large, and they talk about its therapeutic effect.

- **E5P:** I think the radio would cover part of what could be a module of respect. It could link with all the philosophy of the modules of respect, and I believe that it's a very valid instrument for this type of modules, and I think that it could be implanted in all of them... In the way of working out many things through the radio: respect for the other's opinion...the confrontation of ideas, the respect for the word, the taking turns, active listening, all the communication and interaction processes, the conflicts that can be solved through friendship. It is an instrument that gives many, many possibilities.
- On the other hand, they complain about the lack of penetration of the ICTs in prisons.
- **E3Q:** The new technologies are tools that we should give them here. If the new technologies are necessary now for their re-insertion, they have to exist, right? The Constitution states it, and the Penitentiary regulation says that we should encourage their use, that they turn their back on technology, does not comply with this precept.

As for the personal contributions and changes that are produced in them with their taking part in this activity, the incarcerated highlight that it is useful as an avoidance, to improve their training, to create friendships and increase self-esteem.

- **P12A:** Before, I only use to think about how to make a hole to get out of the wall…it's true, and then I had a hole to escape from, and was satisfied and the thoughts that you would express, so that the people would understand. And this gives you a great satisfaction.
- **P14A:** I'm no longer the classical inmate, who does whatever I feel like because I'm a prisoner. This self-disdain. This is a good opportunity.

As for the second part of the question, which asked about the changes they had felt since taking part in this activity, we first show a word cloud (Figure 2) of the words that were more often repeated when speaking about these changes.

The arguments that they have put forward to answer this question are very clear to them, and they are all positive. In the following answers we observe how they have gone to living a very different life in prison thanks in part to everything the activities contributes, as well as the professional workers that work with them:

Figure 2. Changes brought on by taking part in this activity
Source: Author generated

- **P8Q:** I didn't use to sign up to these activities, because I was the bad one. I didn't like it, I liked competing with everyone else…I used to be in the yard… No, it wasn't important..in the past, they didn't let me even speak with you…my own people and all..my gang…I couldn't speak to anyone, and less to the recorder..it was not seen right. Now everyone knows what to say. I'm guessing you have heard about my program on gangs. I created it, because I use to be a member. Of course, it was directed to the youngsters, the ones that are young and have the opportunity to save themselves, and warn them.

In the case of the educators, the changes they highlight are the involvement with the project, the responsibility, the empowerment thanks to these activities, becoming an engine for the prisoners and the educators.

- **E4D:** I think there are changes in every level. The most immediate one is the verbal expression, which this changes. But then, there are more subtle changes as far as self-esteem goes, self-value and value of others. There are also changes in the ability of dialogue in negotiation, of entrepreneurship. The ability of entrepreneurship is surprising, because in the beginning they don't try anything, and then, you can't stop them. The experiences that they live here, and the people that come here, makes them see different things that they have not had a chance to know in their life, and in some cases the radio has given them the opportunity to know alternative ways of life that they could not even imagine existed. This is what it's about, of giving them opportunities. This is what it's being done.

Result Three: Regarding the contributions for their future life expectations

Lastly, as for the contributions that are given to them for their future perspectives, in the case of the imprisoned, they highlight the emotional benefits, attitudinal changes, of behavior, of expression, of communication, and overall, that they are able to change their lives.

- **P7Q:** Yes, to express myself to be a better person, to not be a delinquent anymore.
- **P20H:** That the life we chose before is not the only one, because most of the people believe it, and no, one can live in many different ways, and be happier because the end will not be jail, the end will be with your family, sleeping well, and looking back, proud of what you've accomplished.

And for the educators, their answers referred to the improvement of self-concept that these people have, and the values they acquired. For example, in the case of the mentally ill, it has been fundamental:

- **E5P:** What I was saying, it's not that no one goes to work in the radio, this is not the objective, on the contrary, the objective is that if a patient says that he's mentally ill, and says it through the microphone, is like becoming aware of what he is, what is called "adherence to the treatment", he improves. [...] I have an illness that is called schizophrenia, that manifests in this way, and what do I have to do so it doesn't manifest, or so that we have less possibilities of this happening. Its therapeutic work... First, I'm a person.

Step 4: Discussion and Conclusions

In the following paragraphs, the conclusions will be presented, using as a template the objectives that were planned in the beginning of the investigation.

Objective 1: Outline the different experiments with communication media that are being done in Spanish jails

After performing an exhaustive search and research on the activities that are being done in Spanish prisons that are linked to producing communication media by the imprisoned, encouraging media or digital literacy, we observe that in Spain, there is a large number of experiments dedicated to this, although they are not visible or taken into consideration in any way.

In total, we have gathered 39 experiments in Spain, that are distributed in 14 publications in magazine format, 3 television or cinema experiments, 1 photography, 6 experiments with ICT, and 15 radios stations. We should remember that of the 68 penitentiary centers in Spain, more than half have some kind of activity in place.

In many cases, these projects have a long and distinguishing trajectory. Also, we can conclude that they have an important impact on the inmate population as well as in the society in those cases that the possibility of access exists. However, most of these experiments are not sufficiently recognized by the relevant organisms, and not even by the management team within the prisons, leading to a lack of resources and a greater involvement of the society in these projects.

Objective 2: To learn if the communication media workshops in prisons are relevant and useful to prisoners and educators

The general conclusions that we can extract after learning about the discourse from the educators and the imprisoned are very positive. They have not mentioned any negative aspects in any of the cases. This activity has been highly valued by all those interviewed.

Within the improvements that the prisoners as well as the educators observe, we can find, without a doubt, self-esteem and personal valuation as far as their abilities is concerned. This has to do with the concept that we have mentioned above: Resilience.

Empowerment, the entrepreneurial spirit, the improvement when expressing emotions, or the sense of responsibility are, as a whole, one of the many relevant factors that these types of activities provide for the interns. Also, they gain security, a security that is almost imperceptible and difficult to see in this type of context. They are more open, flexible, and they value friendship. All of these values are the opposite of what is usually generated in prisons.

Lastly, all the benefits that were specifically given to the mentally-ill inmates are emphasized. As compared to their mates, the mentally ill are immersed in apathy and are generally depressed, with an emotional and intellectual paralysis that is almost constant. But those who participate feel their regular therapy complete with the radio.

Objective 3: To learn how participation in communication media that are developed in the context of the prison gives prisoners positive expectations about their future.

Far from thinking that what they are learning will enable them to work in the professional communications field when they are free, all of them coincide in that it gives them a more hopeful view of their future. They speak about the importance of changes in attitude, which was deemed as important as well by the educators. They change routines, have learned to communicate and express themselves better, leading them to understand that this will help them with intra-personal and work relations.

Also, there are inmates who think it important to have learned the internal dynamics of communication media. This is linked with the exercise of healthy education in communication and media literacy, as it will grant them more self-sufficiency and critical consciousness.

On the other hand, to those inmates that have the possibility of using ICT tools, such as in the Quatre Camins (Barcelona) jail, the use will help them in their social/work integration or in their home life.

In the specific case of the prisoners that are mentally ill, as the ones in the Psychiatric Hospital in the Penitentiary Center of Seville, these future expectations could also be more deciding. That they are able to recognize that even if they have a mental illness, they have all the civil rights, and should be treated as people, minimizing the impact of the social and self-stigma.

SOLUTIONS AND RECOMMENDATIONS

After the study has been completed, we can assert in first place, that to create a communication medium in prisons requires perseverance and will power. As any other project with these characteristics, the instability when maintaining a team in the long term will have to be accounted for. As we know, the roaming of the penitentiary population, the exits and the leave permissions, makes it so that in many occasions, when a stable team is created, it has to be redone. Linked to this situation of instability, are the lack of resources or the little willingness that sometimes comes from the jail's own management teams. This leads to the abandoning of the projects. Only when we can count on a professional team that is constantly there, with energy and will power, will the projects continue. But, in the end, it will also come about by itself if it becomes more than an institutionalized objective, a personal objective or an objective of the participating group. This is a common theme in all the experiments with communication media in this context.

In the five projects analyzed, the prisoners, as well as the educators, corroborate the importance that these activities have for the contributing of future perspectives to the lives of the interns, and so that their stigmatized perception become short-lived and be overcome thanks in part to the strengthening of their self-esteem that comes from participating as members of a communication media project.

As for the ICT, while in Catalonia the penitentiary institutions have their own autonomy and have been working on media literacy projects that have had an important social impact and success in their development, in the rest of Spain the fear of adding these tools in the penitentiary setting still exists. This is a form of inequality and a reduction in training and participation for inmates that find themselves outside of this autonomous community.

FUTURE RESEARCH DIRECTIONS

For future research, it is necessary, in first place, to perform a similar analysis of experiments with communication media at the international level, to be able to show that these types of activities have an important trajectory in the case of a few countries. In the same way, we will be able to perform a comparison between the different countries, their policies, and their repercussion, not only in the penitentiary population and their re-insertion, but in society at large

CONCLUSION

This chapter has sought to present a reality, that of Spain, through the case study of five prisons, where the protagonists have been mainly the prisoners, but also their educators. These prisons have been chosen for their important trajectory in the field of the implementation of the media as a therapeutic tool for the transformation of the person and the prison context, as well as to promote a change in their vision of society. It also provides a map, which until now was totally non-existent, of all the educational-communicative practices that are carried out in prisons in Spain. From the vision and belief that education for social change (Barranquero, 2007) can improve the stigma and self-stigma (Goofman, 1989; Contreras-Pulido et al., 2015) of prisoners, we have seen how these workshops bring a real revulsion to those who experience them and open up new expectations for their future life outside prison.

REFERENCES

Barranquero, A. (2007). Concepto, instrumentos y desafíos de la edu-comunicación para el cambio social [Concept, instruments and challenges of media education for social change]. *Comunicar, 15*(29), 115-120. Retrieved from https://goo.gl/vPgYSj

Cabrera-Cabrera, P. (2005). *Nuevas tecnologías y exclusión social. Un estudio sobre las posibilidades de las TIC en la lucha por la inclusión social en España* [New technologies and social exclusion. Studying the possibilities of ICTs in the struggle towards social inclusion in Spain]. Madrid: Fundación Telefónica.

Carbide, J. A., & Gradaílle, R. (2013). Educar en las cárceles: Nuevos desafíos para la educación social en las instituciones penitenciarias [Educating in prisons: New challenges for social education in penitentiary institutions]. *Review of Education*, (360): 36–47. doi:10.4438/1988-592X-RE-2013-360-219

Contreras-Pulido, P., & Aguaded, J. I. (2013). La percepción social a través de la mirada encerrada: el discurso de los presos de Huelva en UniRadio [The social perception through the closed gaze: the discourse of the prisoners of Huelva in UniRadio]. *Razón y Palabra, 83*. Available at: http://goo.gl/KfnOEG (accessed 14/03/2018).

Contreras-Pulido, P., Martín-Pena, D., & Aguaded, I. (2015). Derribando el autoestigma: Medios de comunicación en prisiones como aliados de la inclusión social [Bringing down self-stigma: Media in prisons as allies for social inclusion]. *Cuadernos.Info*, *36*, 15–26. doi:10.7764/cdi.36.708

Flores, G., García, E., & Rodríguez, G. (1999). *Metodología de la investigación cualitativa* [Methodology of qualitative research]. Málaga: Aljibe.

Gil-Cantero, F. (2013). Derechos humanos y reeducación en las prisiones. El derecho a la educación en el modelo 'good lives' [Human rights and re-education in prisons. The right to education in the good lives model]. *Review of Education*, (360): 48–68. doi:10.4438/1988-592X-RE-2013-360-220

Goffman, E. (1989). *Estigma: La identidad deteriorada* [Stigma: Notes on the Management of Spoiled Identity]. Buenos Aires: Amorrortu.

Gozálvez, V., & Contreras, P. (2014). Empowering Media Citizenship through educommunica-tion [Empoderar a la ciudadanía mediática desde la educomunicación]. *Comunicar*, *42*(42), 129–136. doi:10.3916/C42-2014-12

Gozálvez Pérez, V. (2014). *Ciudadanía mediática. Una mirada educativa* [Media citizenship. An educational look]. Madrid: Editorial Dykinson.

Melillo, A., & Suárez-Ojeda, E. N. (2001). *Resiliencia. Descubriendo las propias fuerzas* [Resilience. Discovering your own strengths]. Buenos Aires: Paidós.

Pérez-Tornero, J. M., & Varis, T. (2010). *Media Literacy and New Humanism.* Moscow: UNESCO Institute for InformationTechnologies in Education. Retrieved from https://goo.gl/LCcNoH

Scharager, J., & Armijo, I. (2001). *Metodología de la Investigación para las Ciencias Sociales* [Research Methodology for the Social Sciences] [CD-ROM]: Versión 1.0. Santiago: Escuela de Psicología, SECICO Pontificia Universidad Católica de Chile.

Strauss, A. R., & Corbin, J. M. (2002). *Bases de la investigación cualitativa: Técnicas y procedimientos para desarrollar la teoría* [Basis of qualitative research: Techniques and procedures to develop the theory]. Medellín, Colombia: Universidad de Antioquía.

ADDITIONAL READING

Dejaeghere, J. (2009). Critical Citizens Education for Multicultural Societies. *Interamerican Journal of Education and Democracy*, *2*(2), 223–236.

Del-Álamo, O. (2002). *Conectando... ¿desde prisión? [Connecting... from prison?]* (electronic res.). In Servicio de Observación sobre Internet [Boletín Semanal], (191). Retrieved from http://goo.gl/c2Xunf

Foucault, M. (1998). *Vigilar y castigar: Nacimiento de la prisión* [Discipline & punish: The birth of the prison]. Madrid: Siglo XXI.

Franganillo, J., Burgos, L., García, A., & Tomàs, C. (2006). *Alfabetización digital en la prisión: Una experiencia con jóvenes internos [Digital literacy in prison: An experience with young inmates].* II Congreso Internacional de Alfabetización Tecnológica. Badajoz, Nov. 29-30 / Dec. 1, 2006. Retrieved from https://goo.gl/RwRVup

Freire, P. (1970). *Pedagogía del oprimido* [Pedagogy of the oppressed]. Madrid: Siglo XXI.

Gumucio-Dagron, A. (2010). El cuarto mosquetero: La comunicación para el cambio social [The fourth musketeer. Communication for social change]. *Investigación & Desarrollo, 12*(1), 2-23. Retrieved from http://dialnet.unirioja.es/servlet/articulo?codigo=2382241

Jacquinot-Delaunay, G., Carlsson, U., Tayie, S., & Tornero, J. M. (2008). Empowerment through Media Education: an intercultural approach. In U. Carlsson, S. Tayie, G. Jacquinot-Delaunay & J. M. Tornero (Eds.), Empowerment through media education: An intercultural dialogue (pp.19-33). Göteborg University: The International Clearinghouse on Children, Youth and Media/Nordicom.

Kaplún, M. (1998). *Una pedagogía de la comunicación* [A pedagogy of communication]. Madrid: De la Torre.

Underwood, C., Parker, L., & Stone, L. (2013). Getting it together: Relational habitus in the emergence of digital literacies. *Learning, Media and Technology, 38*(4), 478–494. doi:10.1080/17439884.2013.770403

UNESCO. (2007). *Paris Agenda o 12 Recommendations for media education* (http://goo.gl/vMc0Mc)

UNESCO. (2011). *Declaration of Braga* (http://goo.gl/BQubIR)

KEY TERMS AND DEFINITIONS

Educommunication for Social Change: Media education for social change focuses on more disadvantaged environments, with a transformative outlook and where what is important is the process of change of the collective or community, rather than the final product.

Educommunication or Media Education: Media education goes beyond literacy. It also consists of educating in values, critical awareness and the role that we have as citizens in this mediatized world, where the democratization of technologies and communication must prevail.

Media Literacy: Media literacy is about teaching critical media management strategies, including ICTs.

Self-Stigma: Behind the stigma, people who belong to a particular' labelling' group assume that role or those characteristics that will make it more difficult for them to overcome the state of exclusion.

Social Stigma: It happens when society labels a group, generalizing a series of characteristics, always negative, that will lead them to a state of danger of social exclusion.

Chapter 6
Policies Information Literacy, Equality, and Gender:
The Case of Spanish Prisons

María Antonia Agúndez-Soriano
Colegio Universitario de Estudios Financieros, Spain

Aurora Cuevas-Cerveró
Universidad Complutense de Madrid, Spain

ABSTRACT

The development of information and communication technologies (ICT), especially the internet, means that not all the population has the same opportunities of access and use of these technologies or the training necessary to use them effectively. These technologies are producing socio-economic transformations. They also bring about important changes in the way they work, communicate, behave, and socialize. All these changes constitute a factor of social exclusion and have led to the emergence of the so-called digital divide (BD). This BD has accentuated the social gap and has contributed to the fact that certain population groups, such as female inmates, are considered to be "socially excluded" or "excluded digital," and in the case of these female inmates the gender gap would also be present. The authors presented results of the analysis carried out to know the policies, projects, and programs that are being carried out both in Europe and in Spain in the field of informational and digital literacy for social and labor inclusion, as well as equality and gender policies.

DOI: 10.4018/978-1-5225-5975-7.ch006

INTRODUCTION

The implementation of Information and Communication Technologies (TIC) requires citizens to acquire the necessary skills and abilities to ensure the proper use of TIC, training them to manage the large amount of available information and thus being able to solve their information problems on a daily and work basis throughout their life.

These technological changes bring a risk that can cause and increase the digital social exclusion of some groups or population groups. One of these population groups are women prisoners, these inmates are in clear risk of social and labor exclusion. As a woman and as a prisoner, we must add that most of these women are very poorly qualified, with a low self-esteem profile, school failure, most of them dependent on the male figure, with family, social, psychological problems and lack of freedom. All this causes them to have fewer opportunities of accessing the labor market, being doomed to unemployment or low-paid jobs, all of which makes it difficult to achieve their social and labor integration once they have obtained their freedom.

In prisons where women prisoners are deprived of their liberty, contact with the outside world is usually very limited or completely non-existent. Since they spend several years of their lives in these centers, they should be prepared to live in the information society that awaits them outside once they obtain their freedom. The knowledge about informational competences that they may already have is acquired before entering prison, so that in a brief time these will become obsolete. Therefore, their social and digital exclusion will be greater, the greater their sentence, becoming part of the group called "none -liners" "(Buchmueller et al, 2011).

Therefore, information literacy is presented as a great challenge to solve this situation of inequality for these women prisoners with their subsequent inclusion in society and the acquisition of the necessary knowledge and skills to become informationally literate. The objectives pursued by this research are:

- Determine and know the policies, projects and programs that are being carried out both in Europe and in Spain in the field of information and digital literacy for social and labor inclusion, as well as equality and gender policies.
- Diagnose if these policies are being carried out in the prisons of Spanish women.

The methodology used is a research and analysis methodology to identify existing policies on information literacy at a European level and at a Spanish level and see if they have reached the level of implementation in Spanish female prisons.

BACKGROUND

Information Literacy for Social Inclusion

The European Union (2006) links information literacy with lifelong learning, in its "Action Program in the field of lifelong learning", where it points out that new technologies are an instrument that can lead to social inclusion and that, therefore, people who do not use them for different reasons are excluded from a society of information that is increasingly digitized. Marzal (2007), states that information literacy is closely linked to other contexts such as economic, cultural and social, for this author a person informationally literate should be able to know what information is relevant to evaluate, select and communicate for this way to be able to participate actively within society. Another author Abid (2012), adds a new denomination of information literacy, calls it "information culture", this information culture is the sum of informational, digital and graphic literacy as well as reading and writing, it is a culture of collective exchange and enrichment. Authors such as (Bernhard, 2002, Gómez Hernández, 2002, Ponjuán, 2002) refer to the culture of information in an educational sense. Agúndez (2016: 60) defines information literacy in the following way: "Information literacy comprises a set of competencies that lead to an adequate, reflective, critical and responsible use of information and that contribute to the social inclusion of citizens. For his part, Cuevas (2007) believes that this concept is linked to the historical, economic, cultural and social context, and points out that a person will be informationally literate when he or she is able to decode the relevant information and codify a new message to communicate.

The policies developed in relation to information and digital literacy for social and labor inclusion, as well as equality and gender policies, have generated different programs, projects and plans that aim at literacy in digital skills for the most disadvantaged groups, promoting equality between women and men in terms of training and employment and promoting the social and labor inclusion of population groups at risk of exclusion.

However, it has been possible to see how these policies, more than the acquisition of information skills and abilities that contribute to the digital and informational inclusion of female inmates, are aimed at increasing the connectivity to the internet.

Rights Derived From Tic: A New Human Right

The digital and social exclusion generated by information and communication technologies encourages the creation of a new human right that ensures equality among all citizens. In this sense, information literacy has been supported by different statements that recognize this type of literacy and lifelong learning, and point to it as an essential element for social, cultural and economic development. In addition, it is of mutual agreement that information literacy can end inequality between certain groups and countries by reducing the digital gap between them. The Prague Declaration (2003) states that information literacy encompasses knowledge of one's own information problems and needs, as well as the ability to identify, locate, evaluate, organize and effectively create, use and communicate information to address the issues or problems that arise; it constitutes a prerequisite for effective participation in the Information Society, and is part of the basic human right to lifelong learning. Similarly, the Declaration of Alexandria (2005) considers that information literacy is at the heart of lifelong learning and constitutes a basic human right in the digital world, as well as promotes the social inclusion of all nations. In the same line the Declaration of Fez (2011) highlights the importance of information literacy for social, economic and cultural development. They consider that it is the key for all citizens to participate actively in society.

Information Policies

The information policies initially arose in the face of the transformation of society with the arrival of new technologies. The objective of these policies was and still is to include all citizens in the information society, but this initial objective is still far from being fulfilled, especially in groups such as women prisoners. That is why we will have to continue formulating policies and plans that also include this group and that are truly effective. The definitions on information policies have been numerous, among them Almada de Ascencio, which understands these policies as "the study of guidelines that govern the actions of different sectors or groups of society in the information transfer, its availability, access and recovery as a means of communicating information between creators and users of information ". In the case of Michael W. Hill (1995:279) he describes this concept saying that: Information policies are designed to meet the needs and regulate the activities of individuals, industry and commerce, of all types of institutions and organizations and of national, local, or supranational governments. They must regulate the ability and freedom to acquire, own and store their own information, use it and transmit it. Rowlands (1996) considers that the methodological processes in information policy studies are diverse and speaks of five methodological research instruments that are: Classification, identification of policy issues, reduction of complexity, prospection and reduction of scenarios and oriented research to the case study processes. Years later, this same author groups information policies into five groups: 1. Protection of government information. 2. Information market. 3. Broadcasting and telecommunication. 4. Access to public official information. 5. Information society and information infrastructure. For Cornellá (1997: 39), the information policies "could be framed in three areas: a) informational legislation, b) actions to promote and stimulate the use of information by public agents and c) improvement of the management of information resources in Public Administrations “.

In Europe, regarding these policies, different action plans have been drawn up in recent years that bear some relation to social digital exclusion, since they have literacy goals in digital skills of the most disadvantaged groups, although there are It should be noted that none of these plans have been designed exclusively for the collective of women prisoners. Important references about the information policies have been:

- **The Delors White Paper (1993):** “Growth, competitiveness and employment in Europe: challenges and clues to enter the XXI century” which proposed the strengthening of education and training throughout life.
- **The Bagemann Report:** “Europe and the Global Information Society”, commissioned by the European Council, in which a strategic move was made for teleworking and the creation of companies of remote professional training services.
- **The Action Plan of the Commission of the European Communities:** “Europe in progress towards the information society”, which presents guidelines for incorporating Europe into the information society. These references were points of reference for European information policies.

Since then, different plans and programs have been developed that seek to promote training in digital and information skills so that the entire population can be an active part of society. In the case of Europe, the Digital Agenda for Europe and the Europe 2020 Strategy must be cited as undisputed references.

Digital Agenda for Europe

The European Union has set out to achieve a series of challenges for the development of ICT, which are reflected in the European Digital Agenda, these challenges should be completed by the year 2020. On March 25th, 2010, a resolution draft was presented by the Committee on Industry, Research and Energy to the European Parliament for the creation of a new digital agenda for Europe, which was called Agenda 2015. The objectives of this resolution draft focus on literacy and digital skills and the access to digital technologies by the most disadvantaged social groups as a means of social inclusion and the fight against poverty and inequality. To this end, the entire population must be trained in these skills, contributing to the disappearance of differences between different social groups in terms of digital literacy and Internet use.

With the intention of meeting these objectives, the European Commission proposes a digital literacy and inclusion action plan on level with the EU and the Member States. This action plan includes training in digital literacy for the unemployed and groups at risk of exclusion, increasing accessibility to digital public services, ensuring that equality between women and men in the Information Society is a fact, and contributing to the participation in digital inclusion activities by the civil society. Similarly, among the objectives of the European Digital Agenda 2020, the promotion of digital literacy, training and inclusion is also present. To this end, the Commission proposes that member countries prioritize skills and digital culture within the framework of the European Social Fund by promoting ICT training courses and providing equal access to the digital common space. Other objectives of the Europe 2020 Strategy are:

- Achieve a minimum employment rate of 75% of people from 20 to 64 years.
- Reduce by at least 20 million, the number of people living below the poverty line or at risk of social exclusion, ensuring that the skills required to continue training and the labor market are recognized throughout general education, professional, superior and adult, including non-formal and informal learning and developing collaborations between the educational / training world and the labor world, especially through the involvement of the social partners in the planning of education and the delivery of training.

We understand that these objectives could refer to the inmate population (although no specific mention is made) because it is a disadvantaged group and supports training in digital skills to achieve social and occupational integration.

Following this same line marked by Europe, in Spain there are also policies that establish ICT learning as a way to reduce the social, digital and labor exclusion suffered by some disadvantaged population groups, for which a series of projects and programs have been developed in relation to digital literacy and social and labor inclusion.

All these policies are aimed at literacy training in digital skills of the most disadvantaged groups, including women prisoners. Another objective is to promote equality between women and men in terms of training and employment. Its goal is to promote the social and labor inclusion of these population groups.

National Plan of Action for Social Inclusion (Pnain)

This Plan has among its objectives to promote the social inclusion of the most disadvantaged groups as well as to promote equality and non-discrimination, having the same opportunities in access to education, training and employment. In the elaboration of this Plan, different public bodies have intervened, such as the Ministry of Health and the Secretary of State for Social Services and Equality and have had the participation of the General State Administration through the ministries involved, as well as the State Council of ONG of Social Action and the Economic and Social Council (CES). The PNAIN follows the recommendations of the Council of the European Union for Spain regarding the National Reform Program, specifically addressing recommendation 6 on the need to adopt and apply measures to reduce the number of people at risk of poverty or social exclusion, as well as measures that reinforce policies aimed at increasing the employment of those who do not have access to the labor market. The plan is organized through a series of strategic objectives and specific actions to achieve its final objective, which is the social inclusion of the most disadvantaged groups and equal opportunities in education, training and employment. This plan devotes a section to the prison population in its actions 237 to 240, establishing in actions 238 and 240 respectively, that it is necessary to seek resources to promote the participation of the prison population in training, cultural and labor programs, among others, through the Participation of the Third Social Action Sector (non-profit associations) to achieve this group's social and labor insertion. At the same time, it is intended to guide and educate prison staff and women prisoners on issues of gender violence to alleviate the consequences of this problem.

Throughout this document, the need to achieve social inclusion of the most vulnerable groups and achieve equality is emphasized. As for the prison population, they see, like us, the need to participate in training and work programs to achieve social and labor reintegration.

Inclusion Strategy of the Community of Madrid 2016-2021

The Office of Social Policies and Family of the Community of Madrid has the mission of favoring the integration and social inclusion of people who are in an inferior situation. For this purpose, it has developed a social inclusion strategy. This strategy is based on the principles of active inclusion, such as a sufficient income, employment opportunities and quality social services. It includes four groups of objectives. The first group refers to the development of inclusive policies in employment, education, health or housing; the second group is aimed at strengthening social services and supporting those population groups in situations of exclusion; the third focuses on organizational improvements to improve efficiency; and the last group is dedicated to active participation. Among these social policies are those aimed at the elderly or people with disabilities, to alleviate situations of dependency, to prevent and address situations of abuse and promote gender equality, to guarantee a minimum income in those households that lack resources and work for the inclusion of people who for various reasons cannot be integrated into society, whether for ethnic reasons, sexual orientation or gender or other circumstances that may jeopardize this inclusion.

Digital Agenda for Spain: Inclusion and Digital Literacy

This digital agenda for Spain currently in force has among its objectives to promote inclusion and digital literacy so that all people have access to ICT. In 2013, and following the steps set by Europe, a Digital Inclusion and Employability Plan was drawn up with the aim of improving the digital skills of those most disadvantaged groups of the population, regardless of their age, economic situation or place of residence who cannot or do not know how to use TIC. In this way they can incorporate them into their daily lives and cover their needs both personally and professionally. The way to achieve this goal is to encourage and promote digital literacy programs, advance in terms of equality between men and women and encourage the participation of these groups in digital inclusion activities to reduce their risk of social and digital exclusion. This plan is structured around four axes, among which is providing the most disadvantaged groups access to the Internet and ICT tools to reduce the risk of exclusion; provide the population with the basic digital skills needed to use ICT with emphasis on the older and less qualified population; reduce inequality between men and women regarding the use and access to ICT; allocate resources to acquire digital competences and reorient professional training related to ICT to be able to train future professionals. Each year a review of the plan is made to evaluate the results and determine if it is necessary or not to make any changes or evaluate a possible adaptation of objectives and measures and, if applicable, extend the time scope to meet the objectives already marked in the Digital Agenda for Europe or any new additional objectives that may arise.

It must be said that, although one of the objectives of this plan is to ensure that the most disadvantaged groups have access to the Internet and learn how to use TIC, we find that inmates do not have access to TIC and they do not have an Internet connection in prisons for security reasons.

Even so, we consider that these four axes in which this digital agenda is structured, are necessary to digitally and informationally literate the inmates; contribute to gender equity and achieve their social and labor inclusion by facilitating the learning of the necessary information and digital skills to achieve the full participation of these inmates in society.

Plan of Action for the Equality of Women and Men in the Society of Information

In June 2014, the action plan for equality of women and men in the information society was drawn up (2014-2017). The main objective of this plan developed by the Women's Institute, is the digital inclusion of women in equal opportunities than men to participate actively in the information society. To achieve this goal, measures are taken to provide Internet access as well as training programs to train women in ICT. Likewise, these programs should include learning about access to electronic administration and online public services.

This plan is already at a very advanced stage, but so far these measures have not been carried out in women's prisons. During the development of this chapter, it was found that the inmates still do not have an Internet connection and still do not have formative courses in information literacy. Therefore, it is difficult for these women to actively participate in an information society for which they have not been prepared.

Nowadays, information literacy is considered as one of the requirements to participate actively in society and reduce the risk of exclusion of the most vulnerable groups, as is the case of female inmates. The objectives of all these policies coincide in promoting the social and digital inclusion of these groups through courses or training programs and promoting equality between men and women. But the reality that women prisoners live in Spanish prisons about training in information literacy and even regarding equality between prisoners and inmates is quite different.

Solidarity Ciberaulas Project

The Ministry of the Interior and the "la Caixa" Foundation have signed different collaboration agreements in recent years, the last dated on August 23, 2017. The objective of these agreements is to proceed with the development of the CiberCaixa Solidarias Program, also named EspacioCaixa, in different Spanish penitentiary centers carrying out informative training activities for male and female inmates both young and old who are serving sentences in Spanish prisons. These activities are carried out both by professionals and by seniors who are already retired and who have been trained for this purpose. To achieve these objectives, they have planned to develop a "Preparation for freedom" program, instructing the inmates for their life in freedom. Basic computer courses and workshops are held to bring these inmate population groups closer to new technologies to ease their social and labor inclusion. To carry out this project, the "Fundaci6n la Caixa" installs computer rooms in the prisons. The implementation of the program is carried out in different penitentiary centers, in closed regime: Teixeiro, Villabona, Badajoz, Valencia, Zaragoza, Las Palmas, Seville and Palma de Mallorca, and in open regime: the Centers of Social Insertion of Victoria Kent in Madrid, Guillermo Miranda in Murcia, Dulce Chacón in Cáceres, Mercedes Pinto from Santa Cruz de Tenerife, Carmen Avendaño from Vigo, Evaristo Martín Nieto from Málaga, Marcos Ana in Albacete, Alfredo Jorge Suar Wall from Jerez de la Frontera, Concepción Arenal from Ciudad Real and Jesús Hadad Blanco de León. It must be said that this project does not reach all Spanish prisons.

Equality and Gender Policies

Given that the inequality of opportunities between women and men in training and employment issues within women's prisons exists, this research is directly linked to equality policies and to normative references related to this concept. Equality between women and men is a universal legal principle recognized in various international texts on human rights, including the Convention on the Elimination of All Forms of Discrimination against Women, adopted by the General Assembly of the United Nations in December 1979 and ratified by Spain in 1983. For the European Union it is also a fundamental right and it was expressed in the Treaty of Amsterdam. This treaty enters into force on May 1st, 1999 and it can be seen how measures are adopted to fight against all types of discrimination based on sex, race, religion, disability, age or sexual inclination. This Treaty includes the obligation to promote equality of opportunities between men and women in all Union policies.

Equality Policies in Europe

As for the policies of equality in Europe, from the year 2000, the European Union adopts different directives to fight against gender inequality. These directives are: Directive 2000/43 / EC, on the application of equal treatment of persons in order to fight against discrimination; Directive 2000/78 / EC on the application of the principle of equal treatment in employment and occupation; Directive 2002 / 73CE on the application of the principle of equal treatment for men and women with regard to access to employment, training and working conditions and Directive 2006/54 / EC on the application of the principle of equal treatment between men and women in matters of employment and occupation. Years later, in 2010, the European Commission adopted the strategy of the European Commission for the equality of women and men. This strategy consists of five objectives that are: economic independence; equal salary for the same job; equality in decision-making; dignity, integrity and the end of sexist violence; and equality in foreign action. Likewise, this strategy addresses very important issues related to the roles assigned to the sexes and the instruments necessary to achieve gender equality. A year later, the Council of the EU adopted the second European Pact for Gender Equality (2011-2020).

In addition to these policies, there are institutional bodies that fight for equality between women and men. Among them are the UN Women, created by the United Nations General Assembly for Gender Equality and the Empowerment of Women and the European Institute for Gender Equality. In 2006, the European Parliament and the European Council created this Institute with the aim of elaborating measures in favor of gender equality throughout the European Union. In this struggle is also the Committee for the Elimination of Discrimination against Women (CEDAW), consisting of experts on women's issues from different member states of the UN, whose objective is to end discrimination against women.

Equality Policies and Normative References in Spain

The Spanish Constitution in its article 14, promulgates the right to equality and non-discrimination based on sex. In article 9.2 of this same Constitution, it attributes the obligation of the public powers to promote the conditions so that the equality of the individual and the groups in which they are integrated is real and effective. In Spain, in 1983, the Women's Institute was created with the objective of promoting equality between both sexes. The creation of this institute was the starting point of public policies on gender equality in Spain (Gil, 1996). Thanks to this effort, Spanish society and the different institutions are becoming aware of gender discrimination and inequalities between men and women. In 2007, a law comes into force whose main objective is the right to equal treatment and opportunities between women and men. This new law is known as Organic Law 3/2007, of March 22, for Equal Opportunities between women and men (LOIEMH). This law was a great step forward for society in terms of equality. In its article 1.1 it establishes that women and men are equal in human dignity, and equal in rights and duties. The purpose of this Law is to give effect to the right to equal treatment and opportunities between women and men, through the elimination of discrimination against women, whatever their circumstance or condition, in any area of life. and, singularly, in the political, civil, labor, economic, social and cultural spheres. (LOIEMH, art.1.1).

In relation to education for the equality of women and men, article 23 of this same law includes the elimination of obstacles that hinder effective equality between women and men and the promotion of full equality between them. Another point to highlight within the LOIEMH is related to the Information Society. In its article 28.2, it is established that the Government will promote the full incorporation of women in the Information Society through the development of specific programs, which include access and training in information and communication technologies. This article also includes women at risk of exclusion.

We do not know to what extent the application of this article is effective for all Spanish women. What we can affirm, in the light of this investigation is that, in the case of the group of women prisoners, the article is not respected in what refers to their informational training.

From this law on, different plans and programs arise, such as the Program of actions for equality between women and men in the penitentiary (PAIHMAP). This program is carried out with the collaboration of the Ministry of Equality. The objectives of this law are aimed at eradicating the discriminations that could be detected due to gender, as well as knowing the characteristics of women inmates to adequately attend to their needs, reducing their vulnerability to situations of violence. To develop this program, a Mixed-Observatory Technical Commission was created in 2009, made up of 25 members from different fields (Women's Institute, Universities, Associations, Public Prosecution Staff and Prison Professionals) to examine and evaluate the impact of the program. The most important objective of the program consisted of promoting, examining and evaluating the impact of the program, the diversity of its composition guaranteed us the interconnection with the different social realities, which allowed us to have specialized advice on each of the topics that were undertaken and add a wide social network of collaborators. (Yagüe 2012: 2).

This Technical Committee must meet at least once a year, or when its members deem it necessary, and should promote the formation of working groups to deal with issues in a more specific manner and advance the proposals on the actions that the program contains. In 2014, the Government of Spain approved the Equal Opportunities Strategic Plan. Among the areas of action of this plan is political, economic and social participation; Education; and development of actions within the framework of other sectoral policies. There are also institutional equality bodies. Among these organisms is the Ministry of Health, Social Services and Equality. It is up to this Ministry to propose and carry out government policies on cohesion and social inclusion and equality, as well as to fight against all kinds of discrimination and against gender violence.

Other organizations committed to equality policies are the Women's Institute, a body under the Ministry of Health, Social Services and Equality. Its function is to promote the conditions that make possible the social equality between women and men and the participation of women in political, cultural, economic and social life, and the General Directorate of Women. This body depends on the Office of Social Affairs of the Community of Madrid and aims to achieve real and effective equality between men and women in the different areas of political, economic and social life of the Community of Madrid.

Prison Context

The prison is considered as a social institution oriented to reeducation and social reinsertion, as reflected in article 25.2 of the Spanish Constitution (CE): "prison sentences and security measures will be oriented towards re-education and social reintegration". On the other hand, Article 44.1 of the EC provides "that public authorities promote and protect access to culture, to which everyone has the right". Therefore, it is a fundamental right of the inmates to be able to access the necessary training for their subsequent reinsertion and it is the prison administration that must guarantee compliance. Likewise, the General Penitentiary Organic Law (LOGP) of September 1979, in its article 1 of the preamble, establishes that the penitentiary institutions regulated in said law have as their primary objective the reeducation and the social reinsertion of those sentenced to custodial penalties and penal measures. In article 59 of the same it is enacted that the prison treatment consists of the set of activities directly directed to the attainment of the reeducation and social reinsertion of the convicts. However, even though inmates have the right to training that facilitates their social reintegration, in reality we find that in Spanish prisons access to the Internet is prohibited due to security reasons. This situation leads to a total isolation of women prisoners in the field of ICT, whose knowledge and use is nowadays necessary both to integrate the labor market and to keep informed of what is happening in society. This situation also prevents women prisoners from developing the knowledge and skills necessary to use ICT. Therefore, it is very important to provide these women with adequate resources so that they can access training with the objective of acquiring the necessary information and digital skills to be an active part of the Society the moment they obtain their freedom.

In relation to the activities that are carried out in Spanish prisons, we observe that there are few experiences of training inmates in informational and digital competencies. We have only found seven focused on digital competences, none of which is oriented towards information competencies. 1) Ómnia prisons, is taught in Barcelona and focuses on notions of digital literacy and the construction of a blog for young inmates. 2) Alfadigital, taught in Barcelona, focuses on audiovisual workshops (radio, video, photography and music). 3) Alfablog Digital, this blog aims to compile all the creative productions made by the inmates of the different prisons in Catalonia. 4) Blog of the prison of Al lama, is given in the jail of Al lama (Pontevedra), collects the experiences lived by the prisoners of the modules of coexistence. In addition, it publishes poems and everything related to the activities that take place in the prison. 5) Cyberaula (promoted by la Caixa), extends throughout Spain and includes programs that cover digital literacy. These last two programs are taught to inmates and inmates. 6) The voice of mako, is a blog written by inmates of the penitentiary center of Albolote (Granada). They also have a digital literacy workshop conducted by social education students from the University of Granada. 7) Predis, takes place in the prison of Alcalá-Meco (Madrid) and covers digital literacy. This last experience is imparted to prisoners and disabled prisoners, which limits the scope of the activity. Of these seven experiences, in the Community of Madrid, only the Cyberaula and Predis programs are taught. Catalan penitentiaries have Internet connection in the classrooms since 2000, although they have filters so that inmates and inmates can not access certain pages. During the classes, it is only controlled that the prisoners and prisoners are connected to specific pages to carry out the activity. In the Community of Madrid, we find only one penitentiary center, in which the program "Aula mentor" is developed. Aula Mentor, is a resource center where inmates have a computer room with Internet connect

CONCLUSION

Throughout these pages, the policies of information and digital literacy, equality policies and gender policies for social inclusion that are being developed both in Europe and in Spain have been projected. Perhaps this is a good time to reflect on whether these policies are being done well or if they could be improved. In the current social context, it seems necessary to raise awareness among the population about women prisoners and their reintegration into society. Equality policies, plans and programs in the penitentiary area advance very slowly. It would be necessary to turn these plans and programs into concrete facts, to move from the legislative to the real. These policies should be more than a mere set of good purposes.

It would be very important to be able to evaluate and analyze the achievements made in the application of these plans, as well as the objectives achieved after carrying out the implementation of these policies. Public administrations should give priority to this population group by investing and getting involved in achieving the social and labor reintegration of these women deprived of their liberty.

Currently, information literacy policies in the penitentiary area could be effective and obtain positive results, adapting the formation of prisons to the demands of the information society and the labor market. We are talking about a specific training in information skills, since most of the jobs currently use ICT and the Internet. Considering that the educational level of the inmates is low, access to work is limited, so the information literacy training programs will serve them to be able to adapt to the current demands of society. A necessary condition for these programs to be delivered is to improve technological resources so that they are up to date and ensure free access to the Internet (currently prohibited for security reasons) in prisons during the development of information and digital skills training for female inmates, taking the security and surveillance measures deemed appropriate. In addition, the policies and action models that are applied in the penitentiary centers continue to be oriented and designed for a male profile. Once she enters prison, a woman suffers a double discrimination, that of being a woman and that of being a recluse since we move in a society that still prioritizes the figure and patriarchal schemes and this is taken to all areas including the police, judicial and even in the penitentiary legislation itself (Piñeiro Zabala, 2010). Both in the penitentiary regulations and in the general organic prison law, there is very little presence of articles dedicated to women prisoners. In relation to this, it must be said that Penitentiary Institutions, through the program of actions for equality between women and men in the penitentiary, has committed to introduce the gender perspective in penitentiary policy, as well as a comprehensive plan to adapt the architectural structures where convicted female inmates serve their sentence. Hopefully this will be effective as soon as possible since it is necessary to build exclusive prisons for women with suitable facilities for them, as well as policies that are really aimed at the social and labor reintegration of this group, with training programs that can help meet this objective.

REFERENCES

Abid, A. (2012). *Hacia una cultura de la información*. Universidad de Toluca.

Agenda Digital para Europa. (n.d.). Retrieved October, 15, 2017 from http://www.europarl.europa.eu/ftu/pdf/es/FTU_5.9.3.pdf

Agúndez, M. A. (2016). *Alfabetización informacional para la inclusión social de las mujeres reclusas de la Comunidad de Madrid: un estudio de caso* (Unpublished doctoral dissertation). Universidad Complutense de Madrid, Madrid, Spain.

Almada, M. (1999). Políticas de información y políticas educativas: un vínculo importante para el desarrollo hemisférico. *Boletín de política informática*, *23*(6), 34.

Bernhard, P. (2002). La formación en el uso de la información: una ventaja en la enseñanza superior. Situación actual. *Anales de Documentación*, *5*, 409-435. Retrieved March, 31, 2018 from http://revistas.um.es/Analesdoc/article/view/2271/2261

Buchmueller, S., Joost, G., Bessing, N., & Stein, S. (2011). Bridging the gender and generation gap by ICT applying a participatory design process. *Personal and Ubiquitous Computing*, *15*(7), 743–758. doi:10.100700779-011-0388-y

Comisión Europea. (n.d.a). *Agenda Digital para Europa: 2015.eu, 2010*. Retrieved October 14, 2017 from http://www.europarl.europa.eu/sides/getDoc.do?pubRef=-//EP//NONSGML+REPORT+A7-2010-0066+0+DOC+PDF+V0//ES

Comisión Europea. (n.d.b). *Europa 2020: la estrategia de la Unión Europea para el crecimiento y la ocupación*. Retrieved October, 14, 2017 from http://eur-lex.europa.eu/legal-content/ES/TXT/?uri=LEGISSUM:em0028

Cornellá, A. (1997). *Políticas de información en España*. Barcelona: ESADE.

Cuevas, A. (2007). *La promoción de la lectura como modelo de alfabetización en información en bibliotecas escolares*. Gijón: Ediciones Trea.

Declaración de Alejandría. (2005). Acerca de la alfabetización informacional y el aprendizaje de por vida. *Faros de la sociedad de la información*. Retrieved October, 14, 2017 from http://www.cobdc.org/grups/alfincat/documents.html

Declaración de Fez. (2011). *Alfabetización informacional y mediática*. Retrieved October, 14, 2017 from http://www.unesco.org/new/fileadmin/MULTIMEDIA/HQ/CI/CI/pdf/news/Fez%20Declaration.pdf

Declaración de Praga. (2003). *Hacía una sociedad alfabetizada en información*. Retrieved October, 18, 2017 from http://www.cobdc.org/grups/alfincat/documents.html

Delors, J. Libro Blanco (1993). *Crecimiento, competitividad, empleo. Retos y pistas para entrar en el siglo XXI*. Comunidad Europea. Retrieved October, 5, 2017 from http://biblioteca.cunef.edu/gestion/catalogo/doc_num.php?explnum_id=449

Directiva 2000/43/CE, de 29 de junio de 2000. Aplicación del Principio de Igualdad de Trato de las Personas independientemente de su origen racial o étnico (DOCE L nº 180, de 19 de julio de 2000). (n.d.). Retrieved October, 18, 2017 from http://eur-lex.europa.eu/LexUriServ/LexUriServ.do?uri=OJ:L:2000:180:0022:0026:es:PDF

Directiva 2000/78/CE de 27 de noviembre de 2000, relativa al establecimiento de un marco general para la igualdad de trato en el empleo y la ocupación étnico (DOCE L nº 303/16, de 2 de diciembre de 2000). (n.d.). Retrieved October, 18, 2017 from https://www.boe.es/buscar/doc.php?id=DOUE-L-2000-82357

Directiva 2002/73CE del Parlamento Europeo y del Consejo Europeo de 23 de septiembre de 2002, relativa a la aplicación del principio de igualdad de trato entre hombres y mujeres en lo que se refiere al acceso al empleo, a la formación y a las condiciones de trabajo étnico (DOCE L nº 269/15, de 5 de octubre de 2002). (n.d.). Retrieved October, 18, 2017 from https://www.boe.es/buscar/doc.php?id=DOUE-L-2002-81758

Directiva 2006/54/CE del Parlamento Europeo y del Consejo Europeo de 5 de julio de 2006, relativa a la aplicación del principio de igualdad de trato entre hombres y mujeres en asuntos de empleo y ocupación, la finalidad de esta Directiva es garantizar la aplicación de dicho principio (DOCE L nº 204/23, de 26 de julio de 2006). (n.d.). Retrieved October, 18, 2017 from https://www.boe.es/buscar/doc.php?id=DOUE-L-2006-81416

España Constitución (BOE núm. 311, de 29 de diciembre de 1978). (n.d.). Retrieved October, 15, 2017 from http://www.boe.es/buscar/act.php?id=BOE-A-1978-31229

España Ley Orgánica 1/1979, de 26 de septiembre, General Penitenciaria. (BOE núm. 239 de, 16 de octubre de 1979). (n.d.). Retrieved October, 15, 2017 from http://www.boe.es/buscar/act.php?id=BOE-A-1979-23708

España Ley Orgánica 3/2007, de 22 de marzo, para la igualdad efectiva de mujeres y hombres. (BOE núm. 71 de, 23 de marzo de 2007). (n.d.). Retrieved October, 5, 2017 from http://www.boe.es/buscar/doc.php?id=BOE-A-2007-6115

España Comunidad de Madrid. Consejería de Políticas Sociales y familia. Estrategia de inclusión social de la Comunidad de Madrid 2016-2021. (n.d.). Retrieved October, 25, 2017 from http://www.madrid.org/cs/Satellite?blobcol=urldata&blobheader=application%2Fpdf&blobheadername1=Content-Disposition&blobheadervalue1=filename%3DEstrategia+de+Inclusi%C3%B3n+Social+CM.pdf&blobkey=id&blobtable=MungoBlobs&blobwhere=1352918600937&ssbinary=true

España Ministerio del interior. (2017). *Convenio de colaboración entre la Secretaría General de Instituciones Penitenciarias y la Fundación Bancaria La Caixa para la implementación de «Ciberaulas Solidarias» en centros penitenciarios.* Retrieved October, 5, 2017 from https://www.boe.es/boe/dias/2017/09/20/pdfs/BOE-A-2017-10729.pdf

España Ministerio sanidad, servicios sociales e igualdad. (n.d.). *Plan de Acción para la Igualdad entre mujeres y hombres en la Sociedad de la Información 2014-2017*. Retrieved October, 5, 2017 from http://www.inmujer.gob.es/actualidad/NovedadesNuevas/docs/BorradIIPlanAccionSocInf.pdf

Gil, J.M. (1996). *Las políticas de igualdad en España: avances y retrocesos*. Servicio de Publicaciones de la Universidad de Granada: Instituto Andaluz de la Mujer.

Gómez Hernández, J.A. (2002). La alfabetización informacional como servicio de las bibliotecas. *Referencia*, *7*(1).

Hill, M. W. (1995). Information policies: Premonitions and prospects. *Journal of Information Science*, *21*(4), 273–282. doi:10.1177/016555159502100403

Instituto de la Mujer. (n.d.). Retrieved October, 15, 2017 from http://www.inmujer.gob.es/

Instituto Europeo de la Igualdad de género. (n.d.). Retrieved October, 3, 2017 from http://europa.eu/legislation_summaries/employment_and_social_policy/equality_between_men_and_women/c10938_es.htm

Marzal, M. A. (2007). Proyectos y realidades de la alfabetización en información: una perspectiva conceptual y aplicativa desde España. XVII Encuentro de Bibliotecas de Cajas de Compensación Familiar (Cofenalco) Alfabetización informacional: desafíos y posibilidades.

Naciones Unidas Comité para la eliminación de la discriminación de la mujer. (n.d.). Retrieved October, 15, 2017 from http://www.cinu.org.mx/temas/mujer/cedaw.htm

Organización de las Naciones Unidas mujeres. (n.d.). Retrieved October, 3, 2017 from http://www.unwomen.org/es

Parlamento Europeo. (n.d.). Recomendación 2006/962/CE del Parlamento Europeo y del Consejo, de 18 de diciembre de 2006, sobre las competencias clave para el aprendizaje permanente [Diario Oficial L 394 de 30.12.2006]. Retrieved October, 15, 2017 from http://eur-lex.europa.eu/legal-content/ES/TXT/?uri=CELEX%3A52013DC0359>

Piñeiro, I. (2010). Derecho penitenciario y mujeres. *Noticias jurídicas*. Retrieved October, 16, 2017 from http://noticias.juridicas.com/conocimiento/articulos-doctrinales/4608-derecho-penitenciario-y-mujeres-/

Plan Nacional de acción para la inclusión social. (n.d.). Retrieved October, 10, 2017 from https://www.msssi.gob.es/ssi/familiasInfancia/inclusionSocial/docs/PlanNacionalAccionInclusionSocial_2013_2016.pdf

Ponjuán Dante, G. (2002). De la alfabetización a la cultura informacional: Rol del profesional de la información. In *Congreso Internacional de Información Info 2002*. IDICT.

Programa de acciones para la igualdad entre mujeres y hombres en el ámbito penitenciario. (n.d.). Retrieved October, 15, 2017 from http://www.institucionpenitenciaria.es/web/export/sites/default/datos/descargables/publicaciones/Programa_para_la_igualdad_accesible.pdf

Programa de Intervención con Mujeres. (n.d.). Retrieved October, 15, 2017 from http://www.institucionpenitenciaria.es/web/portal/Reeducacion/ProgramasEspecificos/mujeres.html

Rowlands, I. (1996). Understanding information policy: Concepts, framework and research tools. *Journal of Information Science*, *22*(1), 13–25. doi:10.1177/016555159602200102

Rowlands, I. (1998). Some compass bearing for information policy orienteering. *Aslib Proceedings*, *50*(8), 230–237. doi:10.1108/eb051501

Segundo Pacto Europeo por la Igualdad de Género. (2011-2020). Retrieved October, 15, 2017 from http://eur-lex.europa.eu/LexUriServ/LexUriServ.do?uri=OJ:C:2011:155:0010:0013:ES:PDF

Unión Europea. (1997). *Tratado de Ámsterdam*. Retrieved October, 15, 2017 from http://www.europarl.europa.eu/topics/treaty/pdf/amst-es.pdf

Unión Europea Decisión Nº 1720/2006/CE del Parlamento Europeo y del Consejo de 15 de noviembre de 2006, por la que se establece un programa de acción en el ámbito del aprendizaje permanente. Diario Oficial de la Unión Europea, 24/11/2006. (n.d.). Retrieved October, 15, 2017 from http://europa.eu/legislation_summaries/education_training_youth/general_framework/c11082_es .htm

Yagüe, C. (2012). Políticas de Género y prisión en España. In Condenadas desigualdad: sistema de indicadores de discriminación penitenciaria. Icaria editorial.

KEY TERMS AND DEFINITIONS

Digital Inclusion: Focuses on those population groups that have many difficulties in accessing new information and communication technologies, facilitating access to ICT for incorporation into society.

Equality Policies: These are specific measures implemented by public institutions in order to help overcome inequality between men and women and ensure equal opportunities.

Female Inmates: Women serving a prison sentence for committing some type of crime. Once obtained the freedom suffers of social/labor exclusion.

Gender Gap: The gender gap is present in work, in the economy, in new technologies, etc. The greater the gap, the greater the differences and inequalities between men and women.

Information Literacy: Is to acquire the necessary skills to know how to search, select, evaluate and communicate information in a responsible and critical way to be able to actively participate in the information society. It contributes to the social inclusion of citizenship and therefore of women prisoners.

Information Literacy Policies: These are policies aimed at ending inequalities among citizens in relation to access and use of new technologies, avoiding the so-called digital divide or information gap.

Prisons: The prison is an enclosure where people who have been convicted of committing a crime to serve a custodial sentence are imprisoned. They represent a danger to society.

Social Inclusion: Process to ensure that socially excluded groups of people have the necessary opportunities to be active people in society.

Chapter 7
Prison Blogs, a Place of Freedom Behind Bars:
Notes From a Workshop at the Barcelona Youth Detention Centre

Jorge Franganillo
University of Barcelona, Spain

ABSTRACT

This chapter reports on the cultural workshop which, from 2006 to 2008, encouraged a group of inmates at the Barcelona Youth Detention Centre to produce and publish blogs as a joint project between the Òmnia on-site internet access point, the prison library, and the Faculty of Library and Information Science of the University of Barcelona. The objectives of the project were to promote inmate education, improve their level of information, encourage them to read and write more, instill some ICT skills in them or strengthen those they already had, and broaden their contact with the outside world. Prison libraries are presented as an agent that supports the intellectual, social, and cultural development of inmates and thus can help them on the road to personal betterment. The prisoners' responses are critically assessed; the experience was considered positive, although the insufficient technological infrastructure and the prisoners' rejection of certain social conventions represent obstacles.

DOI: 10.4018/978-1-5225-5975-7.ch007

INTRODUCTION

In the Internet and in the library, prisoners have two useful tools for their cultural enhancement and personal development, as both can improve the conditions under which they move towards social reinsertion and integration. The mission of the library, despite the limitation of being a prison library, can expand almost infinitely. Through the Internet, and through the possibility of having a presence on the web which stretches beyond the necessary limits of the prison confines —and especially, a voice and a role to play in dialogue— prisoners can find a space of free and creative expression that is universal, and where they have equal rights. This space offers them the chance of personal enrichment and of improving their prison surroundings. Contact with and through the web can help dispel the dangers of isolation as, for much of the time, prison life is all the inmates experience, and so the Internet can improve their day to day existence while at the same time guaranteeing them a right.

Providing prisoners with access to the Internet is one of the *Guidelines for Library Services to Prisoners* of the International Federation of Library Associations (IFLA): «Where prison network security permits, prisoners shall be given supervised Internet access for education and treatment purposes, as well as pre-release planning.» (Lehman & Locke, 2006; Sulé, 2006). The Spanish Constitution expressly grants the right to access culture (art. 44.1) through, among other resources, a network of public libraries, and it extends this right (art. 25.2) to people who have been condemned to sentences which deprive them of their freedom. Declarations of a universal nature, such as the Universal Declaration of Human Rights, also express the right of prisoners to access information as an instrument of personal betterment (art. 19 and others). After all, the most general overall objective of imprisonment is to provide the educational tools and means of rehabilitation necessary to facilitate the reinsertion of prisoners into society. The library is precisely one of the institutions that can work efficiently as a framework and as a tool for personal improvement.

However, the reality of prison life seems to be quite different: we need to provide more space for the Internet in prisons to ensure that it is not reduced to insignificance. Both documented evidence and personal experience teach us that providing prisoners with access to what a library represents in general, and the Internet in particular, throws up important, but not insurmountable, challenges. The difficulties stem from weaknesses that tend to be firmly entrenched when we consider low levels of basic schooling; difficulties that result from cultural inequalities, particularly in terms of language and of social prejudices; difficulties brought about by practices that in one way or another govern the lives of people at risk of social exclusion. Moreover, there are difficulties in achieving the motivation necessary to carry out any task, even that of improving one's own condition. The fact of having suffered from one failure after another makes it difficult for prisoners to want to embark on a project; but initial success, even though it may be minimal, is a powerful motivator to continue. This is where the library acquires its greatest importance and also where a workshop to promote culture can set in action what is in fact very much alive, even though it is dormant.

This chapter presents the experience of the cultural workshop that took place from 2006 to 2008 in the then Barcelona Youth Detention Centre (at present located at La Roca del Vallès). It also gives credit to a previous similar experience that was without a doubt an important precedent (Castell, Pallisé, Pedrola, Tomàs, & Burgos, 2006). The workshop encouraged a group of inmates to create and publish personal blogs, and it was brought about as a collaborative effort between the prison library, the Xarxa Òmnia and the University of Barcelona. The objectives were to promote prisoner education, encourage inmates to read and write more, awaken or strengthen their technological skills, improve their IT competences and their digital literacy, and broaden their contact with the outside world. Through the development of these skills, the workshop aimed to promote attitudes and habits that would favour the personal growth necessary for the prisoners to be able to participate in society as citizens, even though they did so from a detention centre.

Therefore, the workshop was designed in compliance with a basic cultural right and in accordance with the principles of the *UNESCO public library manifesto* and the *IFLA Internet manifesto*. Within this double framework, this activity was intended as a step towards eliminating the barriers that impede the circulation of information, particularly those that foster inequality, poverty and both social and technological exclusion. It was conceived within the universal right to freedom of expression and ideas, and the right to seek, receive and impart information through any media, regardless of frontiers. It was founded on the *Spanish Constitution* and current prison legislation in Spain, where it is considered that prison is an instrument of rehabilitation, and not merely punitive (Pérez Pulido, 2011). It benefited from the regional Catalan prison policy which, despite legal grey areas as far as the use of ICT in correctional centres is concerned,[1] already considered the Internet as a new tool for the education and rehabilitation of inmates (Catalonia General Subdirectorate for Rehabilitation and Health Programs, 2011). In fact, in recognition of the advances towards social inclusion of prisoners that this work with ICT represents, it received the City of Knowledge 2007 award from the Internet Global Congress, and the Barcelona Municipal Social Welfare Council Media Award 2007 from Barcelona City Council. Several studies of this project confirm previous findings concerning reading and writing in prison, while at the same time they acknowledge how the availability of Internet access in a prison context can be a powerful tool for learning and readjusting to society (Pérez Pulido, 2010; Rocha & da Silva, 2016).

The workshop reported here was later followed by similar initiatives within Catalonia developed at La Modelo Men's Detention Centre, the Quatre Camins

Detention Centre and the Brians 2 Detention Centre. These experiences have demonstrated how the conjunction of ICT, digital narratives, and social and intercultural education can be highly motivating and enriching (Boó, Sancenón, & Zino, 2014). Among other factors, this is because the development of digital narratives in the prison environment is accessible to people with different levels of ICT knowledge, it allows for a wide range of meaningful learning experiences, and it can produce an end product that is attractive and can be transmitted to others (Zino & Martín, 2012; Elvira-Valdés, 2014). It therefore comes as no surprise that writing an electronic diary has become one of the most popular uses of electronic resources in Spanish prisons (Pérez Pulido, 2010).

DIGITAL LITERACY AND THE PRISON LIBRARY

In Catalan prisons, the library is conceived as a cultural centre: a meeting point for inmates and professionals. In this paradigm of the prison library, we can see the traditional function of informing, educating or entertaining as part of a broader concept in which the library would not be merely a cultural agent, but also an element of integration and a promoter of the personal and sociocultural development of the inmates.

For many years, prison libraries have focused on fostering and motivating inmates' interest in reading and on contributing to their education by bringing the resources of the library, however scarce they may be, within their reach. These institutions offer a wide range of cultural activities and they are rather more than the place where the prisoners go to read the paper, to study or to borrow a book. Several factors have favoured the fact that the objective of Catalan prison libraries is to foster the educational and sociocultural process that enables prisoners to acquire or consolidate skills, attitudes and competences that go far beyond reading and writing. These factors include the fact that the libraries are run by qualified librarians, their activities are user centred, they are modelled on the working of public libraries, and they have adjusted their collections and services to the *Guidelines for Prison Libraries in Catalonia* (Comalat & Sulé, 2007).

Within its cultural programme, the library at the Barcelona Youth Detention Centre included activities to encourage reading and writing (reading clubs, poetry and creative writing workshops, book presentations, etc.) and to introduce inmates to the library collection (bibliographic and commemorative exhibitions, dramatised readings, etc.). It also contemplated other activities that aid the process of resocialising inmates: workshops on sensitisation and information on health, basic social skills, leisure alternatives, conferences and discussions around the events that characterise the daily reality of the outside world (International AIDS Day, International Women's

Day, international conflicts, etc.), and proposals specifically aimed at a young adult audience (urban art, manga, music, video forums, etc.). Together with all this, it also promoted competences and capacities related to the computing environment.

The educational tradition of libraries has evolved and adapted to the new social reality; and it is now, in the context of the information society more than at any other time, that a new approach that opens the way towards a new model of literacy is necessary. So it should not surprise us to find a workshop on digital literacy among the cultural activities offered by a prison library. It is a way to add on-line information to the printed word; and to add computing skills to traditional literacy. The objective should be to move beyond simply improving instrumental capacities: the aim is to develop IT skills as part of a broader literacy, in which the information dimension goes hand in hand with the personal and social dimensions.

A BLOG WORKSHOP IN PRISON

Prison libraries frequently organise a range of different cultural activities that aim to develop and promote the cultural competences and skills of the inmates, especially those related to reading and writing. The involvement of the library is necessary in these tasks, particularly because the value that reading and writing have for the treatment and resocialisation of inmates has been demonstrated (Pérez Pulido, 1997).

Within this rehabilitating context, under the management of the librarian Lola Burgos, the library at the Detention Centre organised a workshop on publishing blogs in collaboration with the University of Barcelona and the Òmnia project, which promotes access to new technologies. Through Aída García, the Òmnia on-site Internet access point at the Detention Centre offered specialised personnel, spaces and the resources necessary to use the new technologies as a valuable educational and socialising instrument, and effectively to develop the activity described herein. Similarly, the cooperation with the University of Barcelona offered teaching and advice via the voluntary participation of the author of this chapter: lecturer in digital communication at the Faculty of Library and Information Science; and also of Cristina Tomàs, a student of the same faculty.

Programming

As soon as we first considered the workshop, we agreed that it should be a tool to foster digital literacy. We were also very aware of the difficulties that typically show themselves in the users of prison libraries, and which may be intensified in young inmates. These can be psychological, educational, cultural, affective and personal problems. We had to try to explain to the inmates the importance of information in the development of any project, even in personal development, given that they would find it extremely difficult to participate in a society that they did not understand or they did not feel they were part of. So, the blog workshop had to be a meeting point for information, technologies and people; it had to be a space where the inmates were not passive receivers, but active participants in the whole process.

The format chosen was the blog: a website that is easy to update where an author or a group of authors publish texts, generally written in a personal and informal style. A blog is an interactive diary in which information appears in chronological order, and where any reader can add comments, always reserving the role of moderator for the author of the blog. In this way, blogs represent a space for both creation and communication, where people express themselves and establish relationships; they share experiences, learn from them together and bring meaning to them.

Setting and Participants

The Barcelona Youth Detention Centre was home to a heterogeneous community, with significant differences between the young offenders who formed part of it: cultural and linguistic differences, and also in their degree of basic literacy and schooling. The majority of them were aged between 18 and 25, and came from disadvantaged backgrounds in which reading is not encouraged as either entertainment or as a system of personal education. Neither is the use of IT as a means of learning new skills or as a tool to earn a living common among such youngsters. Many of the inmates had suffered from affective deficiencies while growing up and later had severally limited education and employment skills, as well as difficulties interacting with other people and with their surroundings. The majority had a certain digital illiteracy, associated with their lack of knowledge of the use of ICT applications (Sulé, 2005; Franganillo & Burgos, 2007).

However, there were signs of change: many of the inmates commonly visited the Centre's library. The prison population uses libraries ten times more than people in the outside world (Pérez Pulido, 2002). A prison library is thus an ideal space to encourage reading; it offers the chance to support the intellectual, social and cultural growth of the inmates, and it can actively contribute to promoting digital literacy and favouring the personal improvement they need. The *Guidelines for Prison Libraries in Catalonia* recognise these capacities and identify the prison library as an effective tool to motivate the habit of reading among the inmates, to stimulate their intellectual and sociocultural development, and to act as an important link with the outside world (Comalat & Sulé, 2007).

Therefore, it was fortunate that the Centre's library and Òmnia point planned an activity that, in addition to stimulating reading and writing among the inmates and forming a connection with the outside world, would help counteract technological exclusion. It must be remembered that the employment and social integration of the prisoners within the outside world of work depends, to an extent, on them mastering IT tools and having the capacity to search for information. So, the prison library can play a decisive role in preparing inmates, when the moment comes, to face their social and working integration successfully.

The Centre's library had personal computers for the inmates to use, but the Òmnia point installed on the premises was the resource that allowed them to use new technologies as a valuable educational and socialising tool, and to develop the activity described herein efficiently. The aim of the Òmnia network, a project run jointly by two regional authority departments —the Department of Welfare and Family; and the Department of Universities, Research and the Information Society— is to provide anybody with access to ICT, irrespective of their age, social and economic situation, where they come from or their level of education. To achieve this objective, three lines of action are adopted:

- **Community Use:** It promotes free access for all and offers spaces that should generate social cohesion, dynamics and exchange.
- **Employment and Social Integration:**It aims to bring information and resources that are useful for employment and social integration within the reach of users.
- **Training:** Users are taught how to use ICT, while aspects of public participation, self-esteem, societal values and personal skills are all worked on.

Foundations and Objectives

In response to the need for new literacy in the digital era, the workshop was designed as an opportunity to develop abilities related to the new multimedia technologies, and not just as a means of practicing instrumental skills. Digital literacy must not be seen as the acquisition of skills and knowledge out of context, because it forms part of a broader literacy in which the information dimension goes hand in hand with the personal and social dimensions (Gutiérrez, 2003). Therefore, the workshop promoted the development of a set of literacies:

- **Literacy per se:** The workshop described herein attempted to improve the capacity to understand what is read, and not only through reading, but also through the practice of writing.
- **Information Literacy:** The workshop aimed to be the context in which to learn to recognise a need for information and to resolver it with the help of the right tools.

- **Library Literacy:** The requirements of the workshop and the role played by the library, which actively participated in it, justified, and indeed made necessary, the use of the library's resources.
- **Digital Literacy:** This ability, in which some of the workshop participants proved to be less than competent, is necessary to handle information deftly in a world that is dominated by digital technology.
- **Media Literacy**. Media culture teaches us ways to behave, gender roles, attitudes towards and visions of the world that are appropriate and inappropriate, and it often does so in subliminal and invisible ways. A person who is media savvy will know how to analyse and criticise the content these media transmit —codes, stereotypes, conventions, values and ideologies— and critically examine the forms they adopt (Kellner, 2004).

Ultimately, the new technologies on their own do not make us wise or freer, partly because real technological skill does not consist of learning to use computers and the Internet, but of making these two tools instruments of learning. With this conviction, the workshop set out four goals:

- To stimulate reading and writing;
- To strengthen creative skills;
- To develop information and technology skills; and
- To encourage individual and group work.

The Internet allows us access to a wide range of information and educational resources; it thus enables the creation of rich and varied learning contexts. But within a prison, the Internet can only realise this potential if, recognising the value of its content, there is no limit placed on access, beyond situations that may compromise security. Internet access without barriers can serve to guarantee the participation of the prisoners in the information society and allow them to maintain the vital points of reference they need with life on the outside.

In response to this argument, the librarian and the Òmnia point manager approved, for the start of the workshop described herein, to provide unlimited Internet access on a trial basis. It would have been a contradiction to plan an activity based on the Internet without real contact with the worldwide web. In keeping with the security protocols of the prison environment, those in charge of the activity took responsibility for controlling the use of the web. Throughout the duration of the workshop, the prisoners would have direct and open access to the Internet, and they could consult whatever they wished, but always under the supervision of those in charge of the workshop. This control was initially established as a security measure, but also as part of the educational process, since education fosters the adoption of responsible attitudes.

Tools

The workshop on creating and publishing blogs was programmed as a series of weekly 2-hour sessions. In accordance with the established objectives, the inmates should each write and publish their own blog. As a publication tool, *Blogger* was used, with the support of the *Flickr* image hosting site, from where the participants took photographs under Creative Commons licences to illustrate their posts, and the *YouTube* video hosting site, which allowed them to incorporate audio-visual content. In this way, the library and Òmnia recognised the variety of forms of information that can be transmitted: on the Internet, the different forms of expression used are texts, photographs, animated images, sounds and videos.

These resources that the Internet offers are characterised by a high degree of participation and a liberal philosophy, as they are not institutional or commercial hosting sites via which an organisation offers products with restricted rights or subject to economic conditions. They are channels through which anybody, in their own name, can post what they create in a straightforward way, and free of charge, in order to share them publicly and open them up to debate among the members of a broad virtual community. Participation, with no interest other than the desire to share one's own reflections and worries, gave these resources intrinsic value that they share with the blog format, a value that was in harmony with the objectives of the workshop and which was something that we felt was worth transmitting.

In addition, these days, libraries are not limited to printed materials: they use a considerable range of tools and supports to achieve their mission, with no distinction between formats or media. So, the activity also dealt with the identification and selection of sources of information from different supports, the use of a word processor (for the spell-checking function) and of programmes for editing images, and the use of various dictionaries, both online and printed. In addition, the young inmates were given advice on general writing techniques and also specific techniques for the web setting.

Through all of this, in addition to promoting the use of different tools and techniques, in the planning of the activity we aimed to ensure that the participants discovered new channels of personal expression and enriched their language (in the broadest sense of the term); when people manage to express themselves and communicate comfortably in different settings, they can better develop their internal capacities to express themselves with freedom and confidence, and they can improve both themselves and their relations with others. In addition, the acceptance of discourse and ways of being that are different from one's own makes integration into one's surroundings possible.

Convinced that a brief printed explanation would be a great help for these young inmates in grasping certain concepts, we prepared some hand-outs which were distributed at the start of the sessions. The inmates' difficulties with attention and comprehension, and the presence of people at an educational disadvantage —people who could not read Spanish and Catalan proficiently, who had been educated in other languages or who had dropped out of school— meant that we had to design materials that were easy to read. To this end, the contents were written following the *Guidelines for easy-to-read materials* by Tronbacke (2010). The texts contained clear arguments, short expositions and simple language; but they were still written in respectful adult language. Moreover, the hand-outs were printed on adequately sized sheets and were attractive, with a clear type face, and useful illustrations.

The advice on writing materials that are easy to read has much in common with the techniques of effective writing for the Internet. In a web setting, straightforwardness, precision and clarity are also key aspects of producing a text that is easy to read and understand. This parallel allowed us to use the hand-outs themselves as examples of good practices in writing for websites. In fact, writing is, essentially, an exercise in summarising that helps to make ideas clear, order them and express them concisely.

DEVELOPMENT

The Barcelona Youth Detention Centre considered education of the inmates to be a broad and complex process that was carried out in widely ranging contexts, both formal and informal, which configured educational realities that were equally diverse. The arrival of summer marks the end of the academic year and it is the moment at which the training which the inmates have received needs to be given some sort of continuity. For the summer of 2006 this uplifting sociocultural project was programmed, which was characterised as having a light-hearted component, suitable for the summer period, while it was also included in the framework of education through leisure. The interest the prisoners showed in the contents of the workshop and the socio-educational dynamics that it generated made it advisable to programme an extension to the activity, which had initially been planned for the aforementioned summer period. So, it was continued and included within the education courses on offer and the treatment programmes as the Detention Centre; now, not so much as a library workshop, but as an activity in its own right.

During the running of the workshop, the principal objective of the organisers of the activity was to manage the contents of some blogs, improve the formal quality of the texts and consolidate habits. In the interpersonal plan, our interventions were aimed at improving the inmates' self-concept and their self-esteem. Special emphasis was placed on ensuring that their posts acquired importance through what they expressed, and not so much for their form, although it was necessary for the inmates to present their texts with a minimum formal quality. Some of the participants were reluctant to make corrections, giving arguments that showed a defensive attitude through which they tried not to recognise their weaknesses. However, through helping them and providing constructive criticism, we tried to assist them in completing the frustrating process that having to revise the language, and in some cases the contents, represented. Gradually, some of the prisoners became used to writing with a word processor, although others continued with pen and paper. They came to use the dictionaries, the spell checkers and the programmes to edit images more and more, and they became advanced users of *Blogger*: they acquired the ability to redefine design templates, download and manipulate images, and carry out other parallel tasks.

It was also necessary to give them guidance in an individual fashion, in simple ways and at basic levels, with guidelines and techniques for intellectual tasks. The majority of the inmates worked intuitively, without following any didactic method, and that meant that they often asked for help when they came to write the content of the blog in their own words or to present a summary of their ideas. This was because they had not acquired some instrumental competences concerning basic school learning and, even as adults, they presented personal characteristics that were more those of adolescents. Examples of this are a lack of attention and of self-control —they always wanted to have everything here and now—, their lack of a general work ethic or their low tolerance of frustration. However, none of this should surprise us if we bear in mind the emotional and intellectual development of some of these young people had stalled at a young age due to the personal situations that they had had to live through.

Just as the first texts of the blogs were characterised by the expression of opinions, experiences and worries that these young people had, which were the fruit of the knowledge that they had accumulated throughout their lives, at a later stage it was necessary to link that prior knowledge with what they had recently learned. The inmates started to show that they valued positively their time spent on personal improvement and they broadened the concept that they had had until then of productive work. Some of them had even expressed on numerous occasions that learning and being informed was akin to a waste of time. Later on, however, they started to accept this learning and they furthermore came to understand that culture, education or training are lifelong experiences, and not just something related to school.

The young people showed a capacity for culture and aesthetics, creativity and ingenuity; they also proved to have a marked desire to write. Proof of this is the curiosity they showed towards the dictionaries: they avidly set about looking for synonymous concepts, for example. The word *freedom* even became the subject of some debate because, according to the dictionary, it is a synonym of *democracy*, and democracy is, even for many people in the outside world, actually a dictatorship: the «dictatorship of the masses», it is said.

Of the proposals for the themes of the blogs, those that stand out include literature, body building, social criticism, human values, hip hop and Latin American music, and the gay scene. The most notable feature is that almost all of these are subjects that move the inmates far away from the stereotype of young offenders and prisoners. In the blog, they had the opportunity to break free from the stereotype of delinquents as they could present themselves just like anybody else, with the same will to share their worries or hobbies in a space of individual writing or in collaboration with others.

The blog and the desire to seek out information helped the prisoners to become expert column writers, increased their interest in learning, opened up effective means of participation and provided new perspective both inside and outside the prison. It should be noted that some of the inmates had no problem in presenting themselves as inmates, maybe because the condition of being a prisoner carries with it certain kudos in their social circles on the outside or because going into prison is just one more stage in their lives.

The inmates realised that blogs are a way to get in touch with what happens in the outside world. Beyond sharing their hobbies or expressing their worries, they showed considerable interest in receiving comments and in exchanges with people on the outside who made contributions, always bearing in mind that the blog is a space for public communication and not for private conversations. In this way, the library and the Òmnia point were able to reformulate and strengthen their function as a link with the outside world.

Some inmates implicitly asked for special individualised attention; maybe they were not used to anyone paying attention to the needs they displayed. This demand for attention could be the symptom of immaturity that was best countered by encouraging them to grow up, and this is what happened, stimulating them and treating them perfectly naturally. In parallel, the more advanced inmates were asked to be patient, and in order to maintain a balanced level of learning, it was suggested that they could take what they had already learned a step further. It is necessary to point out that in general, the young offenders accepted constructive criticism and were pleased to receive the advice that they were given by those running the workshop, which was aimed at improving their writing, spelling and the readability of their work. In the process of creating their texts, the young people were capable of identifying, finding and selecting the information that they needed, and after taking it on board and structuring it, they finally generated new ideas, new opinions and new realities.

We were also aware of a reduction in their rejection, insecurities or fear towards the outside world and towards the so-called official culture, thanks to the first comments that their blogs received. Certain prejudices about the outside world disappeared: the contributions brought about a feeling of being connected, of belonging to society, and they became positive and normalising points of reference. Not only did they stir interest in their own right, they also made the inmates feel that they were interesting. At that moment, the degree of responsibility and commitment on the part of the inmates made it looks as if the project was on the road to success. The inmates not only worked on their blogs on the days when it was programmed, more often than not, they would visit the Òmnia point in their free time as part of their daily routine (Franganillo, Burgos, García, & Tomàs, 2008). Even so, there were still weak points that needed the intervention of those running the workshop.

Some Obstacles

Right from the start of the workshop, we tried to show the young offenders that the blogs were part of an educational and cultural activity, and that their contributions should be seen in this context. They were personal blogs, but they should not be used as a tool for private communication, but rather as a medium for socialising in which, as with any means of public communication, there should be no place for certain declarations or opinions that could show a lack of respect or be offensive to some people. On the whole, the inmate population rejects and does not understand certain social norms and conventions. To this, it is necessary to add that being held in a detention centre affects the inmates' conception of reality and of their own situation. This led to some of the participants reading into certain indications a judgemental attitude, with the consequent refusal to continue participating in the activity.

In order to dispel such notions, and well aware that pointing out that the detention centre was there to act as an educational agent would not be seen as a convincing argument, it was decided to use the example of public libraries and the Òmnia point. We explained what their mission and objectives are, and why there must not be any type of ideological, political or religious censorship. All of that gave rise to the workshop, on many occasions, becoming the pretext for debate and reflection on what education is and what it is for, as well as the reasons behind social norms, rules and the law, or where the limits of freedom are. These were moments of dialogue, respect, acceptance of others and the possibility for some to learn from others, establishing interpersonal relationships and the group cohering. They were, then, enriching and necessary moments (Burgos, García, & Tomàs, 2007).

Results and Repercussions

The Internet allows us access to a wide range of information and educational resources; it thus enables the creation of rich and varied learning contexts. But within a prison, the Internet can only realise this potential if, recognising the value of its content, there is no limit placed on access, beyond situations that may compromise security. Internet access without barriers can serve to guarantee the participation of the prisoners in the information society and allow them to maintain the vital points of reference they need with life on the outside. Taking on the responsibility to provide such access implies a greater educational commitment than acquiring computers or giving courses that teach how to use them (Burbules & Callister, 2001). In response to this argument, the librarian and the Òmnia point manager agreed, for the start of the workshop described herein, to provide unlimited Internet access on a trial basis. It would have been a contradiction to plan an activity based on the Internet without real contact with the worldwide web. In keeping with the security protocols of the prison environment, those in charge of the activity took responsibility for controlling the use of the web. This control was initially established as a security measure, but also as part of the educational process, since education fosters the adoption of responsible attitudes.

The publicity that the project received within different groups of professional and through some mass media increased the interaction between the participants in the activity and Internet users on the outside, thanks to the contributions made by the latter. The prisoners saw these comments as a two-way link between the prison and the outside world (from the inside to the outside, and vice versa): the users on the outside have the chance to change their preconceived ideas and challenge the stereotypes concerning the prison population. Meanwhile the inmates, for their part, far from appearing like people locked up in prison, reflect the typical characteristics of any young person.

The interest that their writing attracted represented, for the inmates, a stimulus for self-appraisal, for learning and for the continuity of the activity; and it helped to consolidate their degree of involvement with the blogs and the need to write interesting posts for their readers. This symbiosis was a constructive exchange. The evolution of the activity, through involvement and commitment, had the effect of ensuring responsible and effective use of the technology and of free access to the Internet. The prisoners learned to act as autonomous users who take responsibility for their blog through making their own decisions. They had the valuable support of the Òmnia point manager and of the librarian, but without being bound by their suggestions.

We can assume that the growth of the blogs was in parallel to the personal, sociocultural and educational growth of the inmates. It is clear that experiences such as this strengthen the prison library and the Òmnia project as socialising and integrating spaces. But only the united action of all the agents involved in the process of learning can establish conditions that genuinely facilitate the inclusion of inmates in society.

CONCLUSION AND DECLARATION

The chaotic overload of information to which we have become accustomed in the new globalised society clearly demonstrates the importance of digital literacy, as a set of skills inevitably linked to other forms of literacy. These skills have emerged in response to the needs of a more complex information environment, with new technology and a greater variety of mass media. The digital world is a tangled and unpredictable setting in which it pays to know how to get around so as to be able to determine the value of its contents, which are often of very low quality. So, digital education faces the challenge of promoting the skills necessary to find, analyse and use the most useful and pertinent information in each situation.

Publishing content on the Internet is an important experience, if one is involved in writing and web design; two disciplines in which it is vital that inmates develop skills associated with reading and writing by means of links that connect one piece of information with others that are related to it. Blogs, as on-line content management systems, are a particularly suitable instrument to teach and learn disciplines that require proficiency in Internet culture, and interactive and hypertext languages. They allow the inmate to practice writing hypertext in a relatively simple way and without the need for great knowledge of graphic design or programming (Orihuela & Santos, 2004). Therefore, the possibility of running the workshop represented an exceptional opportunity to supply them with the tools necessary to acquire skills at handling information and, going even further, to integrate themselves into web culture.

However, nothing is easy behind bars, which may seem evident: having been programmed and with the corresponding authorisation, the workshop activity had to wait six months due to an incident at the Òmnia point which meant that the computers could not connect to the Internet. Indeed, even once that hurdle had been overcome, the Òmnia point was not always up and running: the instability of the electrical power supply and the unsuitability of the computing equipment caused frequent power outages and breaks in the connection. These brought activity to a standstill on numerous occasions, and broke up the continuity of the workshop. All these adverse circumstances are not isolated within a prison setting: the library also faces a series of limitations, especially economic, that effectively silence it, and it may well be thought that so many shortcomings are due to the fact that investing in detention centres is unpopular and does not generate votes at elections.

The prison is a setting in which the Òmnia project faces a challenge, at the same time as it represents a great opportunity for the project to demonstrate that it is a plan that aims to guarantee truly universal access to ICT, and that it must make it possible for everyone to participate, irrespective of their condition. These are some of the principles of the project: noble principles that are only effective if the infrastructure works correctly. The mission of Òmnia within prisons shares the same philosophy as the library and complements its mission. Precisely for that reason, Internet access should be a service integrated within the library, and not physically separated, as it was in the Barcelona Youth Detention Centre. Only if access is offered from the library can Òmnia contribute effectively to overcoming the digital divide and combating several illiteracies at once.

It is known that information management is a profession that includes a rich variety of profiles. Moreover, those of us who work as information professionals have been able to tackle the challenges that spring up in very varied settings efficiently. We still have pending, however, a challenge that we should tackle urgently and without fear: to eliminate the drawbacks that do not allow the prison library to advance along established lines or to create its own path forward. This key piece of the socialising machinery of prisons requires more resources. Guaranteeing access to information is, in addition to a fundamental function, one of the most complex issues a prison library faces. Physical, cultural and technological barriers, as well as those that are inevitable in a prison, make the way forward difficult for the library to become a tool that is suitable for the real needs of the prisoners. Prison libraries need more resources, and are open to any contribution from outside. The authorities should be more involved, and library studies professionals should attend to that need.

REFERENCES

American Library Association. (1989). Presidential Committee on Information Literacy: final report. In G. E. Menshing & T. B. Menshing (Eds.), *Coping with information illiteracy: bibliographic instruction for the information age* (pp. 156–171). Ann Arbor, MI: Pierian Press. Retrieved from http://ala.org/acrl/publications/whitepapers/presidential

Barreiro, M., Novo, I., & Varela, L. (2013). e-Prisons and new technologies: ICT as a mechanism of social inclusions of prisoners. *International Journal of Knowledge Society Research*, *4*(3), 1–10. doi:10.4018/ijksr.2013070101

Boó, E., Sancenón, E., & Zino, J. (2014, January). Una experiencia con las TIC en la educación social de prisiones: nuevas metodologías para nuevos tiempos. *Revista de Educación Social*, no. 18. Retrieved from http://eduso.net/res/pdf/18/e2e10_res_18.pdf

Burbules, N. C., & Callister, T. A. (2001). *Educación: riesgos y promesas de las nuevas tecnologías de la información*. Barcelona: Granica.

Burgos, L., García, A., & Tomàs, C. (2007). El blog desde la prisión: un instrumento de inclusión social. *Educación y biblioteca, 19*(158), 102–109.

Campbell, B. (1990). What is literacy? Acquiring and using literacy skills. *Australasian Public Libraries and Information Services*, (3): 149–152.

Castell, L., Pallisé, J. M., Pedrola, N., Tomàs, C., & Burgos, L. (2004, December). Art pop i curtmetratges a una biblioteca penitenciària. *BiD: textos universitaris de biblioteconomia i documentació*, no. 13. Retrieved from http://www.ub.edu/bid/13tomas.htm

Catalonia General Subdirectorate for Rehabilitation and Health Programs. (2011). *El model de rehabilitació a les presons catalanes*. Barcelona: General Directorate of Penitentiary Services. Retrieved from http://justicia.gencat.cat/web/.content/enllacos/pdf/model_rehabilitacio_presons_catalanes.pdf

Comalat, M., & Sulé, A. (2007). *Directrices para las bibliotecas de prisión de Cataluña*. Barcelona: Collegi Oficial de Bibliotecaris-Documentalistes de Catalunya. Retrieved from http://cobdc.org/publica/directrius/presons_cast.pdf

Elvira-Valdés, M. A. (2014). Presos 2.0: comunicación y TIC en contextos de encarcelamiento. *Perspectivas de la Comunicación, 7*(1), 84–96. Retrieved from http://publicacionescienciassociales.ufro.cl/index.php/perspectivas/article/view/217

Franganillo, J., & Burgos, L. (2007, January-March). Blocs a la biblioteca penitenciària: un taller de dinamització cultural. *Item: revista de biblioteconomia i documentació, 45*, 87-104. Retrieved from http://raco.cat/index.php/Item/article/view/72724/129379

Franganillo, J., Burgos, L., García, A., & Tomàs, C. (2008). Alfabetización digital en la prisión: una experiencia con jóvenes internos. Congreso Internacional de Alfabetización Tecnológica (2nd: November-December 2006: Badajoz). In *Actas del II Congreso Internacional de Alfabetización Tecnológica: superando la brecha digital*. Badajoz: Fundación Ciudadanía; AUPEX; Consorcio Identic. Retrieved from http://eprints.rclis.org/8538

Gutiérrez, A. (2003). *Alfabetización digital: algo más que ratones y teclas*. Barcelona: Gedisa.

Kellner, D. M. (2004). Revolución tecnológica, alfabetismos múltiples y la reestructuración de la educación. In I. Snyder (Ed.), *Alfabetismos digitales: comunicación, innovación y educación en la era electrónica*. Málaga: Aljibe.

Lehman, V., & Locke, J. (2006). *Guidelines for library services to prisoners*. IFLA Professional Reports, no. 92. Retrieved from http://ifla.org/files/assets/hq/publications/professional-report/92.pdf

Orihuela, J. L., & Santos, M. L. (2004, July 24). Los weblogs como herramienta educativa. *Quaderns Digitals*. Retrieved from http://quadernsdigitals.net/datos_web/hemeroteca/r_1/nr_558/a_7751/7751.html

Pauné, M. M. (2011, March 28). La vida en la cárcel, retratada por jóvenes presos. *La Vanguardia*. Retrieved from http://lavanguardia.com/cultura/20110328/54131696311/la-vida-en-la-carcel-retratada-por-jovenes-presos.html

Pérez Pulido, M. (1997). Acerca de las bibliotecas de prisiones y sus servicios. *Educación y biblioteca, 85*, 40–44.

Pérez Pulido, M. (2002). Análisis de la percepción de una biblioteca de prisión por parte de la comunidad reclusa: propuesta metodológica basada en un estudio de caso. *Forinfo: revista iberoamericana de usuarios de información, 18*, 6–34.

Pérez Pulido, M. (2010). Programs promoting reading in Spanish prisons. *IFLA Journal, 36*(2), 131–137. doi:10.1177/0340035210369875

Pérez Pulido, M., & De Angelo, C. (2011). Library services in Spanish prisons: Current state of affairs. *Library Trends, 59*(3), 460–472. doi:10.1353/lib.2011.0009

Rader, H. B. (1990). Information literacy: A revolution in the library. *Research Quarterly, 31*(1), 25–29.

Rocha, D. G. S., & da Silva, L. J. O. L. (2016). Competências e-infocomunicacionais em contexto prisional: Proposta de um modelo de formação. *Ciência da Informação, 45*(2), 41–51. http://revista.ibict.br/ciinf/article/view/3800

Rudolph, J., Smith, P., & Argall, R. (1996). *The library literate*. Dubuque, IA: Kendall/Hunt.

Sulé, A. (2005). Serveis de dinamització cultural. In *Les biblioteques de presó a Catalunya*. Doctoral dissertation. Retrieved from http://tdx.cat/handle/10803/2901

Sulé, A. (2006, June). Recomanacions de serveis bibliotecaris per a interns. *BiD: textos universitaris de biblioteconomia i documentació*, no. 16. Retrieved from http://bid.ub.edu/16sule.htm

Tronbacke, B. (2010). *Guidelines for easy-to-read materials*. Revision by Misako Nomura, Gyda Skat Nielsen and Bror Tronbacke on behalf of the IFLA/Library Services to People with Special Needs Section. The Hague: International Federation of Library Associations and Institutions. Retrieved from http://ifla.org/files/assets/hq/publications/professional-report/120.pdf

Zino, J., & Martín, E. (2012, March). La utilización de las narrativas digitales como factor de empoderamiento en el ámbito penitenciario. *International Conference Digital Storytelling*. Retrieved from http://roderic.uv.es/handle/10550/25600

ADDITIONAL READING

Aguilera, J., & Novella, A. (2007, April 18). «Bloggers des de la presó» [vídeo]. *Telenotícies Migdia*. Televisió de Catalunya, TV3. <http://www.ccma.cat/tv3/alacarta/programa/titol-video/video/226041956>

Berrios, O. (2006, December 21). «Alfabetización digital en prisión: jóvenes internos se asoman a la libertad con sus blogs». *CanalSolidario.org*. <http://canalsolidario.org/noticia/8338>

Burgos, L., & García, A. (2007, January 13). Interview [radio broadcast]. *Trestizaje*. Radio Nacional de España, Radio 3. <https://franganillo.es/trestizaje.mp3>

Burgos, L., & García, A. (2007, April 25). Interview [radio broadcast]. *La Malla*. COMRàdio. <https://franganillo.es/lamalla.mp3>

Burgos, L., García, A., Tomàs, C., & inmates of the Barcelona Youth Detention Centre (2007, February 12). Interview [radio broadcast]. *Siglo 21*. Radio Nacional de España, Radio 3. <https://franganillo.es/siglo21.wma>

Carlos. *Consejos para JASP*. <http://jovenesjasp.blogspot.com.es>

Chicass10, blog from the Teixeiro Detention Facility (A Coruña). <http://chicass10.blogspot.com.es>

Cisquella, G., & Rodríguez, M. (2008, July 2). «A un clic del mundo... y tan lejos de él» [TV programme]. *Cámara Abierta 2.0*. Televisión Española, TVE-2. <http://rtve.es/v/206054>

Criado, M. A. «El blog de la cárcel». *El Mundo*, 28 de abril de 2007. <http://elmundo.es/navegante/2007/04/28/tecnologia/1177773667.html>

Daniel & Michael (inmates of the Barcelona Youth Detention Centre) (2007, January 31). Interview [radio broadcast]. *El matí a quatre bandes*. Radio Nacional de España, Ràdio 4. <https://franganillo.es/mati4bandes.mp3>

Daniel. *Club del libro*. <http://club-dellibro.blogspot.com.es>

Daniel. *Mis segundas partes sí fueron buenas*. <http://todohumor2.blogspot.com.es>

Daniel. *Mucho humor*. <http://todo-humor.blogspot.com.es>

Domingo. *Limón naranja*. <http://limonnaranja.blogspot.com.es>

Domingo. *Mundo de colores*. <http://domingo-mundocolor.blogspot.com.es>

El blog de la cárcel, blog from the A Lama Detention Facility (Pontevedra). <http://blogcarcelalama.blogspot.com.es>

Europa Press. (2007, April 22). «"Bloggers desde la prisión" recibe el premio Ciudad del Conocimiento 2007». *La Vanguardia*. <http://lavanguardia.com/tecnologia/20070420/51332254048>

José Luis. *Cultura y arte*. <http://cultura-arte.blogspot.com.es>

José Luis. *Memorias cautivas*. <http://memoriascautivas.blogspot.com.es>

Juanjo. *Sin mente, pero con ganas*. <http://juanjitoblog.blogspot.com.es>

Michael & Álex. *Amigos tras las rejas*. <http://dabura8.blogspot.com.es>

Molist, M. (2007, May 10). «Bloggers desde la cárcel: la Trinitat emplea el blog como instrumento de inclusión social del preso». *Ciberpaís*, p. 1 & 3. <http://elpais.com/diario/2007/05/10/ciberpais/1178763867_850215.html>

Morán, A. (2007, February 24) «Blogs desde la prisión, parcelas de libertad detrás de las rejas». *Informativos Telecinco*. <http://informativos.telecinco.es/blogs/prision/internet/dn_42337.htm>

Pablo & Aaron. *Los confinados*. <http://confinados.blogspot.com.es>

Río, R. (2007, November 11). «Diario desde la cárcel». *El Periódico*, p. 36–37. <http://elperiodico.com/es/barcelona/20071111/diario-desde-la-carcel-i-5492451> & <http://elperiodico.com/es/barcelona/20071111/diario-desde-la-carcel-ii-5492452>

Yoskairo. *Dominicanízate*. <http://sazon-dominicano.blogspot.com.es>

KEY TERMS AND DEFINITIONS

Media Literacy: Ability to critically assess the accuracy and validity of information transmitted by the mass media (press, television, radio, and the internet) and to produce information via any medium.

Xarxa Òmnia: A program that fosters social inclusion through offering access to ICT tools. The Òmnia network is a preventative, socio-educational, community and support program for collectives who are at the greatest risk of vulnerability. It aims to encourage, both individually as collectively, inclusion and links between the people in the community. It is directed at the general population, paying special attention to people at social risk, especially if they need to improve their capacity to overcome their difficulties in accessing ICT, with the aim of preventing their exclusion from the community.

ENDNOTES

1 The Spanish law *Royal Decree 190/1996 which approves prison regulations* limits (art. 129) the possession of private personal computers to educational or training purposes, when this is justified by the prisoner and supported by a teacher or tutor. It prohibits the transmission of information from storage devices and connections to computer networks. It also leaves it for the internal rules and regulations of each correctional centre to decide on the norms for the use of computers and IT materials as communal tools for the different educational, training and treatment programmes. Although the *Organic Law 1/79 on general prison matters* (art. 51) and the prison regulations (art. 46–47) do not explicitly regulate devices for communicating with the outside world, for example, e-mail or chats, the security protocols at Òmnia points do forbid prisoners from using them.

Chapter 8
Inmate Communication as a Conscientization Approach to Societal Mainstreaming

Benjamina Gonzalez Flor
University of the Philippines Los Baños, Philippines

Leandra Carolina Gonzalez Flor
University of the Philippines Los Baños, Philippines

ABSTRACT

This chapter submits that societal mainstreaming of ex-convicts to have a normal life is possible through inmate communication. Inmate communication is a conscientization approach that consists of a holistic strategy to nourish the head, heart, hand, and soul of an inmate, the prison management, and the society. While restorative justice aims to reintegrate inmates once they have served their sentences, life for an ex-convict outside may no longer be the same. A condescending society condemns "convicts as convicts for life" no matter how much they have changed because of the rehabilitation efforts of the government to reform them. The case in point is the National Bilibid Prison, the biggest prison facility that houses more than 22,000 most dangerous inmates in Metro Manila, Philippines who have committed heinous crimes to serve their sentences. Media materials that can nurture the mind such as poems, songs, bookmarks, jingles, letters, etc. for instance that bear words and thoughts of endearment can build a positive attitude and look forward to an accepting society.

DOI: 10.4018/978-1-5225-5975-7.ch008

INTRODUCTION

Prisoners face maltreatment because they are viewed as menace to society. They are ridiculed and shun upon for the wrong deeds committed. However, it is universally acknowledged that criminals are a product of the society. Radical views tend to suggest that social class structures, socio-economic dynamics and socio-cultural injustices bleed criminality (Maburi, 2009). In essence, the society is obliged to foster prisoners, to an extent, once they serve their sentences and attempt to reintegrate themselves and reduce the likeliness of recidivism in the process. Recidivism is the act of a person repeating an undesirable behavior after they had either experienced negative consequences of the behavior, or had been trained to extinguish that behavior.

Being imprisoned for erring individuals is giving prisoners a chance to rethink while serving their sentences what they have done which could eventually reform them in confinement. Ironically, in the Philippines, life behind bars faces challenges and difficulties that are no better than life outside. Prisoners also experience plights of their own including overcrowding, hunger, poor hygiene and sanitation facilities, violence, lack of rehabilitation measures, and a slow-moving justice system (Philippine prisons overflowing with hungry inmates, 2017). Prison population, including pre-trial detainees and remand prisoners, are currently at a total of 178,661, a 436% increase in 2017 (The Condition of Philippine Prison and Jails). While several programs are being implemented to support prisoners' welfare and development in serving their time, a structured transition program has to be designed and implemented by the Government to further assist prisoners in reintegrating themselves in society.

A proper and smooth reintegration of prisoners in the society does not only ensure their welfare but also lessens the tendency of recidivism. Reintegration programs aim to assist ex-prisoners in acquiring skills, knowledge, and access to government support system that will enable them to start over upon release. Ex-prisoners are envisioned to have a 'second shot' at being productive citizens of the society, and they will also be able to live a dignified life away from the plights of being 'criminals' behind bars.

With these arguments, the Philippines has to start rethinking of its correctional and post-correctional programs that will support prisoners as they seek for reformation and assist them in becoming productive members of the society.

Correctional and post-correctional programs for ex-prisoners are critical for several reasons: 1) to reduce prison population; 2) to reduce the likeliness of recidivism; and 3) to ensure safety and security of the members of the community.

Therefore, could the problem lie on communication? Should management need to be more humane and change how they communicate with inmates? Should they need to talk to them and not at them? Should they think of a more innovative way of communicating their reformation process? This chapter then aims to determine how inmate communication can be used as a tool for ex-convicts' societal mainstreaming.

BACKGROUND

Republic Act 10575 or the Bureau of Corrections (BuCor) Act of 2013 enacted on 24 May mandates that "the state should promote the general welfare and safeguard the basic rights of every prisoner incarcerated in the national penitentiary. It also recognizes the responsibility of the State to strengthen government capability aimed towards the institutionalization of highly efficient and competent correctional services. Thus, the State shall provide for the modernization, professionalization, and restructuring of BuCor by upgrading its facilities, increasing the number of its personnel, upgrading the level of qualifications of their personnel and standardizing their base pay, retirement, and other benefits.

It also recognizes the responsibility of the State to strengthen government capability aimed towards the institutionalization of highly efficient and competent correctional services. In RA 10575, the BuCor is in charge of safekeeping and instituting reformation programs to national inmates sentenced to more than three years. The safekeeping of inmates shall include decent provision of quarters, food, water and clothing in compliance with established United Nations standards. The Custodial Force consisting of Corrections Officers with a ranking system and salary grades similar to its counterpart in the Bureau of Jail Management Penitentiary undertakes the security of the inmates.

National inmates should also be assisted through reformation programs, which will be instituted by the BuCor and should consist of the following holistic approach:

1. Moral and Spiritual Program;
2. Education and Training Program;
3. Work and Livelihood Program;
4. Sports and Recreation Program;
5. Health and Welfare Program; and
6. Behavior Modification Program, to include Therapeutic Community.

Professional Reformation Personnel consisting of Corrections Technical Officers with ranking system and salary grades similar to Corrections Officers must undertake these reformation programs. These officers must be composed of the following:

1. Corrections Technical Officers are personnel employed in the implementation of reformation programs and those personnel whose nature of work requires proximate or direct contact with inmates.
2. Corrections Technical Officers include priests, evangelists, pastors, teachers, instructors, professors, vocational placement officers, librarians, guidance counselors, physicians, nurses, medical technologists, pharmacists, dentists, therapists, psychologists, psychiatrists, sociologists, social workers, engineers, electricians, agriculturists, veterinarians, lawyers and similar professional skills relevant to the implementation of inmate reformation programs.

Section 7 of RA 10575 also articulates the facilities that BuCor has to possess. It states that the BuCor shall operate with standard and uniform design of prison facilities, reformation facilities and administrative facilities, through all the operating prison and penal farms, such as the following:

1. Dormitory;
2. Administration building;
3. Perimeter/Security fences;
4. Hospital/Infirmary;
5. Recreation/Multipurpose hall;
6. Training/Lecture center;
7. Workshop facility;
8. Mess hall/kitchen;
9. Visiting area;
10. Water tank and pump;
11. Reception and diagnostic center; and
12. Service personnel facilities.

In line with RA 10575, there are several government-supported programs that are being implemented in the national prisons, especially at NBP. These programs are categorized as follows:

1. Literacy Program – Alternative Learning Systems by the Department of Education
2. Sports Development
3. Paralegal Services
4. Health/Medical & Dental

5. Religious & Spiritual Program
6. Art Therapy

There are also external livelihood programs conducted by several NGOs, but more specific to municipal prisons. Some of their programs include: 1) Carpentry; 2) Agriculture; 3) Arts and Crafts; 4) Sewing; and 5) Grooming and Cosmetology.

In realizing the provisions of the law especially on modernizing the facilities, it will entail huge amount of money, which the government may not afford to build, furnish, maintain and sustain operational requirements and custodial services. Thus, BuCor through the Private-Public Partnership Center of the National Economic Development Authority with support from the Asian Development Bank sought the assistance of a contracting firm to conduct a feasibility study on how best to improve current prison facilities. However, inasmuch as a number of reforms that need to be instituted would greatly affect major decisions to be made as far as safekeeping, reformation, and administration changes are concerned, a strategic communication analysis to implement the reforms among affected stakeholders was deemed necessary to ensure clarity and understanding of the intents of the law. Anchoring the plan on the intents of the law would be the best stance to promote the public-private partnership program.

As part of its technical assistance, the contracted firm has engaged a communication specialist to: a) conduct a public communications needs analysis involving the project; b) design mechanisms such as, but not limited to, workshops to generate feedback from stakeholders on critical aspects of the project, identify conflicting stances and facilitate communication aimed at finding mutually acceptable modes of collaboration among stakeholders; c) propose communication strategies across multiple stakeholders to address the identified communications needs which should be aligned with the objectives, solutions-orientation and positive messaging of the Philippine PPP program; and develop a communications plan, detailing out the phases of implementation, use of tools, including those online, to improve the engagement process of stakeholders, periodic monitoring and evaluation of the plan, and the cost of the plan. The Plan should also incorporate key message development, positioning and management of issues anticipated to arise in the key areas of the project such as economic and financial aspects, the environment, gender, and social safeguards, among others.

In spite of the significant progress in improving the management of prison facilities in the past decades, however, the Philippines is still struggling to keep up with an ever increasing demand for a more humane and rights-based penology. Prison facilities remain perennially plagued with the lack of physical appropriations and communication space that inmates direly need.

MAIN FOCUS OF THE CHAPTER

Correctional stage interventions must capture needs of various types of offenders and must also take into account their eventual re-integration into their communities. At the post-correctional stage, interventions should in essence re-integrate ex-prisoners back into their communities while addressing their psychological, social and economic resettlement needs. Some suggestions include addressing psycho-social needs of ex-prisoners through counseling, while economic needs can be met through funding or credit for income generating activities. Unfortunately, prisoners are often released from the institutions without adequate preparation for the outside world. The psychological disorientation, social stigma and economic hardships that they experience are at times overwhelming that they become vulnerable to the inevitable consequences of re-offending or recidivism (Maburi, 2009).

Ex-offenders also need compassion and understanding from the criminal justice system. They feel a mixture of joy and anxiety after years of being in prison, and wish to start over but not sure where and how to begin. Their needs include shelter, employment, and counseling. Sometimes, even a simple ride from prison to their destination is enough (Ferner, 2015). Their reintegration into the society should not just begin on Day 1 post-prison sentence but on the first day behind bars. A successful transition back in the community requires several phases to fully motivate ex-prisoners to start over. It was suggested to help prisoners acquire the skills set required to succeed in the community, address personal challenges, and factors associated with their criminal behavior, and establish necessary contacts and relationships in the community prior to their release (Griffiths, Dandurand, & Murdoch, 2007). An example of a 'Success in the Community' matrix that shows each phase of ex-prisoner reintegration and what activities under each life area can be done for an ideal transition is hereby presented (Figure 1).

The Government of Canada, on the other hand, offered a comprehensive crime prevention program that includes effective measures to reduce the risk of recidivism of ex-offenders. It was suggested that a key feature of social reintegration of ex-prisoners into the community is the development of interventions that are designed to reduce the levels of recidivism, including substance abuse and unemployment. Evidence shows that positive reintegration outcomes are attained when factors predisposing a person to criminal behavior are addressed in a holistic fashion and where their physical and social needs of ex-offenders are supported both within the prison and after their release (Travis, Solomon, & Waul, 2001).

Social reintegration encompasses a number of interventions following an arrest that include restorative justice process and suitable treatment while awaiting trial and sentence. Prisoners, in the first place, have experienced a range of social, economic and personal challenges that triggered committing crimes that they had. These

Figure 1. Ex-prisoners' success in the community matrix

PHASE	BASIC LIFE AREAS					
	Livelihood	**Residence**	**Family**	**Health and sobriety**	**Criminal justice compliance**	**Social/civic connections**
Survival	• Gate money • Public assistance • Soup kitchens, pantries • Personal care kits	• Shelter • Family or friend • Street	• Find children • Make contact	• Continuity of medication • Relapse prevention	• Report to supervising authority (court, probation, parole, etc.) • Comply with requirements	• Receive peer support
Stabilization	• Public assistance/workfare • Employment or education training • Clothes for interviews	• Transitional residence • Family or friend	• Supervised visitation • Get refamiliarized • Trial discharge	• Drug treatment and treatment of urgent health and mental issues • Counseling	• Earn reduced supervision	• Join support group or nurturing community • Volunteer work
Self sufficiency	• Job that pays a living wage and provides benefits	• One's own apartment with public subsidy, if necessary	• Reunify • Participate in family counseling • Contribute to others	• Regular health visits paid by health insurance • Ongoing support, 12 step, therapy, community activities	• Satisfy conditions of supervision	• Help others • Contribute to community life
GOAL	• Adequate money for food, clothing, transportation, and personal and family expenses	• Safe, clean, affordable home that accomodates household comfortably	• Reunification with children • Reconciliation with family members	• Physically and mentally healthy, or receiving affordable quality care, including prescriptions	• Abide by laws • Live without community supervision	• Healthy friendships and network of supportive adults • Opportunities to give back, civic participation (voting, etc.)

Source: John Jay Prison Reentry Institute
Matrix originally developed by Ann L. Jacobs when Executive Director of Women's Prison Association, New York, NY.

THE HUFFINGTON POST

societal issues include social isolation and marginalization, physical or emotional abuse, poor employment or unemployment, and involvement in criminal lifestyle at an early age. Meanwhile, physical and mental disabilities, and health issues that might be related to substance abuse and drug addiction, lack or poor formal education/illiteracy/innumeracy, lack of planning and management skills are issues they might face upon release (Griffiths et. al., 2007).

There are three main types of offender reintegration: 1) Institution-based programs; 2) Surveillance-based transition programs; and 3) Assistance-based transition programs.

Institution-based programs are those designed to prepare offenders to re-enter society that include education, mental health care, substance abuse treatment, job training, counseling, and mentoring. On the other hand, surveillance-based programs are the ones centered on supervision of offenders in the community following release. Lastly, assistance-based programs are those designed for ex-prisoners with special needs such as mental illness and substance abuse. Addressing their needs in a holistic approach from correctional to post-correctional stages will help ex-prisoners' divert their attention from committing yet another criminal behavior into one that is more healthy and productive in the society.

Research studies have found that the most successful approach in reducing recidivism among offenders—both upon release over time—are prison-based and community-based therapeutic community models (MacKenzie, 1997). One study found that "prisoners who participated in in-prison and community aftercare programming had a three-year re-incarceration rate of 27% as opposed to prisoners who had failed to participate in aftercare treatment services, and prisoners in the "no treatment" control group, had three-year re-incarceration rates of 82, 79, and 75%, respectively (Wexler, Melnick, Lowe, & Peters, 1999).

It also suggested some interventions to address the dynamic risk factors of offenders that have a higher chance of success if there is adherence to the 'principles of effective correctional treatment' as set out by Bonta, Law, and Hanson (1998). For offender reentry programs, it is becoming clear that successful interventions are those which:

1. Focus on a specific target group of offenders and their specific challenges;
2. Rely on sound methods for assessing the needs and risk factors of offenders;
3. Hold the offenders accountable and responsible for their own choices and their actions;
4. Begin while the offender is in confinement in the correctional institution and continue throughout the offender's transition to, and stabilization in, the community (through care);
5. Are offered as a coordinated effort of all agencies involved and supported by strong agency cooperation (supported by partnerships and interagency cooperation and information protocols, clear definition of respective roles and responsibilities; and a clear articulation of services to be provided and the relevant time frames);

6. Are supported by sound case management practices and adequate information management systems;
7. Reflect the public safety priorities of the community in which they are developed;
8. Engage the community in both the planning and the delivery of the intervention and fosters strong community ownership; and
9. Have a robust evaluation component that allows the program to evolve, self-improve, and remain accountable to the community for crime reduction results.

There are some significant cases of successful correctional and post-correctional programs that have proven that design and implementation of which is possible provided that government structures are in place.

In Louisiana, USA, the State allows younger inmates who qualify to learn a trade such as plumbing, welding, and culinary arts, and also provides hours on anger management and communication sessions. On the other hand, San Quentin Prison, California, offers college-level education to inmates through the Prison University Project, the largest in-prison college program in the California Prison System. A 2013 Study from the National Criminal Justice Reference Service shows that in-prison college education programs did effectively lower recidivism rates; they also stayed crime-free longer than those who did not participate in the program due to having 'a sense of purpose' upon release. Singapore Prison Service, on the other hand, focuses on training staff members of facilities to assist an inmate through a prison-warden matching program where the warden is matched to an inmate whom they can mentor and assist during the course of their sentence and specialize their social reintegration preparation.

Some of these re-integration programs are provided at NBP. However, due to the increasing number of inmates, a more aggressive communication intervention is needed.

The Communication Environment

The Changing Theory and Practice of Communication. The existing communication environment in the Philippines needs to be analyzed to provide an appreciation of strategic options and communication tools that BuCor can use in communicating its plans and programs. At present, stakeholders internally and externally to an organization play a crucial role in achieving organizational goals and objectives. While RA 10575 has to be implemented within 90 days upon execution, it is a reality that many orientations, workshops, seminars, debates, fora, consultations, consensus building, and the like have to be carried out internally and to some extent externally. Of late, participants in the communication process are no longer seen as dominant sources and passive receivers but as co-equals. A slight deception from BuCor can ruin all plans. While the communication process nowadays treats participants as co-equals, credibility of the source is at stake. Public Relations or propaganda no longer work. The goal of communication is not anymore seen as persuasion or rhetoric but as mutual understanding. Therefore, communication campaigns should not be media-centric or source-oriented. Communication undertakings should be directed at not just changing behaviors but at transforming social norms, which determine behaviors. There has also been a pronounced change in communication practice. The role of communication in setting national agenda has been recognized. Laws, national policies, local ordinances are influenced or triggered by media coverage. Media has been known to make or break national leaders. So is mainstreaming noble initiatives such as modernizing, professionalizing, and upgrading the status of penitentiaries.

- **The Use of New Media:** New media refer to digital media such as the Internet, the World Wide Web, mobile devices such as hand phones, netbooks, pods, and social networks such as Facebook, Twitter, Tumbler, BlackBerry Messenger, Skype, IM, and other applications such as YouTube and wikis, cable television, digital radio, etc. Using these tools for greater awareness is the challenge on how to take advantage and transform those into action. Traditional Information, Education, and Communication strategies may not be enough to change people's behavior. Changing the norms such as the gang system in the penitentiaries may be difficult to change. Simply talking about reformation without deliberate action may not happen. BuCor should explore the use of the new media. The eDalaw services can be strengthened. Its website should be enhanced to make it more interactive and transparent. With smart phones, a message carried by BB platform, iPhone, MyPhone platforms has the potential of reaching millions considering that the Philippines' population is more than 100 million. Mobile phones are now becoming the device that every Juan or Maria owns, whether rich or poor. It has become the universally accepted medium for knowledge sharing and reuse.
- **Big Media, Small Media, my Media:** The tool use for national communication campaigns is no longer limited to the big media like national dailies, national television and radio networks. Little media such as community radio stations, community newspapers, and community cable television have been more and more co-opted in national media campaigns. Nowadays, another category besides Big Media and Little Media, have gained much prominence and an increasingly significant role in national media campaigns. This category, known as My Media, involves social networking using digital media such as Facebook, Twitter and YouTube that capitalizes on Web 2.0 or the provision

for user generated content in the World Wide Web, thus encouraging direct participation in the communication undertaking itself. One's Facebook page is actually one's published website. One's Twitter account becomes an individualized television channel considering Twitter's slogan, "Broadcast yourself." Online presence can strengthen people's understanding of the reformation process at NBP and therefore become more accepting of ex-prisoners once mainstreamed.

- **Networking:** Another element that is assuming a dominant role in today's communication undertakings is networking. A network is a structure made up of nodes and links. Networking involves establishing links among like-minded nodes. Networks form the natural structures of living things. Thus, organisms, ecosystems, communities and societies are structured as networks, or networks of networks. Networks may be personal or social, individual or institutional, analog or digital, so long as there are nodes that are connected by links. Information travel via networks, knowledge is shared through networks. Thus, networking has become a built-in, common strategy in most IEC activities or communication campaigns. Since BuCor is working closely with non-government Organizations (NGOs); civil society; and the private sector, linkages should be strengthened. Civil society, itself, is composed of: the Church; media; schools; and socio-civic organizations. Even if non-profit in nature, non-government organizations are differentiated from civil society groups since the former are organizations who perform services parallel to government agencies and are thus registered as such. Similarly, although privately run, NGOs differ from the private sector in the sense that the latter is profit-oriented. Another phrase used for the private sector is the business sector or the corporate sector.
- **Indigenous and Local Communication:** Communication materials like komiks may still be appropriate given the nature of Filipinos who are fun of reading and learning moral lessons from those stories. Reformation can be communicated through this medium more so if these are translated in major local dialects like Ilocano, Cebuano, Ilonggo, and the like. Balagtasan, balitaw, plays, rap, singing, interpretative dances or puppet shows can be explored as presentation of messages in the prison facilities. These will not only bring enjoyment but unleashed the inmates' creativity and talent in expressing themselves and drawing out deep feelings and sentiments of their unfortunate circumstances. Actors like Robin Padilla can be invited for inspirational messages or talks or as endorsers to promote reformation programs.

- **Distance Learning:** The use of electronic media did not only hasten communication but education access as well. More and more universities locally and internationally have offered online courses that range from certificate, diploma, bachelors, masters, and even doctorate degrees. The UP Open University for instance offers all programs 100 percent online. Alternatively, examinations may be conducted at the facilities if needed.
- **Conscientization Approach:** Adult learning stems from experience. According to Freire (1972), hinging experience to real life situations can change how people view one's self in a given environment. As a communication strategy, conscientization digs deeper into relationship of inmates with one another to be liberated from the bondage of ignorance and animosity. However, conscientization requires training of staff and jail guards on how to unleash inmate's inner desire to reform. Some forms of conscientization could include exposure to media collaterals bearing words of endearment, affirmation, light of hope, spiritual reminders, songs, poems among others made visible and accessible to inmates and management. Walls can be transformed into galleries where encouraging communication materials to develop a positive outlook of the future or what is in store for inmates when they leave the penitentiary for good. Through exposure to pictures or text, inmates can reflect on their situations and eventually would act as a reformatory action. For instance, an inmate who is constantly exposed to words of endearment and caring environment would have a positive mindset and might lead to developing the thought of a brighter future ahead. On the other hand, an inmate who is surrounded by ill words and derogatory utterances would further push their morale down and perpetuate wrongdoing. An example would be the song "Tie a yellow ribbon." This song is not only reassuring but inspiring as well because it denotes a happier future.

In other words, a more accommodating and reformatory abode can hasten change, which could consequently provide a communication space for them to act and reflect on their actions. In like manner, staff and jail guards who are exposed to these media collaterals will be reminded to control their temper and have more compassion to people who have erred and are willing to reform.

ISSUES, CONTROVERSIES, PROBLEMS

Based on secondary data gathered by the social scientist, gender specialist, legal officer, BuCor's consultant, and personal observations made, these issues and concerns at NBP can be clustered into the following dominant themes (Flor, 2013):

The Inmates'

- **Physical, Environmental, and Economic Issues:** At present, the overall feeling when one enters the maximum security arena is "barangay-like," or the smallest political unit in the country with businesses operated by inmates (business kiosks, increasing number of inmates, type of goods, income generating activities; business establishments (massage services, hair cut); congested, and livelihood of inmates selling different kinds of street foods, other stuff much like sari-sari (a small shop that sells items in small sachets, quantity or volume) stores. Such establishments make the place rowdy and messy. The environment though clean smells, which may be due to the open canals but also perhaps, lack of sufficient toiletries for better hygiene and sanitation of inmates. In the new facility, definitely these features and accommodations will not be tolerated. However, how will taking away their businesses affect sending of income generated to their families?
- **Social Relationships:** The presence of "gang system" at the NBP numbering 13 or so where each one has allotted space; separate rules; legitimate organizations within NBP; international plaza where all gangs converged as a group were there are suspected clandestine operations. If the gangs need to be disintegrated, what reforms have to be in place? What urge members to form into regional groups? Definitely, this goes back to self-concept of being part of a group. Being "alone" in this kind of environment definitely, one would tend to cling to somebody that they can hold on to or depend on.
- **Security Issues**: While security and safety need to be ensured and in the spirit of disciplinary action, jail guards sometimes resort to violence. This is not at all acceptable because this is a violation of human rights. Jail guards who are ill tempered should be reprimanded or trained to be more emphatic and sympathetic especially to emotionally and psychologically impaired inmates.
- **Emotional and Psychological State:** It was apparent that conditions inside NBP could hasten emotional and psychological stress given the crowded and congested conditions. While the number is not much, inmates who have to be rehabilitated do not get well due to harsh treatments of jail guards.
- **Conjugal Visits:** The cramp cells are not suitable for conjugal and family visits. The "kubol" (booth) system may be a good innovation but kind of embarrassing especially for women and children. The "kubo" (nipa hut) system for high profile prisoners should also be looked into. These are special arrangements made within the penitentiary to sustain peace and order. Once the new facility is in place, most likely this system will die a natural death.

Economically viable businesses will die. The fear that talented inmates may no longer be able to earn a decent living because the new facility is far and no visitors might come to buy their products. However, if these products can commercially be packaged and sold in department stores or other outlets aside from the facility, inmates will earn more. As well, loss of economic activities around facilities will affect many entrepreneurs' socio-economic conditions once these are transferred. The same will affect taxes and money supply in the locality.

The Staff and Employees'

- **Fear of Losing one's Roots.** As the saying goes "there's no life without roots," old employees fear that they will leave their roots behind given the proposed transfer plans. Leaving their abode and transferring to a new location where hardly anyone lives is a hurdle indeed.
- **Lack of Amenities in the new Prison Facility:** Staff and employees are apprehensive that the new place will have no housing facilities, no markets, no school, no churches, no malls, no night life, no recreational outlets, and never would be like Metro Manila. Living in the metro all their lives is something that would be difficult to replicate. Of course, BuCor has to implement the law and for all its intents and purposes they should also be ready to legally and properly provide basic necessities.
- **Wife or Husbands' Lack of Opportunity to Work in the New Facility:** Employees feel that if they will transfer to the new facility, their husbands or wives who are working in the metro may become jobless and thus the family income will not be sufficient to afford their needs.

Support Groups'

While compensatory policies of current proprietors are not pro-workers who are paid dismally (i.e. P18.00/pc and minimum of 25 pieces of handicraft divided by 5 workers or approximately P2,500/month divided by 5), inmates felt that this was a better alternative instead of loitering around or being under the sun. The little amount can somehow help defray personal expenses for self-hygiene, better food, and giving some money to family members when they come to visit them. There is also no assurance that they will establish their business, which is far from the city and may require higher overhead because of the transport cost and hauling services. As well, several civic organizations like Rotary, other NGOs, universities may not be willing to transfer their charitable works in the new facility due to costs to be incurred. There is a possibility that new partners will join and volunteer, though. However, given the new reformation programs, external support groups may no longer be needed. As well, if proprietors can pay inmates with daily wages coupled with SSS contributions and Philhealth insurance made available to families through bank accounts that they can withdraw from, reintegration in the society may be easier and faster. Building inmates' morale is very crucial in values formation. While the current practice is to create bank accounts for inmates' payments for products produced, family members cannot access those. Once the inmate dies, the bank account could either be frozen, goes back to the state or could be a source of corruption. Agricultural production should likewise be made more systematic and to treat inmates not simply as farm labor but producers and earners as well. In the absence of policies or manual of operations, the practice can again be in danger of corruption. Transparency in business operations should be publicized as means for governance communication at various levels through different communication platforms. Establishment of standards that are locally based is recommended instead of international standards, which are too western and may not be culturally acceptable and viable. Standards that are attuned to Filipino realities have to be developed to prepare inmates for reintegration without much difficulty in the outside world.

SOLUTIONS AND RECOMMENDATIONS

Discuss solutions and recommendations in dealing with the issues, controversies, or problems presented in the preceding section.

The following sentence is an example of a figure callout. Figure 1 is an example of a figure caption within a chapter.

Problems on implementation are beyond the scope of this paper. The focus of this argument is on how conscientization as a technique for reformation can be employed. Thus, while problems posed are general, the paper attempted to address the need for more appropriate and pragmatic reformation methods especially for diverse inmates in terms of age, social status, geographical location, occupations, crimes committed, length of sentence, spiritual affiliation, and educational attainment. Inmates have rights to be mainstreamed in order to become productive citizens of a country. While their circumstances are unfortunate, the society who dictates their future has to do something to correct wrong behaviors. Hence, allowing inmates to reflect on what they have done would lead to reformation and reintegration.

In the context of reintegration, therefore, inmate communication as a conscientization approach requires a different view, given the different types of stakeholders. Anchored on the circumstances that inmates are in, more humane and rights-based management is required. The conscientization approach requires different methods that may be used to strengthen reformation and restorative processes at the NBP.

The first is self-reflection. Self-reflection is a process that enables inmates to look into their inner selves and understand why they are imprisoned in the first place. Pictures, drawings, or poems posted around where they "live" as an enabling communication environment can help them to act towards reformation. It builds hope of seeing the light beyond the tunnel signifying that the end of their sentence is near. Their families are waiting to give them the long overdue warm embrace and acceptance (Figure 2).

The second is proactive action. Messages that call for action can conscienticize others to do the same. The process enables inmates to plan on what they are going to do upon their release. In the course of serving their sentence, they can prepare themselves to take short courses or livelihood training. This will prepare inmates to think critically and logically on the expectations that lie ahead. The outcome would be good deeds and readiness to go back to the fold on the hope that an accepting society awaits (Translation of text: Always remember that a smile awaits you: Figure 3).

The third is internalization. Internalization is a process of realizing reflections into a concrete understanding and acceptance towards reformation. Inmates will find time to talk to themselves (intrapersonal) and eventually resolve to change for the better. The internalization of messages can sink into one's mind and lead them to decide that there is a second chance for anyone who would want to take it. The assumption is that the inmate would resolve to change because of the recurring messages exposed to. The hope lingers associated with words of encouragement to

Figure 2. Path to freedom

Figure 3. A joy to cherish

move on so that the reformatory abode can hasten its fruition. (Translation: I am important! Face the mirror and ponder on your feelings. Say these words to your self…I love you! For the wrong things that I have done, my apologies, forgive me. Expect that I will change…To you I thank thee… because you remained steadfast despite everything. Don't forget the goodness of God, that somebody loves you my friend. Simple words, yet liberating…Figure 4)

The fourth is cultivation period. The cultivation process allows weighing the pros and cons of reformation to happen if the constant exposure to a message becomes a part of the daily routine. The nurturing of the mind can lead to changing norms and eventually behaviors. People in general tend to succumb to what is regularly fed may it be through face-to-face interaction or mediated. This is done through posting or providing communication materials which they cannot miss to read in areas they frequent like their bedrooms, dining area, meeting rooms, or the spiritual corner. Doing constant reminders become second nature in the procedure (Figure 5).

The fifth is Conviction to change. The process of change is a holistic involvement of all stakeholders to include management staff, jail guards, volunteers working within NBP in helping inmates in reforming themselves. The support of people surrounding inmates can encourage them to change for the better. The reassuring faces and treatment of fellow inmates can add value to the decision to change. Providing an enabling environment can help inmates realize that there is a better life outside of NBP and they have a right to have that life once more (Figure 6).

Figure 4. Feel important!

Figure 5. A bundle of thoughts

Figure 6. Bars of freedom

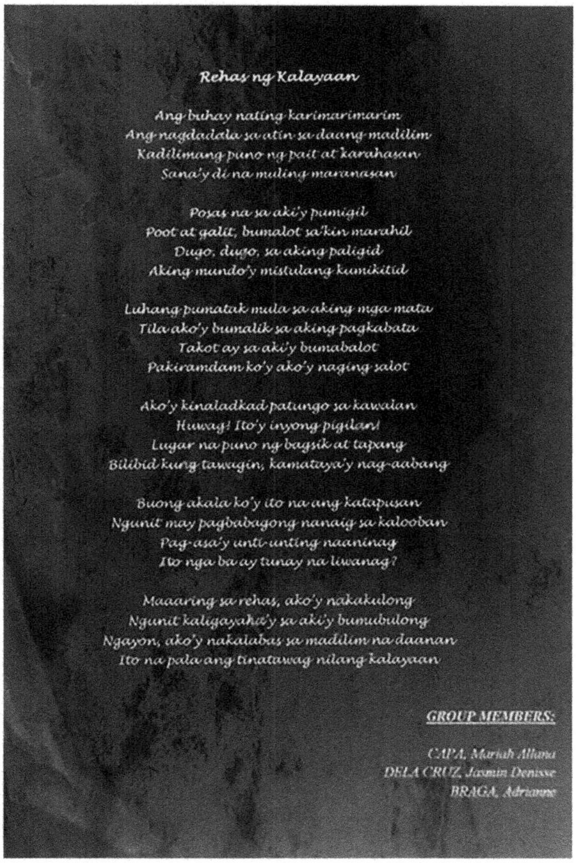

Translation: Bars of freedom. Our disgusting life brings us to a dark path, darkness that is full of bitterness and violence, which hopefully will not be experienced once again. Handcuffs that stopped me; Hatred and spite would have covered me; blood, blood all over the place, which made my world narrower. A tear fell from my eyes making me go back to my childhood; fear enveloped me. I feel that I'm a menace. I was dragged towards emptiness. Don't! Stop this. A place that is full of cruelty and violence. Jail it is called, death awaits. All the while I thought this is the end. However, something persisted from within. Slowly, hope clearly is seen. Is this a clear light? I could be behind bars but happiness whispers that I am out of the dark path which they call freedom.

The sixth is Spiritual anchor. This is one form of conscientization. Believing in a supreme being to hold on to enables people to discern right from wrong. Being an atheist gives men and women liberty to do what they want to do unlike if one was raised as God-fearing. The presence of spiritual guidance within the NBP can help inmates to repent and be sorry for their sins. This is evident at NBP with various denominations in place. However, communicating messages through visual media can strengthen their faith and hope to unleash them from the bondage of committing a crime (Figure 7).

Translation: Beyond the iron grills Serving your sentence for a crime done in the past can turn into sadness sometimes. Almost everything has to be taken away. The family and love ones. Not all crimes were simply committed; sometimes some crimes were inadvertent; may it be an influence or self-decision, you know that there is a reason for doing it. However, if you know that you are repenting, result could be peace with oneself. Remember your old happy self who has no problems and always smiling. Beyond the iron grills, there is hope ready to open; always remember that there is a smile waiting for you. A new life was given to you, offer it to God you because there is nothing more beautiful than the forgiveness of God the father.)

Figure 7. Trust in God

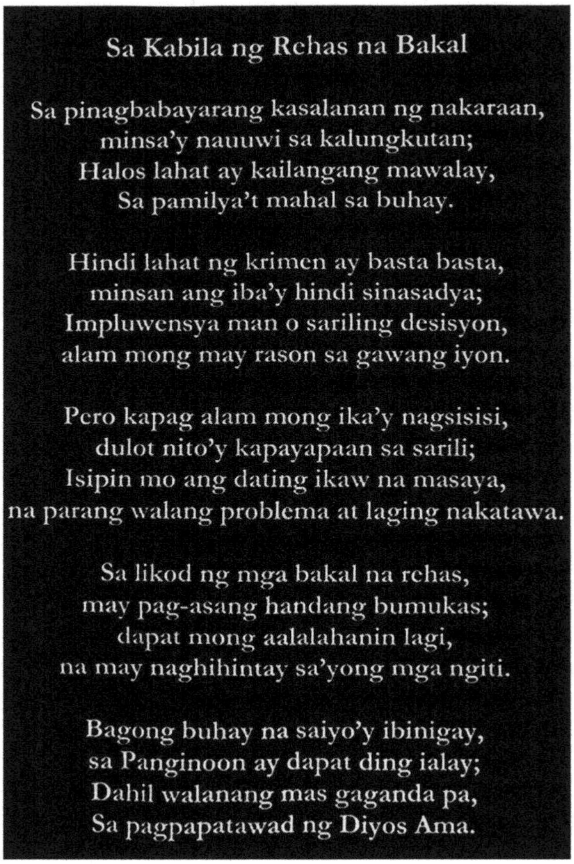

The seventh is Educational preparation. While the conscientization process is education or liberation from a current predicament, educating inmates who cannot read nor write must be done. Some inmates are highly educated but there are more who are illiterates. Alternative Learning Systems (ALS) like those offered by the Department of Education should incorporate in their curriculum anecdotes or short stories that inmates can reflect on instead of straightforward ABCs or 1,2,3s or grammar and syntax. Reformation should not only be communicated during reformation sessions but embedded in lessons as well. This implies that the ALS curriculum should be customized for inmates different from the generic program meant for everyone.

The eight is familial connection. NBP should strengthen communication with family members through guarded computer-mediated communication. Regular meet-ups online can liven one's day and encourage inmates to have good behavior and forth-coming parole. Seeing their children on camera would motivate them to reform faster which connote that the desire to become good is heightened.

The ninth is Local Government Units and NBP partnerships. LGUs must promote NBP's program on reformation and restorative justice. LGU support is necessary to ensure that inmates should be mainstreamed and treated like normal people or citizens again.

The tenth is Believing in oneself. If inmates do not believe in themselves, who would? Inmate communication can inculcate in a prisoner's mind that indeed they have done wrong but it is not the end of the world. They need to have the conviction that they can be good members of the society again. They are now educated and can fend for their families. The belief in what one can do could empower them to carryout a more humane and upright life. If one believes in oneself, one can do anything including reformation (Figure 8).

Translation:

Bars...
One does not feel anything but remorse and sadness;
An angry heart raves, which was denied of freedom;
Of the many offenders why only a few are punished?
As if justice is blind in looking at who have sinned.
Inside the room, you are shut in despair;
You want to be free but you committed a crime to society;
Might be difficult to think but you have to pay;
For the sins that you need to ponder upon.
If you think that everything is the end for you;
And that there is no hope for people like you;

Figure 8. Temporary isolation

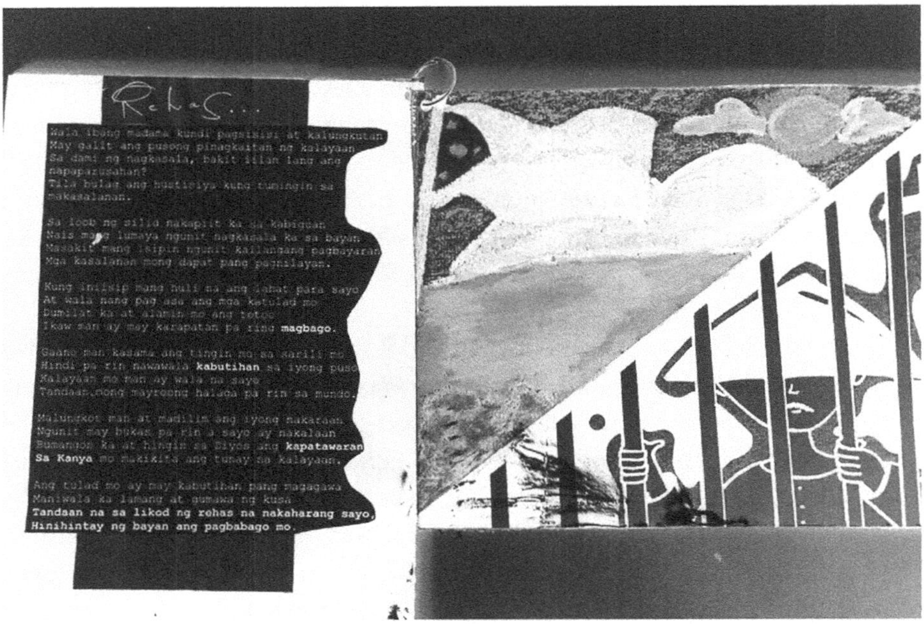

Open your eyes and search for the truth;
You also have the right to change.
No matter how much you see yourself to be bad;
Some goodness still lingers in your heart;
You might have lost your freedom;
Remember that you are still important in this world.
Your past maybe sad and dark;
Tomorrow awaits you;
Wake up and ask God for forgiveness;
You can see in Him the real freedom.
People like you can still do good things;
Just believe and volunteer to do good things;
Remember behind the bars in front of you;
The society waits for your reformation.

The eleventh is Last Song Syndrome (LSS). Songs like "Tie a yellow ribbon" when played regularly within the premises of the NBP through Public Address system can lighten one's day. The message is so encouraging and the beat quite entertaining. NBP can ask prominent local singers to compose songs of hope to have a brighter future and produced professionally. These songs can also be mainstreamed through TV, radio, and YouTube like memes, which could spread like a virus. Listeners would unconsciously accept ex-convicts when they are mainstreamed.

The twelfth is Speedy trial. The slow-moving justice system in the Philippines perpetuates the propensity to err while in prison. Restlessness, ambivalence, and lack of belongingness can hinder the desire to do well, which could sometimes lead to unnecessary or unwanted brawls. The justice system should put and observe fast and fair hearing of cases so that erring individuals would have a longer time to be with their families and love ones as fast as they can. Giving the verdict at the earliest time possible also communicates that what they have done warrants release or service.

The thirteenth is *Use of new media over traditional media.* BuCor has installed eDalaw that inmates can use to connect with their families back home especially in far-flung areas. It is an Internet video chat which allows inmates to talk for 30 minutes with their love ones during special occasions like Christmas. However, this is not regular and bandwidth is weak. Seeing the faces of family members while chatting can create higher hopes of going back home therefore leads to good behavior within the penitentiary. New media can also be used by BuCor to inform the public about what they are doing to reform the inmates so that it can transform negative perceptions about them. BuCor can have a Facebook account, twitter, or Instagram to update the public of their reformation process, the changes that are being done, and could even be a medium to encourage volunteerism as tutors, perhaps.

FUTURE RESEARCH DIRECTIONS

Inmate communication as a methodological framework has to be tested prior to implementation. It is suggested that management staff and jail guards have to be trained on how communicate with a heart without sacrificing discipline or rules that have to be implemented. The manner of communicating towards reformation is something novel that may not be easily accepted by management.

Localized visual media should be developed which should be written in the dialect. Songs, jingles that could be played regularly must likewise be composed and tested.

Appropriate treatment should likewise be revisited. Inmates should know that they have rights as prisoners. Treating them as people is a must. They may have done something bad against societal standards but prisoners have also the responsibility to look after themselves while cases are being tried or sentences being served.

A study in implementing inmate communication should be explored to ensure that it works. A manual on inmate communication duly designed and endorsed by BuCor should be done.

CONCLUSION

Treating inmates inhumanely is against the law. Communicating reformation properly can conscientize prisoners to do well and serve their sentence without any complication.

Correctional and post-correctional reform programs are crucial for prisoners to ensure that they live a dignified life while serving their sentence, and motivate them to focus on their transition upon release. Not only will the knowledge and skills acquired in these programs, as well as emotional, mental, and religious support can help divert their attention from re-offending upon release but they will also become productive members of the society. The benefits of having strong correctional and post-correctional reform programs can create ripples of positive impacts in the society and that nation as a whole because it assures safety, security, and productivity of its citizens. In order to realize these plans, however, strict implementation of policy, resources, political will, and government support system should be in place to properly conduct inmate communication.

RA 10575 remains to be BuCor's strongest point in establishing correctional and post-correctional reform programs but plenty of machinery should be in place first before these can be designed and implemented. In this case, changes in the National Level would prove to be more effective than having the Institution implement programs themselves.

It should be noted, however, that the Government can begin strengthening the Justice System first and give everyone access to an effective and sound trial. In this way, there is a likelier chance that the Correctional System will be managed better and programs for the inmates can be prioritized.

Base on the foregoing, the Philippine Government can begin strengthening the criminal justice system and ensure proper court trials are conducive, and restorative justice measures can be accessed. It is also critical to train jail staff members to be compassionate, and serve as mentors and support system for prisoners to be motivated towards working on their transition and reformation. The country can begin to design and implement inmate communication little by little, step by step. It can work on what the country has at the moment, and build a stronger BuCor that does not only look after criminals but help them transition back to becoming productive members of the society without ending up re-offending.

ACKNOWLEDGMENT

Photos and poems included in the paper were produced by Dr. Flor's students in DEVC 10 (Introduction to Development Communication) in SY 2013-2014 as a class requirement at the University of the Philippines Los Baños.

REFERENCES

Bonta, J., Law, M., & Hanson, R. K. (1998). The Prediction of Criminal and Violent Recidivism among Mentally Disordered Offenders: A Meta-Analysis. *Psychological Bulletin, 123*(2), 123–142. doi:10.1037/0033-2909.123.2.123 PMID:9522681

Ferner, M. (2015, September 9). These programs are helping prisoners live again on the outside. *The Huffington Post.* Retrieved from https://www.huffingtonpost.com/entry/if-we-want-fewer-prisoners-we-need-more-compassion-when-they-re-enter-society_us_55ad61a5e4b0caf721b39cd1

Flor, B. (2013). *Design of a communication strategy and communication plan to support the RPF-PPP Project.* Academic Press.

Freire, P. (1972). *Pedagogy of the oppressed.* New York: Herder and Herder.

Griffiths, C., Dandurand, Y., & Murdoch, D. (2007). *The social reintegration of offenders and crime prevention.* The International Centre from Criminal Law Reform and Criminal Justice Policy. Retrieved from https://www.publicsafety.gc.ca/cnt/rsrcs/pblctns/scl-rntgrtn/index-en.aspx

Maburi, T. (2009). *Re-integration of ex-prisoners back into society: What more can we do?* Retrieved from http://www.newtimes.co.rw/section/read/12648/

MacKenzie, D. L. (1997). Criminal Justice and Crime Prevention. In L. Sherman, D. Gottfredson, D. MacKenzie, J. Eck, P. Reuter, & S. Bushway (Eds.), *Preventing Crime: What Works, What Doesn't, What's Promising. Report to the United States Congress*. Washington, DC: US Department of Justice.

Philippine prisons overflowing with hungry inmates as Duterte's drug war intensifies. (n.d.). Retrieved from http://www.abc.net.au/news/2017-09-20/philippine-prisons-overflowing-as-war-on-drugs-intensifies/8959448

Republic Act No 10575. (n.d.). Retrieved from http://www.lawphil.net/statutes/repacts/ra2013/ra_10575_2013.html

The Condition of Philippine Prison and Jails. (n.d.). Retrieved from http://www.preda.org/media/research-documents/the-condition-of-philippine-prisons-and-jails/

Travis, J., Solomon, A. L., & Waul, S. (2001). *From prison to home – The dimensions and consequences of prisoner re-entry.* Retrieved from https://www.urban.org/research/publication/prison-home-dimensions-and-consequences-prisoner-reentry/view/full_report

Wexler, H. K., Melnick, G., Lowe, L., & Peters, J. (1999). Three-year Reincarceration Outcomes for In-prison Therapeutic Community and Aftercare in California. *The Prison Journal, 79*(3), 321–336. doi:10.1177/0032885599079003003

ADDITIONAL READING

Executive Edge: The Filipino Inmates' Right to Livelihood I https://www.rappler.com/business/features/101486-executive-edge-karaw-craftventures-paul-orpiada

House Bill 2054 I http://www.congress.gov.ph/legisdocs/basic_16/HR02054.pdf

Laguna Provincial Jail. Programs and Projects I http://www.laguna.gov.ph/jail/programs-projects#DECONGESTION_PROGRAM

New Bilibid Prison Visit I http://www.marriageandbeyond.com/2012/06/14/new-bilibid-prison-visit-part-1-bucors-mandate-and-reformation-program/

Philippine Jails 511% congested, audit finds I http://www.philstar.com/headlines/2017/06/16/1710620/philippine-jails-511-congested-audit-finds

Philippine prisons overflowing with hungry inmates as Duterte's drug war intensifies I http://www.abc.net.au/news/2017-09-20/philippine-prisons-overflowing-as-war-on-drugs-intensifies/8959448

Policy Guidelines for BJMP Livelihood Projects I https://www.bjmp.gov.ph/files/guidelines_livelihood.pdf

Prisons and rehab overcrowding in the Philippines I http://www.aljazeera.com/indepth/inpictures/2016/12/prisons-rehab-overcrowding-philippines-161207091046623.html

Republic Act No 7438 I http://www.chanrobles.com/republicactno7438.htm

Republic Act No 9344 I http://www.chanrobles.com/republicactno9344.htm

The Condition of Philippine Prison and Jails I http://www.preda.org/media/research-documents/the-condition-of-philippine-prisons-and-jails/

World Prison Brief. Philippines I http://www.prisonstudies.org/country/philippines

KEY TERMS AND DEFINITIONS

Believing in Oneself: Refers to the process of inmates taking upon themselves the responsibility that they can still reform and once more get mainstreamed.

Conviction to Change: Depicts inmates' assertion to reform and convincing oneself that there is life after their sentence is served.

Cultivation Period: Is the regularity of exposure to communication media that eventually gets into the system of the viewer.

Inmate Communication: Is a conscientization approach that consists of a holistic strategy to nourish the head, heart, hand, and soul of an inmate, the prison management, and the society.

Recidivism: Is that act of a person to repeat an undesirable behavior after they a bad experience or negative consequence of exhibiting one, or had been trained to extinguish that behavior.

Reformation: Pertains to the process of changing norms and behavior to become a better person.

Reformatory Abode: Refers to NBP as penitentiary mirrors a place that prisoners come out clean and productive as members of society.

Chapter 9
Communication Technologies for Social Integration of Inmates in Nigeria

Janet Aver Adikpo
Eastern Mediterranean University, Cyprus

Peter Iorper Ugondo
Kwararafa University, Nigeria

ABSTRACT

In recent years, political instability has resulted in the rising wave of unemployment, poverty rate, and insecurity, all which have attendant effect on the crime rate across Nigeria. Presently, the prison population is 68,259: a number which has soared from 44,450 in year 2000. Several reports on the activities of the Nigerian prisons services widely indicate that there is a disturbing crime rate. Going by these statistics, the focus of this chapter is on the use of communication technologies skills for rehabilitation and reintegration of inmates into society. Since communication technologies provide a unified learning process for knowledge sharing, prisoners need to have access to these new forms of information exchange. This clearly implies that inmates need info-communication skills to prevent recidivism. Using the backdrop of the Nigeria's prison terrain, the chapter recommends an overhaul of the prisons with a reliable information and communication framework.

DOI: 10.4018/978-1-5225-5975-7.ch009

INTRODUCTION

Over the years, Nigeria has remained the most populous country in Africa. With a current estimation of over 190 million people, Nigeria is projected to experience a fast population growth of over 390 million by year 2050 (Central Intelligence Agency World Factbook, 2017). The growing population has brought with it, several persistent daunting issues such as the absence of political will, corruption, brain drain, increased crime rate occasioned by financial practices, widespread poverty, unemployment, migration, to mention but few. As a developing country, the rising wave of (specifically) unemployment rate, persistence in poverty and unabated insecurity, all have attendant effect on the crime recorded across Nigeria. This explains the congestion of prisons and a further inability for adequate plans for the social integration of inmates.

The Nigerian Prisons Service[1] is saddled with the responsibility of welfare of the inmates through ensuring lawful jurisdiction, ascertain the root cause for anti-social conduct, as well as providing safe and secure conditions to improve and reintegrate them into the society upon release. Several reports of the activities of the Nigerian prisons services widely indicate that there is a disturbing crime rate with which a better effective criminal justice system would have remanded more people. According to the World Prison Brief Data (2017), the prison population of Nigeria presently is 68,259; a number which has soared from 44,450 in year 2000. Given the above estimations, (also provided by WPB), the prison population rate is 36 per 100,000 of the nation's population.

Going by the statistics of prisoners, it is interesting to note that there is a considerably low number of prisoners in Nigeria. Danbazau (2017) revealed that what is worrisome about the prisons is that facilities are built to carter for convicts but seventy per cent of population in prison are those awaiting trials. The training and productivity of inmates is another important focus of the Nigerian Prison Service, to ensure self-sustenance, affirmative and dignified orientation of the culpable people. However, these operations have not fared well, due to constraints that will be discussed in the background of this chapter. Suffice it to say, that these issues account for the reason why the vision of integration has not been effectively carried out.

BACKGROUND

Despite that Nigeria has continued to grapple with hindrances, there are still prospects and the prisons authorities have continued to sue for the integration of inmates through skill-acquisition trainings in the area of furniture, soap-making, fabrication, aluminium and metal works, mechanised and non-mechanised agricultural practices, social entrepreneurship and several other business profiteering methods. These are the major ways through which the prisons services have continued reforms to rehabilitate and reintegrate inmates into the society (Asokhia & Agbonluae, 2013).

It is worthy of note that the Nigerian situation is one that is peculiar to most developing nations the world over, and to say the least, some developed economies also encounter some of these issues in their prison sector. The welfare of prisoners is primarily targeted towards preparing them to recuperate from the lifestyles that prompted them to commit crime in the first place, and in a lot more precise manner, enable them to fit back into the dynamic society. Even as there is no stated universal prison standards, the United Nations pronouncement of the standard minimum rules for the treatment of prisoners[2] using the provisions and core instruments of the human rights as a guiding principle. According to United Nations Office on Drugs and Crime (2015), the pronouncement contained in the standard minimum rules for treatment of prisons have greatly influenced the advancement, guidelines and performance of prison management across nations. On the Africa continent, several attempts have been made by governments to improve on the conditions in the prisons, yet, a lot is still desired (Dissel, 2001; Sarkin, 2008; Allen, 2010; International Committee of the Red Cross, 2012; Bureau of Democracy, Human Rights and Labor, 2013).

Looking at the Nigerian situation, the standards of communication differ significantly when compared with that which is derivable in other developed and/or developing climes. This deplorable state has raised questions, captured by Adetula and Fatusin (2010) that it seems an encounter with the prisons influences individuals to become hardened criminals when unleashed to the society. In another assertion, Araromi (2015) asserts that the central reason why inmates have problem adjusting to society is tied to the manner in which they were locked up in the first place, and what they eventually encountered while in prison. The National Human Rights Commission of Nigeria reports these hideous conditions comprising the absence of befitting social amenities compounded by overcrowding, which is perpetuated by inaccessibility to prompt justice all of which are a clear contrast to the requirement of the universally accepted human rights and standards for persons in prison custody (National Human Rights Commission, 2016).

The most striking issue is that those who have spent time detained in the prisons will have to reintegrate in a society, different from what they were accustomed to. Interestingly, the several efforts to reintegrate prison inmates into society has continued to yield positive results. However, there is not yet any outright process to meet the needs for social integration of inmates. This is due largely to the ever-changing aspects of social living which also requires a continued search for solutions.

One very striking trend that inmates need to be trained to keep up with is the information and communication technologies. Apart from the need to have working knowledge of the basic computer and telecommunications skills, the cyberspace is a handy means through which other forms of skills acquisition trainings for inmates can be consolidated. With the barrage of opportunities brought about by ICTs, it is very pertinent that prison inmates be trained to also have info-communication skills. This notion is upheld that it is critical for individuals in society to have access and familiarise with communication technologies because this brings about a reliable means through which knowledge can be created, gained and shared (Dijst, 2004; Warschaurer, 2004; Helsper, 2008; Goggin, 2012; Walsham, 2012; Baym, 2015).

For inmates, communication technologies are considered fundamental in increasing and equipping knowledge needs for possible empowerment opportunities (Tenibiaje, 2012). Thus, increased knowledge of inmates is an index of social integration. Therefore, through information and communication technologies, there is a unification of learning processes, information gathering and exchange, knowledge sharing, and so many more. The possibility of adopting the use of these new technologies will also offer many other alternative skills to inmates. This clearly emphasises the necessity of info-communication skills especially for the inmates so as to prevent the likelihood of slipping back to the criminal way of life. This goes to show, that with the success recorded in the use of communication and information technologies across the globe today, inmates will be able to adjust easily and better by living an up-to-date life.

Based on the existing literature, researches previously conducted on prison inmates in Nigeria reveal that they have access to various forms of traditional media such as television, radio (some are allowed to own), newspapers and magazines. However, there is none which has focused on the need to introduce the use of communication technologies either to enhance their rehabilitation process(es) or enable them socially integrate to society in any way.

The focus of this study is bothering on the welfare in form of skills for rehabilitation and reintegration in society. There exist a wide margin between society's and the prison's population use of communication technologies in Nigeria's terrain. The main aim is to bring bare, the need for prisoners across Nigeria to have access to the new forms of information exchange because this has not been adequately implemented. Using the framework of the primary aims of the entire publication (which is to promote digital literacy in prisons and promote better social integration), appropriate policy recommendations will be offered to benefit the prison authority and by extension, the government of Nigeria.

MAIN FOCUS

Social integration is conceptualised to be synonymous to adaptation, acculturation, and assimilation. According to Ware, Hopper, Tugenberg, Dickey and Fisher (2008), social integration which used to be a practice in ensuring that mentally derailed people were cared for, has found relevance in discourses on diverse issues. This indicates that the concept has assumed newer formations and quality. This chapter conceives the notion that if adequately utilised for social integration, communication technologies will play a lead role in improving the quality of life of prison inmates for eventual reintegration into their communities.

As a correctional institution, the prisons assume a crucial role in the process of re-socialising previously culpable individuals through working practices, educational, cultural and recreational activities. The basic questions raised in are premised on whether the prison inmates in Nigeria do have access to, and whether they adequately utilise the superfluity of technologies that are not widely adopted to facilitate livelihood in the society. It became necessary to project the Nigerian scenario of prison inmates, to solicit for suitable frameworks with which the desired standards and treatment can benefit the prison system.

One of the new ways through which social values and skills learned in recent time is by the use of communication technologies. As instruments of socialization and education, communication technologies have spurred massive citizen awareness, for collecting, processing, sharing, protecting and storing information. Despite assuming a prestigious position first as the foundation which also act as a driving force since the 21st century, the prison institutions are reportedly lagging behind in the adoption of new technologies (Tsend-Ayush, 2017). This has paved way for utopian and dystopian shades of opinion in the application of communication technologies in prison services.

The main arguments of the latter group are audibly uphold that there is low literacy rate among prison detainees. Also that there is likelihood that exposing prison inmates to communication technologies will aid crime. However, this chapter firmly submits that rather than a disadvantage, the misgivings about communication technologies are rather contained in the potentials, reason been that through its educative and secure accessibility, technologies holds sway for effective service delivery for the prison institution.

DIFFUSION OF INNOVATION: APPLICABILITY TO SOCIAL INTEGRATION OF PRISONERS

The theoretical frame of reference for this study is based on the underpinnings of diffusion of innovation theory. Historical accounts reveal that during the early 20th century was when agriculture experienced a technological boost (Valente & Rogers, 1995; Dimitri, Effland, Conklin, 2005; Anderson, 2010; Rogers, 2010; Pinilla, 2017). First, a 1962 study conducted on rural sociology by Everett Rogers blazed the trail when it focused on the level of adoption of hybrid seeds and techniques of mechanized farming.

Rogers' ground-breaking research is said to have established the synergy existing of the diffusions of innovation theory for various themes across disciplines and works of life (Easley & Kleinberg, 2010). Thus, for the purpose of this chapter, the sociological and communication perspectives are considered. On its own, diffusion is a phenomenon that describes natural proliferation of occurrences in the social system, while an innovation can be in form of a new idea, technology, culture, etc. Therefore, the theory of diffusion is utilised to justify the elements, patterns, stages and possible variations that exist in the process.

The diffusion of innovations theory categorises that there are different degrees at which diffusion occurs in the society as well as how people tend to respond. In the process of diffusion, there are key players consisting of innovators, early adopters, early majority, late majority and the laggards. At three stages of diffusion (that is, adoption, diffusion and late adoption), there is variation in the process innovations are embraced in the society, usually it starts slow and eventually there is a hype in the adoption when more information has reached more members of the social system (Dearing, 2009; Ruiz-Mercado, Masera, Zamora & Smith, 2011; Webster, Caputi, Perreault, Doan, Doutis & Weaver, 2013; Dinkel, Schaffer, Snyder & Lee, 2017).

In between these stages, the innovators feature prominently as those who are the first to try out an innovation followed by the early adopters who adopt a change based on the need they identify. Those who are in the early majority tend to also adopt ideas just like the innovators and early adopters, but need to be substantial convinced about an innovation before they embrace it. The late majority eventually adopt an innovation but do so with reluctance, while it is very difficult to convince the laggards about innovations.

Using the backdrop of the key stages and actors above, it is imperative to apply the tenets of the diffusion of innovations theory to current discourse on the need for information and communication technologies in reintegration of prisoners back into society. It is a truism that information and communication technologies have greatly impact on how things are done in the society. This diffusion has resulted in the need for individuals to adopt the use in various ways, be it as a skill, means of communication, information sharing, knowledge acquisition, commercial transactions. However, the inability of prisoners to live among other members of society has resulted to alienation.

Glaringly, while other members of the society have the will to adopt innovation, the case is not so with the prisoners. For instance, a prisoner who is naturally an innovator unconsciously becomes a laggard because of the confinement of imprisonment. The theory of diffusion of innovation clearly presents an individuals' natural disposition and openness to innovation, but the reality for prisoners is not the case. As critical tools for growth and development (either collectively or individually), reintegration of prisoners cannot be successful achieved in todays' globalised world without addressing the info-communication skills of the prisoners. Therefore, since every individual has a peculiar way of responding to innovation, exposure to technological innovations will further enhance their well-being upon release from incarceration.

The emphasis on the need to ensure that prisoners are successfully re-integrated is tailed by the need for financial empowerment, to have unhindered access to justice, improved social status, living conditions, shelter, food and water. This need is targeted towards ensuring that the public safety is ensured in the case of those who lived reckless lives at the detriment of other members of society. In line with the main beliefs of 'social integration' whose sociological roots presupposes that connections should exist between individuals and the general public (Tselios, Noback, Dijk & McCann, 2015; Tselios, McCann & Dijk, 2017), access to modern forms of information and communication is a relevant index to ascertain the level of success.

Equally important, connecting prisoners with mainstream society necessitates basic requirements such as proficiency in language use, knowledge of laws and adoption of common sets of values. Diffusions of innovations explains how individuals can access the desired social support, therefore, early exposure to innovations will also tend to have maximal impact on their integration with other individuals and groups. This leads us to the need for prisoners to become employable, create job opportunities, building social relationships as well as develop sense of belonging.

ISSUES, CONTROVERSIES, PROBLEMS

The industrial revolution recorded to have begun in the late 18th century, brought about a full swing of technological innovation (Berg, 2005; Lucas, 2010; Hudson, 2014). Consequently in the latter years that followed, this growing trend became effective in the major industries like textiles, power and steel as well as machinery (Horn, Rosenband & Smith, 2010; Rosen, 2012). This spread eventually has spread to all subsectors of all economies in developed and developing nations across the globe. Without exception, world leaders have upheld the dire need to promote the ideals of the fourth industrial revolution[3] to effectively enhance interdependence so as to foster collective response for advanced impact of innovation on societies. For instance, technology was the spotlight during the World Economic Forum Annual Meeting of 2016, which was themed: 'mastering the fourth industrial revolution'. The year's report clearly emphasized that technological innovations are essential through the gradually transformation of livelihoods and social interactions (Reyes, Bacani, Horch, Rienstra & Walter, 2016).

Importantly too, technology has paved way for deliberations on reshaping social innovations and integration for all-inclusive government policies. The same goes for the African continent that has high vulnerability of socio-cultural and economic watershed. Mawasha (2017) affirms that the digitalization holds very great capacity to energize development of nations in Africa, through enabling social entrepreneurship and service delivery.

To achieve this need, policies in Nigeria are now targeted towards reaching wide-ranging advancement of industrial development through digital skill acquisition and inclusive partnership. In the past, communication technologies were more or less considered as a threat to cybersecurity than offer opportunities for national development. However, the changing face of the cyberspace is accompanied by measures that have largely curtailed the many threats that were hitherto apparent (Australian Computer Society, 2016; Wall, 2017).

The government has cashed in on this improvement by its poise to formulate and adopt policies that enhance the utilisation of communication technologies for national development. Hence, the federal government speedily approved the National Policy for Information Technology and established National Information Technology Development Agency (NITDA) all in 2001 and the National Information and Communication Technology (ICT) Policy was also formulated in the following year (Adeyemo, 2011; Babalola, 2013; Neji, 2016). These government policies and agencies have the visionary aim to promote the use of information and communication technologies and foster socioeconomic development in the country.

Of course, there are visible benefits especially in e-governance and mobile telephony but a policy framework that will accommodate the integration of communication technologies for prison administration and maximise the potentials of communication technologies for social integration of inmates is conspicuously absent. That is not all, even with the presence of communication technologies, those dedicated to prison administration are highly negligible when compared to its use in the wider society.

The reality of communication technology revolution is yet to reflect in prison policies for social integration of inmates in Nigeria. Therefore, this chapter seeks to canvass for a policy framework that will fully integrate communication technologies in Nigerian prisons to enhance as well as facilitate social integration of inmates. Concurrently, efforts made to also examine other related strategies, with specific focus on the need for specific short and long term action plans appropriate for the application of communication technologies for the re-integration of inmates.

WELFARE OF INMATES IN NIGERIA

In Nigeria, treatment of inmates is regulated by the Prisons Act, Laws of the Federation of Nigeria 1990. More than 70 per cent of the inmates are later released into the society without visible means of livelihood which, in most cases ultimately leads such individual to commit crime again. The concern expressed in many quarters is mainly about the welfare of inmates, stressing the need for proper funding of prisons in order to achieve the goals of rehabilitating inmates and to ensure greater efficiency (Araromi, 2015; Muhammad, Gwangndi & Hassan, 2017).

The latest common rehabilitation strategy of inmates in Nigeria is vocational skills acquisition. In the Female Maximum and Medium Security Prisons, Kirikiri - Apapa in Lagos State Nigeria, about 36 resident inmates of the female prisons graduated with various vocational skills, such as: tie and dye, fashion designing, soap making, among others at the pre-release ceremony in the Kirikiri Prisons' premises. While at the Kaduna Central Prison more than sixty inmates are trained in tailoring and basic computer appreciation. As a result these skills acquisition endeavours benefitted the over one hundred prisoners who were exonerated in year 2016 (Akoni, 2017).

Adult schooling is another means with which rehabilitation is conducted in the Nigerian Prisons. Media reports reveal that The Plateau State Command of Nigerian Prisons registered twenty two inmates to sit for the 2017 Basic Literacy Examination (News Agency of Nigeria, 2017; *The Nigerian Expression*; Vanguard, 2017). At the Ikoyi Prison School, about thirty-six out of fifty-nine inmates who sat for the 2017 Unified Tertiary Matriculation Examination (UTME) scored 180 and above (*Nigeria Today*, 2017). This was is an improvement from only about thirty-six inmates who registered for the same exam in the previous year. A combined number of over 120 inmates from Ikoyi and Kaduna prisons registered for the 2017 Unified Tertiary Matriculation Examination conducted by Joint Admission and Matriculation Board (Obike, 2017; Popoola, 2017). Meanwhile, the total number of inmates from Ikoyi and Kirikiri prisons in Lagos alone who registered for the West African Senior Secondary Examination in the last three years are reported to be up to three hundred and thirty-two (*The Nation,* 2017a, 2017b; *Vanguard, 2017*).

Despite the successes recorded in ensuring that inmates are empowered to integrate in the society upon release, there are several problems militating against actualizing the desired rehabilitation in the Nigerian Prisons. According to Ayade (2010), of all the problems encountered in the rehabilitation of prison inmates, overcrowding causes the overstretching of the limited resources. Other issues are inadequate funding, poor infrastructures, illiteracy, and improper follow-up on inmates post-release (Obioha, 2011; Chukwudi, 2012; Ugwumba & Usang, 2014; Adebisi & Oyewo, 2015; Fasanmi, 2015; Adeagbo, Asubiojo, Obadare & Akindojutimi, 2016; Opafunso & Adepoju, 2016).

In the case of congestion of prisons, a precise reference is to the Kirikiri Prisons, which presently holds 3,526 inmates in a 1,200 capacity for residence (Awopetu, 2014; Isah, 2017). The number of awaiting trials constitutes more than three quarter of population. There are a lot of factors responsible for this congestion, for example there is a present programme of Lagos State Government where people are raided on daily basis and dumped in prisons with minor offences. Elsewhere in developed societies, these kind of offences are not supposed to be brought to prisons, so when individuals are arrested and thrown into prison upon any slightest provocation, the result is congestion. Unfortunately, this has resulted to cases of fire incidences, disease outbreaks and jail breaks. A very good instance of such provocations has resulted to a huge fire outbreak at the Kuje Prison in Abuja, for which the Prisoners Against Injustice in Nigeria (PAIN) claimed responsibility (Sahara Reporters, 2017), the reason stated as an effort to draw attention of the world to the pathetic state of prisons and corruption within prison services.

A study by Uche, Uche, Ezumah, Ebue, Okafor and Ezegbe (2015) on the effectiveness of rehabilitation by the Nigerian Prisons Services found that programmes fall short of actualisation primarily as a result of inadequacy in funding either by the absence of it of misappropriation of same. This shortfall is corroborated by Onyekachi (2016) that the inadequate funding which limits rehabilitation also negates the effectiveness of the prison administration. In no small measure, inadequacy in funding for Nigerian prisons has brought about an overburden occasioned by misappropriation of financial resources, wrecked structural facilities and an almost non-functional system. To curb the problem with funding of prisons in Nigeria, the suggestion by Ugwumba and Usang (2014) is that Nigeria should consider the privatization policy to eliminate sole funding as is obtained in most advanced economies. If this is done, there is a sure tendency for private sector participation especially in the area of agriculture, and several avenues through which revenue can be generated while the prison inmates adopt independent strategies to empower and hasten their reintegration into society.

The state of infrastructures in prisons across Nigerian is widely decried, especially by government officials, prison administrators and inmates alike, and academics on their part have advocated widely for policy change for a favourable rehabilitation of prisoners. As long as there is a delay in finding a lasting solution those remanded in prisons (most of whom are young offenders) will be released back into the society with a higher tendencies to re-engage in criminal activities.

COMMUNICATION TECHNOLOGIES FOR SOCIAL INTEGRATION OF INMATES

Controversies circumvent the usefulness of communication technologies for enhancing the integration of inmates in Nigeria. These controversies are nurtured by too much fear of the negative effect of these technologies. Of a truth, technological revolution was said to lead to loss of job, less social interaction, and others, but today, the reverse is the case. People have found more avenue to interact beyond geographical spaces. People interact freely on social platforms like Facebook, Twitter, and by making use of mobile applications like Viber, Telegram WhatsApp, Snap-chat, etc. Also, the loss of jobs that technologies were presumed to occasion is nowhere to be found. Rather, more job opportunities (skilled and semi-skilled) are created in terms of use, maintenance and repair, marketing and distribution, as well as software development. The potentials of communication technologies for driving social integration of inmates in Nigeria is under serious cross fire on the grounds of security, illiteracy, digital divide, and legality.

Several scholars uphold the fact that the ability of inmates to access, adapt, and create new knowledge using communication technologies is critical to social integration in today's era (Mossberger, Tolbert & Stansbury, 2003; Warschauer, 2003; Dahlman, 2008; Celebic & Rendulic, 2011; Joseph, 2012; Digard, diZerega, Yaroni & Rinaldi, 2016). The point is, when inmates are excluded, during incarceration, they are also isolated from opportunities that would ordinarily expose them to the use of new technologies. These technologies useful for inmates to be gainfully employed, and motivated to develop the capacity to achieve social integration after release from custody tend to diminish.

With the use of communication technologies prisoner can retain family and community ties, thereby making it easy for an eventual reintegration. Lockitt (2011) and Jungen (2016) corroborate that apart from adding tax revenues and reducing welfare costs, communication technologies can relieve the need to build additional prisons. Therefore, applying communication technologies in social integration of inmates need to be prioritised.

Similarly, in the educational programs for inmates, digital literacy (e-learning) has proved capable of facilitating the learning ability of people. Pillera (2015) holds strongly that communication technologies have important tools for interactive learning, and for prisoners, the new form of learning with the support of technologies will enrich potential and increase the chances of rehabilitation. This underscores the fact that communication technologies are crucial for efficient and effective social integration of inmates and Nigeria is not an exception.

Literacy is one of the culprits for social deviance and reason for the offences that take people to prison. This is particularly on the part of inmates because most of them are unable to read and/or write, and so considered unfit to use communication technologies. In a study on literacy, information and communication technology as tools for empowerment of inmates, Tenibiaje (2012) found that illiteracy was very high among prison inmates while observing that two-thirds of the inmates sampled in that study agreed that they can neither read a newspaper nor write a letter.

However, these technologies transcend the barriers of literacy and language. All it takes for one to effectively use technologies is basic education and through the application of communication technologies, the emotional isolation of inmates can be eliminated. Therefore, to curb illiteracy is to prevent the likelihood of prison inmates to return to prison after their acquittal while quickening the process of re-integrated.

The nature of education available for inmates in Nigeria today, strengthens the need for incorporating communicating technologies in those literacy programmes. So since education necessitates for communication to be effective, communication technologies now assumes the position as the bedrock for effective education. The use of communication technologies will definitely enhance knowledge acquisition among inmates.

Generally speaking, the prison officials in Nigeria make use of communication technologies such as mobile phones, computers and tablets and so on. Since their usage is not inclined to official duty, this proves that the same can be applicable for the benefit of prison inmates. In Tsend-Ayush (2017), the purposes for which communication devices are commonly used in prison institutions across the globe are for voice calls, chatting, texting, playing music, watching videos, storing information and sometimes video conferencing.

Another trend is that of the satellite TV and video technology which can enhance distance communication for prison administrators to ensure order and discipline, track the whereabouts of inmates, monitor visitation patterns and also record medical history in prisons. To a great extent, this will eliminate unnecessary formation of gangs and security threats. For an efficient service also, there is need for the prisons to have secured intranet and internet networks, computers and other peripheral devices in managing daily activities of prison administration.

According to Araromi (2015), the Nigerian Prisons Regulations (item 42), visitors who are either family of friends for a certain time of the month. Such visitor cannot be left alone with the inmate, but must be in the presence of a prisoner warden. Although inmates could make calls using their visitors' phones and in other cases, using the mobile phones in the presence of prison personnel. Also, regulations authorises inmates to write and receive letters, and to be assisted in case they are unable to read and write. This makes letter writing the most common and accepted means of communication between inmates and the outside society. One of the reasons that communication technologies will be most fitting to compliment or substitute letter writing among inmates is literacy barrier; but inmates are not allowed to own any technological device.

It is no longer news that communication technologies are used in vocational and educational training facilities for inmates across prisons in Nigeria; but these vocational and adult literacy programmes are organised by non-governmental organisations like Prison Fellowship Nigeria, and Small and Medium Enterprises Development Agency of Nigeria (SMEDAN), etc. In fact, the United Nations (1990) declared that prison inmates should be provided with education necessary for their rehabilitation. In assessing rehabilitation services in Nigerian prisons, Asokhia and Agbonluae (2013) found that four adult remedial educational programmes and two educational development project were available in Edo State prisons.

The use of communication technologies by inmates according to respondents is very common in adult literacy where the inmates are trained on the use of computer for taking examinations. For instance, inclusion of computer studies in school curricula and the creation of computer-based test by Joint Admissions and Matriculation Board (JAMB) for examinations paved way for inmates to also learn to operate computers. This way, inmates across the country are allowed to access such facilities within the purview of prison yards.

Communication technologies can therefore be very impactful through educational programmes for inmates. This is affirmed that by participating in the programs, inmates would have access to digital literacy (Tsend-Ayush, 2017). This is a good means through which the rehabilitation process for prisoners can be enhanced. Bearing in mind that communication is very important for human existence (specifically those who are imprisoned), maintaining regular interactions with family and friends can help to alleviate the pain of imprisonment. All of above-mentioned processes could definitely increase the chances of a successful rehabilitation. It is therefore, important for prison establishments to strive for new means of using communication technologies for social integration.

SOLUTIONS AND RECOMMENDATIONS

From the foregoing, it is clear that there is no clear-cut framework on what specifically happens to prisoners when they are freed. It is obvious that the seeming rehabilitation of inmates has not sub-peddled the rate of those going into jail. In very common cases, those who were initially acquitted end up committing similar, if not, worse crimes that those which they were initially incarcerated for. This implies that the challenges faced by the Nigerian prisons have largely crippled its ability to efficiently carryout the desired rehabilitation of prison inmates. As earlier observed, it seems as if the prison has further criminalised those whose paths enter the prisons.

As the population grows, the rate of crime also has skyrocketed in recent times. One great contributing factor is the global upsurge in the rate of crime, insecurity and mobility. These are unforeseen circumstances, and factors that are out of reach of any government across the globe. However, one thing is sure, issues such as illiteracy, lack of basic amenities and infrastructures, lack of or insufficient funding are within the reach of the federal government.

The challenges faced by prisoners upon re-entry to society are not only found in Nigeria but has continued to affect families of offenders even in the most developed societies. For instance, in the United States of America, cases of recidivism are reportedly as rampant, if not, occurs as often as or even more than those convicted for first time offences (Bureau of Justice Statistics, 2017). In the case of Nigeria, the major issue of overcrowding is as a result of too many inmates awaiting trial. This has overstretched the available facilities which were provided for fewer number of inmates.

With a modern strategy, it is possible to imbibe a teaming spirit between the public and private sector; a collaboration that will go a long way in eradicating the pitiful state of prison service in Nigeria. Rather than resort to a single funding source as earlier discussed, individuals, non-governmental, multi-national organisations have a great role-play in ensuring that the crisis in the prisons sector is solved. The government should as a matter of urgency initiate privatisation of part or all of the prisons, to encourage an all-participatory administration. This practice has been put in place in most developed societies and has proven effective for the rehabilitation and re-integration of the prison inmates. The involvement of the private sectors can also lead to an industrial breakthrough for inmates to put to use their skills acquisition programmes they undergo while serving their jail sentences.

As the government sue for diversification of the economy, it is necessary for this same policy to be extended to those who are in prison. By this, the establishment of agencies to regulate information and communication technologies is a welcomed developed, which must be utilised to grow the prisoners the same way other members of the society are benefitting. A total overhaul of the prisons with a reliable information and communication framework in all prisons is recommended, as it will go a long way in facilitating learning, skills acquisition, and eventual job creation for inmates. Those in prison need to have devoted number of house to surf the internet, use mobile applications, and other computer based programmes.

If this is done, a new shade of entertainment will be introduced for inmates, other than the traditional practice of listening to radio and watching television on limited occasions. Adopting the use of these new technologies will also offer many other alternative skills to inmates. This clearly emphasises the necessity of info-communication skills especially for the inmates. This goes to show, that with the success recorded in the use of communication and information technologies in society today, the inmates will be able to adjust easily and better by living an up-to-date life.

FUTURE RESEARCH DIRECTIONS

This study primarily outlined the challenges of Nigeria's prison population, and clearly proposed the use of communication technologies for the reintegration of inmates. The authors propose that focus on future research be considered about challenges of government policies for information and communication technologies in the Nigerian prisons. Another possible area of research is to assess the challenges during their post-incarceration and reintegration.

REFERENCES

Adeagbo, O. O., Asubiojo, B. O., Obadare, S. O., & Akindojutimi, B. F. (2016). Re-Integration of Prison Inmates in Nigeria: Advocating for Library Support. *The International Information & Library Review*, *48*(3), 169–175. doi:10.1080/10572317.2016.1204872

Adebisi, K. S., & Oyewo, O. O. (2015). Prisons and security challenges in a democratic Nigeria. *Research on Humanities and Social Sciences*, *5*(6), 124–129.

Adetula, G. A., & Fatusin, A. F. (2010). The prison subsystem culture: Its attitudinal effects on operatives, convicts and the free society. *Psychological*, *18*(1), 232–251.

Adeyemo, A. B. (2011). E-government implementation in Nigeria: An assessment of Nigeria's global e-government ranking. *Journal of Internet and Information Systems*, *2*(1), 11–19.

Akoni, C. (2017). Hope rises as varsity empowers pre-release Kirikiri female inmates. *Vanguard*. Accessed online on 29/9/2017 from https://www.vanguardngr.com/2017/06/hope-rises-varsity-empowers-pre-release-kirikiri-female-inmates/

Allen, R. (2010). *Current situation of prison overcrowding*. Accessed on 21/09/2017 from http://www.prisonstudies.org/sites/default/files/resources/downloads/current_situation_of_prison_overcrowding_paper.pdf

Anderson, K. (2010). Globalization's effects on world agricultural trade, 1960–2050. *Philosophical Transactions of the Royal Society of London. Series B, Biological Sciences*, *365*(1554), 3007–3021. doi:10.1098/rstb.2010.0131 PMID:20713399

Araromi, M. A. (2015). Prisoners' rights under the Nigerian law: Legal pathways to progressive realization and protection. *Journal of Sustainable Development Law and Policy (The)*, *6*(1), 169–198. doi:10.4314/jsdlp.v6i1.8

Asokhia, M. O., & Agbonluae, O. O. (2013). Assessment of rehabilitation services in Nigerian prisons in Edo State. *American International Journal of Contemporary Research*, *3*(1), 224–230.

Australian Computer Society. (2016). *Cybersecurity threats challenges opportunities*. ACS. Accessed on 19/09/2017 from https://www.acs.org.au/content/dam/acs/acs-publications/ACS_Cybersecurity_Guide.pdf

Awopetu, R. G. (2014). An assessment of prison overcrowding in Nigeria: Implications for rehabilitation, reformation and reintegration of inmates. *IOSR Journal of Humanities and Social Science*, *19*(3), 21–26. doi:10.9790/0837-19362126

Ayade, E. A. (2010). *Problems of Prisons Overcrowding in Nigeria: Some lessons from South Africa and America. LLM, Human Rights* (Unpublished Thesis). Central European University, Legal Studies Department, Budapest, Hungary.

Babalola, Y. T. (2013). Nigeria's information infrastructure policy: Implications for e-government. *Arabian Journal of Business and Management Review*, *2*(11), 8–15.

Baym, N. K. (2015). *Personal connections in the digital age*. John Wiley & Sons.

Berg, M. (2005). *The age of manufactures, 1700-1820: Industry, innovation and work in Britain*. Routledge.

Bureau of Democracy, Human Rights, and Labor. (2013). *Report on International Prison Conditions*. BDHRL, United States Department of State. Accessed on 21/09/2017 from https://www.state.gov/documents/organization/210160.pdf

Bureau of Justice Statistics. (2017). *Re-entry trends in the U.S.: Recidivism*. Accessed on 30/11/2017 from https://www.bjs.gov/content/reentry/recidivism.cfm and https://www.bjs.gov/index.cfm?ty=tp&tid=17

Celebic, G., & Rendulic, D. I. (2011). *Basic concepts of information and communication technology: Handbook*. Zagreb: Open Society for Idea Exchange.

Central Intelligence Agency. (2017). *World Factbook*. Accessed on 8/10/2017 from https://www.cia.gov/library/publications/the-world-factbook/geos/ni.html

Chukwudi, F. (2012). Challenges of Reforms in the Nigerian Prison System: Lessons from USA and South Africa. *Journal of Social Science and Public Policy*, *4*(36).

Dahlman, C. (2008). Technology, globalization, and international competitiveness: Challenges for developing countries. In D. O'Connor & M. Kjollerstrom (Eds.), *Industrial Development for the 21st Century* (pp. 29–83). University of Chicago Press.

Danbazau, A. (2017). 70% of prison inmates are awaiting trial. *Vanguard*. Accessed from https://www.vanguardngr.com/2017/06/70-prison-inmates-awaiting-trial-danbazau/

Dearing, J. W. (2009). Applying diffusion of innovation theory to intervention development. *Research on Social Work Practice*, *19*(5), 503–518. doi:10.1177/1049731509335569 PMID:20976022

Digard, L., diZerega, M., Yaroni, A., & Rinaldi, J. (2016). *A New Role for Technology? Implementing video visitation in prison*. New York, NY: Vera Institute of Justice. Accessed online on 23/11/2017 from https://storage.googleapis.com/vera-web-assets/downloads/Publications/video-visitation-in-prison/legacy_downloads/video-visitation-in-prison_02.pdf

Dijst, M. (2004). ICTs and accessibility: an action space perspective on the impact of new information and communication technologies. In M. Beuthe, V. Himanen, A. Reggiani, & L. Zamparini (Eds.), *Transport developments and innovations in an evolving world* (pp. 27–46). Heidelberg, Germany: Springer-Verlag. doi:10.1007/978-3-540-24827-9_3

Dimitri, C., Effland, A. B., & Conklin, N. C. (2005). *The 20th century transformation of US agriculture and farm policy* (Vol. 3). Washington, DC: US Department of Agriculture, Economic Research Service.

Dinkel, D., Schaffer, C., Snyder, K., & Lee, J. M. (2017). They just need to move: Teachers' perception of classroom physical activity breaks. *Teaching and Teacher Education*, *63*, 186–195. doi:10.1016/j.tate.2016.12.020

Dissel, A. (2001). *Prison conditions in Africa (A report). Centre for the Study of Violence and Reconciliation.* Accessed from on 21/09/2017 from http://www.csvr.org.za/docs/correctional/prisonconditions.pdf

Easley, D., & Kleinberg, J. (2010). *Networks, Crowds and Markets: Reasoning about a Highly Connected World.* Cambridge University Press. doi:10.1017/CBO9780511761942.020

Fasanmi, A. (2015). In the shadow of being forgotten: Women incarcerated in Nigerian prisons and the health implications. *Agenda (Durban, South Africa)*, *29*(4), 67–78.

Goggin, G. (2012). *Cell phone culture: Mobile technology in everyday life*. New York: Routledge.

Helsper, E. (2008). *Digital inclusion: an analysis of social disadvantage and the information society*. London: Department for Communities and Local Government.

Horn, J., Rosenband, L. N., & Smith, M. R. (Eds.). (2010). *Re-conceptualizing the industrial revolution*. Cambridge, MA: The MIT Press.

Hudson, P. (2014). *The industrial revolution*. Bloomsbury Publishing.

International Committee of the Red Cross. (2012). *Water, sanitation, hygiene and habitat in prisons: Supplementary guidance*. ICRC. Retrieved from https://www.icrc.org/eng/assets/files/publications/icrc-002-4083.pdf

Isah, M. (April 26, 2017). Assessing infrastructural deficit in Nigerian prisons. *PR Nigeria*. Accessed online on 19/9/2017 from https://prnigeria.com/general/prawa/prison-service-prawa/

Joseph, T. D. (2012). Literacy, information and communication technology as tools for empowerment of inmates. *European Journal of Educational Research*, *1*(2), 117–126. doi:10.12973/eu-jer.1.2.117

Jungen, A. (2016). GPS ankle bracelet monitoring of low-risk offenders costs more than anticipated. *La Crosse Tribune*. Accessed online 20/9/2017 from http://www.govtech.com/public-safety/GPS-Ankle-Bracelet-Monitoring-of-Low-Risk-Offenders-Costs-More-than-Anticipated.html

Lockitt, G. W. (2011). *Technology in prisons*. Winston Churchill Travelling Fellowship. Retrieved September 20, 2017 from https://www.wcmt.org.uk/sites/default/files/migrated-reports/797_1

Lucas, A. R. (2010). Narratives of Technological Revolution in the Middle Ages. In A. Classen (Ed.), *Handbook of Medieval Studies: Terms-methods-trends* (pp. 967–990). Berlin: De Gruyter. doi:10.1515/9783110215588.967

Mawasha, M. (2017). *The fourth industrial revolution - an African perspective.* Accessed on 30/09/2017 from https://www.fin24.com/Opinion/the-fourth-industrial-revolution-an-african-perspective-20170921

Mossberger, K., Tolbert, J., & Stansbury, M. (2003). *Virtual reality: Beyond the digital divide.* Washington, DC: Georgetown University Press.

Muhammad, Y. A., Gwangndi, M. I., & Hassan, A. S. (2017). The Rights of Prisoners in Nigeria and the Role of Prisons and Modern Penology. *JL Pol'y & Globalization, 60*, 71–80.

National Human Rights Commission Nigeria. (2009). *Report of Prison Audit.* Accessed on 21/09/2017 from https://www.state.gov/documents/organization/265500.pdf

Neji, M. O. (2016). *Information and Communication Technology utilization and implementation on adult education programmes in Nigeria* (Master Thesis). University of Nigeria, Nsukka.

News Agency of Nigeria. (2017). *205 inmates enrolled in formal, non-formal education in plateau state.* Accessed online on 22/11/2017 from http://punchng.com/205-inmates-enrolled-in-formal-non-formal-education-in-plateau/

Nigeria Today. (2017). *59 Ikoyi Prisons inmates sit for 2017 UTME.* Accessed online on 19/9/2017 from http://www.nigeriatoday.ng/2017/05/59-ikoyi-prisons-inmates-sit-for-2017-utme/

Obike, G. (2017). *Over 120 inmates register for JAMB.* Accessed online on 19/9/2017 http://thenationonlineng.net/120-inmates-register-jamb/

Obioha, E. E. (2011). Challenges and reforms in the Nigerian prisons system. *J Soc Sci, 27*(2), 95–109.

Office of the High Commissioner, United Nations Human Rights. (2017). *Standard Minimum Rules for the Treatment of Prisoners.* OHCHR. Accessed on 20/09/2017 from http://www.ohchr.org/EN/ProfessionalInterest/Pages/TreatmentOfPrisoners.aspx

Onyekachi, J. (2016). Problems and prospects of administration of Nigerian prison: Need for proper rehabilitation of the inmates in Nigeria Prisons. *Journal of Tourism & Hospitality (Los Angeles, Calif.), 5*(228), 2167–0269.

Opafunso, Z. O., & Adepoju, O. O. (2016). Prison reforms system and inmates welfare in Nigeria. *Arts and Social Sciences Journal*, *7*(1), 1–6.

Orakwe, W. I. (2017). *History of Nigerian Prisons Service*. Accessed on 14/09/2017 from http://www.prisons.gov.ng/history_of_nps

Pillera, G. (2015). E-Literacy and access to internet as inmate's right: European ICT frameworks in correctional education. *ICERI2015 Proceedings*, 344-353.

Pinilla, V. (2017). *Agricultural crisis in Spain (19th and 20th centuries)*. SEHA.

Popoola, S. (2017). *Over 120 inmates register for JAMB*. Accessed online on 19/9/2017 from http://www.thecaveat.info/2017/05/over-120-inmates-register-for-jamb.html

Reyes, A., Bacani, C., Horch, D., Rienstra, D., & Walter, J. (2016). *World Economic Forum Annual Meeting 2016 Mastering the Fourth Industrial Revolution*. Geneva: World Economic Forum.

Rogers, E. M. (2010). *Diffusion of innovations* (4th ed.). New York: The Free Press.

Rosen, W. (2012). *The Most Powerful Idea in the World: A Story of Steam, Industry and Invention*. Chicago: University of Chicago Press.

Ruiz-Mercado, I., Masera, O., Zamora, H., & Smith, K. R. (2011). Adoption and sustained use of improved cookstoves. *Energy Policy*, *39*(12), 7557–7566. doi:10.1016/j.enpol.2011.03.028

Sahara Reporters. (2017). *Fire Attack on Kuje Prison in Abuja*. Accessed online on 19/9/2017 from http://saharareporters.com/2017/07/21/fire-attack-kuje-prison-abuja

Sarkin, J. (2008). Prisons in Africa: An evaluation from a human rights perspective. *Sur. Revista Internacional de Direitos Humanos*, *5*(9), 22–51. doi:10.1590/S1806-64452008000200003

Tenibiaje, D. J. (2012). Literacy, information and communication technology as tools for empowerment of inmates. *European Journal of Educational Research*, *1*(2), 117–126. doi:10.12973/eu-jer.1.2.117

The Nation. (2017a). *How Ikoyi prison inmates fared in UTME*. Accessed online on 19/9/2017 http://thenationonlineng.net/ikoyi-prison-inmates-fared-utme/

The Nation. (2017b). *322 prisons inmates registered for WASSCE*. Accessed online on 19/9/2017 from http://thenationonlineng.net/322-prisons-inmates-registered-for-wassce/

The Nigerian Expression. (2017). *22 inmates in Jos register for examination*. Accessed online on 19/9/2017 from http://thenigerianexpression.com/2017/08/12/22-inmates-in-jos-register-for-examination/

Tselios, V., McCann, P., & van Dijk, J. (2017). Understanding the gap between reality and expectation: Local social engagement and ethnic concentration. *Urban Studies (Edinburgh, Scotland)*, *54*(11), 2592–2612. doi:10.1177/0042098016650395

Tselios, V., Noback, I., Dijk, J., & McCann, P. (2015). Integration of immigrants, bridging social capital, ethnicity, and locality. *Journal of Regional Science*, *55*(3), 416–441. doi:10.1111/jors.12160

Tsend-Ayush, G. (2017). The Impact of Information and Communication Technologies on Prison Institutions. *Hadmernok*, *12*(1), 278–289.

Uche, I. B., Uche, O. A., Ezumah, N. N., Ebue, M. O., Okafor, A. E., & Ezegbe, B. N. (2015). Effectiveness of Rehabilitation Programmes in the Nigerian Prisons: A Study of Perception of Inmates in Enugu Prison. *Mediterranean Journal of Social Sciences*, *6*(S2), 164-170.

Ugwumba, N. C. F., & Usang, E. E. (2014). The challenges of rehabilitation and reintegration of ex-convicts from Nigerian prisons. *Journal of Science, Engineering and Technology*, *3*(2), 59–64.

United Nations. (1990). *UN basic principle for treatment of prison inmates* (Resolution 45/III). UN.

United Nations Office on Drugs and Crime. (2015). *The United Nations Standard Minimum Rules for the Treatment of Prisoners (the Nelson Mandela Rules): An updated blueprint for prison management in the 21st century*. Accessed on 20/09/2017 from https://www.unodc.org/documents/justice-and-prison-reform/Brochure_on_the_UN_SMRs.pdf

Valente, T. W., & Rogers, E. M. (1995). The origins and development of the diffusion of innovations paradigm as an example of scientific growth. *Science Communication*, *16*(3), 242–273. doi:10.1177/1075547095016003002 PMID:12319357

Vanguard. (2017a). *22 inmates of Jos prison adult education scheme register for examination*. Accessed online on 19/9/2017 from https://www.vanguardngr.com/2017/08/22-inmates-jos-prison-adult-education-scheme-register-examination/

Vanguard. (2017b). *Kaduna Prison trains 60 inmates in tailoring, ICT*. Accessed online on 19/9/2017 https://www.dailytrust.com.ng/news/general/kaduna-prison-trains-60-inmates-in-tailoring-ict/180008.html

Wall, D. S. (2017). Crime, security and information communication technologies: The changing cybersecurity threat landscape and its implications for regulation and policing. In R. Brownsword, E. Scotford, & K. Yeung (Eds.), *The Oxford Handbook of Law, Regulation and Technology* (pp. 1076–23). Oxford University Press. doi:10.2139srn.3005872

Walsham, G. (2012). Are we making a better world with ICTs? Reflections on a future agenda for the IS field. *Journal of Information Technology*, *27*(2), 87–93. doi:10.1057/jit.2012.4

Ware, N. C., Hopper, K., Tugenberg, T., Dickey, B., & Fisher, D. (2008). A theory of social integration as quality of life. *Psychiatric Services (Washington, D.C.)*, *59*(1), 27–33. doi:10.1176/ps.2008.59.1.27 PMID:18182536

Warschauer, M. (2003). *Technology and Social inclusion: Rethinking the digital divide*. Cambridge, MA: MIT Press.

Warschauer, M. (2004). *Technology and social inclusion: Rethinking the digital divide*. Cambridge, MA: MIT Press.

Webster, C. A., Caputi, P., Perreault, M., Doan, R., Doutis, P., & Weaver, R. G. (2013). Elementary classroom teachers' adoption of physical activity promotion in the context of a statewide policy: An innovation diffusion and socio-ecologic perspective. *Journal of Teaching in Physical Education*, *32*(4), 419–440. doi:10.1123/jtpe.32.4.419

World Prison Brief Data. (2017). *Nigeria*. Accessed on 14/09/2017 from http://www.prisonstudies.org/country/nigeria

ADDITIONAL READING

Ackerman, G. (2017). *Efficacious technology management: A guide for school leaders*. Hack Science Network.

Apulu, I., & Ige, E. O. (2011). Are Nigeria SMEs effectively utilizing ICT? *International Journal of Business and Management*, *6*(6), 207. doi:10.5539/ijbm.v6n6p207

Asaolu, O. S. (2006). On the emergence of new computer technologies. *Journal of Educational Technology & Society*, *9*(1).

Asaolu, O. S. (2012). Improving software integration and development for engineering education in Nigeria. *African Journal of Computing and ICT*, *5*(5), 1–7.

Britz, J. (2010). *The Oxford handbook of Information and Communication Technologies*. Wiley.

Couldry, N. (2007). Communicative entitlements and democracy: The future of the digital divide debate. In The Oxford handbook of information and communication technologies. Oxford.

Fashanu, T. A., & Asaolu, O. S. (2012). Adoption of ICT and its Comparative Impact on Private and Public High Schools in Lagos State, Nigeria. *International Journal of Science & Emerging Technologies*, *3*(1).

Shehu, M. I., Othman, M. F. B. & Osman, N. B. Nigerian justice system: The ideal, hope and reality. *Sahel Analyst*: Journal of Management Sciences, 15(3).

Shin, M. J., & Cassidy, T. D. (2015). Designing a fashion driving forces website as an educational resource. *International Journal of Fashion Design. Technology and Education*, *8*(2), 173–183.

Tsatsou, P. (2011). *Digital divides in Europe: Culture, politics and the Western-Southern divide*. Berlin, Germany: Peter Lang.

KEY TERMS AND DEFINITIONS

Diffusion: A process through which ideas, information and knowledge spread in the social system.

Info-Communication Skills: A means through which diffusion and information exchange is carried out.

Information and Communication Technologies: A unified term used to refer to computer-based and telecommunication processes through which information is gathered, processed, shared, and stored.

Information Exchange: A process of sending and receiving information either physically or electronically and/or both.

Prison Population: The number of people who have been imprisoned for various forms of punishable crimes.

Recidivism: A tendency that someone is has been convicted will commit the same crime, if not, a more serious one.

Rehabilitation: Is rebuilding one's character to improve their well-being and relevance to society.

Reintegration Tools: A technique used to enable an individual who been imprisoned fit in a social group or the social system as a whole.

Skill Acquisition: A process through which a prisoner attains mastery of the basics of a task with the aim to render service(s) for financial freedom.

Social Reintegration: A process through which a person who has been imprisoned gains freedom and returns to live among other members of the society.

ENDNOTES

1 The Nigerian Prison Service is a government agency, which has been operational since 1861 but it was not until 1971 when a pronouncement was made for the reorganisation and a decree in 1972 clearly spelt out the goals for reform and rehabilitation of detainees for committing culpable offences (Orakwe, 2017).

2 The Standard Minimum Rules for the Treatment of Prisoners was adopted in 1955 by the United Nations Congress on the prevention of crime and the treatment of offenders, which took place in Geneva-Switzerland. However, the approval came by the Economic and Social Council resolutions in July 1957 and May 1977 respectively (OHCHR, 2017).

3 Industrial revolution is widely discussed using four stages: first (industrialization and urbanization of agrarian areas); second (expansion of existing industries); third (technological advancement) and fourth (revolution of digital technology). This fourth stage of industrial revolution has birthed popular technological inventions such as nanotechnology, 3-dimension printing, quantum computing, robotics, and many more.

Chapter 10
New Media Usage and the Impact on Inmates' Technological Profiles and Their Infocommunicational Skills

Ana Melro
University of Aveiro, Portugal

Daniela Graça
University of Aveiro, Portugal

Lídia Oliveira
University of Aveiro, Portugal

ABSTRACT

We live in a period of new literacies development, specifically the technological ones. Contact with new media or changes in more traditional ones leads to a need for different social, intellectual, and educational tools. As a consequence of the new demands of the twenty-first century, teaching had to be updated and monitored in order to foster the inclusion of individuals at school, work, socially, and digitally. The learning of technological tools should not marginalize individuals for their geographic, economic, and/or social characteristics, and should happen in an equitable way regardless of the teaching context. Media education is a factor that can favorably contribute to the process of the inmate inclusion in "free society" and to reduce recidivism. The chapter intends to reflect on the integration of the new media in the Portuguese education system in general, and later to analyze it in micro contexts, by comparative observation of the "citizen-inmate."

DOI: 10.4018/978-1-5225-5975-7.ch010

INTRODUCTION

ICT have an important role in various areas of the current Portuguese society. They exist as informal support of human relations and as an instrument for citizenship. On the other hand, social reintegration after prison is a key theme in the Portuguese penal system and its legislation, being reflected, in 2012, in the upgraded name of the Direção-Geral de Serviços Prisionais — "General Directorate of Prison Services" — to Direção-Geral de Reinserção e Serviços Prisionais — "General Directorate of Reintegration and Prison Services".

This dichotomy between a more dependent and existing online society, the importance of inmates reintegration lead us to question if the existence of Internet access in the school prison has been a reintegration key point.

Literature reveal that education is a pivotal factor in the preparation of the inmate for his return and integration in the society as well as in the prevention and reduction of recidivism. And the present schooling guidelines reinforce the importance of the technology base knowledge in the curriculum of any individual. Therefore the acquisition of such competences is of extreme importance, and cannot be ignored in the education that is offered to all those that sit in the margin of society.

As it is considered that the insertion of the new media did not occur at the same time in all social contexts, the inmates and free individuals will be analyzed in more depth (using statistics of the inclusion of new media in Portuguese schools).

Additionally, it is still important to understand what is not evident with the distribution of technology, that is, whether digital inclusion is carried out in contexts considered to be disadvantaged (namely, prisons) and, if so, how it is handled, as defended by Warschauer (Warschauer, 2006 [2003]) it is not sufficient to have the physical means (computers, mobile phones, among others), it is necessary to acquire the skills that allow its satisfactory use.

From the analysis of the historical development of the decades that accompanied the technological evolution in Portugal one starts an understanding of the technological profile of the individual, more specifically, her/his respective infocommunicational competences. The central objective of this chapter is to outline what is known as the technological profile of the competent individual in media usage, which, as mentioned, not only refers to access to new media, but above all by indicators of literacy, social interaction, among others.

This aspect led to the construction of a model based on macro, micro and meso factors, that is, in the first, the social, political and economic characteristics of society; at the micro level are the idiosyncrasies of the individual (family, career and school, social class, skills, among others) and the meso level (intermediate) is considered the specific access to different types of infrastructure, (possession of new media, available internet connections, among others).

BACKGROUND

In Portugal, the integration of new media happened gradually. In 1856 appeared the telegraph which linked the Terreiro do Paço to Cortes and the Palace of Necessities to Sintra[1]. The first experiments carried out with the telephone happened in 1877, with the aim of connecting Lisbon to Carcavelos and the observatories of the Escola Politécnica and Tapada da Ajuda (Santos, 1999, p. 1). And it was in the early 20th century that the first Morse radio contacts were established[2]. These were the first media that allowed people to communicate and since then, although a little slowly, they have been evolving and the need to integrate more and better communication and information technologies has arisen.

Nevertheless, the technology explosion in Portugal, like in the rest of the world, was not linear, since the research and development around it is a process that can last for decades until its massive use. Thinking back to the beginning of the 1950s, the memory that may arise with the media is related to radio and telephone. In fact, it was these same technologies that enabled and encouraged the development of television in the late 1950s in Portugal and of the mobile phone in the 1990s (Williams, 1966/1989, p. 101).

It was in the 70's that the first computers appeared in Portugal, first only available in business and universities; but in the early 1980s they started to reach some homes, with a smaller size and more affordable price.

The 1990s are profitable in technology development and dissemination. Televisions change as well as computers, and become more frequent: the percentage of households with television rises from 91.3% in 1991 (Vieira, 2001, p. 55) to 97% in 1999[3]. There are also laptops, in 1990, only 5% of Portuguese households have a computer, a percentage that increases to 31.4% in 1999[4] "and from that date onwards the PCs explode at homes" (Roberto, 2010, p. 43).

Family relations, work and leisure contexts assume visible differences. Initially (1957), access to television was carried out in public spaces (cafés, associations' spaces open to the public, such as scouts, among others). Only a few months later (1958) the television started to appear more frequently in family space (in 2009 it existed in 99.9% of Portuguese households (Cardoso & Espanha, 2009, p. 3)), around which all members of the family met to attend the available programs. In the 1980s, computer introduced new habits in the workplace (and, more recently, in school), Tasks developed only manually, gained greater efficiency with the help of this technology. In the 90's, the mobile phone was the third screen that changed some of the routines implemented, eliminating the spatial-temporal barriers. All these devices have gained a presence in the individuals' daily lives so close and so indispensable that makes them always with them, assuming almost a second skin relationship.

Table 1 gives information regarding integration and evolution of some media in Portugal.

By the end of the 20th century, more and more equipment was encircling people: television, radio, video, telephone, fax and computer; a situation that has been changing at the turn of the century and that, even today, it is almost impossible to know what else will be created and made available to individuals to have access to information, to share knowledge, to interact with other people, etc. If in the past the privileged means for these activities were television and radio, today there are endless devices where it is possible to collect and share information, the main characteristics are - and they have to be, in order to satisfy users - speed, reliability and versatility.

As McLuhan (2008 [1964]) states, "Any technology generates new pressures and needs in the society that engendered it. New needs and new technological responses emerge from our adoption of existing technologies in an endless process" (McLuhan, 2008 [1964], p. 190). This process also occurs because the developed technologies are not always spread by society as the creators intended, and are therefore considered as a failure, moreover, either the actual artefact itself or the production of content with the support of this artifact is intended to be more widespread, because as Jenkins, Ford and Green (2013) refer to "if it doesn't spread, it's dead"(2013, p. 1).

Table 1. Telecommunication services evolution in Portugal

1874								telegraph
	1876							telephone
		1920						radio
								telex
			1930					television
				1960				color television
								mobile phone
								high fidelity
								telecopy
					1975			data
								teletext
								videotext
								videoconference
								stereo television
						1990		newspaper printing
							1993	electronic mail
								Internet

Source: Santos (1999, p. 5)

For McLuhan (2008 [1964]) this relationship of reception, adoption, and integration of technologies, to the point of becoming intrusive and ubiquitous in individuals' lives, takes on a relationship of service, but not in a logic of being to serve the purposes of individuals, but rather individuals corresponding to the expectations of media. The author even considers that "a narcissistic subliminal awareness and a numbness in relation to these images of ourselves are produced" (McLuhan, 2008 [1964], p. 60). However, in order for a new medium to be inserted into a group or society, McLuhan (2008 [1964]), says that there must be a "massive social surgery" (McLuhan, 2008 [1964], p. 77). Nowadays, this massive social surgery does not happen, it applies for groups to adapt to the monotonous, such is the speed at which new technologies, tools and applications arise.

In Portugal, the integration of new media crossed three essential moments. The first great moment occurred during the dictatorship period, between 1933 and 1974. At this time, the content transmitted by the Portuguese media had a tight ideological control from the Government. The newspapers were not professionalized, had a very weak business and financial structure; the radios belonged mostly to the Government and to the Catholic Church, and when they didn't, they had to account for these two institutions and / or serve their interests; television began its regular broadcasts in 1957 (although several attempts have been made since 1953), but, like radio, under full Government domination and with little coverage in terms of national territory (Cardoso, Costa, Conceição, & Gomes, 2005, p. 75).

A second period began with the revolution of April 1974. With it freedom of expression was implemented, however, the mainstream media were nationalized (Cardoso *et al.,* 2005, p. 75), that is to say, the Government was the main holder of the Portuguese media, which, although uncensored, continued to constitute some control over the information conveyed.

The third, and last, period was Portugal's accession to the EEC in 1986. This was a crucial period for the definition of what the media would be in Portugal, and to which the economic climate of confidence contributed. The existing structures have been modernized and conditions have been created for the creation of new ones. The written press was privatized; the radio structures were reorganized; and new and private television projects appeared: SIC in 1992 and TVI in 1993 – private television channels (Cardoso *et al.*, 2005, p. 76).

As it turned out, the Country's political context was one of the main drivers of the integration of media or its restructuring. In this way, the Government has always assumed a preponderant role in the introduction of technology in the main sectors of activity, and continues to assume. For example, in 1965, in education, the school television project came up, meaning it was through television that students from more isolated backgrounds (especially rural ones) had access to the classroom and school contents.

But it was, especially, from the end of the 90's, and related to the strong spread of computers and the Internet in Portugal at that time, that the Government has paid more attention to the technology sector. In 1997 the Green Paper on Information Society in Portugal was launched. This document had as main guidelines the improvement of efficiency of public administration, through the streamlining of procedures; make public documents increasingly digital and therefore easier to access; promote the creation of digital libraries; equip schools with more and better technological tools; make companies more competitive by favoring their online presence; to legislate the production and dissemination of online content; among others (Gil & Amaro, 2011, p. 62).

Meanwhile, in 2005, the Technological Plan was launched, with three main axes - Knowledge, Technology and Innovation - and being addressed to Citizens, Companies, Public Administration and Research and Teaching[5]. As part of the Technological Plan, the Portuguese Government created the Digital Agenda 2015 in 2010[6], the reformulation of which until 2020 was carried out in 2013. The intervention areas of the Digital Agenda 2015 were, once again, businesses, citizens, health, education and the energy sector. In 2013 these areas of analysis were aimed at the following: "access to broadband and the digital market; investment in Research and Development (R & D) and Innovation; improving digital literacy, qualification and inclusion; combating fraud and tax evasion, contributory and benefits; response to societal challenges; entrepreneurship and internationalization of the ICT sector."[7]

Also worthy of mention is the Schools Technological Plan[8]. Since 2007 the Government has some ongoing projects to promote technological development in schools and students, teachers and non-teachers. The most well-known projects, and with greater public visibility, were the e-school, e-teacher and e-opportunities; ICT skills; among others. The primary objective of the first two was the access of teachers and students from primary and secondary education to portable computers and broadband internet.

In relation to the Digital Agenda 2015, is important to mention Portugal INCoDe.2030[9], as an innovative and more recent project (2017), which implements a strategy for the digital development of the country, with the aim of positioning Portugal in the group of top European countries in digital skills.

Table 2 presents a summary of the emergence of the first media in Portugal, the years of its introduction in the country are identified, which may not have been the year in which they were available to the common user, but were used in large companies and universities, such as the computer, the internet and mobile phones. It also shows the number or percentage of users at the time of its appearance (or approximate), as well as the last year available in the official statistics; the type

Table 2. Integration of studied media in Portugal and some indicators

	Television	Computer	Internet	Mobile Phone[10]
Introduced in	1957	1970	1990	1989
Amount of users	1959: 3.1256 receptors[11] 2011: 4.015.832 TV appliances[12] (subscription TV, 2012: 76,6%[13])	1990: 5% of the household[14] 2012: 66,1% of the household[15]	1997: 88.670 subscribers 2011: 2.212.412 subscribers[16]	1990: 6.584 subscribers 2011: 20.003.783 subscribers[17]
Equipment	Television and TDT appliance or box (expensive)	Computer (desktop or portable) not too expensive	Fixed and portable connection (expensive)	Mobile phone (not too expensive)
Cost (approximated values)	100€ (TV) + 25€ (TDT appliance) + 30€/month (box)	300€ (laptop) + 100€ (software)	10€/month	Monthly fee of € 10 on average with access to voice, text and free internet
Language	Portuguese	English	English	Portuguese
Necessary skill	No special skills needed	Writing, reading, English, calculus, searching, ...	Writing, reading, English, calculus, research, social skills, ...	Simplified writing, reading, research, social skills, ...

Source: Adapted from Warschauer (2006 [2003], p. 92)

of equipment needed for its actual use; the cost of the equipment, currently, in approximate values; the language of which it is necessary to have some knowledge for an effective and complete use and other skills required for its use.

Considering that one of the prisons' objectives should be to provide individuals with educational instruments that favor their social reintegration, access to the Internet from the establishment of incarceration is a demandable right. Indeed, in the current context of a multicultural society, literacy must be multiple, in order to mitigate the division between prison and society, not only social but also digital.

Inmates should be able to learn about and assimilate the technological and social changes that will enable them to successfully readapt in the future. From the point of view of Burgos, Garcia & Humbert Oliván (2007), it is necessary to develop technological and information capacities integrated in a broad literacy, in which the informative, personal and social dimensions do not dissociate.

In fact, new technologies alone do not make individuals wiser or freer. They simply give them the learning tools and instruments for possible progress as an individual. It seems, therefore, to be crucial that digital literacy be integrated into a broader and more inclusive evolutionary process (Burgos et al., 2007), in which individuals in reclusion are included (Agúndez Soriano, 2016; Graça, 2016).

It should be considered that teaching in the specific context of incarceration will serve as a form of socialization, contact with the outside, and learning by participating (Rocha & Oliveira, 2014). For individuals whose motivation is low or nil and / or whose experience with the school was traumatic prior to incarceration, it is crucial to provide a stimulating teaching practice that allows the individual to identify and relate in a healthy way to the school, now in reclusion (Hurry, Brazier, Snapes, & Wilson, 2005). The context and format of teaching are indeed determinants of successful learning. A direct interaction with learning, a regular relationship with the study, with teachers, trainers or tutors, with the tasks and objectives to be achieved, allows the individual-inmate to feel integrated into a social group outside the prison in the school community, which results in a positive, pro-social, normal-life self-identity (Pike, 2014).

The same idea is shared by Farley & Pike (2016) in "Engaging prisoners in education: Reducing risk and recidivism", which demonstrates that the existence of a school course can promote the stability of the environment in the prison establishment by keeping the individual occupied, goal oriented which will subsequently contribute to reducing the risk of recurrence. It also explains that if school attendance of prisoners had a greater incentive on the part of the institutions, of the prison system and that if the education of individuals was considered as a potential method of reducing security risks and instability in establishments, many of the challenges the system face would be reduced (Farley & Pike, 2016).

In Portugal, access to the Internet in prisons takes place in schools and only in subjects related to information and communication technologies. There are some exceptions where access does not only occur within these disciplines as in the case of individuals attending specific projects or university education. In these cases there is always monitoring and supervision of a technician of the establishment who has the responsibility to guide the use of the Internet (Graça, 2010, 2016).

MAIN FOCUS OF THE CHAPTER

Issues, Controversies, Problems

In the Portuguese case it is more about the exceptional use of the system, infrastructure, organization, human resources, than a new investment, in a new scenario, with new ways.

Cunha & Bastos (2007) point out, in an analysis of the therapeutic role of prison, that "the rhetoric of the intramural reintegration programs is the transfer of resources from the community to the prison, even when the investment in the external environment has already proven to be crucial" (Cunha & Bastos, 2007, p.

980), inferring that the organization of the efforts' distribution, whether economic, structural, etc., should focus on the problem before it becomes one, that is, the individual before this become a recluse.

Regardless of any research that is known or planned, it is possible to define, in abstract, some obstacles to the application of the Internet in reclusion. In this exercise, the safety factor will certainly be the one that comes first, since the use of a technology is considered in a context in which the individual should be restricted to a set of rules, namely that of controlled contact with the outside of the place of imprisonment.

In order to ensure the stability of the safety factor, there is a need to work on other factors, such as human resources management and infrastructures. The first is to ensure the technical control and monitoring of the possible use of the Internet, the second is to generate the appropriate space. This narrative of needs, which aims to reach a point of comfort in the existence of the possibility of Internet use by the prisoners, gives rise to the last, and not less relevant, factor: the economic one.

The citizen, whose place in the network occupies an increasing space, must understand the language of this context as he/she understands the language of reality outside the Internet. Thus, "The traditional scheme focused on literacy, which for many years represented the minimum necessary to prepare citizens, needs to be redefined." (Borges, Bezerra, Diomondes, & Coutinho, 2013, p. 3) with a set of skills adapted to the present reality.

The social organization that we live in today brings the condition that each individual has a virtual place, that he/she occupies a space in the network. Physical and virtual existences seem to be becoming inseparable. This new reality gives rise to the emergence of a new citizen profile, one in which the infocommunicational competences are part of the basic skills that a citizen should receive and acquire.

The current change, therefore, is cultural because we are migrating from a position of viewers - people who receive ready, uniform and standardized information content via TV and radio, for example - for participants - people who seek, evaluate and decide how to take advantage of the information available on the Internet. (Borges & Oliveira, 2011, p. 295).

Borges *et al.* define a model of infocommunicational competences by agglomerating those that come from information and communication, and adding them to the operational area, in a symbiotic and organic scheme in which the weight of each of the parts is variable according to the experience verified. (Borges *et al.,* 2013).

Borges & Oliveira conclude by stating that "infocommunicational competences in digital environments can be characterized as the convergence of knowledge, skills and attitudes that enable them to act appropriately in digital environments, mobilize their resources and new contacts, articulating them for the production of meaning and knowledge, based on legal and ethical precepts." (Borges & Oliveira, 2011, p. 321).

The curricular programs of the technological areas and disciplines present the competency profile that is considered to define the technologically competent citizen, an individual "capable of appreciating and considering the social, cultural, economic, productive and environmental dimensions resulting from technological development." (Borges & Oliveira, 2011).

In the competences' implementation study in Information and Communication Technology (Costa et al., 2008), the National Technology Standards and Performance Indicators of the International Society for Technology in Education (ISTE) was presented, which produced, in parallel to the competence framework in ICT for teachers, the ICT competence reference for students that says that the competent individual in Information and Communication Technologies should be able to use technology, to research, analyze and evaluate information; solve problems and make decisions; to effectively and creatively use production tools; to communicate, produce and edit; and to be an informed, responsible and contributing citizen.

Silva (2008) says that when talking about ICT skills two inseparable things are referred: "the existence and commercial expansion of devices with certain characteristics, namely the basic infrastructure, and the instrumental capacity to use them." The author considers that computer literacy (or digital), digital literacy and digital inclusion are synonymous when they refer exactly to the situation described above. And that individuals who claim to have these competencies are considered digital literate, info-included or digital natives.

In the history of technological development there is a time when generations are born into a technology-driven environment. Indeed, since 1980, "digital natives" have emerged, individuals who share a global culture that is defined not only by age but also by the possession of certain attributes and experiences related to how they interact with information technologies, the information itself, among them, with other people and institutions (Palfrey & Gasser, 2008, p. 364). These are individuals who have learned how to use technology as previous generations have learned to use books. They are, therefore, instruments of learning with which they have grown and which help shape thinking and reasoning in a new way.

When technology becomes an indicator for a new reading of the individuals' literacy, it is necessary to determine in which domains of knowledge there will be transformation. The first domain of knowledge that the individual faces in this process is the operational and instrumental domain of the technology (hardware), since the first requirement in the contact with the indicator [technology] is the physical one. In this the user is required to recognize technological equipment - computer, smartphone, tablet, etc. -, and physically start the moment of use. The second contact lies in the area of the experimental cognitive domain, in which the individual is asked to understand the existence and organization of software - operating systems, desktop applications, online applications - and is able to use it to achieve the objectives his/her action requires. The next step, in which the user uses the tools provided by technology - software - for production - research, selection, treatment and analysis of information - knowledge, communication, information manipulation - enters the infocommunicational domain.

This framework of relations is, due to the dependence of the existence of other literacies: interrelational; as a result of the various domains that integrate it. Multidimensional; because it is difficult to quantify and evaluate. Complex; by the changeable and variable nature dependent on the location, organization and social structure: geo and sociocultural.

This development process of infocommunicational competences is influenced by the individual, more particularly by the characteristics that the individual has previously and that will mark his route in the three domains. Therefore, in order to make the best course and achieve the best infocommunicational competence acquisition, it is therefore with a flexible and adaptable behavior that is certainly resilient and curious, critical, responsible and ethical. These characteristics, to a greater or lesser extent, are, for example, those that may dilute the disadvantages of the starting point resulting from pre-existing literacies, or blur the possible asymmetry resulting from the geo and socio-cultural condition from which the individual starts.

SOLUTIONS AND RECOMMENDATIONS

The research intended to apply the training model in two Portuguese prisons, to male and female inmates. This double application allowed the collection of data and information to carry out a correct analysis of the participants' profile, the feasibility of the training model, and the results that come from it, either through the enhancement of the participant's infocommunicational competencies or by the adaptability to the context to which was intended.

The training action format, integrated into a case study, has given researchers the dual advantage of allowing the target audience to learn and provide data on it. That is, the training moments that were constituted as exercises allowed the participant to learn by testing their knowledge and, simultaneously, result in information about the training action and the participant population.

Due to the methodological strategy used, whose basis was a training action and that, therefore, is conditioned by all the inherent characteristics of the same, two main methods were considered to obtain data: direct observation and questionnaire survey. In effect, the format of training action allowed for a privileged witness resulting from the necessary interaction between trainer and trainee, in which direct observation was unavoidable. Thus, a research-action / research-participant scenario was set up, in which the researcher was actively involved in the dynamics that are simultaneously his / her research locus.

Due to the methodological strategy used, whose basis was a training action and that, therefore, is conditioned by all the inherent characteristics of the same, two main methods were considered to obtain data: direct observation and questionnaire survey. In effect, the format of training action allowed for a privileged witness resulting from the necessary interaction between trainer and trainee, in which direct observation was unavoidable. Thus, a research-action / research-participant scenario was set up, in which the researcher was actively involved in the dynamics that are simultaneously his / her research locus.

The selection factors were, in order of importance: (i) age, (ii) remaining time of punishment, (iii) length of time served, (iv) number of times in confinement, (v) participation in a curricular year or training course in the establishment, (vi) level of schooling achieved, (vii) physical and mental state.

Of the nine participants who started the training at the Female Santa Cruz do Bispo Prison (FSCBP), six concluded it. Two participants withdrew from the training because they started working; the third withdrawal was due to the exit from the Prison. In the analysis of the sessions, only eight participants were considered due to the fact that one of the initial participants (who starting work) participated only in the first session.

From the Male Santa Cruz do Bispo Prison (MSCBP), the training began with 16 participants. Of these 16, two individuals participated only in the beginning of the action - an individual was transferred from the Free Drug Unit (FDU), within which the training action took place, for the main building of the prison, thus not being able to attend the training and two individuals attended almost all of the training but left the FDU and the prison due to fulfillment of two-thirds of the penalty or completion of the same. In the training, the FDU received a new inmate who, for showing interest, was integrated into the training group. Thus, a total of 17 individuals attended the training course, of which only 13 completed.

Figure 1 shows that 87% of respondents used the Internet prior to reclusion, which corresponds to seven of the eight participants in the training action (only participant 3 indicated that they did not use the Internet prior to reclusion).

In response to the question "Do you use or already used the Internet in reclusion?" Responses were obtained from all eight participants. Figure 2 (EPSCBF) shows that 37% (three participants) of the respondents answered affirmatively.

Figure 3 shows that 82% of the respondents (14 participants) used the Internet prior to reclusion, and that three did not use it (18%).

Figure 1. Internet usage before reclusion (FSCBP)

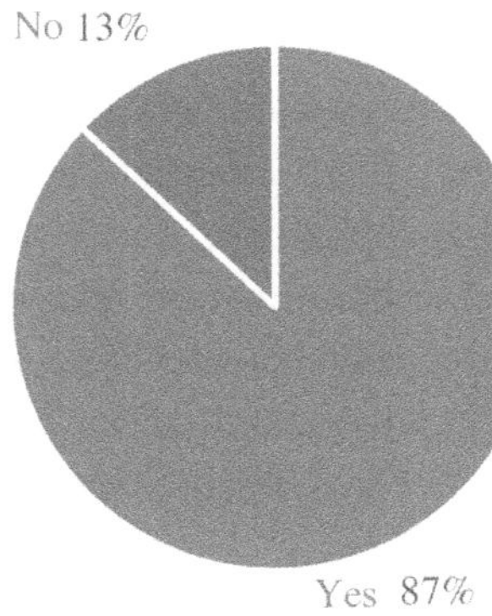

Figure 2. Internet usage during reclusion (FSCBP)

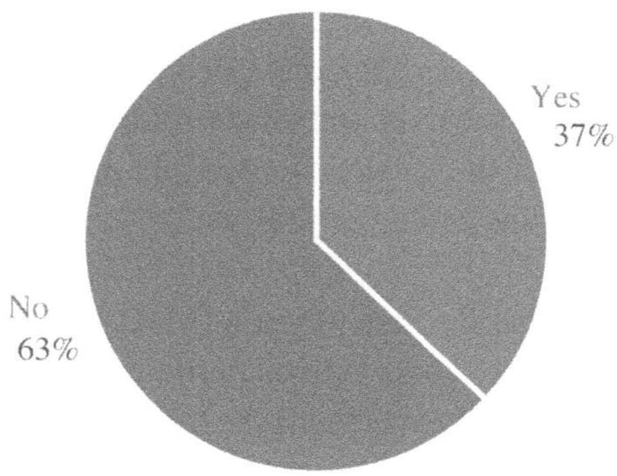

Figure 3. Internet usage before reclusion (MSCBP)

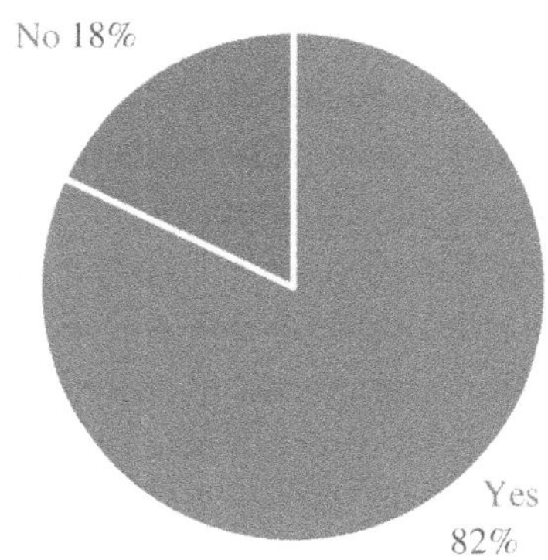

The answers to the question "Do you use or had already used the Internet in reclusion?", represented visually in Figure 4, indicate that 71% of the sample (12 participants) did not used the Internet while in reclusion; and 29% (5 participants) indicate that they have already done so.

While answering the question, some participants shared that their Internet usage stated in the questionnaire survey was illegal. That is, their access to the Internet in the establishment happened outside the law, did not happen in a school context, for example. If it was indicated that it happened in the case of some of the participants in the training course in the Female Santa Cruz do Bispo Prison. Considering this aspect, it should be assumed that the data in Figure 4 is not reality representative since some participants, knowing the anonymity under which they are protected in the scope of this investigation, decided to point out the truth of the facts, and others, either by fear or out of respect for the institution, did not do so. In summary, although it is considered that this aspect is not decisive in the investigation, it is believed that the percentage related to the "Yes" answer may actually be higher.

Analyzing participants' general satisfaction, which can be seen from the answers given throughout the case study, it is considered that the training action had a very positive impact not only on the infocommunicational knowledge of the trainees, but also on their relation with learning and also in their self-image and self-esteem.

An analysis of the obtained responses at all stages of the training activity shows that, apart from some organizational and structural issues, the training action is to the liking of all participants. In fact, learners are satisfied with the learning they have gained, and possibly more relevant, they have acquired the motivation to learn and the will to acquire more knowledge.

Thus, it is possible to affirm that there are no doubts about the added value of the application of similar training actions in the context such as the one found and for target audiences such as the one presented here.

Figure 4. Internet usage during reclusion (MSCBP)

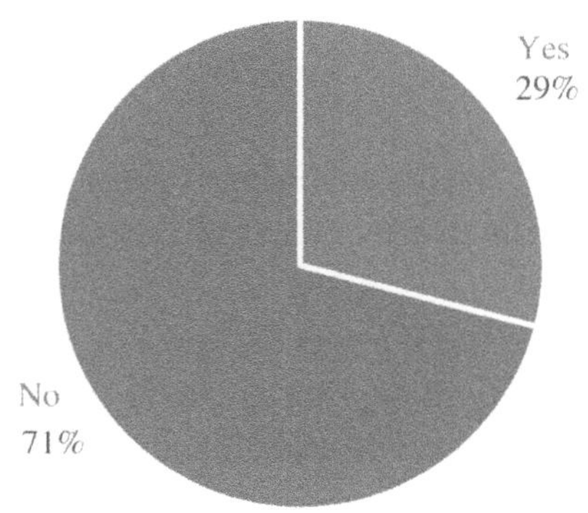

FUTURE RESEARCH DIRECTIONS

The first suggestion was actually proposed by a participant in the training course administered at the Santa Cruz do Bispo Prison. In response to the question about suggestions for improvement of the training action in the final evaluation, one of the participants suggested a pilot project to be carried out in that same facility and in the same unit, the Free Drug Unit. The trainee considered that that context would be the ideal to apply the model of Internet designed by the participant group. Because it is considered a valid suggestion and potential, it is included here.

Another suggestion concerns the organization of training sessions. As it is possible to confirm by reading this work, the moments of teaching result, for the most part, as moments of 'normality' for the inmates. In fact, the moments of training were moments of learning that should focus as much on this aspect and ignore the context as much as possible. One of the reasons for this is that participants can experience, within normal rules a teaching-learning context, doing things that cannot go beyond that moment. So, the suggestion is to have ludic moments in the training session.

In the case of this training action in which the theme allows access to the Internet these ludic moments are, moreover, a learning moment. The format may be that in each session a trainee choose something they would like to share with the group, be it a song, a video, news, etc. Thus, as a closing moment of the session, a trainee researches what they want to share, with supervision of the trainer, and displays it to the group, being able at the end of the visualization / hearing to have a moment of discussion about the choice made.

Innovation and creativity, while not unique to digital infocommunicational scenarios, should be viewed as crucial in the contemporary context of production and consumption of digital content (on and offline). In this sense, the authors challenge the readers to design and implement a research project in a prison context that aims to develop innovation and creativity skills using digital tools as a way to broaden the aesthetic and professional horizon of the inmates.

CONCLUSION

The research work developed and presented here fits the problem of the development of infocommunicational skills in the context of the use of digital tools, online, in the context of imprisonment.

Specifically on the use of the Internet for learning purposes, both experiences have shown that, within conditions appropriate to the prison context, this possibility exists and is practiced albeit in very restricted and conditioned ways.

Thus, it is concluded that in a one-to-one relationship in which the organics and dynamics of the prison are maintained and not disturbed, and when there is justification and authorization for use, Internet access may exist in a school context and / or training for the learning purpose.

Considering the target audience to which this research is directed, it is important that the structure of the topics addressed in the training action is designed for different levels of knowledge and for trainees with very little or no knowledge about the general theme. For this reason, the thematic program tested and presented includes the basis for all themes included in order to provide a simple and clear framework to any participant. This way of presenting and transmitting knowledge has shown to be motivating for the trainees by allowing them to understand effectively the origin of things. As a result, this construction of knowledge makes them curious and makes them want to know more, and the cycle repeats itself.

In order to maintain the interest and motivation of the trainees and because the thematic allows it, thematic flexibility must exist. That is, the thematic structure that is presented acts as the basis from which to add related topics that interest the participants in the training action or that the trainer considers relevant for the specific group with whom the teacher is working.

It cannot be ignored that the general theme of the training action, alone, provokes interest and curiosity in the participants, either because they have reduced qualifications and skills, or because of the context in which the training takes place.

Indeed, before a population with low level of knowledge it is verified that any learning is an added value in the increase of skills and knowledge of the individual, and even in the construction of the person as a citizen and professional. In the case of this research, specifically in the attempt to provide the individual with basic infocommunicational skills, the advantages become more obvious not only because individuals who already use the technologies do so inefficiently with respect to the positive return in professional success, but also because the learning they eventually receive post-reclusion will be more likely to be informal and therefore not geared to an effective and efficient use of information and communication technologies in order to achieve a place of success in the future, but oriented towards trivial use.

The results obtained with both case studies applied in prisons participating in this research show that there was a very positive impact not only on the infocommunicational knowledge of the individuals, but also on the relationship acquired with learning. The gain of knowledge and skills brought, in turn, a positive increase in the self-image and self-esteem of the participants. In fact, the satisfaction of the trainees with the obtained learning increases the motivation to learn and the will to acquire more knowledge.

Considering all the difficulties they face following their detention, this contribution is undoubtedly an added value for the future of these people. And it is argued that training actions such as those applied in this research should be a constant in Portuguese prisons, always with necessary adaptation to the structures and dynamics of each one, and to the profiles of the individuals involved.

ACKNOWLEDGMENT

This research received no specific grant from any funding agency in the public, commercial, or not-for-profit sectors.

REFERENCES

Agúndez Soriano, M. A. (2016). *Alfabetización informacional para la inclusión social de las mujeres reclusas de la Comunidad de Madrid: um estudio de caso.* Universidad Complutense de Madrid.

Borges, J., Bezerra, L., Diomondes, S., & Coutinho, L. (2013). Competências infocomunicacionais: Um conceito em desenvolvimento. *Tendências Da Pesquisa Brasileira Em Ciência Da Informação, 5*(1), 1–23.

Borges, J., & Oliveira, L. (2011). Competências infocomunicacionais em ambientes digitais. *Observatorio (OBS*), 5*(4).

Burgos, O., García, V., & Humbert, C. (2007). El blog desde la prisión: un instrumento de inclusión social. *Educacion Y Bibliotecas, 19*(158), 102–109.

Cardoso, G., da Costa, A. F., Conceição, C. P., & Gomes, M. do C. (2005). Processo de mudança estrutural na sociedade portuguesa. In G. Cardoso, A. F. da Costa, C. P. Conceição, & M. do C. Gomes (Eds.), A Sociedade em Rede em Portugal (1a, Vol. 17, pp. 31–80). Porto: Campo das Letras.

Cardoso, G., Espanha, R., & OberCom. (2009). *A Internet em Portugal 2009.* Lisboa: OberCom.

Costa, F., Rodrigues, Â., Peralta, M., Cruz, E., Reis, O., Ramos, J. L., … Valente, L. (2008). Competências TIC. Estudo de Implementação (vol. 2). Lisboa.

Cunha, M., & Bastos, C. (2007). As instituições híbridas. Reclusão e laços sociais. *Análise Social. Revista Do Instituto de Ciências Sociais Da Universidade de Lisboa, 42*(185), 977–983.

Farley, H., & Pike, A. (2016). Engaging prisoners in education: Reducing risk and recidivism. *Journal of the International Corrections and Prison Association, 1*(1), 65–73.

Gil, H., & Amaro, F. (2011). e-Inclusão: dos 7 aos 77. In U. de Aveiro (Ed.), 61st Internacional Council for Educational Media and the XIII International Simposium on computers in Education (ICEM&SIIE'2011) (pp. 60–65). Aveiro.

Graça, D. (2010). *Utilização da internet nos estabelecimentos prisionais portugueses: realidade ou utopia?* Universidade de Aveiro.

Graça, D. (2016). *Desenvolvimento de Competências Infocomunicacionais em Contexto Prisional - Proposta de um Modelo de Formação para a Utilização da Internet no Contexto Prisional Português*. Univeridade de Aveiro e Universidade do Porto - Portugal.

Hurry, J., Brazier, L., Snapes, K., & Wilson, A. (2005). *Improving the literacy and numeracy of disaffected young people in custody and in the community*. London.

Jenkins, H., Ford, S., & Green, J. (2013). *Spreadable media: creating value and meaning in a networked culture*. New York: New Iorque University Press.

McLuhan, M. (2008). *Compreender os Meios de Comunicação - Extensões do Homem. Antropos*. Lisboa: Relógio D'Água. (originally published 1964)

Palfrey, J., & Gasser, U. (2008). Opening Universities in a Digital Era. *New England Journal of Higher Education, 23*(1), 22–24.

Pike, A. (2014). *Prison-based transformative learning and its role in life after release*. Open University.

Roberto, J. (2010). Anos 1990-1999. As novas tecnologias. In Visão/Expresso (Ed.), *Os nossos anos* (Vol. 9). Lisboa: Planeta DeAgostini.

Rocha, D., & Oliveira, L. (2014). Informação e comunicação em plataformas digitais: novos desafios para o sistema prisional português. In A. M. da Silva, B. Passarelli, & F. Ramos (Eds.), *e-Infocomunicação - Estratégias e aplicações* (pp. 169–200). São Paulo: Senac.

Santos, R. (1999). História das Telecomunicações em Portugal. *Biblioteca on-Line de Ciências Da Comunicação*, 1–11.

Silva, A. M. (2010). Inclusão digital e literacia informacional em Ciência da Informação. *Revista Prisma. Com*, (7).

Vieira, J. (2001). Crónica em imagens 1990-2000. In J. Vieira (Ed.), *Portugal Século XX* (Vol. 10). Lisboa: Círculo de Leitores;

Warschauer, M. (2006). *Tecnologia e inclusão social: a exclusão digital em debate*. São Paulo: Editora Senac.

Williams, N. (n.d.). 1974/1984. In *Cronologia Enciclopédica do Mundo Moderno* (Vol. 8). Lisboa: Círculo de Leitores;

KEY TERMS AND DEFINITIONS

Education System: Also in the area of Public Administration (local and central), it is responsible for the definition of levels, curricula, infrastructures construction, among all the areas that compose Pre-school education (with the prevalence of private administration in some cases), secondary education and higher education (with prevalence of private administration also in some cases).

Infocommunicational Skills: Skills acquired or taken for the use of technological artifacts (hardware and software), of various nature: operational, informational, communicational, and ethical.

Inmate: Citizen who is in a situation of imprisonment in an official prison, to serve a sentence for a criminal or illegal act committed.

New Media: All the media that have undergone transformation to adapt to the new technological requirements or that have been created in the light of the new demands of the citizen.

Prison: Place of execution of the sentence attributed to the citizen in situation of imprisonment, in the Portuguese case, belonging to the domain of the Central Public Administration.

Reintegration: Capacity that, on the one hand, the citizen has to adjust to the society and find work and / or training that allows him/her to participate actively in that same society. And, on the other hand, the social context itself to provide the necessary tools for this reintegration of the individual.

Technological Profile: Profile of the individual regarding their use of technology and new media.

ENDNOTES

1 http://www.infopedia.pt/$telegrafo-em-portugal.

2 http://telefonia.no.sapo.pt/.

3 http://www.pordata.pt/.

4 http://www.marktest.com/wap/a/n/id~109c.aspx.

5 http://www.planotecnologico.pt/default.aspx?idLang=1&site=planotecnologico.

6 http://www.umic.pt/images/stories/noticias/PWP_AgendaDigital2015.pdf.

7 http://www.ei.gov.pt/iniciativas/detalhes.php?id=29.

8 http://www.pte.gov.pt/pte/PT/Projectos/index.htm.

9 http://www.incode2030.gov.pt/en/home.

10 Prepaid mobile phone users are not counted, which may substantially increase the indicator.

11 Crónica em imagens 1950-1960 (J. Vieira, 2000, p. 214).

12 Anuário Estatístico de Portugal 2011 (INE, 2012a, p. 289).

13 http://www.marktest.com/wap/a/n/id~19fc.aspx, visualized in February 6th, 2013.

14 Anos 1990-1999. As novas tecnologias (Roberto, 2010, p. 43).

15 http://www.pordata.pt/, visualized in February 6th, 2013.

16 http://www.pordata.pt/, visualized in February 5th, 2013.

17 http://www.pordata.pt/, visualized in February 5th, 2013.

Chapter 11
Restricted Communication:
Social Relationships and the Media Use of Prisoners

Bettina Zbinden
University of Hamburg, Germany

ABSTRACT

The aim of this research is to point out the patterns of media use of an inmate before the incarceration and the communication habits, as well as the compulsorily restricted media use during imprisonment. The purpose is to get insight of how the prisoners deal with the change of their situation and the subsequent use of traditional media such as letters and phone calls in order to keep in touch with their family and other social contacts. Deriving from the media repertoire approach, the research question is focused on the media use before and during imprisonment, which should clarify the change of patterns. In order to conduct a detailed exploration of a media repertoire on the personal level, the data collection has been conducted through semi-structured in-depth interviews with female prisoners from the German female prison TAF (Teilanstalt für Frauen) at the JVA Billwerder.

INTRODUCTION

Digital change is an everyday challenge for individuals, but also for society. Every part of modern life is somehow connected online. Humanity relies heavily on contiguous technological improvements and digital success. Even addiction to the Internet has become a growing issue in society and research (Griffiths, 2016). In Germany 88% of

DOI: 10.4018/978-1-5225-5975-7.ch011

the population has access to the Internet (Internet Live Stats, 2016). However, what about the part of society who is excluded from the Internet? What about prisoners whose media consumption is regulated by institutions and by the state?

Media develops exponentially quickly and change evolves in an ongoing process. Prisons regulations on the other hand are rigid and fixed. Long ago, our society decided what the correct manner of punishment must look like, as the French philosopher Michel Foucault claimed in 1977. These theories of punishment and rehabilitation have changed over time, yet media access in penal institutions still is appears rather old fashioned. In times of social media as an important factor of the maintenance of social relationships, incarceration means not only a big cut in the lives of prisoners, but also for their communication as a means of social sustenance and contact outside prison. This research sheds light on the understudied field of media use and incarceration in women's prisons in Germany. The aim is to get insight on the process of change in an individual in terms of media use at the time of imprisonment. The interest lies in the manner of communication, such as the media use of an inmate in order to sustain their respective social relationships. Therefore, the following research questions are guiding throughout this research:

- **RQ1**: How are the patterns of media use of an individual changing in the case of imprisonment?
- **RQ2**: How does the change of the media repertoire affect the social relationships of a female prisoner?
- **Sub RQ**: What role does the lack of social media play in the shift of the communicative figurations?

Since the nature of the topic of this study poses some ethical considerations a basic premise must be outlined here. "Do offender perceptions really matter? Clearly, some would argue that they don't, maintaining that it is for society rather than criminals to determine the purpose or meaning of punishment" (Van Voorhis, 1997, p. 139).

This study looks at the prisoner as an important individual which is part of our society, and therefore needs to be reintegrated after incarceration. This reintegration makes it relevant for the society who demands punishment, as well to give them a chance to regain respect and prove that they deserve a second chance. Therefore, offender perceptions matter as they help us to understand the situation from the point of view of a prisoner. The everyday, but also long term, needs of prisoners are taken seriously and therefore this study is interested in their perceptions in order to ascertain a better understanding for society at large, but also with regards to the rehabilitation process as a whole.

Though this study does not examine the victims who may have suffered as a result of the prisoners' actions, they are not forgotten. This study does not intend to diminish the seriousness of the delinquency and the horror they may have lived through.

BACKGROUND

Prisons in Germany are still very much unchanged from 50 years ago. Even though the focus of imprisonment lies today more on the rehabilitation of the prisoners, it still maintains the characteristics of total institutions or prisons in the sense of Goffman's and Foucault's ideas. Yet the communication tools and the digitalization of media is evolving outside the prison walls at an exponential pace, and therefore challenging prisons to keep pace with the newest technology and developments of media. Being cut off from society is one major aspect of imprisonment, but as the literature shows, it is debatable whether this is the right treatment for criminals. The question of how to penalize people in an accurate way is still prevailing and vastly different solutions have evolved over time. However, society cannot agree on another solution, therefore nothing changes, as Foucault stated in his work (Foucault, 1977). This applies to today's prisons, even though the aspect of rehabilitation and the new digitalized communication forms do not keep speed with the structures of today's prisons. Little research has been done on the media use of prisoners in a qualitative, user-centered way, as for example the media repertoire approach suggests. Conducted research on media use in prison is mostly focused on structural components in terms of access and use in a quantitative manner. Another research gap has been identified in the field of female prisoners where only recent studies show interest in their respective treatment (Haverkamp, 2012).

Female Prisoners

2016 the ratio of women living in Germany is 51% (Statista, 2018). Yet, the World Female Imprisonment List shows that only 5,9% of the total prison population in Germany are women[1]. This lies in the average number of worldwide female prisoners (Walmsley, 2015). The reason for these low female prison population rate are due to the differences of male and female criminality and the severity of their respective delinquencies (Haverkamp, 2011).

Dünkel, Kestermann and Zolondek (2005) demonstrate in their comparative research that female prisoners are not treated in an appropriate way according to their needs. The study makes clear that women need different treatment in prisons than men due to their background and different characteristics. The most relevant factors hereby are that most of the imprisoned women experienced physical and/ or sexual violence in their past, some of them even in their childhood. Often the women have children and therefore need to fulfill the duties of a mother. A big number of female prisoners are drug addicts, which stresses the need of medical and psychological support. In many cases the addiction and craving for drugs is a factor for their condemned delinquency. Furthermore, it is common that they suffer from other mental illnesses. Hence it is important to treat female inmates in an appropriate way to their respective needs since most of the time the women are 'over secured' (Übersicherung) and do not get the special treatment from qualified staff (Dünkel, Kestermann & Zolondek, 2005). Haverkamp supports those statements and adds that women's crime has to be treated as an "independent social phenomena" (Haverkamp, 2011, p. 114). After all, it is challenging to get society involved in this issue since social change, meaning increasing emancipation, does not cause increasing female criminal acts and therefore under this light man and women should not be treated equally for once. Another concern of Haverkamp are ideological biases surrounding scientific work related to the implied affairs. Her empirical work aims to research women's imprisonment according to the European Prison Rules (2006). The European Prison Rules are a 'soft law' containing recommendations of the Committee of Ministers to member states (Council of Europe, 2006).

The criminal justice of Hamburg lists only four regulations about imprisoning women:

- § 70(1) "The search of male prisoners are only carried out by men, the search of female prisoners are only carried out by women. It has to be taken care of the feeling of shame"
- § 70(2) "[...] If a body search involves undressing [...] in case of male prisoners only men are allowed to be present, in case of female prisoners only women and it has to be conducted in a closed room. Other prisoners are not allowed to be present."
- § 98(3) "Women and men are in general accommodated in separate institutions or departments."
- § 100 "Mothers with children. Institutions or departments for women should have the facilities to accommodate mothers with their children." (HmbStVollzG, 2009).

Though the regulations of female imprisonment offer much flexibility, Haverkamp designates the German women's prisons as acceptable and conforming to the European Prison Rules. She identifies the work with female inmates as humane and the tenor shows dignity towards the prisoners (Haverkamp, 2011). Even though her data collection did not take place at a prison in Hamburg, one can infer that her conclusions may be applicable for the purposes of this study. According to the framework of the Teilanstalt für Frauen (TAF) at the Justizvollzugsanstalt (JVA) Billwerder the guiding principles are highly oriented towards an approach specified for women. The elaboration of the details of this approach are discussed in a following chapter. At this point it is important to provide some insights about the basics of prisons in Hamburg and especially the conditions of the TAF.

Teilanstalt für Frauen (TAF) at JVA Billwerder

There is room for 102 female inmates in 'house 3', a stand-alone building in the west of the terrain of the JVA Billwerder. 40 cells in the north wing which are used as a remand center. 62 rooms in the west wing for the women to serve their penal sentence in a closed prison. There is additionally a mother-child unit which has a maximum capacity of four mothers with their child.

The TAF follows a strict timetable for the weekdays and as well for the weekends. A weekday starts for the prisoners at 6:15am when the cell doors get unlocked and ends at 6:30pm when they get looked in again. All prisoners are locked up for the night in their single cell. The whole day is precisely structured and organized, such as work or leisure time. During the day, the inmates are allowed to shower, cook together and visit each other, unless otherwise ordered, according to an individual's situation. Several sports and leisure activities, such as yoga classes, step-aerobic, gospel choir, painting and crafting lessons, are offered to all the female inmates at arranged times during their free time (JVA Billwerder, 2015).

Once per week the prisoners have the possibility to do grocery shopping and have the option to buy toothpaste, cigarettes, and such. The prisoners can purchase their goods through a so called "Sichteinkauf" (JVA Billwerder, 2015, p. 10). The 'Listeneinkauf' differs from the 'Sichteinkauf' as stated: Shopping in prisons is either arranged with a list – 'Listeneinkauf', similar to a catalogue where the inmates order their requested products in advance or the penal institution has an in-house like supermarket where the prisoners can actually have a look at the products and then buy them – 'Sichteinkauf' (Höflich et al. 2014, pp. 295-6).

The detainees are given the possibility to order books of their choice out of a catalogue at the central library, the Hamburger Öffentlichen Bücherhallen (HÖB).

The prisoners have the possibility to make phone calls with the landline of the prison, aware of the fact that the calls might be monitored by the Landeskriminalamt (LKA), the state criminal office (JVA Billwerder 2015). The TAF offers 2 phones for the remand center and 2 for the regular station, all of them situated in the common room of the respective units. The mother-child unit has a phone as well as the therapeutic station, the TvS. This means the TAF has 6 phones for total for 102 inmates. The prisoner's phone calls are not timely but financially limited to a 100€ monthly. The provider of the landline is called Telio, a company from Hamburg which solely provides communication services for prisons and other monitored institutions throughout Europe. They offer different products,[2] however, the TAF makes use of the 'PHONio' a telephone system for prisoners where each inmate has an account which they can charge money. With a pin code the prisoners can access their account through the phone and see how much credit they have left. The prison has full control over the phone and the transactions, meaning the phone calls (Telio, 2016). However, the prices for the connection are higher than the offers from a regular telephone service. The Commercial and Industrial Chamber Berlin, the Industrie- und Handelskammer (IHK) Berlin, unveiled in their report in 2014, that a prisoner using the Telio phone service pays per month 275% more than the cheapest offer of a standard phone service. This shows that the inmates are not given the possibility to make a phone call in line with market conditions. The IHK estimates the margin of 66%, which is evaluated as high (Eberle, 2014, p. 34). However, the company Telio lowered their rates in 2015 due to high pressure from prisons and press. Yet, as new reports show, the prices are still high. A review of the Senat of Berlin (2015) shows in a summary what prisoners have to pay for 5 minutes of Telio phone services for a) a call within Berlin, b) a call outside of Berlin and c) a call to a German mobile phone:

1. Ortsgespräch 5 Minuten: 0,42 Euro,
2. Ferngespräch außerhalb Berlins 5 Minuten: 0,60 Euro,
3. deutsches Mobilfunknetz 5 Minuten: 2,10 Euro
4. (Straßmeier, 2015, p. 2)

Calls to foreign countries are clearly more expensive and the prices vary in between 1,14 Euro and 10,74 Euro per 5 minutes, depending on the country and if the connection passes through a landline or a mobile phone (Straßmeier, 2015). However, this issue will be uncommented for now, but further discussed in a later chapter.

The TAF has in their common rooms a TV available for all prisoners. Upon request a TV to put in the individual cell can be borrowed from the JVA for the price of 10€ per month according to the head of the TAF, Rosemarie Höner-Wysk.

Behind the building there is a separate courtyard for the female prisoners, where they are allowed to spend one hour per day outside.

The visiting hours are limited to two hours every second week. This means "two x two hours per month" (JVA Billwerder 2015, p. 15). However, to sustain the relationship between a mother and her children there is the possibility to receive a "longterm visit" (JVA Billwerder 2015) of four hours once per month. Yet the prisoner must make a request and needs to be determined as 'suitable.'

An in-house medical center takes care of the health of the imprisoned women. The institution offers a general medicine service, dental treatment, psychiatric service, and gynecologist. The penal institution offers a variety of care, consulting, and treatment services: Psychological service, pastoral care, external addiction counseling, advisory service for debtors, support for released prisoners, acupuncture sessions, social education and additional external consulting services. The inmates are encouraged to complete an apprenticeship or work at one of the four provided work areas, such as IT/computer, economics/administration, services and agriculture/environment. The weekly working time is 35 hours. Besides the job, it is also possible to get a basic education or to attend vocation workshops. The penal institution is deliberated to provide the prisoners a secure and gentle way out of jail. Therefore, the staff of the TAF regularly checks on the development of their inmates to propose a possible transfer to the open prison JVA Glasmoor.

Of note in the conceptual framework of the JVA Billwerder (2015) is the strict division of female and male prisoners. Even though the female prison is part of a penal institution for male prisoners it is highly separated from this part. There is no sight from the male tract to the female tract and vice versa.

It is stated that it is of great importance that female inmates must be treated differently than male prisoners:

Using the same models and approaches which are suitable for male prisoners would not meet the criteria for the needs of women and even connote them with a disadvantage."[3] (JVA Billwerder 2015, p. 7). Hereby the TAF refers to the study of Dünkel, Kestermann and Zolondek (2005) which has been discussed earlier. However, the study only briefly addresses Haverkamp's main conclusion: communication. Communication within the prison but as well with the outside world. One of the most striking characteristics between the male and the female inmates is the "indirect and talkative culture of communication. (Haverkamp, 2011, p. 818).

METHODS

A qualitative methods approach is the most suitable way of proceeding to answer the aforementioned research questions. The research is highly based on the approach and research design of the pilot study by Hasebrink & Domeyer (2012). Since the study focuses on media repertoires as meaningful practices, the qualitative approach is helpful to ascertain the whole picture of an individuals' pattern of media use. However, a disadvantage of the qualitative approach is that, even though the data collection provides much information, it is tied to an individual case which makes it hard to generalize the subsequent findings. Yet, it is evident to take a qualitative approach since the study is interested in the individual person.

Research Design

In order to conduct a detailed exploration of a media repertoire on the personal level, the data collection has been conducted through semi-structured in-depth interviews. Therefore, it is possible to get detailed explanations which help to illuminate the users' subjective perspective on their media repertoires. The sampling group for the interviews were the female prisoners of the TAF at the JVA Billwerder in Hamburg, Germany. A purposive sampling has been pursued to draft five interviewees. The first criterion was very open in restricting the age group between 18 and 50 years. This age gap has been chosen for the reason of their affinity to digitalized media. The second criterion was predicated on their duration of imprisonment. In order not to overtax the challenge of the remembrance of certain patterns of media use in their past, meaning before imprisonment, it was necessary that the interviewee was not being imprisoned for more than one to two years at the point of the interview. This is also contingent on their familiarity and use of new media technology before imprisonment since the aim of this research is to detect the change of media use and therefore the interviewees should have used new technology and preferably social networking sites (SNS) before their sentence. The data has been collected in August 2016.

The interview guide of the semi-structured interviews was based on the study of Hasebrink & Domeyer (2012) connected with the study of Haverkamp (2011). The overall guiding structure was linked to the basic assumption of Hepp and Hasebrink, that communication happens within a set of actors about a certain topic through specific media practices and media ensembles.

Visualizing Cards

As conducted in the study of Hasebrink and Domeyer (2012), a strategy within the interviews was the use of cards to visualize the relationship of the interviewee with his/her media repertoire, and to make it easier for the person to talk about sensitive or unconscious topics. As Haverkamp (2011) suggests in her study, it is useful to give the interviewees some sort of task to establish space and a chance for the interviewee to back off a bit, if the interview should be too demanding or stressful. Haverkamp accomplishes this by giving the interviewee a self-completion survey. However, this study works with cards as suggested by Hasebrink & Domeyer (2012). Similar to the procedure suggested by those authors, the portion with the cards during the interviews of this research have been conducted as following:

1. In a first step the interviewee was asked to note down on a set of green cards all the media she used before imprisonment. It did not matter which level the interviewee chose to describe her used media. For example, she could write TV or simply a specific media production such as *Berlin - Tag und Nacht.*[4] The interviewee was also free in terms of how many cards, meaning how many media components she noted down.
2. The next step concerned the percentage of the respective time devoted to a specific medium. Here the interviewee was asked to roughly state in percentage their time budget on yellow cards.
3. As third step, the interviewee was asked to take a white card, note down 'me' and place it in the middle of a round table. Then she had to place the cards with the described media around the 'me' in the center, representing the closer a certain media was to the middle the higher was the subjective relevance for the media user.
4. Thereafter, the interviewee was given a set of blue cards where she could state the purpose of the use of this specific medium and its main functions. The interviewee was asked to state her motivation why she uses specific media.
5. In a last step, which was not included in the Hasebrink and Domeyer study, the interviewee was asked to note down on red cards the involved actors she linked to the respective media. This additional set of cards was derived from the communicative figurations approach since Hasebrink and Domeyer stated in their study (2012) that the social context was very relevant. Therefore, this category has been added.

After the completion of the five steps, the interviewee was asked to depict her current situation of media use in the case of imprisonment. They were allowed to rearrange the order, add new cards or put old ones away, for example the card of the Internet, since it is not available for these prisoners.

Thus, the interviewee created two expositions of media use, one before and one during imprisonment. The original display was photographed and afterwards copied into a digital diagram.

This method of visualization cards was applied to create a comfortable interview situation and to stimulate talk about the media repertoire. However, the diagrams in connection with the detailed explanation is an interesting visualization of the change of the respective media repertoire and therefore used in the findings to demonstrate and sum up the interview. Figure 1 shows an example of the visualization of the media repertoire of Agnes Lakis before imprisonment and figure 2 while imprisonment.

Figure 1. Media repertoire of Agnes Lakis before imprisonment

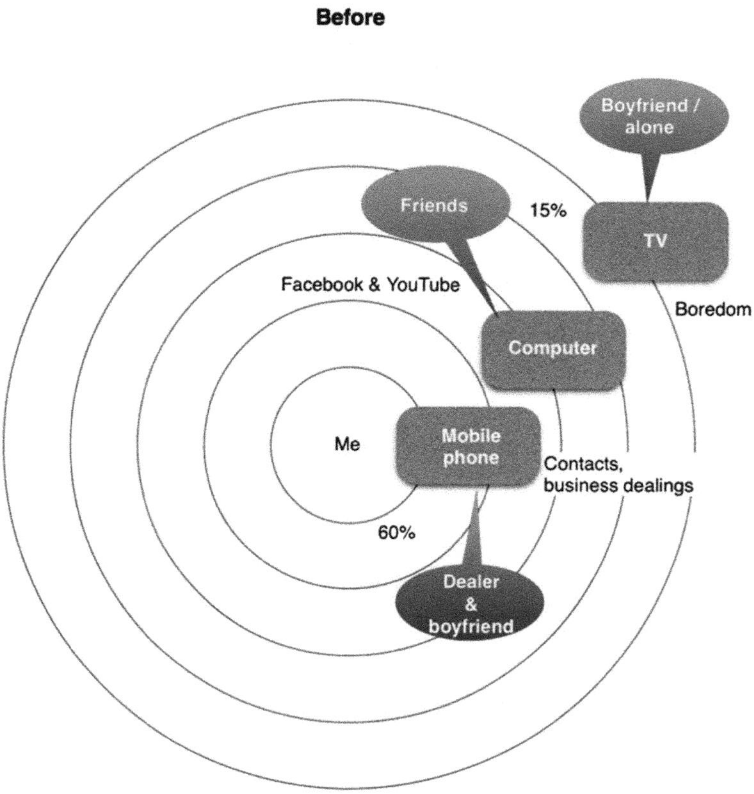

Coding / Analysis

The qualitative content analysis has been conducted based on the media repertoire study of Hasebrink and Domeyer (2012). Therefore, the coding process was a mixture between inductive and deductive coding since the first step of analysis was to code the transcripts according to the thematic categories of the suggested analytical framework previously presented. After the first coding round, a memo with striking statements has been created and therefore new categories added. The results of the analysis of each category of the media user is portrayed in the chapter of the findings, where the comparison of all the cases can be found as well.

Figure 2. Media repertoire of Agnes Lakis while imprisonment

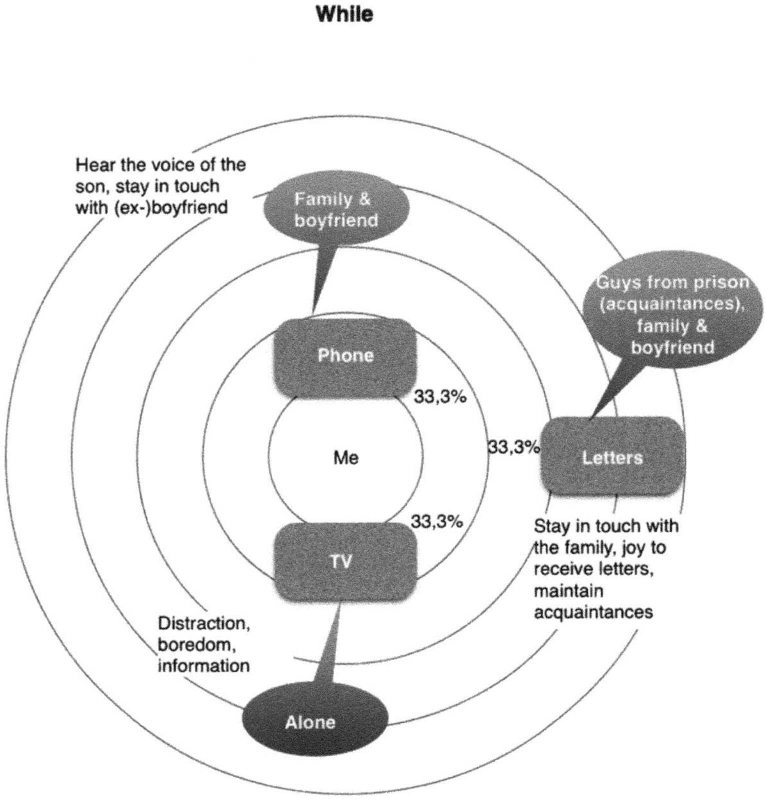

Anonymization

Ethical considerations are an integral part of this research since the interviewees are nevertheless prisoners which must be protected by the anonymization of their data. Therefore, in the transcripts, all indicators of either location or time have been excluded and the attributes have been replaced with a high level of abstraction (Meyermann & Pozelt, 2014).

The original audio file of the interviews are stored on a separate data carrier. The initial order of the conducted interviews was given a number, whereas on a disconnected storage medium the order has been changed and then allocated with a new name for each interview. The names have been picked randomly from an online name generator machine (Name Generator, 2016).

Within the description of the key findings and the discussion about an interviewees' media repertoire, the aggregation of information method was followed. This type of anonymization is characterized by the oversimplification of information due to the set up of categories. Therefore, the concrete age is replaced by an age group. For example: Age: 27 // Aggregation: 25 to 30 years old or Job: Hairdresser // Aggregation: craftsperson (Meyermann & Pozelt, 2014). In order to have a consistent and clear method of anonymization, a protocol of the process has been conducted. This not only provides a sustainable documentation of the process but assures a coherent application of the pseudonyms and aggregations. This insures the possibility of further analysis to conduct a de-anonymization. The protocol of anonymization is saved on a separate data carrier as well (Meyermann & Pozelt, 2014).

According to those provisions, the chances of a de-anonymization would only be possible with an excessive effort to assign the personality of a participant being interviewed for this research.

MAIN FOCUS OF THE CHAPTER

The key findings of each interviewee demonstrate some similarities but also some key differences. This chapter sets out the comparison of the main findings and lays them into a larger theoretical perspective. The chapter follows the structure according to the framework of the media repertoire. However, the focus lies more on the change of the media repertoire and the respective resulting media habits of the prisoners at the present time of imprisonment in order to answer the research questions. Therefore, each category will be directly compared with the situation before and during imprisonment. In order to set out a clear evaluation the research questions are mentioned here again.

- **RQ1:** How are the patterns of media use of an individual changing in the case of imprisonment?
- **RQ2:** How does the change of the media repertoire affect the social relationships of a female prisoner?
- **SubRQ:** What role does the lack of social media play in the shift of the communicative figurations?

In order to come to a conclusion for the first research question, it is imperative to regard the media components, empirical indicators, and the relevance of the media repertoire. Only this combination makes it possible to see the change in media use. As previously stated, the change is made visible by comparing the categories before and during imprisonment right after each other.

Relevant Media Components Before Imprisonment

The key findings of the interviews show that each of the participants had a somewhat diverse media repertoire in terms of components before imprisonment. Their relevant components were varying between three to five media elements, which is rather modest compared to Hasebrink and Domeyer (2012).[5] The components were not very different from each other and most of the time contained overlapping media types from interviewee to interviewee. All of them had experience with social media and each of them possessed a Facebook account. Everyone focused a lot on the digital media and as well on the SNS which constituted a large portion of their respective media repertoires. The attitude towards the SNS or other digital media was mainly positive, however some would often point out that they were, or were not, addicted and therefore giving social media a somewhat negative review. The word 'addiction' has been mentioned throughout the interviews which makes it seem that this is a common term in prison jargon. However, this will be discussed further on.

Relevant Media Components While Imprisonment

According to the restriction of the prison regulations it was not surprising that the media components decreased to mainly three to four media components. Here it was interesting that they all named the components on the media type level, even though they used different levels to describe their media use before imprisonment. This goes align with the established prison jargon mentioned above, what demonstrates an assimilation between the prisoners. This could be connected to Foucault (1977) and Goffman (1961/2009) stating that the prison itself generates a closed group of society, what reinforces the factor of exclusion from the outside world, which makes it difficult for reintegration after they get released. However, the main components during imprisonment are the phone, TV, and letters. Some mentioned books or the radio as well. All the inmates make use of the provided media.

This first category shows that the number of the components did not change drastically but the components themselves changed. The only component which was mentioned outside but as well inside prison was the television.

Empirical Indicators for the Description of Repertoires Before Imprisonment

As already mentioned in the methodology portion, the frequency and duration is a challenging aspect to get a clear picture from, especially when the participants have to remember how their media use was in the past. Therefore, it is not surprising that some of the interviewees could not draw a concrete picture of their media use in terms of duration and frequency. Some of them would even contradict themselves throughout the interview. However, to get an insight of their media use it is enough to see how intensely they made use of a certain medium. Interesting to note is that most of them used their mobile phones very excessively and were online very often before imprisonment. Most of the participants stated that their media repertoires were very much part of their daily routines and therefore embedded in daily life. Only one interviewee mentioned that most of her media consumption was luxury and therefore separated from her daily routines.

The change of the media repertoire becomes evident while not only looking at prohibited media (like SNS), but also at media they used before and during imprisonment, such as the TV, which the next section demonstrates.

Empirical Indicators for the Description of Repertoires While Imprisonment

The media consumption during incarceration is even more embedded in the daily routines of each interviewee than before. The participants could give clear numbers of how long they were using a specific media. This is tied to the highly regulated structure of the prison's daily life. Since every day looks the same, the inmates even organize their media consumption around the structure which is highly routine as well. This combines the theoretical framework of Goffman and Foucault, given that the structure of the prison generates the behavior of the prisoners and creates a closed circle of the institution. Jewkes goes even further since, the prisoners are by themselves and watching TV for an significant amount of time due to the long lock-up times. Therefore, they are even losing their social contacts in prison and become lonely, what only reinforces the "Foucauldian conclusion that personal media have one great, unspoken advantage as far as prison authorities are concerned, and that is to normalize the regulation and surveillance of inmates" (Jewkes, 2002, p. 222).

Another a big issue in terms of duration and frequency were the high costs of the Telio phone rates which restrict the inmates as well in their freedom to make phone calls the length they desire to their social contacts in the outside world.

Being limited to a 100€ per month by rates which could easily be two Euros for a five minute call brings the prisoners into a disadvantage in terms of sustaining their social relationships. This factor has been brought up as a big topic for almost all the interviewees.

Actors Involved in the Media Consumption Before Imprisonment

The shift in the communicative figurations gets clear by looking at the actors involved in the media consumption before and during imprisonment. Also the change of the relevance of the media repertoire before and during imprisonment demonstrate the change in the constellation of the social relationships, which is tied to the second research question. The sub research question will come into play as well, discussing the maintenance of social relationships in prison without social media. An interesting factor here to note is that most of the interviewees were not very embedded in a vast social group of friends before imprisonment. Most of them had no substantial hobbies, which meant that they did not have a large circle of friends who were sharing the same interests. Almost all of them are in more or less stable relationships and almost every participant was in a good standing with their families, meaning with their parents and their siblings. However, most of the interviewees' parents got divorced, but still they were at least in touch with one of their biological parent and had a seemingly close relationship. An important distinction to make here is the social environment of the ones who were drug addicted. Since the consumption of drugs is an essential part of the everyday lives of the addicts, all the actions are driven by the need and organization of drugs. Therefore, they were stating that besides their drug addiction, there was nothing else. For example, Agnes described her hobbies: "Making money, consuming drugs, you don't do a lot more if you're a drug addict"[6] (Agnes, 03:12). This shows how focused they were on drugs and not on social relationships, which makes it interesting to see that when they are imprisoned, the drug addicted persons were in a better condition than before in terms of health and social relationships, which will be discussed in the following subchapter.

Actors Involved in the Media Consumption Before Imprisonment

Without exception, all of the participants were in touch with at least one of their respective parents during imprisonment, whom they stated would support them and be there for them. It is mostly the mother who is a continuously important figure in the inmate's lives. This supports Dünkel, Kestermann and Zolondek's study about female prisoners which concluded that women attempt to maintain their social relationships, even while imprisoned (Dünkel, Kestermann and Zolondek's, 2005). However, an interesting case is Agnes, who is the only one solely in touch with her family when she is imprisoned. She was also the only interviewee who has more social contacts during imprisonment than when she is outside of the prison. For Agnes, it is not only the physical but also the mental health which improves in prison. "Since I'm imprisoned I gained 20 kilo, even though you can't see it. (laughs) But they feed you until you're healthy again… if you are... There was a time when I weighed 40 kilos… Yeah I was not always so well when I was out there. But even though I do not want to stay here"[7]. (Agnes, 24:28). On those terms, Agnes benefits from the rigid structures of prison life. However, her elaboration on the reason why she does not want to stay here supports Foucault and Goffman's view that the prison is just a constructed reality "[…] outside is the reality. Here I can be clean as much as I want but what counts is later when I'm out there again. […] Everything is different outside. Here everything is structured and they structure a lot for you. Everything is forbidden and you get punished if you're doing it anyways. There is nobody out there who says 'you, you you' or who tells you that you have to work or that you have to eat something now"[8] (Agnes, 17:25). This demonstrates the future perspective in this case for Agnes, that she cannot rely on an established circle of social relationships who support her no matter what once she gets released.

For the other participants, this phenomenon was reversed. The number of social relationships shrank to roughly three main people. Yet, though they were imprisoned, the quality of those relationships did not diminish. However, some of the interviewees felt some kind of pressure to prove to their families that they were on the right track and had potential to become 'better'. Some of the participants described some actions to protect their family members in order not to hurt them. An interesting case here is Grazia, whose mother does not even know that she is imprisoned. Regardless, she is constantly in touch with her mother, who is a very important figure in her overall network of social relationships.

It was different for those imprisoned women who had children by themselves. Three out of five interviewees are mothers by themselves and all of their respective relationships to their children seemed problematic. Though they are making an effort to fulfill the duties of motherhood, some of them get rejected by their own children. Dünkel, Kestermann and Zolondek address this issue by stressing the importance of the provision for longer visits and suggesting more privacy for the time spent with the children. Obstacles should be removed in order to enable the children boundless physical closeness. This is not only relevant for the mother but even more for the children and their development (Dünkel, Kestermann and Zolondek, 2005, p. 11). Yet, a problem which the interviews of this research demonstrated is that some children are not visiting their mothers in prison and/or are not even communicating with them, which makes it obviously difficult for a balanced and healthy relationship between the mother and their respective children.

In terms of friendships there is the factor of selectivity on one hand, but also the fear of being forgotten. The first one is a determined decision, whereas the second is a passive happening on their respective friends' side. Since the prisoners have restrictive access to communication media, they must be very conscious of who they choose to call or receive visits from, since time is not an expendable resource. This leads to a decrease of social contacts and makes it possible for the inmates only to focus on the most relevant ones.

Many of the interviewees claimed that they have been forgotten by the outside world, meaning their former friends. Therefore, the phenomenon of real and true friendship has been questioned often: "Those are no friends. Friends are here for you if you get in trouble"[9] (Stacy, 27:51) "[...] half of my alleged friends will not even notice that I have been gone"[10] (Agnes, 28:41) "[...] after I turned myself in - whoosh - everybody was gone. Nobody reached out to me"[11] (Carlin, 58:12).

It is difficult to say what the determinant factor is for these perceived feelings of abandonment. There are two possible reasons: one of them is that due to their delinquency their friends do not want to be in touch with the person anymore. The other reason could be that the effort to send a letter or set an appointment for a phone call is too much to ask, and people are simply too used to sending quick messages and notifications on SNS or WhatsApp. Some of the inmates even said that it would be easier for them if they would have access to Facebook so they could still be in touch with their friends.

Not one single person of the interviewees stated that they were establishing new friendships in prison. According to Haverkamp (2011) this is not a surprising since she got a description of distrust and intrigues about the atmosphere in women's prison. Dünkel, Kestermann and Zolondek stress on the importance of social contacts within prison in order to provide a secure and positive atmosphere. They suggest that the penal institution should organize a wider offer of programs and activities between the inmates (Dünkel, Kestermann & Zolondek, 2005). This seems to be a challenging aim, since the interviewees of this research did state that they do not want to get involved with the other inmates and therefore are not engaging in making new friends and other important social relationships inside the prison. Only one participant stated that she has established some friendships in prison. The others seemed to have a very strong opinion about that topic and clearly avoiding any kind of social contact in prison. This leads as well to the fact that all of them are watching TV by themselves and were not going to the common room to watch with other inmates, since, as Jewkes states, the situation of TV watching in a common room in prison is characterized by power relations. This demonstrates again that the prisoners are losing touch with the outside contacts, but at the same time not establishing new contacts. They become lonely and therefore it is hard for them to establish new relationships once they will get released, which aligns with Jewkes but also with the Foucauldian perspective (Jewkes, 2002).

The atmosphere with the staff was stated to be okay, but not so warm that they could be a substitute for other tight social relationships. The line between prisoners and staff is still strict and fulfills the character of the total institution as Goffman states that there are two parties which are opposing each other (Goffman, 1961/2009).

Most of the participants have two persons who are visiting them on a regularly basis. Even though this is just every second week for two hours, the interviewees seemed to be fine with their visits and did not express desire for other people to visit. Tough, some of the participants were hesitating answering this question and it seemed that there were other people they would like to see but they were aware of the circumstances and therefore denied the wish.

The following categories are important for the research questions one and two but also in order to get an impression of a possible answer of the sub RQ, which is tied to social media.

Relations Between the Components of Media Repertoires Before Imprisonment

Many of the interviewees stated that the most important media for them before imprisonment was either the mobile phone or the Internet. As already noted, all the participants were highly connected to the online and social media world. Even though they were using several other media, the focus was always on the SNS and Internet. However, the relevance was not always this elevated. They were using the Internet constantly but more since it is so highly connected to everyday life. Interesting was to note that they were stating often that they were or were not addicted to certain things, stressing on the word 'addiction', as already discussed above.

Relations Between the Components of Media Repertoires While Imprisonment

The relations and relevance of the components changed significantly for all the participants at the point of imprisonment. All of them stated that the phone is the most important medium of their repertoire since it keeps them in touch with their families and loved ones. This is interesting to see, since this means that social relationships are highly important for the prisoners and that somehow social media would be useful for them as well to keep up their social contacts (Grieve et al., 2013), as some of the participants stated as well.

Another factor to support this argument is the problem of high prices for the Telio phone calls. This is again connected to the new technology and trend of just having a mobile phone outside of prison. Therefore, it is really expensive for prisoners to make calls and waste their 100€ limit on their phone account with high rates for communication through mobile phone, which is very common outside prison. Thus, claiming that Internet would not cost that much and would offer more ways to get in touch with already established friendships but also meeting new people in order to construct a healthy social circle of friends awaiting the prisoners once they get released, therefore they would not fall back into old routines. However, as literature shows, prison staff dreads the Internet as a possible hole in their security system. There would be technical regulations and ideas of how to use the Internet accordingly (Vogel, 2009), yet not elaborated on social media. This leads to a finding, that between Internet access and social media access there is a big difference. The new digital media developments make it challenging for prisons to provide secure SNS access and still keep it monitored. Traditional media such as the phone and letters are obviously to a significant degree easier to control and regulate.

Books are rarely read in prison, only when they do not have access to the TV. The relevance of the TV was the biggest change, from almost no emotional attachment, to becoming the 'best friend' or the peephole to the outside world. This aligns with Vandebosch (2001) who states that the television is an important medium for inmates. However, looking at the constellation of actors, the inmates spend a lot of their time alone in their cell watching TV. This is what Jewkes (2002) ascribes as the downside of TV watching. But Vandebosch describes the TV as a helpful tool to cope with the situation inside prison (Vandebosch, 2001), which has been demonstrated in the interviews of this study as well. All the participants of this research stated that use of the TV helps them to relax but also to avoid negative thoughts such as guilt or other related sentiments about their situation in prison. Therefore they would not want to miss the TV.

General Principles Guiding the Composition of Media Repertoires Before Imprisonment

The participants seemed not to be very self-reflexive in terms of their media use and therefore guiding principles of their media repertoires are difficult to definitively ascertain. For example, compared to the study of Hasebrink & Domeyer (2012) none of the participants of this research mentioned high and low prestige media, while it had been an important topic for the participants of the previous studies. One plausible factor could be that the interviewees of this specific research are not highly educated and did not seem to be very reflexive about their media consumption and therefore did not mind if they were consuming low or high media content.

However, compared to literature, it demonstrates that for media consumption before imprisonment, the participants tended towards an instrumental approach, (Rubin, 1984), since they were not very focused on the media itself but using it as a essential tool to organize their daily life.

General Principles Guiding the Composition of Media Repertoires While Imprisonment

The change of the principles is highly connected to the structure and regulations of the quotidian life in prison. Media consumption become an important part of every interviewee's routines. Therefore, the guiding principles are not only for diversion and overcoming boredom, but also become embedded habits in the inmates' structure. It is less important what they are consuming but when and for what reasons. Here it is very striking that the TV consumption is most important once they are alone in their cells and need to pass time, but as well to avoid uncomfortable feelings of guilt or desperation, as supported by Vandebosch's (2001) conclusion that TV is an important coping tool for prisoners. This means that the general principles guiding the composition became a ritualized (Rubin, 1984), since media consumption is heavily embedded in their daily lives and become an enormously important component for all the interviewees.

Experience of Change

Though the change of media repertoire was drastic in terms of the media components, the participants did not seem to be very disturbed by this. Only some of them would mention that they extremely miss the Internet or the access to SNS. After getting used to the prison rules they stated that they can, or must, deal with the situation. Some stated that they are missing other things more, like the time they can spend outside of prison, or their freedom of decisions. However, one could argue that part of the freedom is also the freedom to get information and access to the Internet. Stacy, for example, argued that she would not have lost her friends if she still could message them on Facebook. This leads to the drastic change of friendships of the prisoners. The experience in terms of social relationships was meaningful and even hurtful for the inmates. Interesting to note here is that all the prisoners could keep their relationships with their families, but almost none with their friends or at least just with one or two. As they are not establishing new friendships in prison, those social relationships are not being replaced and therefore leaves a blank spot in the lives of the inmates. In order of media use, some even argued that it was nice to send letters since they never sent letters before and ascribed a special value to this specific medium.

An important factor which needs to be stressed here, is the dominant connection to the delinquency of the inmates, referred to by themselves. All the participants stated throughout the interview, that they were sorry for what happened or what they did and that they have accepted their respective sentence, meaning the way they are being punished. This meant as well for the topic of this researcher that the inmates were not making demands in terms of getting Internet access or better communication tools. They seemed to see themselves as not eligible to actively put in a claim. Due to the in-depth questions of the interview, the inmates were giving insights in their desires which have been previously discussed.

Future Perspective in Relation to Media Consumption and Social Relationships

Two of the interviewees mentioned that they want to take classes and computer courses to be up-to-date once they get out of prison. The future perspective of the participants, in terms of media use, especially social media use, were divided into two sides: One side was arguing that they are going to activate their Facebook profile again to prove that they are back and succeed managing live outside prison. Interesting here is the factor of taking/choosing a new identity on SNS. Griffiths (2016) describes this phenomenon in his research about addictive behaviors, with people representing themselves differently which was a big argument for them to use the Internet and online communication. Some of the participants were stating that social media might be helpful in order to meet new friends and people outside their established circle of friends. This was connected to the possibility of choosing the degree of how much they would reveal of their personal self, meaning of their criminal history. Especially for women who are drug addicted this might be an important future strategy to meet new people. Dünkel, Kestermann and Zolondek (2005) state that most of the female prisoners who are suffering of a drug addiction do have an significant low self-esteem. Combined with Griffiths findings about identity on SNS this could be an advantage for prisoners once they get released, to find new social contacts and even friendships.

An interesting factor which the investigation along the research on this topic demonstrated was that, maybe not Facebook, but other SNS are important for prisoners, such as the knast.net. This is a platform where a lot of ex-prisoners are telling their story and giving advice to future prisoners or desperate partners, family members and friends. They can act anonymously but can talk about the lived experience. This could maybe be a solution for prisoners to get warm with social media again after they have been released. However, this was not part of the research and will show in some years after the participants of this study will be released.

Interesting is that the women who seemed to be highly embedded in a big social circle of friends, were claiming that they will delete their online profiles. They felt betrayed by their friends and did not want to be surrounded by the old social relationships anymore. This shows the possible downside of SNS for prisoners, which leads to the overall topic of a healthy social environment in order not to fall back into new criminal actions.

SOLUTIONS AND RECOMMENDATIONS

This research identified a significant academic gap in terms of qualitative research of media use in woman's prisons. Literature shows a major interest in prison facilities and structures but also in the individual prisoner. Studies on female inmates became just popular in recent years (Haverkamp, 2011). Media studies about individual media use in prisons in the digital age have yet not been conducted. Therefore the combination of those research fields makes this study significant and the importance cannot be underestimated. It helps to understand the change of an individual's media repertoire and the sense making process behind it. Additionally the issue of the lack of SNS in prisons has been addressed and elaborated on.

The findings of this research demonstrate that the media repertoire of prisoners did change drastically once they were imprisoned. The components changed in terms of new vs. old media but also in the variety and number of devices they had available in prison. The biggest changes, however, were the empirical indicators such as time and duration but also the change of the relevance of the media components and the overall guiding principles of the respective media repertoire. The media use during imprisonment seemed to be a ritualized approach in order to soften the Foucauldian rigid structures but as well to get entertainment and distraction to make time pass faster, which supports the study of Vandebosch (2001).

In terms of social relationships, the change was evident as well, however it was clear that the inmates tried with the given tools and opportunities to keep in touch with some social contacts, which endorses the findings of Dünkel, Kestermann and Zolondek (2005) that female prisoners stay embedded in their social environment during their sentence. However, prison regulations do not offer a lot of freedom in terms of contacts to the outside world. Therefore selectivity comes into play while dealing with the respective social relationships. This research showed that the fall back to traditional communication tools like letters and landline phone calls did still enable the prisoners to maintain some of their contacts with the outside world. Interesting to note is, that with those people they were still in touch, the prisoners claimed that even with the restricted and downgraded media use they were able to keep the quality of the social relationships with their most important contacts.

The core of the social relationships therefore seems to be possible to maintain. Even though it means that the person outside of prison needs to make an effort in either visiting, receiving phone calls at regulated times, or writing letters. However, this seems to be problematic for some of the (own) children but as well for the extended circles of friends. Almost all of the inmates' relationships to friends they had outside of prison got cut at the time of incarceration. Further research here is needed to overcome the determined factor of why they are not in touch anymore. However, some of the participants stated that it would be different if they still had access to SNS so as to sustain their relationships with their friends. Here the question of healthy relationships and 'true friendship' comes into play, since some of the interviewees stated that the friends they had before were even partially responsible for the crime they had committed. A following question regarding the rehabilitation process is therefore if prisoners have a disadvantage or advantage without access to SNS?

The research demonstrated that the difference between Internet access and access to SNS concerns diverse approaches. A relevant question which arises here is whether there is a need for Internet in prisons. The perspective of the prisoners show that this is not their primary need or concern. Even though news articles and prison magazines are filling the void left by Internet access, this study has demonstrated that the urge to go online is only partially evident. The qualitative analysis showed that for them it was more a luxury than an essential need, and they did not feel an enormous disadvantage in terms of communication.

FUTURE RESEARCH DIRECTIONS

Clearly this research shows only one side of the communicative figurations, meaning the individual perspective. Therefore, further research is needed to get an overall picture of the maintenance of social relationships with traditional media during imprisonment. Interesting would be to research an individuals social environment, including the different actors of their media repertoire. Another suggestion would be to take a mixed methods approach as suggested by Hasebrink & Domeyer (2012) in order to first get the prisoners into the mood (for example if they would create a media use diary) which would help the conversation go deeper and be more precise. A highly relevant follow-up study could be to conduct the interviews with male prisoners and explore the differences or similarities. The importance of such a study affirms in the fact that male prisoners remain the vast majority of the total prison population worldwide. Even a combination of a longitudinal study could help to gain a better understanding of how media consumption changes over time in prison and how the respective social relationships are affected by the changing media use.

CONCLUSION

In summary, the whole topic is highly connected to the way society punishes people, but also resocialization, which asks for an interplay of research from different academic disciplines. Satisfying both sides is a delicate balancing act, not only the security of society, but also the social health of prisoners in order to give them a prospect at reintegration into so-called society.

REFERENCES

Billwerder, J. V. A. (2015). Rahmenkonzept für die Teilanstalt für Frauen in der JVA Billwerder. Hamburg: Academic Press.

Bourdieu, P. (1979/2013). *Distinction: A Social Critique of the Judgement of Taste*. London: Routledge.

Council of Europe. (2006). *European Prison Rules*. Strasbourg: Council of Europe Publishing.

David, M., & Sutton, C. D. (2011). *Social Research. An Introduction* (2nd ed.). London: SAGE Publications.

DiIulio, J. J., Jr. (1987). Governing Prisons: A Comparative Study of Correctional Management. New York: The Free Press.

Dünkel, F., Kestermann, C., & Zolondek, J. (2005). *Reader Internationale Studie zum Frauenstrafvollzug. Bestandsaufnahme, Bedarfsanalyse und "best practice"*. Retrieved from www.rsf.uni-greifswald.de/fileadmin/mediapool/lehrstuehle/duenkel/Reader_ frauenvollzug.pdf

Eberle, S. (2014). *Gutachten. In der Strafvollstreckungssache vertreten Tuch Rechtsanwalt Dr. Jan Oelbermann. Aktenzeichen 509 StVK 179/13. Gericht: Landgericht Stendal*. Berlin: IHK Berlin.

Facebook. (2016). *Monster World*. Retrieved from https://www.facebook.com/monsterworld/

Foucault, M. (1976). Alternatives to the Prison. Dissemination or Decline of Social Control? *Theory, Culture & Society, 26*(6), 12-24.

Foucault, M. (1977). *Discipline and Punish. The Birth of the Prison*. New York: Vintage Books. A Division of Random House, inc.

Goffman, E. (2009). Asylums: Essays on the Social Situation of Mental Patients and Other Inmates (2nd ed.). New Brunswick, NJ: Transaction Publishers. (originally published 1961)

Grieve, Indian, M., Witteveen, K., Anne Tolan, G., & Marrington, J. (2013). Face-to-face or Facebook: Can social connectedness be derived online? *Computers in Human Behavior*, *29*(3), 604–609. doi:10.1016/j.chb.2012.11.017

Griffiths, M. D., Kuss, D. J., Billieux, J., & Pontes, H. M. (2016). The evolution of Internet addiction: A global perspective. *Addictive Behaviors*, *53*, 193–195. doi:10.1016/j.addbeh.2015.11.001 PMID:26562678

Gruber, A. (2013). *Internet im Knast. Häftlinge sind offline.* Retrieved from http://www.zeit.de/digital/internet/2013-09/internet-gefaengnis-jva-tegel

Hasebrink, U., & Domeyer, H. (2012). Media repertoires as patterns of behaviour and as meaningful practices: A multimethod approach to media use in converging media environments. *Participations*, *9*(2), 757–779.

Hasebrink, U., & Popp, J. (2006). Media repertoires as a result of selective media use. A conceptual approach to the analysis of patterns of exposure. *Communications*, *31*(3), 369–387. doi:10.1515/COMMUN.2006.023

Haverkamp, R. (2011). *Frauenvollzug in Deutschland: eine empirische Untersuchung vor dem Hintergrund der Europäischen Strafvollzugsgrundsätze*. Berlin: Duncker & Humblot. doi:10.3790/978-3-428-53523-1

Helmreich, W. B. (2009). *Asylums: Essays on the Social Situation of Mental Patients and Other Inmates*. New Brunswick, NJ: Transaction Publishers. VII-XVII.

Hepp, A., & Hasebrink, U. (2013). Human interaction and communicative figurations. The transformation of mediatized cultures and societies. *Communicative Figurations. Working Paper* (2).

Hepp, A., & Hasebrink, U. (2016). *How to research cross-media practices? Investigating media repertoires and media ensembles from a qualitative point of view*. Manuscript.

Höflich, P., Schriever, W., & Bartmeier, A. (2014). *Grundriss Vollzugsrecht. In Das Recht des Strafvollzugs, der Untersuchungshaft und des Jugendvollzugs* (4th ed.). Berlin: Springer Verlag.

Hötzel, Y. (2010). *Debatten um die Todesstrafe in der Bundesrepublik Deutschland von 1949 bis 1990*. Berlin: Walter de Gruyter GmbH & Co. doi:10.1515/9783110248777

Internet Live Stats. (2016). *Germany Internet Users*. Retrieved from http://www.internetlivestats.com/internet-users/germany/

Jewkes, Y. (2002). The Use of Media in Constructing Identities in the Masculine Environment of Men's Prisons. *European Journal of Communication, 17*(2), 205–225. doi:10.1177/0267323102017002693

Justizbehörde. (2009). *Hamburgisches Strafvollzugsgesetz – HmbStVollzG*. Retrieved from http://www.landesrecht-hamburg.de/jportal/portal/page/bshaprod.psml;jsessionid=37F3E1C4D07790374AF2A33E2FB481CC.jp17?showdoccase=1&st=null&doc.id=jlr-StVollzGHA2009rahmen&doc.part=X&doc.origin=bs

Justizbehörde. (2016). *Justizvollzugsanstalten in Hamburg*. Retrieved from http://www.hamburg.de/justizbehoerde/justizvollzugsanstalten/

Justizbehörde Hamburg. (2016). *JVA HSand Flyer*. Hamburg: Author.

Katz, E., Blumler, J. G., & Gurevitch, M. (1973). Uses and Gratifications Research. *Public Opinion Quarterly, 37*(4), 509–523. doi:10.1086/268109

Kes, H. (2013). Aktion Internet 2020. *Trotzdem,* (48).

Kim, S.J. (2016). A repertoire approach to cross-platform media use behavior. *New Media & Society, 18*(3), 353-372.

Langelid, T. (2009). *Nordic Prison Education - A Lifelong Learning Perspective.* Copenhagen: Norden.

Laubenthal, K. (2015). *Strafvollzug* (7th ed.). Berlin: Springer- Verlag. doi:10.1007/978-3-642-54819-2

Levy, M., & Windhal, S. (1984). Audience Activity and Gratifications. A Conceptual Clarification and Exploration. *Communication Research, 11*(1), 51–78. doi:10.1177/009365084011001003

Meyermann, A., & Porzelt, M. (2014). Hinweise zur Anonymisierung von qualitativen Daten. In *Forschungsdaten bildung informiert* (1). Frankfurt am Main: Deutsches Institut für Internationale Pädagogische Forschung. Retrieved from www.forschungsdaten-bildung.de/fdb-informiert

Name Generator. (2016). *Pseudonym Generator*. Retrieved from http://www.namegenerator.biz/pseudonym-generator.php

RTL 2. (2016). *Berlin - Tag und Nacht*. Retrieved from http://www.rtl2.de/sendung/berlin-tag-und-nacht

Rubin, A. M. (1984). Ritualized and Instrumental Television Viewing. *Journal of Communication, 34*(3), 67–77. doi:10.1111/j.1460-2466.1984.tb02174.x

Sollund, R. (2008). Tested Neutrality: Emotional Challenges in Qualitative Interviews on Homicide and Rape. *Journal of Scandinavian Studies in Criminology and Crime Prevention, 9*(9), 181–201. doi:10.1080/14043850802450138

Statista. (2016a). *Number of monthly active Facebook users worldwide as of 2nd quarter 2016 (in millions)*. Retrieved from https://www.statista.com/statistics/264810/number-of-monthly-active-facebook-users-worldwide/

Statista. (2016b). *Anzahl der Gefangenen und Verwahrten in den Justizvollzugsanstalten in Deutschland nach Bundesländern am 31*. Retrieved from https://de.statista.com/statistik/daten/studie/72216/umfrage/gefangene-und-verwahrte-in-justizvollzugsanstalten-nach-bundeslaendern/

Statista. (2018). *Bevölkerung - Einwohnerzahl in Deutschland nach Geschlecht von 1995 bis 2016 (in 1.000)*. Retrieved from https://de.statista.com/statistik/daten/studie/161868/umfrage/entwicklung-der-gesamtbevoelkerung-nach-geschlecht-seit-1995/

Steiner, M., & Lestigni, V. (2016). Die Telio-Tarifparade! *Lichtblick, 1*(366), 12–20.

Straßmeir, A. (2015). *Antwort über Knasttelefonie von Telio zu teuer*. Berlin: Senatsverwaltung für Justiz und Verbraucherschutz.

Telio. (2016). *Telio. Innovative Technologien für den Vollzug*. Retrieved from http://www.tel.io/de/

Van Voorhis, P., Lee Browning, S., Simon, M., & Gordon, J. (1997). The Meaning of Punishment: Inmates' Orientation to the Prison Experience. *The Prison Journal, 77*(2), 135–167. doi:10.1177/0032855597077002003

Vandebosch, H. (2001). Media Use as an Adaptation or Coping Tool in Prison. *Communications, 4*(26), 371–387.

Vogel, B. (2009). *The Prison Library Primer: A Program for the Twenty-First Century*. Plymouth: Scarecrow Press, Inc.

Walmsley, R. (2015). *World Female Imprisonment List* (3rd ed.). London: Institute for Criminal Policy Research.

Walmsley, R. (2016). *World Prison Population List* (11th ed.). London: Institute for Criminal Policy Research.

Widmann, M. (2015). *Neues von der Anstalt*. Retrieved from http://www.zeit.de/2015/40/hamburg-gefaengnis-hahnoefersand

Yuan, E. (2011). New Consumption across multiple Media Platforms. *Information Communication and Society*, *14*(7), 998–1016. doi:10.1080/1369118X.2010.549235

Zwischenbericht des Senats. (2016). *Gemeinsamer Zwischenbericht zum Ausbau der Kooperation auf dem Gebiet des Strafvollzuges*. Hamburg: Author.

ADDITIONAL READING

Dünkel, F., Kestermann, C., & Zolondek, J. (2005): *Reader Internationale Studie zum Frauenstrafvollzug. Bestandsaufnahme, Bedarfsanalyse und "best practice"* (www.rsf.uni-greifswald.de/fileadmin/mediapool/lehrstuehle/duenkel/Reader_frauenvollzug.pdf, 20. October 2016).

Grieve, Indian, M., Witteveen, K., Anne Tolan, G., & Marrington, J. (2013). Face-to-face or Facebook: Can social connectedness be derived online? *Computers in Human Behavior*, *29*(3), 604–609. doi:10.1016/j.chb.2012.11.017

Hasebrink, U., & Domeyer, H. (2012). Media repertoires as patterns of behaviour and as meaningful practices: A multimethod approach to media use in converging media environments. *Participations*, *9*(2), 757–779.

Hasebrink, U., & Popp, J. (2006). Media repertoires as a result of selective media use. A conceptual approach to the analysis of patterns of exposure. *Communications*, *31*(3), 369–387. doi:10.1515/COMMUN.2006.023

Haverkamp, R. (2011). *Frauenvollzug in Deutschland: eine empirische Untersuchung vor dem Hintergrund der Europäischen Strafvollzugsgrundsätze*. Berlin: Duncker & Humblot. doi:10.3790/978-3-428-53523-1

Jewkes, Y. (2002). The Use of Media in Constructing Identities in the Masculine Environment of Men's Prisons. *European Journal of Communication*, *17*(2), 205–225. doi:10.1177/0267323102017002693

Van Voorhis, P., Lee Browning, S., Simon, M., & Gordon, J. (1997). The Meaning of Punishment: Inmates' Orientation to the Prison Experience. *The Prison Journal*, *77*(2), 135–167. doi:10.1177/0032855597077002003

Vandebosch, H. (2001). Media Use as an Adaptation or Coping Tool in Prison. *Communications*, *4*(26), 371–387.

KEY TERMS AND DEFINITIONS

Communicative Figurations: Media communication happening within a specific social (sometimes public) context.

JVA (Justizvollzugsanstalt): German term for a correctional institution. Female and male prisons are usually strictly separated. They can be closed or open institutions.

Media Repertoire: The whole range of media consumed by one individual.

Semi-Structured In-Depth Interviews: Interview technique where the researcher follows not a strict questionnaire but gives more freedom to the interviewee to decide what is important to point out for him/her.

SNS: Social networking sites such as Facebook, Twitter, Instagram, etc. Online platforms where the communication is interactive, and an individual can build a social community.

Traditional Media: Offline media such as letters, phone calls for a landline, in-cell TV, and face-to-face visits.

Visualizing Cards: Method to visualize the media repertoire of an individual.

ENDNOTES

1 Record date: 31.03.15.

2 Interesting here is the product multio. It is an all-in-one system where prisoners can not only make phone calls and watch TV but have access to limited internet pages. However most of the prisons do still make use of the PHONio and therefore we do not go into detail here.

3 Original: "Eine Gleichsetzung mit Modellen bzw. eine Orientierung an Ansätzen, die sich im Männervollzug bewähren, würde letztendlich den Bedürfnissen von Frauen nicht gerecht werden und eine Benachteiligung bedeuten" (JVA Billwerder 2015, p. 7).

4 A German TV reality soap opera series broadcasted on weekdays since 2011 (RTL 2, 2016).

5 In their study they had a participant who mentioned 15 media components.

6 Original: "Geld beschaffen, Drogen nehmen, viel macht man ja eigentlich nicht als Drogenabhängiger" (Agnes, 03:12).

7 Original: "Und in Haft obwohl ich mich auf 20 Kilo zugenommen hab, auch wenn du das nicht siehst. (lacht) Aber die füttern einen halt gesund, wenn man.. ich hab schon mal 40 Kilo gewogen. Ja also mir ging's draussen nicht immer so gut, ne. Aber trotzdem möchte ich nicht hier bleiben". (Agnes, 24:28).

8 Original: "[...] draussen ist ja die Realität. So hier drinne kann ich so viel clean sein wie ich will, es kommt auf später darauf an was draussen ist. [...] Draussen ist alles anders. Hier ist alles strukturiert und hier wird viel strukturiert für dich. Es ist alles verboten du kriegst Strafen wenn du das dann trotzdem machst. Draussen ist keiner der sagt 'du, du, du' oder der sagt du musst jetzt arbeiten oder du musst jetzt was essen." (Agnes, 17:25).

9 Original: "Das sind keine Freundinnen. Freundinnen ist wenn du in Schwierigkeiten bist und wenn die für dich da sind" (Stacy, 27:51).

10 Original: "[...] die Hälfte meiner angeblichen Freunde werden es gar nicht gemerkt haben dass ich solange weg bin" (Agnes, 28:41).

11 Original: "[...] dann hab ich mich gestellt und zack waren sie weg. Keiner meldet sich" (Carlin, 58:12).

Chapter 12
Prison and Social Reintegration:
The Voice of a Formerly Freedom-Deprived Individual

Maria A. Añez
Universidad del Zulia, Venezuela

ABSTRACT

This study uses the voice of a formerly freedom-deprived individual, resorting to his memory, perception, and the exchange of the information acquired during his tenure in jail to interpret and understand the implications and manners of thought of those who live the prison reality. Following the qualitative methodology as the approach in the case study, this investigation demonstrates that in spite of the years that have passed, and of the efforts undertaken by the governments to make changes, jails continue being frequently damaged spaces, and in their interiors reigns a particular way of life in which violence is a necessary consequence, where socially diminished individuals retrain, with insufficient programs of attention, limited offers and opportunities of access amongst other restrictions, which end on disrespect and violation of their human rights because many times, more than stimulation for their rehabilitation, which is the proclaimed goal of the penitentiary system, jail is constituted into a place of development of their criminal career.

DOI: 10.4018/978-1-5225-5975-7.ch012

INTRODUCTION

Article 272 of the Venezuelan Constitution proclaims that it is the duty of the Venezuelan State to guarantee "the rehabilitation of the inmate and respect for their human rights". However, deprivation of liberty is transmuted under the shadows of an ideal of humanization and a utopia of re-socialization, in which the individual could serve his sentence in an appropriate space in respect and guarantee his dignity as a person, which allows them to overcome the conditions of original disadvantage, exclusion or social marginalization.

The country's penitentiary history carries with it a series of problems that trigger successive protests due to prison conditions - especially in the areas of health, work and recreation, judicial delays, property, violence, mistreatment of prisoners and visitors, abuse and corruption by prison officials, the possession and sale of arms and drugs, discrimination of women prison; causing strikes and riots in the prison establishments in the country.

In addition to this, it is impossible to avoid that in the penitentiaries of the country, in addition to the organization and formal norms of these institutions of social control, an intramural culture underlies, an underworld with its own codes and rules governs the daily life of people deprived of freedom.

Some efforts have been made by the national government to appease the crisis and to improve the penitentiary system, implementing various programs, plans, policies and / or projects without obtaining the expected success. It is precisely because of a prison emergency, that the constitutional mandate to create "an autonomous penitentiary entity" is fulfilled, in order to provide comprehensive care of the prisoner, considering the responsibility of the State and Society in the preventive treatment of delinquency and re-education of the individual.

At the end of the year 2013, the last known official figures, the Ministry with Penitentiary Competency reports a total of 53,917 (50,541 males and 3,376 females) inmates housed in 50 establishments, of which 69.31% remain in unprocessed status, in addition to providing assistance to 28,776 graduates with benefits from the penal system, in 06 night centers, 33 supervised residency centers and 30 technical units for supervision and guidance. (MPPSP, 2013: 26)

During this period, the national press - since no official statistics are released - reports 226 cases of injuries and the death of 248 people deprived of their liberty, mainly produced (71.9%) for the use of firearms, to some of these cases (12.7%) are added to high levels of violence, simultaneously using resources such as bullets, stabbings, dismemberments and hangings (Provea, 2014). However, in its management report the ministerial office states that "80% of the country's prisons are free of weapons" (MPPSP, 2013: 120).

From these premises arises the concern of a study that using the voice of the ex-inmate, resorting to its memory, perception and information exchange, acquired during his tenure in jail, how this experience was lived and how was their Process to return to social life, to interpret and understand the ways of thinking of those whom have lived prison reality, from their own jargon.

THEORETICAL FOUNDATIONS

From justifications to abolitionists, even in modernity, the reason of existence for punishment is questioned as a coercive mechanism, contemplating institutional violence on the hands of the State, hence the theoretical-philosophical discussions on the question why Punishment ", that is, the legitimation of the power of any political community to exercise structured violence on one of its members, is perhaps the most classic problem of the philosophy of law. (Ferrajoli, 1997: 247).

At the end of the eighteenth century, with the position of the bourgeoisie as a social class that ascended to political power to the detriment of the aristocracy, the correctionalist phase begins, in which the deprivation of liberty is institutionalized as the main form of criminal sanction. Nevertheless, for the last three decades of the nineteenth century, a reorientation of the punitive ideology and the identification of the human sciences arose, from which the terms used interchangeably, such as re-socialization, reinsertion, re-education, rehabilitation, etc., Expressions which suggest that the inmate suffers from a deficiency in his social adaptation that must be remedied. (Sandoval, 1982)

Rehabilitation is a compound word that comes from French and Latin: the French particle re means return or repetition and the Latin term habilis means competent, so the word denotes a return to competency, based on four main components: work, education, moral influence and discipline. (Mathiesen, 2003)

In the medical tradition, rehabilitation refers to a problematic condition - such as an illness - which must be restored to its previous state of health or condition; thus, applied to the criminal context, the term should only be used to refer to situations such as rehabilitation Abuse. Hence, its broad and differential use alludes to the positivist idea of crime as a synonym for a social ill that must be rehabilitated to return to normal. (Villagra, 2008)

The idea of rehabilitation is then advocated as "the reform of the delinquent via the application of treatments, based on previous clinical studies of the delinquent's personality" (Linares, 1981, p. 14), so that they recognize a moldable subject whose Behavior will respond to the expected "normal, moral, adapted" canons. (Castagno et al., 2011)

In parallel, the word reinsertion in a broad and general sense refers to "the act of re-inserting a person into the legal social order in which the citizens of a certain community relate and of which this person was marginalized", generating no less controversy about its functionality. (Villagra, 2008: 3)

For some, resocialization as a declared purpose of the criminal sanction, is a very broad and unfeasible concept, condemned to not achieve the expected success, since after the release from prison, it is only possible to expect minimal adaptation as a result, but never the complete integration to top social values, coupled with the fact that there are penalties that, by nature, exclude an aim to reform, as well as criminals whose treatment would be useless, due to their age, tendencies, crime committed or the duration of the penalty. (Sandoval, 1982)

At the practical level, the purpose of re-socializing implies the implementation of a treatment within a penitentiary regime, which leads to two objections; The first one relates to the material conditions available to carry out such treatment, and the second one relates to the criminal legal cases involved in the enforcement of the sentence. (Leal and García, 2002)

The guideline contained in article 272 of the constitutional text, finds obstacles in its attainment, since the custodial sentence challenges its re-education and socially readapting function, consequently questioning the idea of re-socialization.

In addition, the system is not equipped with sufficient resources for social restoration, so that once the sentence is extinct, the prisoner is given back his dignity, rights and honor; on the contrary, resources are allocated almost exclusively to the construction of more Prisons, so that rehabilitation only constitutes an ideology declared for the benefit of the prison system itself. (Mathiesen, 2003)

Methodology

This research was carried out using the qualitative methodology, following the approach of the case study, in which a phenomenon is defined, placing it in a time and space to perform a deep study of the how and why of that phenomenon. Thus, we study the Venezuelan prison system, for a better understanding of the world of life of the subject within the Venezuelan prisons.

To carry out this research, a collection of spontaneously produced discursive material (narrations) was planned through in-depth interviews with an ex-inmate about their life before, during and after their sentence was extinct[1]. In the words of Kvale (1996: 6), it is a matter of "obtaining descriptions of the interviewee's world, regarding the interpretation of the meanings of the phenomena described", it is sought to document the opinion of the interviewee on the subject, to unveil and represent feelings and Unobservable events. (Simons, 2011).

The in-depth interview seeks to obtain information on a given problem from a list of topics in relation to which the interview is focused, without subjecting itself to a formalized structure in advance, approaching the individual extensively for a considerable period of time, who is expected to have a relatively complete knowledge of the opinion or point of view of the subject on that issue. (Merlino, 2009, Rodríguez et al., 1999)

In that sense, in order to organize the interview sessions, a question bank was designed as a guiding instrument for the interview, structured in four sections, namely: the first one aimed at contextualizing life before deprivation of liberty; the second to internalize intramural experience, a third block of questions sought to investigate their current life situation, and finally, questions that were designed to extract the interviewee's perception of the prison and the process of social reintegration.

The interview process was carried out with a single informant of 56 years of age, whose life experience accumulates two periods of fulfillment of a 22-year sentence of imprisonment in the former National Prison of Maracaibo. A total of five meetings were held with an average duration of 40 minutes each, in which the interviewee in a retrospective to the past gave his life experience. Considering that in these sessions were sufficient to cover all the aspects included by the researcher in her question bank, the discourse regarding the data that this informant could offer was exhausted.

After the meetings were exhausted by the repetitiveness of the discourse and the approach of all the items contemplated in the instrument, the researcher proceeded to unravel the respective dialogues. Using a table for analysis line by line, we proceeded to label categories, subcategories and concepts emerged from the discourse following the analytical method of Strauss and Corbi (2002), which allows to explain at the same time to describe, performing a descriptive analysis and relational data. Also, to organize and facilitate the approach to the interpretation of results, we proceeded to diagram the relationships between categories and concepts, which are present in the narratives resulting from the in-depth interview.

Discussion of the Results

Prison is perceived as a "overwhelming and dangerous place" (Inmate A, Personal Communication, March 17, 2015), the view of it as an institution of social control, is that it is a melting pot for "the sadist, rapist, murderer and many More, ... it is a cycle that makes men worse, and those ones that improve, do so because they see the true reality lived in the inside "so that rather than" appease the wrath of the human being (Inmate A, Personal Communication, March 26, 2015), constitutes a space of contention, where the confined goes mad (Inmate A, Personal Communication, April 28, 2015) and corruption deafens (Inmate A, Personal Communication, April

Figure 1.

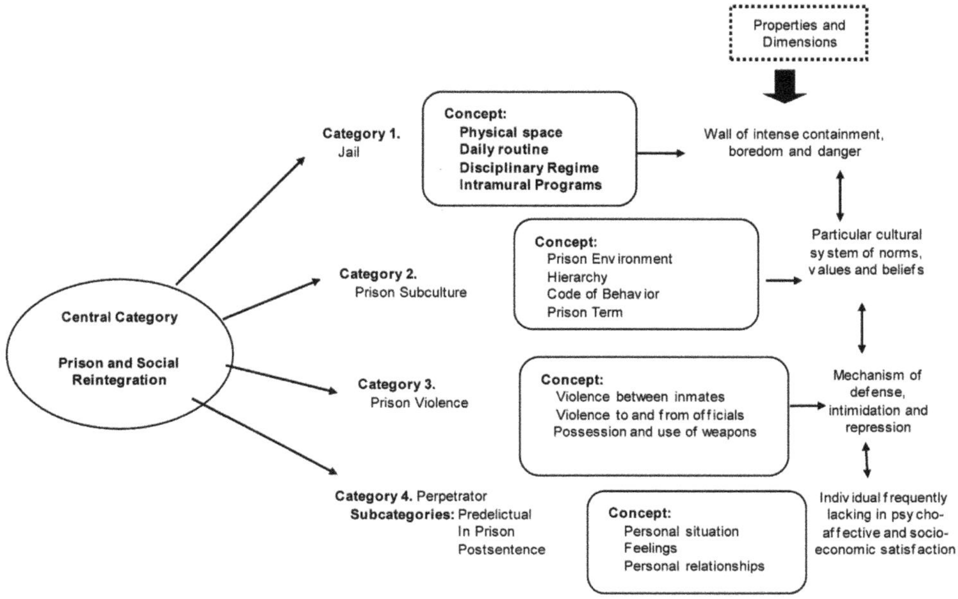

28, 2015). Despite the guarantee of rehabilitation and respect for human rights, proclaimed in Article 272 of the Constitution, the positivist postulates inside the prisons do not fade, when entering the establishment the individual knows the center of observation, "a restricted area they were arriving to, they lasted there for 30 days, after which they assigned him to one of the 40 pavilions" (Inmate A, Personal Communication, March 26, 2015). On the other hand, the informal organization of the enclosure also makes its diagnosis of the intern who is just entering, "tried to see if one was clothed or not" (Inmate A, Personal Communication, March 26, 2015).

Its physical infrastructure consisted of two-story pavilions, identified with letters and/or numbers, divided into four cells per floor. "They were boards but with rags" composed of Furniture and furnishings, such as "bunks, a television, a little armoire, a kitchen," most of which were provided with sacrifice from their families (Inmate A, Personal Communication, April 14, 2015).

The daily routine begins with the count, "they woke us up at 6:00, at 6:00 we were all awaken by number, the number was counted by their respective area, pavilions" (Inmate A, Personal Communication, April 14, 2015), "in the morning the first thing they went over is the number, the Guard counts three times, one in the morning, one at noon and one in the afternoon and there the prisoner is in command" (Inmate A, Personal Communication, March 26, 2015) "on passing the number that was at 6:00 we went out to the field, to carry out our duties, some worked in shoemaking, others cleaned, others went to the classes, others went to the dining room" (Inmate A, Personal Communication, April 14, 2015).

The evening countdown is around 5:00 p.m., so everyone should be in their cells, "that's where the problems came, in the confinement, because everyone is locked in, everyone Wants to call the shots, everyone wants to command" (Inmate A, Personal Communication, April 14, 2015). "After the Guard came out there were holes in each pavilion and people could go out, but not everyone could leave, only those who could, those that had carte blanche" (Inmate A, Personal Communication, April 14, 2015).

For some, their routine included cooking their own food with the provisions provided by their families or those who have access through the informal trade that takes place inside the establishments, while for others "everything is violence, everything is a knife and everything is, and everything is an empire, as they call it trash talking" (Inmate A, Personal Communication, April 14, 2015).

In order to reprimand unruly behavior, the authorities resort to confinement, subjecting the person to a disciplinary regime that neutralizes the individual's behavior through isolation in "dungeons" located in areas of "maximum" security. Punishment results in more confinement, more boredom, more exclusion. (Inmate A, Personal Communication, April 14, 2015)

Thursdays and Sundays are the most anticipated days of the week (Inmate A, Personal Communication, March 26, 2015), the days of the conjugal and family visit, moments in which the reach of affective bonds, give a respite to the reality that surrounds the prison environment, "the visit came and you would see the girls, I saw the lady" (Inmate A, Personal Communication, March 26, 2015), so that family support and the mother in particular, constitutes a fundamental pillar during the period of fulfillment of sentence.

This emotional need, regardless of the established regulations, indicates situations of governmental uncontrol and even dangerous to the family environment that attends the visit in the penitentiary establishments, "came to ask for a weekend visit, Friday, Saturday and Sunday, the family went to visit, everyone could see it, they slept in there Friday, Saturday and Sunday imagine everything that could take place those three days" (Inmate A, Personal Communication, April 16, 2015).

Overcoming boredom is a necessary challenge, "there is much boredom there, too much boredom" and "confinement drives the person mad if you do nothing" (Inmate A, Personal Communication, April 16, 2015).

The opportunities to develop a trade are precarious, "in these jails, study, study, there is no use for work, work is for mules, because I worked like a mule you know, I won't be fooled, work is for mules, that's why I made my decision to study "(Inmate A, Personal Communication, April 28, 2015).

Charging for the services rendered - of any kind - is another way of obtaining a living of their own in the prisons of the country, "as I gave classes they paid me, my work, even the car, the head of the gang and the the students paid me my fees, I paid them, the head of the gangs gave me ten thousand bolívares every six months, but those ten thousand bowls that I got from him were to pay for the tuition for the university" (Inmate A, Personal Communication, April 16, 2015).

In this context, inmates who genuinely have the initiative to overcome, occupy idle time and a positive attitude to make changes in their lifestyle, choose to carry out educational activities - in the limited range of options to which they have access - and / Or sports that allow access to the benefit of redemption of penalty for work and study (Inmate A, Personal Communication, April 16, 2015):

... I started to study first grade, second grade, third grade, fourth grade, fifth grade and sixth grade, they gave me the sixth grade ballot, and I told him," Mommy crowned, I passed all, now I'm going to study high school, "I said. I started to study, I did a course of facilitator, of ... Robinson I and Robinson II ... (Inmate A, Personal Communication, March 17, 2015)

... I was studying at the UNA (National Open University) engineering this ... what is it called ... industrial engineering, I was studying industrial engineering out there, ... but it got difficult, because I did not have money for books and what I had for books, I got monthly exams and I had to - as one says - struggle to pass my subjects and it was difficult for me. (Inmate A, Personal Communication, March 17, 2015)

... I was enticed to study law and I really wanted to get into it, as I told you, to move around in something, to be someone there in whatever, but to be given the opportunity and that was the only opportunity It was given to me, you understand me, there was no other opportunity and I could not despise it ... (Inmate A, Personal Communication, March 17, 2015)

However, prison is a monster in which "one had to survive every day" (Inmate A, Personal Communication, March 17, 2015), an underworld with a particularly violent social organization, in which the attitude of the inmate determines his life experience in these establishments, so the interviewee narrates: "I will not go back to prison meat God, that's a lie, I'm going to see what can I do around here, I'm not going to let myself die, and I started, I started until I succeeded thanks to God" (Inmate A, Personal Communication, April 16, 2015).

Indeed, in these institutions, the so-called prison subculture in a micro-social space that envelops and consumes (Inmate A, Personal Communication, March 17, 2015), in which bullying validates the worth and reputation and consequently the life of the inmate (Inmate A, Personal Communication, March 17, 2015; Inmate A, Personal Communication, April 16, 2015 Inmate A, Personal Communication, April 28, 2015), where ironically crime is unpunished (l. 888), in which drugs, alcohol and homosexuality constitute a means of relief to the confinement (Inmate A, Personal Communication, March 17, 2015; Inmate A, Personal Communication, April 16, 2015 Inmate A, Personal Communication, April 28, 2015), in which the technology, which access illegally - internet and cell phones - is used to satisfy illicit desires (Inmate A, Personal Communication, April 16, 2015), overlapping with the corruption of the officials responsible for ensuring the safety, proper functioning and order of the institution:

... those same officials, those same watchmen see how each inmate moves and how each individual survives there, they themselves are the promoters of everything, those same watchmen and the same guards, because they are the ones who volunteer themselves to everything There, for armament, for drugs, they are the ones that put everything there ... The Guard was the one that introduced the armament, the Guard was the one that brings in the drugs, ... they were the ones that brought everything to the inside you know ... first they talk and then they give him his cut, they bring in the goods and then they receive the other part, that's the business with the mafia ... it's a means of corruption that is there through the prisoner, the leaders in the Inside and the ones that have the institution, the command, the Guard or the officials that cooperate with the inmate. (Inmate A, Personal Communication, April 16, 2015)

The family not only suffers the vexations of a degrading treatment fro[the authority, but they are also at the mercy of the whims of the leaders of the prison in protection of their loved inmates:

... when he gets to the family, the sisters, the mother, those in the same boat, they want the sisters, they have sex with them, they marry them, they have children with them and they also make their families, but seeing it hindsight that is a kind of subjugation that has taken place first, because they attack the son and if the mother does not fulfill what they say they kill the child, whom is inside, then the mothers and daughters have to adapt to the environment inside, Because they are the only ones who can go see him, their loved ones... the family is so fucked... (Inmate A, Personal Communication, April 16, 2015)

In this type of social organization, the formation of small groups or "bands" as a symbol of fraternity, protection and defence (Inmate A, Personal Communication, March 17, 2015; Inmate A, Personal Communication, April 28, 2015) in which its members play roles and possess a Hierarchy that grants them a certain level of command and power.

In this way, the existence of "the gang bosses (prans), the chariot, the band of the chariot" (Inmate A, Personal Communication, March 17, 2015), who constitute the leading leaders of this system of informal organization and whose authority is contrasted with the one that the officials of The institution, "... there was a government, just like, the president was the pran, the band of the car are the governments was just inside..." (Inmate A, Personal Communication, April 28, 2015) "...there was the intern inside, the prisoner, we..."(Inmate A, Personal Communication, March 26, 2015)

This structure denotes a code of behavior that must be acknowledged, adopted and respected coercively by all prisoners under penalty of punishment or rebuke by the negative leaders of the penitentiary establishment. In this way, the leaders are not questioned, respected, the visit is sacred, before corruption and illicitness turns their eyes and so many other social norms that govern the life inside the prisons. Some clear examples of these rules are evidenced in the narratives of the interviewee:

...to the bourgeoisie they have submitted and pay for the tariff... (Inmate A, Personal Communication, April 14, 2015)

...that is bataneo, and that is paid with death... (Inmate A, Personal Communication, April 14, 2015)

...we were respected, we closed up and nobody touched anything, I went, when I arrived I found my things just because they already knew that if I realized who they were they were going to die ... (Inmate A, Personal Communication, April 14, 2015)

...the drug there was like liquor for me, I got to consume marijuana, it was the only thing that I consumed there, nothing else, there are many drugs, many, but I just consumed that and that because it encouraged me and me Motivated my work to my chores, that's what I did, when I was depressed, I looked bad, then I came and motivated me without needing them to tell me, I got motivated being there I had to do it because there it is like I told you it is a tribute that must be paid ... (Inmate A, Personal Communication, April 16, 2015)

Respect the visitors, the wife, respect the couples, they do not mess with the couples, whomever messes with a spouse is sentenced to die, that they kill him, the same population, because there they respect all that, there is a Code, the offender has his code and that code is respected. (Inmate A, Personal Communication, April 16, 2015)

...never a prisoner ..., can have contact with an official, they can never be seen together because that means the are already telling on others, if there is a crime, and an intern talking to a caretaker, or to the Guard, it is Very delicate, there we cannot contact between them nor talk to them, because our code does not allow it, ... (Inmate A, Personal Communication, April 16, 2015)

Verbal communication is identified by a particular prison term whose meaning is suited during their tenure, thus recreating an intra-prison dictionary, in which the most frequent words denote the meanings of the way of life in these institutions.

The words of the prison jargon to which the interviewee refers in his dialogues are the following:

- **Agua:** "It is that the government is going to bring them in and take them away" (Inmate A, Personal Communication, March 26, 2015);
- **Bataneo:** "... in a prison that is a crime ..." (l. 808), means robbing the belongings of a prisoner (Inmate A, Personal Communication, March 26, 2015);
- **Bandiar:** To hit (Inmate A, Personal Communication, March 17, 2015);
- **Bicha:** Unhappy (Inmate A, Personal Communication, March 26, 2015);
- **Burguesito:** Who likes to get everything done for him (Inmate A, Personal Communication, March 26, 2015);
- **Candela:** Problematic situation (Inmate A, Personal Communication, March 26, 2015);
- **Caricariar:** "Is that a band comes and kills them" (Inmate A, Personal Communication, March 26, 2015);
- **Chulo:** "Is a dead inmate" (Inmate A, Personal Communication, March 26, 2015);
- **Cobra Peaje:** "Its is a person that comes and talks to you and asks you, on visitation days and asks you for money n behalf of the mob boss, this because he knows that you or your family has the money " (Inmate A, Personal Communication, April 16, 2015);
- **Convive:** Friend, partner. (Inmate A, Personal Communication, March 17, 2015);
- **Culebra:** Enemy, person with whom you have a problem (Inmate A, Personal Communication, March 17, 2015);
- **Emproblemao, Guerriao:** In trouble (Inmate A, Personal Communication, March 17, 2015);
- **Mansalbear:** "To come at you from Behind your back, and you can't see the person" (l. (Inmate A, Personal Communication, March 17, 2015), to act with treachery;

- **Nero:** "Is a person that does not smoke, drink, hang out with the mob, does not walk around bothering others" (Inmate A, Personal Communication, April 16, 2015);
- **Obligaito:** Vaccine or fee, a tribute that must be paid. (Inmate A, Personal Communication, April 16, 2015);
- **Pajuo, Sapo:** Person that tells on others (Inmate A, Personal Communication, April 14, 2015);
- **Pran:** "Head of a gang" (Inmate A, Personal Communication, April 14, 2015);
- **Prote:** Payment to obtain some benefit or protection (Inmate A, Personal Communication, April 14, 2015).

In addition to this particular form of communication, some nicknames are used, those label the image and personality of the prisoner. Some of them are known as plastic boys (Inmate A, Personal Communication, April 14, 2015), hair gum (Inmate A, Personal Communication, April 14, 2015), golden top (Inmate A, Personal Communication, April 14, 2015), golden knight (Inmate A, Personal Communication, April 14, 2015), the latter two assumed by the interviewee as their own performance within the penitentiary.

This internal coexistence is also marked with a seal of violence, both between inmates and those that arise from and towards prison officials and the National Guard as guarantors of the external security of prisons.

The malandreo, or bullying - knife and gun in hand - is a defense mechanism in prison (Inmate A, Personal Communication, April 14, 2015; Inmate A, Personal Communication, March 26, 2015), so life in these establishes is a deadly war where the strongest survives - physically and psychologically- "... you have to play to be alive because you are going to be killed ..." (Inmate A, Personal Communication, March 26, 2015).

In this way, to be respected by the use of knives or firearms (Inmate A, Personal Communication, March 26, 2015), is a way to ensure survival, to repel attacks (l. 554-555, 677, 683) and to inflict fear "I did not let go of my knife ..." (Inmate A, Personal Communication, March 26, 2015), "... they forced me to take the knife..." (Inmate A, Personal Communication, March 26, 2015), "...we took up arms because they were forcing them on us, life becomes impossible and they were going to keep us under their thumb, our things are not ours, but for others." (Inmate A, Personal Communication, April 14, 2015)," ...to me if I was pressured, and I had to surrender, but I would not let myself submit, I let myself be humiliated and I did not let myself be told how to act like a mule, give, give, and give ... "(Inmate A, Personal Communication, April 16, 2015).

Hence, fights (Inmate A, Personal Communication, April 14, 2015), homicides (1,951) and deaths on commission (l. 738), injuries (l. 1150), threats and the barbarity (l. 738), ".. the best defense is the attack, never wait for them to attack you and you keep quiet, no on the contrary you defend yourself and pum, you pull, and pam, you dominate the person or you injure him..." (Inmate A, Personal Communication, April 28, 2015).

Violence as a means of coercion and intimidation floods the justice system even before entering it, from the beginning the police authorities are presented with scenarios of abuse of power and underground repression as a means of confession and unlawful punishment of criminal conduct, "they hit me and they electrocuted me, and I never told them anything, and they hit me and hit me ... and they put me down because I did not say anything to them" (Inmate A, Personal Communication, March 17, 2015).

Once inside the penitentiary system, the use of physical and psychological force by the authority, mainly by the hands of the National Guard is positioned as a means of punishment, "... all the guards entered and beat us all up..." (Inmate A, Personal Communication, April 14, 2015). "I called the official" officer, I do not want him here for another minute"... and because of that I got beaten up" (Inmate A, Personal Communication, April 14, 2015).

In addition, the inmates repel this violence in a context of reciprocity to the official in total disregard for authority, "...officials at night could not enter because there dominated by the power of the knife," you know, and also, gunpowder, they could not go in there because they were shot at, too, so they would just come in the morning, run their number in the afternoon and leave, run their number all complete, and sometimes when they came around to get Someone, they came in a group, quite a few of them, and the Guard also came in to get whom they had come for and took him away" (Inmate A, Personal Communication, April 14, 2015).

The offender is characterized by being mainly a young man (Inmate A, Personal Communication, March 17, 2015), with a low level of education, originating from a large and unstructured family nucleus, where the mother plays a primordial role, in which affective and socioeconomic deficiencies, together with the bad companies, are the catalyst and justifier of a criminal career with no return, "you know why me, why we entered jail for the first time?, because there wasn't a pattern a control in our family, we lived all our life since childhood, in a messed up way ..." (Inmate A, Personal Communication, March 17, 2015):

Mommy ehh, she was practically my father and my mother, because I did not know my father. (Inmate A, Personal Communication, March 17, 2015)

We are five brothers. Two females and three boys. (Inmate A, Personal Communication, March 17, 2015)

I have been with them very little since we have been separated as kids. (Inmate A, Personal Communication, March 17, 2015)

I was barely able to read and I was looser. (Inmate A, Personal Communication, April 14, 2015)

I began to mischief to wander because I did not have a profession, I had nothing. (Inmate A, Personal Communication, March 17, 2015)

In the prison context, the conditions of exclusion and marginalization tend to intensify, so that the original family disintegration is transferred to their own families, "my brother ... and he had his wife, he married a minor, had two babies, he lost his wife in there... "(Inmate A, Personal Communication, April 14, 2015), "... I never had a wife, a wife, a girlfriend, I lived with a knife and studied... "(Inmate A, Personal Communication, March 26, 2015), "... God does not want to give me my wife and my children, I'm 56 years old and I do not have babies around, because I did not have time to fall in love with a girl, I did not have time to think about a home" (Inmate A, Personal Communication, April 16, 2015) "...sometimes I had sex there I paid to be able to do it, but I never had a girlfriend, a wife who visited me, nobody, mother was the only one who came to visit me" (Inmate A, Personal Communication, April 28, 2015).

In this way, feelings of loneliness and restlessness are generated in the prisoner, "I said my God why do I get this destiny, I do not deserve it, tell me what I have done,... and tears came to me while I was alone" (Inmate A, Personal Communication, April 28, 2015) "and he told me patience because the executioner does not ask for clemency,... because if I am bad and I am casting a scabbard and when it is my turn to suffer, there I will ask for mercy" (Inmate A, Personal Communication, April 28, 2015). Thus, he assumes himself as an evil being "I was very bad inside, because I would not let myself cast a scabbard ... he would not let me beat him, he would not let me be humiliated" (Inmate A, Personal Communication, April 28, 2015). "I wanted to kill myself, ... I did not want to go on with my life ...I wanted to die" (Inmate A, Personal Communication, March 17, 2015). "... I lived under siege" (Inmate A, Personal Communication, April 28, 2015).

Consequently, the internal self defines itself as an object of the system:

I am a punished inmate and I belong to the Ministry and they do with the prisoners what they want, when one is already punished one is not a citizen, and one is an inmate and the government sends him anywhere, sends him to where he is until he completes his sentence, after he completes his sentence, he becomes a citizen again, but the world keeps an eye on it, he has it, he has it, he cannot enter anything, no one gives you work. (Inmate A, Personal Communication, April 14, 2015)

In the first meeting with the prison world, it is common to assume a reluctant and quarrelsome position as a defense mechanism, "copied with the world too ..." (Inmate A, Personal Communication, March 17, 2015), "... I could not look at myself, the one I was looking at I was sparing him the knife, I am not telling you, I lived in isolation, then came the moment that I did not leave a dungeon ... "(Inmate A, Personal Communication, March 26, 2015), " ... all the felons were afraid of me" (Inmate A, Personal Communication, April 16, 2015). "I saw that people feared me, they were afraid of me, because I got a lot of fame (l. 1175) ... if I did not do it, they would have me underneath ... " (Inmate A, Personal Communication, April 16, 2015).

The support of the family is a fundamental pillar for coping with imprisonment, especially of the mother who constitutes a preconditioning unconditional figure for the support and emotional and economic assistance during the sentence period:

...And then there was Mommy, my little old lady next to us..." (Inmate A, Personal Communication, March 17, 2015)

...Then when we are condemned, this mother, Mother, hears, twelve and a half years...(Inmate A, Personal Communication, March 17, 2015)

...I graduated from high school and my mother was there ... "(l. 208-209)

...I was not visited by anybody, the only one who visited me was my late mother ... (Inmate A, Personal Communication, March 17, 2015)

...That gave me that strength and that will was her...(Inmate A, Personal Communication, March 17, 2015)

...Mommy I promised you that I would be someone in life and I will do it...(Inmate A, Personal Communication, March 17, 2015)

I had my kitchen, I had my television, I had my bed, I had my window, to my bookstore, my library, all that mother brought for me...(Inmate A, Personal Communication, March 17, 2015)

Resuming a positive attitude towards life despite the circumstances is a challenge in which the family plays a fundamental role, another important ally are the activities and programs that are possible to develop within the prison, allowing the inmate to cope with the daily life of confinement of another way, so as to transform despair is a peaceful state that empowers you emotionally to live in conditions of social isolation:

I told her 'Mommy I'm tired of this scabbard, I'm going back to incarceration, they're going to kill me like a dog here and I do not want them to kill me, I want to be someone in life, since I was not outside, I'll try to do it here, here where you cannot, I promise Mommy from now on to change my life' and I started to study(Inmate A, Personal Communication, March 26, 2015).

and from that door there are students, they are another person, but from the door there are animals (Inmate A, Personal Communication, March 26, 2015)

...I already graduated and I am a high school graduate, I already trained, since I am not the same truant as before, and I am not I'm the same dry coconut from before, I already have another image in my mind, my knowledge, I arrived and my mom was there (Inmate A, Personal Communication, April 14, 2015)

There the blows, the need, even the hunger made me change ... (Inmate A, Personal Communication, April 16, 2015)

Faith and religious belief is also an aspect that the human being holds to maintain the strength and hope that sustains him mainly in the most difficult moments of his prison experience, "... thank God that gave me that strength of will ... "(Inmate A, Personal Communication, March 26, 2015)," ... I did not want to continue living, I even tried to take my life and God did not let me, I sought problems, for people to kill me and God did not want that... "(Inmate A, Personal Communication, April 16, 2015), "I did not know what to do with my life, because no one took it from me, sometimes God spoke to me" (Inmate A, Personal Communication, April 16, 2015), "I am alive, thanks to God, God allowed me everything" ((Inmate A, Personal Communication, April 16, 2015), "... I speak with God and God hears me ..." (Inmate A, Personal Communication, March 17, 2015).

With the passing of time, the status of the prisoner in the prison and the attitude towards this experience of life, it is possible to reassume the positioning of the self, exalting the importance of the self within the context in which it unfolds.

With the passage of time, the status of the prisoner in the prison and the attitude towards this experience of life, it is possible to reassume the positioning of the self, exalting the importance of self within the context in which it develops:

I'm good, when I concentrate on something like that, it's the last one, but I get to the end as it is, so do not take me into account or see that I'm out there (Inmate A, Personal Communication, April 28, 2015)

immediately saw that I was great (Inmate A, Personal Communication, April 28, 2015)

I was one of the best in there (Inmate A, Personal Communication, April 28, 2015)

However, despite any effort undertaken, being locked up, together with the conditions under which seclusion elapses and the prisoner's life history, become a trigger that directly affects the physical and mental health of the individual during and even after the sentence has been served:

My mommy died one year before my eleventh year here, as I told you I was not allowed to see it, they told me three days after they died, I got sick, everything came over me and I turned ... everything went dark for me, my self-esteem was put again here (pointing down), when I left I did not find what to do, I went to university did not let me enroll as a high school graduate, I wanted to work I was not allowed because I was ex-convict and I was alone, I was alone because I did not have a house, I did not have a wife, I did not have children or anything, and the one I had was a little sister of mine, so she took me in, I lived for some time with her, then I fell into the second fall. (Inmate A, Personal Communication, April 14, 2015)

Over time I had to make that decision because I could not get a job and at the University they would not let me study, so I was forced to go out and steal. (Inmate A, Personal Communication, April 14, 2015)

The devil again absorbed me and put me to steal there again. (Inmate A, Personal Communication, April 28, 2015)

That same feeling of loneliness and longing that is secured in prison, accompanies the ex-prisoner after the end of his sentence, because it is often uphill to not only overcome the stigma of life in prison, but also erase the traces of a turbulent history of life before her:

I changed, you see, one changes, I now ... of course I always have something, I'm always alone. (Inmate A, Personal Communication, April 16, 2015)

I've never been married, and I've never had a princess, I had a girlfriend because I was punished, I never had that pleasure like other people like every citizen, like every human being, I did not go through that, I did not have children, I did not have an education, my education was there in prison...now I am lacking a wife, children and a house. (Inmate A, Personal Communication, April 16, 2015)

the friendships that I have are very few and sincere because friends are not. (Inmate A, Personal Communication, March 26, 2015)

I changed, thank God and my deceased mother, because that is what I have, and mommy left, all I have left is God in my heart, I have no one else and I have been optimistic. (Inmate A, Personal Communication, April 28, 2015)

This same stigma that implies being an ex-inmate, coupled with the degree of instruction and trade or professionalization of the subject, provides scarce and precarious employment opportunities to the individual, "... I went there as a kitchen assistant to work because I was a prisoner, pay, no one gave me work ... "(Inmate A, Personal Communication, April 28, 2015), "they made me to work as a watchman... "(Inmate A, Personal Communication, April 28, 2015).

With education and professionalization, the satisfaction of the fulfillment of other personal goals contributes to alleviate the vacuum of affective deficiencies: "... the studies are very beautiful I fell in love with them, I did not fall in love with anyone, I fell in love with them, my studies ... "(Inmate A, Personal Communication, April 16, 2015)," today I am a lawyer, I am studying engineering ... "(Inmate A, Personal Communication, March 17, 2015).

However, the longing to form and establish a family is always present "... already an improved person, I feel happy, not very happy I still lack more parts, to look for a wife, a house, my children, to form my home before I retire, I have a long life ... "(Inmate A, Personal Communication, April 28, 2015) " ... I know that, perhaps here I cannot get a wife or my children, it can be somewhere else, in another country..." (Inmate A, Personal Communication, April 28, 2015).

In this experience of life, the discrediting of the judicial system penetrated by corruption and injustice (Inmate A, Personal Communication, March 17, 2015), in which public defenders "...were doing their process, their paperwork and now, ready and I paid my penance ... "(Inmate A, Personal Communication, March 17, 2015), without providing psychosocial support or support to address the problems associated with crime (Inmate A, Personal Communication, March 17, 2015).

In a perspective to the past, the twenty-two years transited in the National Prison of Maracaibo in the fullness of his youth, marked the existence of the interviewee, however, it was possible to turn the negative conditions of the prison, to restructure his life in spite of the circumstances, the stigma and the temptations that in the middle are presented (Inmate A, Personal Communication, April 28, 2015):

I was left with beautiful memories and bad memories and an overcoming and a liberation, because I freed myself, I freed myself from those demons that were in me. (Inmate A, Personal Communication, April 16, 2015)

I went through prison, jail did not happen for me. (Inmate A, Personal Communication, March 17, 2015)

I practically got myself in jail, did you hear me? I did not go to prison when I arrived. (Inmate A, Personal Communication, March 17, 2015)

I have achieved what is called ... something that not everyone achieves in hell, I succeeded. (Inmate A, Personal Communication, March 26, 2015)

Nowadays, I am another person, I am very proud. (Inmate A, Personal Communication, April 28, 2015)

I am now as it is said of the middle class, I already belong to the middle class, I am a lawyer and the lawyer enters the middle class, the bourgeois above and the middle society are all graduates, ..., I am no longer society, of the poor. (Inmate A, Personal Communication, April 28, 2015)

In this sense, reinsertion, redemption, rehabilitation or, as it prefers to be called the perspective of a new enterprise and reborn in society after prison life, requires motivation, self-determination and family and social support, to overcome the unfavourable socioeconomic conditions that accompany the individual before, during and after the completion of the sentence:

My rehabilitation was that I arrived there ignorant and a dry coconut and the necessities that I survived there inside made me make decisions of a mature man, of a decisive¡¡ man, you understand me. I decided it was my studies, I decided to be someone in life, take advantage of my studies and not letting myself be led by bands or vandalism or lead, or assassinate, become a hit man, because there come assassins, they kill themselves. (Inmate A, Personal Communication, April 28, 2015)

On leaving to take control of everyone who was going out the respective institution and rehabilitate it once to a job, a job for anyone who goes out and is rehabilitating, companies work for them, I would do, to create companies, shoemaking, eh masonry and such, but exclusively for them, and there they are rehabilitated more and society accepts them more, and they can work in other institutions, because institutions do not allow them to go there because they are prisoners, they are thieves, they are murderers and they are going to spoil the company, that is what the entrepreneurs think, you understand me, because I already lived it the first time because I came from there, I continued to steal and I went to jail the second because of that, because no gave me support, the government does not help those who go outside, rather they close the doors. (Inmate A, Personal Communication, April 28, 2015)

FINAL CONSIDERATIONS

Although the corrosive aspects of the penitentiary system have been addressed by scholars and specialists in the area, their exposure by experienced subjects reveals not only the contradictions of the formal discourse by the official spokesmen but also proclaims the call for help and inclusion of those who suffer the ravages of the country's prison situation.

Venezuelan prisons become institutions whose social organization is regulated by the rules imposed by the prison subculture above the formal system, amid inhuman conditions of confinement and coexistence. In this hostile environment, a new system of life is built for the inmate, conformed by a code of conduct imbued with values, beliefs and principles that regulate social interaction in prison, whose non-observance can have harmful consequences for the life and physical integrity of the prisoner who is deprived of freedom.

This investigation reveals that, despite the years that have passed and the efforts made by the governments of the day, prison remains a frequently deteriorated space envisaged as a wall of restraint, boredom and danger, within which a way of life instituted by A particular system of norms, values and beliefs, in which violence is a necessary consequence assumed as a defense, intimidation and repression mechanism, recycling socially diminished individuals, often lacking the satisfaction of psycho-affective and socio-economic needs, Many of the times more than impelling the rehabilitation of the intern is constituted in a place of perfection of the criminal race.

In fact, penitentiary establishments, despite refractions and maintenance, continue to be dismal, inadequate and unhygienic spaces, whose occupation exceeds the installed capacity for their shelter, with a limited routine of activities and few opportunities for study and occupation, combined with A disciplinary regime of punishment and penance by force of more isolation and more confinement.

In this context, the inmate builds a system of beliefs, values, attitudes, ideologies, stereotypes and images from their life-world immersed in the prison subculture. Thus, within the penitentiary establishments, a daily life marked by codes of behavior, a particular form of verbalization and structures of command and power is built, which must be adapted not only to the prisoner but also to his family group, the process of de-culturization and imprisonment that takes place in Prison environment also clothes those who attend the visit of their loved ones.

Prison violence is not only physical but also psychological, not only leaves the mark of scarring on the skin but also inside these people who live daily fear of losing along with their freedom, their life.

Violence, becomes an accessory penalty to confinement, enhanced by the drug and arms trade within prisons. Because of this, the physical and psychological force employed among the inmates themselves and reciprocally from and to authority is the catalyst for unpunished punishable acts within the prison - intimidation, injury, rape, corruption, homicide - overlapping by fear and indifference.

Another aspect that seems invariable in the time and coincident with the criteria of selectivity of the penal system is the characterization of the deprived of freedom, as a young man, who is single, of low education level, originating of numerous families, with economic deficiencies and affective breaches from childhood, whose criminal beginnings are presented as an opportunity to obtain income not possible by legal means and whose actions are self-justify in the individual and social conditions that have marked their existence.

Thus, in spite of the proclaimed "new adult penitentiary regime", for the proper social transformation towards the new man implemented through strategies of dialogue, persuasion and respect for human rights, under a daily and permanent schedule of educational, labor, Sports, cultural and recreational facilities to ensure their subsequent reinsertion to society after their release from prison (MPPSS, 2013), the current management of the penitentiary system, is still strongly criticized and questioned, as inadequate conditions of imprisonment, prison overcrowding, procedural delay, violence and insecurity, among many other aspects, are still present in life in prison, making illusory the ideal of re-socialization proclaimed in the Constitution.

REFERENCES

Asamblea Nacional Constituyente. (1999). Constitución de la República Bolivariana de Venezuela. 1999. Caracas, Venezuela. Gaceta Oficial No. 36.860 de fecha 30 de diciembre de 1999.

Castagno, Malek, Renzone, & Correa. (2011). Significaciones de la (re)inserción social de sujetos privados de la libertad, desde la teoría de las Representaciones Sociales. VII Encuentro Interdisciplinario de Ciencias Sociales y Humanas. Vol. 1, No. 1. Facultad de Filosofía y Humanidades. Universidad de Córdoba, Argentina.

Ferrajoli, L. (1997). *Derecho y Razón. Teoría del Garantismo Penal*. Editorial Trotta.

Kvale, S. (1996). Interviews: An Introduction to Qualitative Research Interviewing. Thousand Oaks, CA: SAGE Publications.

Leal & García. (2002). Discurso y Garantismo: consideraciones acerca de los fines de la pena. Fronesis, 9(2), 85-120.

Linares, M. (1981). *El Sistema Penitenciario Venezolano. Instituto de Ciencias Penales y Criminológicas*. Universidad Central de Venezuela.

Mathiesen, T. (2003). *Juicio a la Prisión. Una Evaluación Crítica*. Ediar, S.A.

Merlino, A. (2009). La Entrevista en Profundidad como Técnica de Producción Discursiva. In Investigación Cualitativa en Ciencias Sociales. Cengage Learning.

Ministerio del Poder Popular Para el Servicio Penitenciario. (2013). Caracas, Venezuela: Memoria y Cuenta.

Programa Venezolano de Educación-Acción en Derechos Humanos. (2014). *Situación de los Derechos Humanos en Venezuela. Informe Anual Enero-Diciembre 2013*. Derechos de las personas privadas de libertad. Caracas, Venezuela. Pág. 415-432.

Rodriguez, Gil, & García. (1999). *Metodología de la Investigación Cualitativa* (2nd ed.). Ediciones Aljibe.

Sandoval, E. (1982). *Penología. Parte General*. Universidad Externado de Colombia.

Simons, H. (2011). *El Estudio de caso: teoría y práctica*. Ediciones Morata, S.L.

Strauss & Corbin. (2002). *Bases de la Investigación Cualitativa. Técnicas y Procedimientos para Desarrollar la Teoría Fundamentada*. Editorial Universidad de Antioquía.

Villagra, C. (2008). Reinserción: Lecciones para una Política Pública. *Revista Debates Penitenciarios, 6*, 3-18.

ENDNOTE

1 For the purposes of this working paper, the interviews were translated using English idioms to convey the message intended by the interviewee, instead of using literal translations which would have stripped the text of sense.

Compilation of References

Abid, A. (2012). *Hacia una cultura de la información*. Universidad de Toluca.

Adeagbo, O. O., Asubiojo, B. O., Obadare, S. O., & Akindojutimi, B. F. (2016). Re-Integration of Prison Inmates in Nigeria: Advocating for Library Support. *The International Information & Library Review, 48*(3), 169–175. doi:10.1080/10572317.2016.1204872

Adebisi, K. S., & Oyewo, O. O. (2015). Prisons and security challenges in a democratic Nigeria. *Research on Humanities and Social Sciences, 5*(6), 124–129.

Adetula, G. A., & Fatusin, A. F. (2010). The prison subsystem culture: Its attitudinal effects on operatives, convicts and the free society. *Psychological, 18*(1), 232–251.

Adeyemo, A. B. (2011). E-government implementation in Nigeria: An assessment of Nigeria's global e-government ranking. *Journal of Internet and Information Systems, 2*(1), 11–19.

Agenda Digital para Europa. (n.d.). Retrieved October, 15, 2017 from http://www.europarl.europa.eu/ftu/pdf/es/FTU_5.9.3.pdf

Agúndez Soriano, M. A. (2016). *Alfabetización informacional para la inclusión social de las mujeres reclusas de la Comunidad de Madrid: um estudio de caso*. Universidad Complutense de Madrid.

Agúndez, M. A. (2016). *Alfabetización informacional para la inclusión social de las mujeres reclusas de la Comunidad de Madrid: un estudio de caso* (Unpublished doctoral dissertation). Universidad Complutense de Madrid, Madrid, Spain.

Agúndez-Soriano, M. A. (2015). *Alfabetización informacional para la inclusión social de las mujeres reclusas de la Comunidad de Madrid: un estudio de caso* (Unpublished doctoral dissertation). Universidad Complutense.

Akoni, C. (2017). Hope rises as varsity empowers pre-release Kirikiri female inmates. *Vanguard*. Accessed online on 29/9/2017 from https://www.vanguardngr.com/2017/06/hope-rises-varsity-empowers-pre-release-kirikiri-female-inmates/

Alberoni, F. (1989). *Génese*. Lisboa: Bertrand.

Allen, R. (2010). *Current situation of prison overcrowding*. Accessed on 21/09/2017 from http://www.prisonstudies.org/sites/default/files/resources/downloads/current_situation_of_prison_overcrowding_paper.pdf

Almada, M. (1999). Políticas de información y políticas educativas: un vínculo importante para el desarrollo hemisférico. *Boletín de política informática*, *23*(6), 34.

American Library Association. (1989). Presidential Committee on Information Literacy: final report. In G. E. Menshing & T. B. Menshing (Eds.), *Coping with information illiteracy: bibliographic instruction for the information age* (pp. 156–171). Ann Arbor, MI: Pierian Press. Retrieved from http://ala.org/acrl/publications/whitepapers/presidential

Añaños, F., Fernández, M. P. & Llopis, J. J. (2013). Aproximación a los contextos en prisión. Una perspectiva socioeducativa. *Pedagogía social. Revista interuniversitaria*, (22), 13-28.

Añaños, F. (2013). Formación educativa previa ante las discriminaciones: Las mujeres reclusas en España. *Review of Education*, (360), 91–118. Retrieved from http://www.mecd.gob.es/dctm/revista-deeducacion/articulosre360/re36006.pdf?documentId=0901e72b814a77e6

Anderson, K. (2010). Globalization's effects on world agricultural trade, 1960–2050. *Philosophical Transactions of the Royal Society of London. Series B, Biological Sciences*, *365*(1554), 3007–3021. doi:10.1098/rstb.2010.0131 PMID:20713399

Aranda, M. J. (2005). *Reeducación y reinserción social: Tratamiento penitenciario: análisis teórico y aproximación práctica* (Unpublished doctoral dissertation). Universidad Nacional de Educación a Distancia.

Araromi, M. A. (2015). Prisoners' rights under the Nigerian law: Legal pathways to progressive realization and protection. *Journal of Sustainable Development Law and Policy (The)*, *6*(1), 169–198. doi:10.4314/jsdlp.v6i1.8

Asamblea Nacional Constituyente. (1999). Constitución de la República Bolivariana de Venezuela. 1999. Caracas, Venezuela. Gaceta Oficial No. 36.860 de fecha 30 de diciembre de 1999.

Asokhia, M. O., & Agbonluae, O. O. (2013). Assessment of rehabilitation services in Nigerian prisons in Edo State. *American International Journal of Contemporary Research*, *3*(1), 224–230.

Australian Computer Society. (2016). *Cybersecurity threats challenges opportunities*. ACS. Accessed on 19/09/2017 from https://www.acs.org.au/content/dam/acs/acs-publications/ACS_Cybersecurity_Guide.pdf

Awopetu, R. G. (2014). An assessment of prison overcrowding in Nigeria: Implications for rehabilitation, reformation and reintegration of inmates. *IOSR Journal of Humanities and Social Science*, *19*(3), 21–26. doi:10.9790/0837-19362126

Ayade, E. A. (2010). *Problems of Prisons Overcrowding in Nigeria: Some lessons from South Africa and America. LLM, Human Rights* (Unpublished Thesis). Central European University, Legal Studies Department, Budapest, Hungary.

Babalola, Y. T. (2013). Nigeria's information infrastructure policy: Implications for e-government. *Arabian Journal of Business and Management Review, 2*(11), 8–15.

Barbelet, J. (2001). *Emotion, Social Theory and Social Structure - a macrosociological approach.* Cambridge, UK: Cambridge University Press.

Barranquero, A. (2007). Concepto, instrumentos y desafíos de la edu-comunicación para el cambio social [Concept, instruments and challenges of media education for social change]. *Comunicar, 15*(29), 115-120. Retrieved from https://goo.gl/vPgYSj

Barreiro, M., Novo, I., & Varela, L. (2013). e-Prisons and new technologies: ICT as a mechanism of social inclusions of prisoners. *International Journal of Knowledge Society Research, 4*(3), 1–10. doi:10.4018/ijksr.2013070101

Baskas, R. S. (2016). Creating a Curriculum and Accommodating Teaching Methods at a Federal Prison's Special Housing Unit. *ERIC*, 1–14.

Batra, R., Jasso, T., & Stevens, Y. (2012). Learning behind bars: Exploring prison educators' facilitation of inmates' self-directed learning through Garrison's model. *11th Annual College of Education & GSN Research Conference*, 2–9.

Baym, N. K. (2015). *Personal connections in the digital age*. John Wiley & Sons.

Benito Rangel, F., Espartero Martínez, P., García Marijuán, J. A., Garrido Martínez, A., & López-Araujo, J. F. (2002). La Ciencia y Práctica Penitenciaria en una Sociedad en Cambio: Apuntes para una Reflexión de Futuro. *Revista Electrónica de Ciencia Penal y Criminología, 4*(1).

Berg, M. (2005). *The age of manufactures, 1700-1820: Industry, innovation and work in Britain.* Routledge.

Bernhard, P. (2002). La formación en el uso de la información: una ventaja en la enseñanza superior. Situación actual. *Anales de Documentación, 5*, 409-435. Retrieved March, 31, 2018 from http://revistas.um.es/Analesdoc/article/view/2271/2261

Bernsmann, S., & Croll, J. (2013). Lowering the threshold to libraries with social media: The approach of Digital Literacy 2.0, a project funded in the EU Lifelong Learning Programme. *Library Review, 62*(1-2), 53–58. doi:10.1108/00242531311328168

Berrio, C. (2012). Entre la alfabetización informacional y la brecha digital: Reflexiones para una reconceptualización de los fenómenos de exclusión digital. *Revista Interam. Bibliot., 35*(1), 39–53.

Bhambra, G. K. (2014). Connected Sociologies. London: Bloomsbury.

Billwerder, J. V. A. (2015). Rahmenkonzept für die Teilanstalt für Frauen in der JVA Billwerder. Hamburg: Academic Press.

Bobes, M., & García, A. (2010). El Uso de las TIC como Herramienta Educativa y Terapéutica en el Contexto Penitenciario. El Proyecto Òmnia en las Prisiones Catalanas. *Revista de Educación Social*. Retrieved from http://www.eduso.net/res/?b=14&c=131&n=3

Boltansky, L., & Chiapello, È. (1999). *Le Nouvel Esprit du Capitalisme*. Paris: Gallimard.

Bonta, J., Law, M., & Hanson, R. K. (1998). The Prediction of Criminal and Violent Recidivism among Mentally Disordered Offenders: A Meta-Analysis. *Psychological Bulletin*, *123*(2), 123–142. doi:10.1037/0033-2909.123.2.123 PMID:9522681

Boó, E., Sancenón, E., & Zino, J. (2014, January). Una experiencia con las TIC en la educación social de prisiones: nuevas metodologías para nuevos tiempos. *Revista de Educación Social*, no. 18. Retrieved from http://eduso.net/res/pdf/18/e2e10_res_18.pdf

Booth, A. (2002). Evidence-based librarianship: One small step. *Health Information and Libraries Journal*, *19*(2), 116–119. doi:10.1046/j.1471-1842.2002.00373.x PMID:12389610

Borges, J., & Oliveira, L. (2011). Competências infocomunicacionais em ambientes digitais. *Observatorio (OBS*)*, *5*(4).

Borges, J., Bezerra, L., Diomondes, S., & Coutinho, L. (2013). Competências infocomunicacionais: Um conceito em desenvolvimento. *Tendências Da Pesquisa Brasileira Em Ciência Da Informação*, *5*(1), 1–23.

Bourdieu, P. (1979/2013). *Distinction: A Social Critique of the Judgement of Taste*. London: Routledge.

Buchmueller, S., Joost, G., Bessing, N., & Stein, S. (2011). Bridging the gender and generation gap by ICT applying a participatory design process. *Personal and Ubiquitous Computing*, *15*(7), 743–758. doi:10.100700779-011-0388-y

Burbules, N. C., & Callister, T. A. (2001). *Educación: riesgos y promesas de las nuevas tecnologías de la información*. Barcelona: Granica.

Bureau of Democracy, Human Rights, and Labor. (2013). *Report on International Prison Conditions*. BDHRL, United States Department of State. Accessed on 21/09/2017 from https://www.state.gov/documents/organization/210160.pdf

Bureau of Justice Statistics. (2017). *Re-entry trends in the U.S.: Recidivism*. Accessed on 30/11/2017 from https://www.bjs.gov/content/reentry/recidivism.cfm and https://www.bjs.gov/index.cfm?ty=tp&tid=17

Burgdorf, A. M. (2012). *Women in Prison: Planning the Getaway Vocational Education in a Southern Women's Correctional Institution* (Unpublished doctoral dissertation). The University of Memphis.

Burgos Oliván, L., García Villar, A., & Tomás Humbert, C. (2007). El Blog desde la Prisión: Un Instrumento de Inclusión Social. *Educación y Biblioteca*, *158*, 102–109.

Burgos, García, & Humbert. (2007). El blog desde la prisión: un instrumento de inclusión social. *Educacion Y Bibliotecas*, *19*(158), 102–109.

Burgos, L., García, A., & Tomàs, C. (2007). El blog desde la prisión: un instrumento de inclusión social. *Educación y biblioteca, 19*(158), 102–109.

Burgos, O., García, V., & Humbert, C. (2007). El blog desde la prisión: un instrumento de inclusión social. *Educacion Y Bibliotecas, 19*(158), 102–109.

Cabrera-Cabrera, P. (2005). *Nuevas tecnologías y exclusión social. Un estudio sobre las posibilidades de las TIC en la lucha por la inclusión social en España* [New technologies and social exclusion. Studying the possibilities of ICTs in the struggle towards social inclusion in Spain]. Madrid: Fundación Telefónica.

Campbell, B. (1990). What is literacy? Acquiring and using literacy skills. *Australasian Public Libraries and Information Services*, (3): 149–152.

Caparrós, M. (2014). *A Fome*. Lisboa: Círculo de Leitores.

Cardoso, G., da Costa, A. F., Conceição, C. P., & Gomes, M. do C. (2005). Processo de mudança estrutural na sociedade portuguesa. In G. Cardoso, A. F. da Costa, C. P. Conceição, & M. do C. Gomes (Eds.), A Sociedade em Rede em Portugal (1a, Vol. 17, pp. 31–80). Porto: Campo das Letras.

Cardoso, G., Espanha, R., & OberCom. (2009). *A Internet em Portugal 2009*. Lisboa: OberCom.

Caride Gómez, J. A., & Gradaílle Pernas, R. (2013). Educar en las cárceles: Nuevos desafíos para la educación social en las instituciones penitenciarias. *Review of Education*, (360): 36–47. doi:10.4438/1988-592X-RE-2013-360-219

Carou García, S. (2017). *Primer grado penitenciario y estado de derecho: El estatus jurídico de los reclusos en régimen de máxima seguridad*. Barcelona: Bosch.

Castagno, Malek, Renzone, & Correa. (2011). Significaciones de la (re)inserción social de sujetos privados de la libertad, desde la teoría de las Representaciones Sociales. VII Encuentro Interdisciplinario de Ciencias Sociales y Humanas. Vol. 1, No. 1. Facultad de Filosofía y Humanidades. Universidad de Córdoba, Argentina.

Castell, L., Pallisé, J. M., Pedrola, N., Tomàs, C., & Burgos, L. (2004, December). Art pop i curtmetratges a una biblioteca penitenciària. *BiD: textos universitaris de biblioteconomia i documentació*, no. 13. Retrieved from http://www.ub.edu/bid/13tomas.htm

Castells, M. (2004). *A Galáxia Internet – Reflexões sobre a Internet, Negócios e Sociedade*. Lisboa: Fundação Caloust Gulbenkian.

Castells, M. (2010). *The Rise of Network Society*. Oxford, UK: Blackwell Publishers.

Castells, M. (2012). *Redes de Indignación y Esperanza*. Madrid: Alianza.

Castillo-Algarra, J., & Ruiz-García, M. (2007). Un reto educativo en el siglo XXI: La educación de los delincuentes en el sistema penitenciario. Una perspectiva de género. *Review of Education, 9*, 301–315.

Catalonia General Subdirectorate for Rehabilitation and Health Programs. (2011). *El model de rehabilitació a les presons catalanes*. Barcelona: General Directorate of Penitentiary Services. Retrieved from http://justicia.gencat.cat/web/.content/enllacos/pdf/model_rehabilitacio_presons_catalanes.pdf

Celebic, G., & Rendulic, D. I. (2011). *Basic concepts of information and communication technology: Handbook*. Zagreb: Open Society for Idea Exchange.

Central Intelligence Agency. (2017). *World Factbook*. Accessed on 8/10/2017 from https://www.cia.gov/library/publications/the-world-factbook/geos/ni.html

Chukwudi, F. (2012). Challenges of Reforms in the Nigerian Prison System: Lessons from USA and South Africa. *Journal of Social Science and Public Policy*, *4*(36).

Civallero, E. (2007). Aplicación de la metodología de investigación-acción en prácticas bibliotecológicas basadas en la evidencia. *73rd IFLA General Conference and Council. World Library an Information Congress*.

Cobo del Rosal, M., & Boig Reig, J. (1982). Derechos fundamentales del condenado. Reeducación y reinserción social. Comentarios a la Legislación penal, 217-227.

Collins, R. (2008). *Violence: A Micro-sociological Theory*. Princeton, NJ: Princeton University Press.

Comalat, M., & Sulé, A. (2007). *Directrices para las bibliotecas de prisión de Cataluña*. Barcelona: Collegi Oficial de Bibliotecaris-Documentalistes de Catalunya. Retrieved from http://cobdc.org/publica/directrius/presons_cast.pdf

Comisión Europea. (n.d.a). *Agenda Digital para Europa: 2015.eu, 2010*. Retrieved October 14, 2017 from http://www.europarl.europa.eu/sides/getDoc.do?pubRef=- //EP//NONSGML+REPORT+A7-2010-0066+0+DOC+PDF+V0//ES

Comisión Europea. (n.d.b). *Europa 2020: la estrategia de la Unión Europea para el crecimiento y la ocupación*. Retrieved October, 14, 2017 from http://eur-lex.europa.eu/legal-content/ES/TXT/?uri=LEGISSUM:em0028

Comité de Ética, C. S. I. C. (2011). *Código de Buenas Prácticas Científicas del CSIC/Code of Good Scientific Practices of CSIC*. Madrid: Consejo Superior de Investigaciones Científicas (CSIC). Retrieved January 7, 2018, from https://www.cnb.csic.es/documents/CBP_CSIC.pdf

Connor, E. (Ed.). (2007). *Evidence-based librarianship: case studies and active learning exercises*. Oxford, UK: Chandos Publishing. doi:10.1533/9781780631080

Contreras-Pulido, P., & Aguaded, J. I. (2013). La percepción social a través de la mirada encerrada: el discurso de los presos de Huelva en UniRadio [The social perception through the closed gaze: the discourse of the prisoners of Huelva in UniRadio]. *Razón y Palabra, 83*. Available at: http://goo.gl/KfnOEG (accessed 14/03/2018).

Contreras-Pulido, P., Martín-Pena, D., & Aguaded, I. (2015). Derribando el autoestigma: medios de comunicación en prisiones como aliados de la inclusión social. *Cuadernos.Info, 36*(36), 15–26. 10.7764/cdi.36.708

Cordeiro, A. D. (2018, March 3). Activista acusado pela sexta vez por denunciar condições nas cadeias. *Público*. Retrieved from https://www.publico.pt/2018/03/03/sociedade/noticia/academico-enfrenta-tribunais-pela-sexta-vez-por-denunciar-situacao-das-prisoes-portuguesas-1805085

Cornellá, A. (1997). *Políticas de información en España*. Barcelona: ESADE.

Costa, F., Rodrigues, Â., Peralta, M., Cruz, E., Reis, O., Ramos, J. L., … Valente, L. (2008). Competências TIC. Estudo de Implementação (vol. 2). Lisboa.

Council of Europe. (2006). *European Prison Rules*. Strasbourg: Council of Europe Publishing.

Crétenot, M. (2014). *From national practices to European guidelines: interesting initiatives in prisons management*. Rome: European Prison Observatory.

Cronin, J. (2011). *The path to successful reentry: The relationship between correctional education, employment and recidivism*. University of Missouri, Institute of Public Policy.

Cuevas, A. (2007). *La promoción de la lectura como modelo de alfabetización en información en bibliotecas escolares*. Gijón: Ediciones Trea.

Cuevas-Cerveró, A. (2007). *La promoción de la lectura como modelo de alfabetización en información en bibliotecas escolares* (Unpublished doctoral dissertation). Universidad Carlos III.

Cuevas-Cerveró, A. (coord.). (2009). IDEIAS, Inclusión digital y educación informacional para salud. Madrid: Universidad Complutense.

Cuevas-Cerveró, A., & García, M. A. (2010). IDEIAS. Un modelo de evaluación para inclusión digital y alfabetización informacional orientado a salud. *El Profesional de la Información, 19*(3), 240–245. doi:10.3145/epi.2010.may.03

Cunha, M., & Bastos, C. (2007). As instituições híbridas. Reclusão e laços sociais. *Análise Social. Revista Do Instituto de Ciências Sociais Da Universidade de Lisboa, 42*(185), 977–983.

Cushman, M., & Mclean, R. (2008). Exclusion, Inclusion and Changing the Face of Information Systems Research. *Information Technology & People, 21*(3), 213–221. doi:10.1108/09593840810895993

Dahlman, C. (2008). Technology, globalization, and international competitiveness: Challenges for developing countries. In D. O'Connor & M. Kjollerstrom (Eds.), *Industrial Development for the 21st Century* (pp. 29–83). University of Chicago Press.

Danbazau, A. (2017). 70% of prison inmates are awaiting trial. *Vanguard.* Accessed from https://www.vanguardngr.com/2017/06/70-prison-inmates-awaiting-trial-danbazau/

Daunis Rodríguez, A. (2016). *Ejecución de Penas en España*. Editorial Comares.

David, M., & Sutton, C. D. (2011). *Social Research. An Introduction* (2nd ed.). London: SAGE Publications.

De Marcos Madruga, F. (2014). Las nuevas tecnologías en los centros penitenciarios y sus implicaciones jurídicas. In *Sistema penitenciario y nuevas tecnologías* (pp. 225–249). Valladolid: Lex Artis.

Dearing, J. W. (2009). Applying diffusion of innovation theory to intervention development. *Research on Social Work Practice, 19*(5), 503–518. doi:10.1177/1049731509335569 PMID:20976022

Declaración de Alejandría. (2005). Acerca de la alfabetización informacional y el aprendizaje de por vida. *Faros de la sociedad de la información*. Retrieved October, 14, 2017 from http://www.cobdc.org/grups/alfincat/documents.html

Declaración de Fez. (2011). *Alfabetización informacional y mediática*. Retrieved October, 14, 2017 from http://www.unesco.org/new/fileadmin/MULTIMEDIA/HQ/CI/CI/pdf/news/Fez%20 Declaration.pdf

Declaración de Praga. (2003). *Hacía una sociedad alfabetizada en información*. Retrieved October, 18, 2017 from http://www.cobdc.org/grups/alfincat/documents.html

Del Pozo, F. J., Jiménez, F., & Turbi, A. (2013). El tratamiento con mujeres: Actuación socioeducativa y sociolaboral en prisiones. *Pedagogía Social. Revista Interuniversitaria*, (22), 57-72. Retrieved January 12, 2018, from http://www.redalyc.org/html/1350/135031394005/

Delors, J. Libro Blanco (1993). *Crecimiento, competitividad, empleo. Retos y pistas para entrar en el siglo XXI*. Comunidad Europea. Retrieved October, 5, 2017 from http://biblioteca.cunef.edu/gestion/catalogo/doc_num.php?explnum_id=449

Desmurget, M. (2012, January). *TV Lobotomie : La vérité scientifique sur les effets de la télévision*. Paper presented at Forum Social Local du Morbihan.

Díez Ripollés, J. L. (2011). La Dimensión Inclusión/Exclusión Social como Guía de la Política Criminal Comparada. *Revista Electrónica de Ciencia Penal y Criminología (RECPC), 13-12*, 1-36.

Digard, L., diZerega, M., Yaroni, A., & Rinaldi, J. (2016). *A New Role for Technology? Implementing video visitation in prison*. New York, NY: Vera Institute of Justice. Accessed online on 23/11/2017 from https://storage.googleapis.com/vera-web-assets/downloads/Publications/video-visitation-in-prison/legacy_downloads/video-visitation-in-prison_02.pdf

DiIulio, J. J., Jr. (1987). Governing Prisons: A Comparative Study of Correctional Management. New York: The Free Press.

Dijst, M. (2004). ICTs and accessibility: an action space perspective on the impact of new information and communication technologies. In M. Beuthe, V. Himanen, A. Reggiani, & L. Zamparini (Eds.), *Transport developments and innovations in an evolving world* (pp. 27–46). Heidelberg, Germany: Springer-Verlag. doi:10.1007/978-3-540-24827-9_3

Dimitri, C., Effland, A. B., & Conklin, N. C. (2005). *The 20th century transformation of US agriculture and farm policy* (Vol. 3). Washington, DC: US Department of Agriculture, Economic Research Service.

Dinkel, D., Schaffer, C., Snyder, K., & Lee, J. M. (2017). They just need to move: Teachers' perception of classroom physical activity breaks. *Teaching and Teacher Education*, *63*, 186–195. doi:10.1016/j.tate.2016.12.020

Directiva 2000/43/CE, de 29 de junio de 2000. Aplicación del Principio de Igualdad de Trato de las Personas independientemente de su origen racial o étnico (DOCE L nº 180, de 19 de julio de 2000). (n.d.). Retrieved October, 18, 2017 from http://eur-lex.europa.eu/LexUriServ/LexUriServ.do?uri=OJ:L:2000:180:0022:0026:es:PDF

Directiva 2000/78/CE de 27 de noviembre de 2000, relativa al establecimiento de un marco general para la igualdad de trato en el empleo y la ocupación étnico (DOCE L nº 303/16, de 2 de diciembre de 2000). (n.d.). Retrieved October, 18, 2017 from https://www.boe.es/buscar/doc.php?id=DOUE-L-2000-82357

Directiva 2002/73CE del Parlamento Europeo y del Consejo Europeo de 23 de septiembre de 2002, relativa a la aplicación del principio de igualdad de trato entre hombres y mujeres en lo que se refiere al acceso al empleo, a la formación y a las condiciones de trabajo étnico (DOCE L nº 269/15, de 5 de octubre de 2002). (n.d.). Retrieved October, 18, 2017 from https://www.boe.es/buscar/doc.php?id=DOUE-L-2002-81758

Directiva 2006/54/CE del Parlamento Europeo y del Consejo Europeo de 5 de julio de 2006, relativa a la aplicación del principio de igualdad de trato entre hombres y mujeres en asuntos de empleo y ocupación, la finalidad de esta Directiva es garantizar la aplicación de dicho principio (DOCE L nº 204/23, de 26 de julio de 2006). (n.d.). Retrieved October, 18, 2017 from https://www.boe.es/buscar/doc.php?id=DOUE-L-2006-81416

Dissel, A. (2001). *Prison conditions in Africa (A report). Centre for the Study of Violence and Reconciliation.* Accessed from on 21/09/2017 from http://www.csvr.org.za/docs/correctional/prisonconditions.pdf

Dores, A. P., Pontes, N., & Loureiro, R. (2016). *Manifesto para uma nova cultural penal.* Academic Press.

Dores, A. P. (1996). *O Movimento Informático nas Escolas Portuguesas: Análise Sociológica do Caso do Projecto Minerva.* Lisboa: ISCTE.

Dores, A. P., Pontes, N., & Loureiro, R. (2016). *Manifesto for a new penal culture.* Rome: European Observatory of Prisons.

Dünkel, F., Kestermann, C., & Zolondek, J. (2005). *Reader Internationale Studie zum Frauenstrafvollzug. Bestandsaufnahme, Bedarfsanalyse und "best practice".* Retrieved from www.rsf.uni-greifswald.de/fileadmin/mediapool/lehrstuehle/duenkel/Reader_frauenvollzug.pdf

Durkheim, É. (1960). *De la division de travail social.* Paris: PUF.

Durkheim, É. (1973). *O suicídio: estudo de sociologia*. Lisboa: Editorial Presença.

Durkheim, É. (2002). *As Formas Elementares da Vida Religiosa*. Oeiras: Celta.

Easley, D., & Kleinberg, J. (2010). *Networks, Crowds and Markets: Reasoning about a Highly Connected World*. Cambridge University Press. doi:10.1017/CBO9780511761942.020

Easton, S. (2011). *Prisoners' Rights. Principles and practice*. London: Routledge.

Eberle, S. (2014). *Gutachten. In der Strafvollstreckungssache vertreten Tuch Rechtsanwalt Dr. Jan Oelbermann. Aktenzeichen 509 StVK 179/13. Gericht: Landgericht Stendal*. Berlin: IHK Berlin.

El Confidencial. (2013, August 24). ¿Viven bien los presos en las cárceles españolas? *El Confidencial Digital*. Retrieved from http://www.elconfidencialdigital.com/te_lo_aclaro/Viven-bien-presos-carceles-espanolas_0_2113588622.html

Elvira-Valdés, M. A. (2014). Presos 2.0: comunicación y TIC en contextos de encarcelamiento. *Perspectivas de la Comunicación, 7*(1), 84–96. Retrieved from http://publicacionescienciassociales.ufro.cl/index.php/perspectivas/article/view/217

Elvira-Valdés, M. A. (2014). Presos 2.0: Comunicación y TIC's en Contextos de Encarcelamiento. *Perspectivas de la Comunicación, 7*(1), 84–96.

Elvira-Valdés, M. A., & Durán-Aponte, E. (2014). Estudiar en mayúsculas: La educación formal en instituciones penitenciarias venezolanas. *Sophia, 10*(1), 64–73. Retrieved from http://www.scielo.org.co/pdf/sph/v10n1/v10n1a06.pdf

Ely, J. W. (2012). *Effects of Occupational Education Programs Offered by the Oklahoma Department of Career and Technology Education, Skills Centers Division, on the Recidivism Rate of Selected Groups of Released Offenders in Oklahoma* (Unpublished doctoral dissertation). Oklahoma State University.

Emasealu, H. U., & Popoola, S. O. (2016). Information Needs, Accessibility and utilization of Library Information Resources as Determinants of Psychological Well-being of prison Inmates in Nigeria. *Brazilian Journal of Information Science, 2*(2010), 29–46.

Engels, F. (1975). *A situação da classe trabalhadora na Inglaterra*. Lisboa: Editorial Presença.

España Comunidad de Madrid. Consejería de Políticas Sociales y familia. Estrategia de inclusión social de la Comunidad de Madrid 2016-2021. (n.d.). Retrieved October, 25, 2017 from http://www.madrid.org/cs/Satellite?blobcol=urldata&blobheader=application%2Fpdf&blobheadername1=Content-Disposition&blobheadervalue1=filename%3DEstrategia+de+Inclusi%C3%B3n+Social+CM.pdf&blobkey=id&blobtable=MungoBlobs&blobwhere=1352918600937&ssbinary=true

España Constitución (BOE núm. 311, de 29 de diciembre de 1978). (n.d.). Retrieved October, 15, 2017 from http://www.boe.es/buscar/act.php?id=BOE-A-1978-31229

España Ley Orgánica 1/1979, de 26 de septiembre, General Penitenciaria. (BOE núm. 239 de, 16 de octubre de 1979). (n.d.). Retrieved October, 15, 2017 from http://www.boe.es/buscar/act.php?id=BOE-A-1979-23708

España Ley Orgánica 3/2007, de 22 de marzo, para la igualdad efectiva de mujeres y hombres. (BOE núm. 71 de, 23 de marzo de 2007). (n.d.). Retrieved October, 5, 2017 from http://www.boe.es/buscar/doc.php?id=BOE-A-2007-6115

España Ministerio del interior. (2017). *Convenio de colaboración entre la Secretaría General de Instituciones Penitenciarias y la Fundación Bancaria La Caixa para la implementación de «Ciberaulas Solidarias» en centros penitenciarios.* Retrieved October, 5, 2017 from https://www.boe.es/boe/dias/2017/09/20/pdfs/BOE-A-2017-10729.pdf

España Ministerio sanidad, servicios sociales e igualdad. (n.d.). *Plan de Acción para la Igualdad entre mujeres y hombres en la Sociedad de la Información 2014-2017.* Retrieved October, 5, 2017 from http://www.inmujer.gob.es/actualidad/NovedadesNuevas/docs/BorradIIPlanAccionSocInf.pdf

Europa Press. (2017, April 15). El Gobierno confirma que los internos de la prisión "no tienen conexión a Internet para estudiar", según Cs. *20 minutos.* Retrieved from http://www.20minutos.es/noticia/3012115/0/gobierno-confirma-que-internos-prision-no-tienen-conexion-internet-para-estudiar-segun-cs/

Europa Press. (2017, March 23). Las cárceles catalanas empiezan a conectar por videoconferencia a presos y abogados. *La Vanguardia.* Retrieved from http://www.lavanguardia.com/vida/20170323/421130274867/los-carceles-catalanas-empiezan-a-conectar-por-videoconferencia-a-presos-y-abogados.html

Facebook. (2016). *Monster World.* Retrieved from https://www.facebook.com/monsterworld/

Fara, P. (2009). *Science: a Four Thousand Years History.* Oxford, UK: Oxford University Press.

Farley, H., & Pike, A. (2016). Engaging prisoners in education: Reducing risk and recidivism. *Journal of the International Corrections and Prison Association, 1*(1), 65–73.

Farley, H., Pike, A., Hopkins, S., & Byrne, C. (2015). Bringing digital literacies to students in prison: challenges and opportunities. In *Proceedings of the 15th EPEA Training Conference (EPEA 2015)* (pp. 1–1). University of Southern Queensland.

Fasanmi, A. (2015). In the shadow of being forgotten: Women incarcerated in Nigerian prisons and the health implications. *Agenda (Durban, South Africa), 29*(4), 67–78.

Fassin, D. (2017). *Prison worlds: An ethnography of the carceral condition.* Cambridge, UK: Polity Press. Retrieved from https://www.google.com/books?hl=pt-PT&lr=&id=qZFNDwAAQBAJ&oi=fnd&pg=PR3&dq=Prison+Worlds+an+Ethnography+of+the+Carceral+&ots=1ba538Uv7H&sig=tXWSErGMJ-kRDfEI2GGPvUsUuNg

Fernández Díaz, C. R. (2015). Las Relaciones del Interno con el Mundo Exterior y su Importancia para la Reeducación y Reinserción Social. *Revista Electrónica de Ciencia Penal y Criminología (RECPC)*, *17*(7), 1-26.

Fernández, R. (2011). *Exclusión social de mujeres presas: Análisis de necesidades y su percepcion del proceso de rehabilitacion en el centro penitenciario de Villabona* (Unpublished doctoral dissertation). Universidad de Oviedo, Departamento de Psicología.

Ferner, M. (2015, September 9). These programs are helping prisoners live again on the outside. *The Huffington Post*. Retrieved from https://www.huffingtonpost.com/entry/if-we-want-fewer-prisoners-we-need-more-compassion-when-they-re-enter-society_us_55ad61a5e4b0caf721b39cd1

Ferrajoli, L. (1997). *Derecho y Razón. Teoría del Garantismo Penal*. Editorial Trotta.

Ferreira, E. V. (1997). *Crime e Insegurança em Portugal: Padrões e Tendências (1985-1996)*. Oeiras: Celta.

Fine, M. (2001). *Changing Minds: The Impact of College in a Maximum-Security Prison. Effects on Women in Prison, the Prison Environment, Reincarceration Rates and Post-Release Outcomes*. Academic Press.

Firouzi, O. (2016). *Reducing the prison population in Europe: does community justice work?* Rome: European Observatory of Prisons.

Flamer, E. (2012). *Recidivism, Disciplinary History, and Institutional Adjustment: A Quantitative Study Examining Correctional Education Programs* (Unpublished doctoral dissertation). University of Phoenix.

Flor, B. (2013). *Design of a communication strategy and communication plan to support the RPF-PPP Project*. Academic Press.

Flores, G., García, E., & Rodríguez, G. (1999). *Metodología de la investigación cualitativa* [Methodology of qualitative research]. Málaga: Aljibe.

Fong, J. (2008). Facilitating education in prisons. In E. W. C. Leung, F. L. Wang, L. Miao, J. Zhao, & J. He (Eds.), Advances in Blended Learning (Vol. 5328, pp. 1–15). Berlin: Springer. doi:10.1007/978-3-540-89962-4_1

Foucault, M. (1976). Alternatives to the Prison. Dissemination or Decline of Social Control? *Theory, Culture & Society*, *26*(6), 12-24.

Foucault, M. (1975). *Surveiller et punir: naissance de la prison*. Paris: Gallimard.

Foucault, M. (1977). *Discipline and Punish. The Birth of the Prison*. New York: Vintage Books. A Division of Random House, inc.

Foucault, M. (2004). *A Hermenêutica do Sujeito*. São Paulo: Martins Fontes.

Franganillo, J., & Burgos, L. (2007, January-March). Blocs a la biblioteca penitenciària: un taller de dinamització cultural. *Item: revista de biblioteconomia i documentació, 45*, 87-104. Retrieved from http://raco.cat/index.php/Item/article/view/72724/129379

Franganillo, J., Burgos, L., García, A., & Tomàs, C. (2008). Alfabetización digital en la prisión: una experiencia con jóvenes internos. Congreso Internacional de Alfabetización Tecnológica (2nd: November-December 2006: Badajoz). In *Actas del II Congreso Internacional de Alfabetización Tecnológica: superando la brecha digital*. Badajoz: Fundación Ciudadanía; AUPEX; Consorcio Identic. Retrieved from http://eprints.rclis.org/8538

Franganillo, J., Burgos, L., García, A., & Tomàs, C. (2006). Alfabetización digital en la prisión: una experiencia con jóvenes internos. In *Alfabetización digital en la prisión: una experiencia con jóvenes internos* (pp. 102–118). Badajoz: II Congreso Internacional de Alfabetización Tecnológica. Retrieved from http://www.franganillo.net/franganillo2006.pdf

Freire, P. (1972). *Pedagogy of the oppressed*. New York: Herder and Herder.

García España, E., & Díez Ripollés, J. L. (2011). *Realidad y Política Penitenciarias*. Valencia: Tirant lo Blanch.

Garland, D. (2001). *The Culture of Control – Crime and Social Order in Contemporary Society*. Oxford, UK: Oxford University Press.

Garland, D. (2003). *The Culture of Control. Crime and Social Order in Contemporary Society*. Oxford, UK: Oxford University Press.

Gil, H., & Amaro, F. (2011). e-Inclusão: dos 7 aos 77. In U. de Aveiro (Ed.), 61st Internacional Council for Educational Media and the XIII International Simposium on computers in Education (ICEM&SIIE'2011) (pp. 60–65). Aveiro.

Gil, J.M. (1996). *Las políticas de igualdad en España: avances y retrocesos*. Servicio de Publicaciones de la Universidad de Granada: Instituto Andaluz de la Mujer.

Gil-Cantero, F. (2013). Derechos humanos y reeducación en las prisiones. El derecho a la educación en el modelo 'good lives' [Human rights and re-education in prisons. The right to education in the good lives model]. *Review of Education*, (360): 48–68. doi:10.4438/1988-592X-RE-2013-360-220

Goffman, E. (2009). Asylums: Essays on the Social Situation of Mental Patients and Other Inmates (2nd ed.). New Brunswick, NJ: Transaction Publishers. (originally published 1961)

Goffman, E. (1989). *Estigma: La identidad deteriorada* [Stigma: Notes on the Management of Spoiled Identity]. Buenos Aires: Amorrortu.

Goggin, G. (2012). *Cell phone culture: Mobile technology in everyday life*. New York: Routledge.

Gómez Hernández, J.A. (2002). La alfabetización informacional como servicio de las bibliotecas. *Referencia, 7*(1).

González Cussac, J. L. (2013). Tecnocrimen. In *Nuevas amenazas a la seguridad nacional. Terrorismo, criminalidad organizada y tecnologías de la información y la comunicación*. Valencia: Tirant lo Blanch.

Gozálvez Pérez, V. (2014). *Ciudadanía mediática. Una mirada educativa* [Media citizenship. An educational look]. Madrid: Editorial Dykinson.

Gozálvez, V., & Contreras, P. (2014). Empowering Media Citizenship through educommunication [Empoderar a la ciudadanía mediática desde la educomunicación]. *Comunicar*, *42*(42), 129–136. doi:10.3916/C42-2014-12

Graça, D. (2010). *Utilização da internet nos estabelecimentos prisionais portugueses: realidade ou utopia?* Universidade de Aveiro.

Graça, D. (2016). *Desenvolvimento de Competências Infocomunicacionais em Contexto Prisional - Proposta de um Modelo de Formação para a Utilização da Internet no Contexto Prisional Português*. Univeridade de Aveiro e Universidade do Porto - Portugal.

Grieve, Indian, M., Witteveen, K., Anne Tolan, G., & Marrington, J. (2013). Face-to-face or Facebook: Can social connectedness be derived online? *Computers in Human Behavior*, *29*(3), 604–609. doi:10.1016/j.chb.2012.11.017

Griffiths, C., Dandurand, Y., & Murdoch, D. (2007). *The social reintegration of offenders and crime prevention*. The International Centre from Criminal Law Reform and Criminal Justice Policy. Retrieved from https://www.publicsafety.gc.ca/cnt/rsrcs/pblctns/scl-rntgrtn/index-en.aspx

Griffiths, M. D., Kuss, D. J., Billieux, J., & Pontes, H. M. (2016). The evolution of Internet addiction: A global perspective. *Addictive Behaviors*, *53*, 193–195. doi:10.1016/j.addbeh.2015.11.001 PMID:26562678

Gruber, A. (2013). *Internet im Knast. Häftlinge sind offline*. Retrieved from http://www.zeit.de/digital/internet/2013-09/internet-gefaengnis-jva-tegel

Gutiérrez, A. (2003). *Alfabetización digital: algo más que ratones y teclas*. Barcelona: Gedisa.

Harlow, C. W. (2003). *Education and Correctional Populations. Bureau of Justice Statistics Special Report*. U.S. Department of Justice, Office of Justice Programs Revised. Retrieved from https://www.bjs.gov/content/pub/pdf/ecp.pdf

Hasebrink, U., & Domeyer, H. (2012). Media repertoires as patterns of behaviour and as meaningful practices: A multimethod approach to media use in converging media environments. *Participations*, *9*(2), 757–779.

Hasebrink, U., & Popp, J. (2006). Media repertoires as a result of selective media use. A conceptual approach to the analysis of patterns of exposure. *Communications*, *31*(3), 369–387. doi:10.1515/COMMUN.2006.023

Haverkamp, R. (2011). *Frauenvollzug in Deutschland: eine empirische Untersuchung vor dem Hintergrund der Europäischen Strafvollzugsgrundsätze*. Berlin: Duncker & Humblot. doi:10.3790/978-3-428-53523-1

Hawley, J. (2011). *Prison Education and Training in Europe: A Review and Commentary of Existing Literature, Analysis and Evaluation. Education And Training*. Retrieved from http://ec.europa.eu/justice/news/consulting_public/0012/Fullreport_en.pdf

Helmreich, W. B. (2009). *Asylums: Essays on the Social Situation of Mental Patients and Other Inmates*. New Brunswick, NJ: Transaction Publishers. VII-XVII.

Helsper, E. (2008). *Digital inclusion: an analysis of social disadvantage and the information society*. London: Department for Communities and Local Government.

Helsper, E. (2012). A Corresponding Fields Model for the Links between Social and Digital Exclusion. *Communication Theory*, *22*(4), 403–426.

Hendry, J. D. (2000). Social inclusion and the information. *Library Review*, *49*(7), 331–336. doi:10.1108/00242530010344192

Hepp, A., & Hasebrink, U. (2013). Human interaction and communicative figurations. The transformation of mediatized cultures and societies. *Communicative Figurations. Working Paper* (2).

Hepp, A., & Hasebrink, U. (2016). *How to research cross-media practices? Investigating media repertoires and media ensembles from a qualitative point of view*. Manuscript.

Hill, M. W. (1995). Information policies: Premonitions and prospects. *Journal of Information Science*, *21*(4), 273–282. doi:10.1177/016555159502100403

Hirschi, T. (1969). *Causes of Delinquency*. Berkeley, CA: University of California Press.

Hobsbawn, E.J. (1997). *A era das revoluções*. Rio de Janeiro: Paz e Terra.

Höflich, P., Schriever, W., & Bartmeier, A. (2014). *Grundriss Vollzugsrecht. In Das Recht des Strafvollzugs, der Untersuchungshaft und des Jugendvollzugs* (4th ed.). Berlin: Springer Verlag.

Horn, J., Rosenband, L. N., & Smith, M. R. (Eds.). (2010). *Re-conceptualizing the industrial revolution*. Cambridge, MA: The MIT Press.

Hötzel, Y. (2010). *Debatten um die Todesstrafe in der Bundesrepublik Deutschland von 1949 bis 1990*. Berlin: Walter de Gruyter GmbH & Co. doi:10.1515/9783110248777

Hudson, P. (2014). *The industrial revolution*. Bloomsbury Publishing.

Hulsman, L. (1993). El enfoque abolicionista: Políticas criminales alternativas. El Poder punitivo del Estado. Criminologia critica y controlo social. *NeoPanopticum - Derecho, criminologia y ciencias sociales*, 75–104.

Hurry, J., Brazier, L., Snapes, K., & Wilson, A. (2005). *Improving the literacy and numeracy of disaffected young people in custody and in the community*. Retrieved from http://www.nrdc.org.uk/publications_details.asp?ID=28#

Hurry, J., Brazier, L., Snapes, K., & Wilson, A. (2005). *Improving the literacy and numeracy of disaffected young people in custody and in the community*. London.

Illich, I. (1971). *Deschooling Society*. Preservenet.

Imel, S. (1990). *Vocational Education in Corrections. Trends and Issues Alerts*. Columbus: ERIC.

Instituto de la Mujer. (n.d.). Retrieved October, 15, 2017 from http://www.inmujer.gob.es/

Instituto Europeo de la Igualdad de género. (n.d.). Retrieved October, 3, 2017 from http://europa.eu/legislation_summaries/employment_and_social_policy/equality_between_men_and_women/c10938_es.htm

Instituto Nacional de Estadística. (2017, September). *Unemployment rate in Spain*. Retrieved from http://www.ine.es/dyngs/INEbase/es/operacion.htm?c=Estadistica_C&cid=1254736176918&menu=ultiDatos&idp=1254735976595

International Committee of the Red Cross. (2012). *Water, sanitation, hygiene and habitat in prisons: Supplementary guidance*. ICRC. Retrieved from https://www.icrc.org/eng/assets/files/publications/icrc-002-4083.pdf

Internet Live Stats. (2016). *Germany Internet Users*. Retrieved from http://www.internetlivestats.com/internet-users/germany/

Isah, M. (April 26, 2017). Assessing infrastructural deficit in Nigerian prisons. *PR Nigeria*. Accessed online on 19/9/2017 from https://prnigeria.com/general/prawa/prison-service-prawa/

Jenkins, H., Ford, S., & Green, J. (2013). *Spreadable media: creating value and meaning in a networked culture*. New York: New Iorque University Press.

Jensen, G.F., & Jones, D. (1976). Perspectives on Inmate Culture: A Study of Women in Prison. *Social Problems*, *54*(3), 590–603.

Jewkes, Y. (2002). The Use of Media in Constructing Identities in the Masculine Environment of Men's Prisons. *European Journal of Communication*, *17*(2), 205–225. doi:10.1177/0267323102017002693

Jewkes, Y. (2009). The role of the Internet in the twenty-first-century prison. Insecure technologies in secure spaces. In *Technologies of Insecurity. The surveillance of everyday life* (pp. 171–188). Routledge-Cavendish.

Joseph, T. D. (2012). Literacy, information and communication technology as tools for empowerment of inmates. *European Journal of Educational Research*, *1*(2), 117–126. doi:10.12973/eu-jer.1.2.117

Jungen, A. (2016). GPS ankle bracelet monitoring of low-risk offenders costs more than anticipated. *La Crosse Tribune*. Accessed online 20/9/2017 from http://www.govtech.com/public-safety/GPS-Ankle-Bracelet-Monitoring-of-Low-Risk-Offenders-Costs-More-than-Anticipated.html

Justice Action. (2011). Computers in Cells: Maintaining Community Ties and Reducing Recidivism. *Justice Action*. Retrieved from http://search.proquest.com/docview/1033447378?accountid=13042%5Cnhttp://oxfordsfx.hosted.exlibrisgroup.com/oxford?url_ver=Z39.88-2004&rft_val_fmt=info:ofi/fmt:kev:mtx:journal&genre=article&sid=ProQ:ProQ:ncjrs&atitle=Computers+in+Cells:+Maintaining+Commun

Justizbehörde Hamburg. (2016). *JVA HSand Flyer*. Hamburg: Author.

Justizbehörde. (2009). *Hamburgisches Strafvollzugsgesetz – HmbStVollzG*. Retrieved from http://www.landesrecht-hamburg.de/jportal/portal/page/bshaprod.psml;jsessionid=37F3E1C4D07790374AF2A33E2FB481CC.jp17?showdoccase=1&st=null&doc.id=jlr-StVollzGHA2009rahmen&doc.part=X&doc.origin=bs

Justizbehörde. (2016). *Justizvollzugsanstalten in Hamburg*. Retrieved from http://www.hamburg.de/justizbehoerde/justizvollzugsanstalten/

Karam, M. L. (1996). A Esquerda Punitiva. *Discursos Sediciosos – Crime, Direito E Sociedade*, (1). Retrieved from http://emporiododireito.com.br/a-esquerda-punitiva-por-maria-lucia-karam/

Katz, E., Blumler, J. G., & Gurevitch, M. (1973). Uses and Gratifications Research. *Public Opinion Quarterly*, *37*(4), 509–523. doi:10.1086/268109

Kellner, D. M. (2004). Revolución tecnológica, alfabetismos múltiples y la reestructuración de la educación. In I. Snyder (Ed.), *Alfabetismos digitales: comunicación, innovación y educación en la era electrónica*. Málaga: Aljibe.

Kes, H. (2013). Aktion Internet 2020. *Trotzdem,* (48).

Kim, S.J. (2016). A repertoire approach to cross-platform media use behavior. *New Media & Society, 18*(3), 353-372.

Knight, V. (2015, July). Some Observations on the Digital Landscape of Prisons Today. *Prison Service Journal*, *220*, 3–9.

Knight, V. (2016). *Remote Control. Television in prison*. London: Palgrave Macmillan.

Kuhn, M. (2016). *How the Social Sciences Think about the World´s Social - Outline of a Critique*. Stuttgard: Ibidem.

Kvale, S. (1996). Interviews: An Introduction to Qualitative Research Interviewing. Thousand Oaks, CA: SAGE Publications.

Lahire, B. (2012). *Monde pluriel. Penser l'unité des sciences sociales*. Paris: Seuil.

Langelid, T. (2009). *Nordic Prison Education - A Lifelong Learning Perspective*. Copenhagen: Norden.

Laubenthal, K. (2015). *Strafvollzug* (7th ed.). Berlin: Springer- Verlag. doi:10.1007/978-3-642-54819-2

Leal & García. (2002). Discurso y Garantismo: consideraciones acerca de los fines de la pena. Fronesis, 9(2), 85-120.

LEAP. (2016). Law Enforcement Against Prohibition. *LEAP*. Retrieved March 26, 2016, from: http://www.leap.cc

Lehman, V., & Locke, J. (2006). *Guidelines for library services to prisoners*. IFLA Professional Reports, no. 92. Retrieved from http://ifla.org/files/assets/hq/publications/professional-report/92.pdf

Lehmann, V., & Locke, J. (2005). *Guidelines for library services to prisoners*. The Hague, The Netherlands: IFLA Headquarters.

Levy, M., & Windhal, S. (1984). Audience Activity and Gratifications. A Conceptual Clarification and Exploration. *Communication Research, 11*(1), 51–78. doi:10.1177/009365084011001003

Linares, M. (1981). *El Sistema Penitenciario Venezolano. Instituto de Ciencias Penales y Criminológicas*. Universidad Central de Venezuela.

Lochner, L., & Moretti, E. (2004). The Effect of Education on Crime: Evidence from Prison Inmates, Arrest, and Self-Reports. *The American Economic Review, 94*(1), 155–189. doi:10.1257/000282804322970751

Lockitt, G. W. (2011). *Technology in prisons*. Winston Churchill Travelling Fellowship. Retrieved September 20, 2017 from https://www.wcmt.org.uk/sites/default/files/migrated-reports/797_1

Lombarte, S., & García, I. (2005). Estudio de un caso sobre el uso de las tecnologías de la información y la comunicación para la inclusión social. *Teoría de la educación: Educación y cultura en la Sociedad de la Información, 6*(1). Retrieved January 12, 2018, from http://www.redalyc.org/articulo.oa?id=201021059007

Lucas, A. R. (2010). Narratives of Technological Revolution in the Middle Ages. In A. Classen (Ed.), *Handbook of Medieval Studies: Terms-methods-trends* (pp. 967–990). Berlin: De Gruyter. doi:10.1515/9783110215588.967

Maburi, T. (2009). *Re-integration of ex-prisoners back into society: What more can we do?* Retrieved from http://www.newtimes.co.rw/section/read/12648/

Machado, H. (in press). Cabo esconde fortuna da droga a chefe da PJ. *Correio da Manhã*. Available at: http://www.cmjornal.pt/portugal/detalhe/gnr_esconde_fortuna_da_droga_a_chefe_da_pj

MacKenzie, D. L. (1997). Criminal Justice and Crime Prevention. In L. Sherman, D. Gottfredson, D. MacKenzie, J. Eck, P. Reuter, & S. Bushway (Eds.), *Preventing Crime: What Works, What Doesn't, What's Promising. Report to the United States Congress*. Washington, DC: US Department of Justice.

Maculan, A., Ronco, D., & Vianello, F. (2014). *Prisons in Europe: overview and trends*. Rome: European Observatory of Prisons.

Maia e Costa, E. (2003). Prisões: a lei escrita e a lei na prática em Portugal. In A. P. Dores (Ed.), *Prisões na Europa - um debate que apenas começa - European prisons – starting a debate* (pp. 93–102). Oeiras: Celta.

Martín Moral, M. F. (2014). La utilización del sistema de videoconferencia en el marco de las instituciones penitenciarias. In *Sistema penitenciario y nuevas tecnologías* (pp. 45–60). Valladolid: Lex Artis.

Martinson, R. (1974). What works? Questions and answers about prison reform. *The Public Interest*, (35): 22–54.

Marzal, M. A. (2007). Proyectos y realidades de la alfabetización en información: una perspectiva conceptual y aplicativa desde España. XVII Encuentro de Bibliotecas de Cajas de Compensación Familiar (Cofenalco) Alfabetización informacional: desafíos y posibilidades.

Mata y Martín, R. M. (2014). Sistema penitenciario y nuevas tecnologías. In *Sistema penitenciario y nuevas tecnologías* (pp. 9–25). Valladolid: Lex Artis.

Mathiesen, T. (2003). *Juicio a la Prisión. Una Evaluación Crítica*. Ediar, S.A.

Mawasha, M. (2017). *The fourth industrial revolution - an African perspective*. Accessed on 30/09/2017 from https://www.fin24.com/Opinion/the-fourth-industrial-revolution-an-african-perspective-20170921

McLuhan, M. (2008). *Compreender os Meios de Comunicação - Extensões do Homem. Antropos*. Lisboa: Relógio D'Água. (originally published 1964)

Melillo, A., & Suárez-Ojeda, E. N. (2001). *Resiliencia. Descubriendo las propias fuerzas* [Resilience. Discovering your own strengths]. Buenos Aires: Paidós.

Merlino, A. (2009). La Entrevista en Profundidad como Técnica de Producción Discursiva. In Investigación Cualitativa en Ciencias Sociales. Cengage Learning.

Merton, R. K. (1970). Estrutura social e Anomia. In Sociologia - Teoria e Estrutura. S. Paulo: Mestre Jou.

Meyermann, A., & Porzelt, M. (2014). Hinweise zur Anonymisierung von qualitativen Daten. In *Forschungsdaten bildung informiert* (1). Frankfurt am Main: Deutsches Institut für Internationale Pädagogische Forschung. Retrieved from www.forschungsdaten-bildung.de/fdb-informiert

Ministerio del Interior. (2018). *Módulos terapêuticos*. Retrieved from http://institucionpenitenciaria.es/Reeducacion/ProgramasEspecificos/modulosTerapeuticos.html#c2

Ministerio del Poder Popular Para el Servicio Penitenciario. (2013). Caracas, Venezuela: Memoria y Cuenta.

Mossberger, K., Tolbert, J., & Stansbury, M. (2003). *Virtual reality: Beyond the digital divide*. Washington, DC: Georgetown University Press.

Mouzelis, N. (1995). *Sociological Theory: What Went Wrong? – diagnosis and remedies*. London: Routledge.

Muhammad, Y. A., Gwangndi, M. I., & Hassan, A. S. (2017). The Rights of Prisoners in Nigeria and the Role of Prisons and Modern Penology. *JL Pol'y & Globalization*, *60*, 71–80.

Naciones Unidas Comité para la eliminación de la discriminación de la mujer. (n.d.). Retrieved October, 15, 2017 from http://www.cinu.org.mx/temas/mujer/cedaw.htm

Name Generator. (2016). *Pseudonym Generator*. Retrieved from http://www.namegenerator.biz/pseudonym-generator.php

National Human Rights Commission Nigeria. (2009). *Report of Prison Audit*. Accessed on 21/09/2017 from https://www.state.gov/documents/organization/265500.pdf

Neji, M. O. (2016). *Information and Communication Technology utilization and implementation on adult education programmes in Nigeria* (Master Thesis). University of Nigeria, Nsukka.

Newman, G. R. (2011). Crime and Punishment around the World. Santa Barbara, CA: Abc-clio.

News Agency of Nigeria. (2017). *205 inmates enrolled in formal, non-formal education in plateau state*. Accessed online on 22/11/2017 from http://punchng.com/205-inmates-enrolled-in-formal-non-formal-education-in-plateau/

Nietzsche. (1997). *A Genealogia da Moral*. Lisboa: Guimarães.

Nigeria Today. (2017). *59 Ikoyi Prisons inmates sit for 2017 UTME*. Accessed online on 19/9/2017 from http://www.nigeriatoday.ng/2017/05/59-ikoyi-prisons-inmates-sit-for-2017-utme/

Nordic Council of Ministers. (2005). *Nordic Prison Education. A lifelong learning perspective*. Copenhaghen: Temanord.

Novak, M. (2001). *A Etica Católica e o Espírito do Capitalismo*. S.João do Estoril: Principia.

Novo-Corti, I., & Barreiro-Gen, M. (2014). Barreras Físicas y Barreras Virtuales: Delito y Pena en la Era Digital. Nuevas Políticas Públicas para la Reinserción. RiHum So - Revista de Investigación del Departamento de Humanidades y Ciencias Sociales Universidad Nacional de La Matanza, 2(5), 85-104.

O'Neill, L., MacKenzie, D. L., & Bierie, D. M. (2007). Educational Opportunities Within Correctional Institutions: Does Facility Type Matter? *The Prison Journal*, *87*(3), 311–327. doi:10.1177/0032885507304351

Obike, G. (2017). *Over 120 inmates register for JAMB*. Accessed online on 19/9/2017 http://thenationonlineng.net/120-inmates-register-jamb/

Obioha, E. E. (2011). Challenges and reforms in the Nigerian prisons system. *J Soc Sci*, *27*(2), 95–109.

Oborne, P. (2008). *The Triumph of the Political Class*. London: Pocket Books.

Office of the High Commissioner, United Nations Human Rights. (2017). *Standard Minimum Rules for the Treatment of Prisoners*. OHCHR. Accessed on 20/09/2017 from http://www.ohchr.org/EN/ProfessionalInterest/Pages/TreatmentOfPrisoners.aspx

Oguz, E.S. & Kurbanoglu, S. (2013). Strengthening Social Inclusion in Multicultural Societies Through Information Literacy. *Bilgi Dunyasi = Information World, 14*(2), 270- 290.

Onofre, E. M. C. (2009). Educação Escolar na Prisão na Visão dos Professores: um hiato entre o proposto e o vivido. *Reflexão E Ação, 17*(1), 227–244.

Onyekachi, J. (2016). Problems and prospects of administration of Nigerian prison: Need for proper rehabilitation of the inmates in Nigeria Prisons. *Journal of Tourism & Hospitality (Los Angeles, Calif.)*, *5*(228), 2167–0269.

Opafunso, Z. O., & Adepoju, O. O. (2016). Prison reforms system and inmates welfare in Nigeria. *Arts and Social Sciences Journal*, *7*(1), 1–6.

Orakwe, W. I. (2017). *History of Nigerian Prisons Service*. Accessed on 14/09/2017 from http://www.prisons.gov.ng/history_of_nps

Organización de las Naciones Unidas mujeres. (n.d.). Retrieved October, 3, 2017 from http://www.unwomen.org/es

Orihuela, J. L., & Santos, M. L. (2004, July 24). Los weblogs como herramienta educativa. *Quaderns Digitals*. Retrieved from http://quadernsdigitals.net/datos_web/hemeroteca/r_1/nr_558/a_7751/7751.html

Pager, D. (2003). The mark of a criminal record. *American Journal of Sociology*, *108*(5), 937–975. doi:10.1086/374403

Paladines, J. V. (2013). Feminismo Punitivo, cuando el género se redujo al castigo. *Defensa Y Justicia, Revista Institucional de La Defensoría Pública Del Ecuador*, (5). Retrieved from http://www.rebelion.org/docs/174609.pdf

Palfrey, J., & Gasser, U. (2008). Opening Universities in a Digital Era. *New England Journal of Higher Education*, *23*(1), 22–24.

Palidda, S., & Garcia, J. Á. B. (Eds.). (2010). *Criminalización racista de los migrantes en Europa*. Comares Editorial.

Parlamento Europeo. (n.d.). Recomendación 2006/962/CE del Parlamento Europeo y del Consejo, de 18 de diciembre de 2006, sobre las competencias clave para el aprendizaje permanente [Diario Oficial L 394 de 30.12.2006]. Retrieved October, 15, 2017 from http://eur-lex.europa.eu/legal-content/ES/TXT/?uri=CELEX%3A52013DC0359>

Pauné, M. M. (2011, March 28). La vida en la cárcel, retratada por jóvenes presos. *La Vanguardia*. Retrieved from http://lavanguardia.com/cultura/20110328/54131696311/la-vida-en-la-carcel-retratada-por-jovenes-presos.html

Pérez Pulido, M. (1997). Acerca de las bibliotecas de prisiones y sus servicios. *Educación y biblioteca*, *85*, 40–44.

Pérez Pulido, M. (2002). Análisis de la percepción de una biblioteca de prisión por parte de la comunidad reclusa: propuesta metodológica basada en un estudio de caso. *Forinfo: revista iberoamericana de usuarios de información*, *18*, 6–34.

Pérez Pulido, M., & De Angelo, C. (2011). Library services in Spanish prisons: Current state of affairs. *Library Trends*, *59*(3), 460–472. doi:10.1353/lib.2011.0009

Pérez-Tornero, J. M., & Varis, T. (2010). *Media Literacy and New Humanism*. Moscow: UNESCO Institute for InformationTechnologies in Education. Retrieved from https://goo.gl/LCcNoH

Perkinson, R. (in press). Some US prisons as bad as Abu Ghraib. *Straits Times Interactive*.

Philippine prisons overflowing with hungry inmates as Duterte's drug war intensifies. (n.d.). Retrieved from http://www.abc.net.au/news/2017-09-20/philippine-prisons-overflowing-as-war-on-drugs-intensifies/8959448

Picotti, L. (2007). Intercettazioni "Illegali" tra Nuove Tecnologie e Vecchi Strumenti Penali. *Diritto dell'Internet, 2*.

Pike, A. (2014). *Prison-based transformative learning and its role in life after release*. The Open University.

Pike, A., & Adams, A. (2012). Digital exclusion or learning exclusion? An ethnographic study of adult male distance learners in English prisons. *Research in Learning Technology*, *20*(4), 363–376. doi:10.3402/rlt.v20i0.18620

Pillera, G. (2015). E-Literacy and access to internet as inmate's right: European ICT frameworks in correctional education. *ICERI2015 Proceedings*, 344-353.

Piñeiro, I. (2010). Derecho penitenciario y mujeres. *Noticias jurídicas*. Retrieved October, 16, 2017 from http://noticias.juridicas.com/conocimiento/articulos-doctrinales/4608-derecho-penitenciario-y-mujeres-/

Pinilla, V. (2017). *Agricultural crisis in Spain (19th and 20th centuries)*. SEHA.

Plan Nacional de acción para la inclusión social. (n.d.). Retrieved October, 10, 2017 from https://www.msssi.gob.es/ssi/familiasInfancia/inclusionSocial/docs/PlanNacionalAccionInclusionSocial_2013_2016.pdf

Pollock, J. M. (2004). *Prisons and prison life. Cost and consequences*. Los Angeles, CA: Roxbury Publishing Company.

Ponjuán Dante, G. (2002). De la alfabetización a la cultura informacional: Rol del profesional de la información. In *Congreso Internacional de Información Info 2002*. IDICT.

Popoola, S. (2017). *Over 120 inmates register for JAMB*. Accessed online on 19/9/2017 from http://www.thecaveat.info/2017/05/over-120-inmates-register-for-jamb.html

Programa de acciones para la igualdad entre mujeres y hombres en el ámbito penitenciario. (n.d.). Retrieved October, 15, 2017 from http://www.institucionpenitenciaria.es/web/export/sites/default/datos/descargables/publicaciones/Programa_para_la_igualdad_accesible.pdf

Programa de Intervención con Mujeres. (n.d.). Retrieved October, 15, 2017 from http://www.institucionpenitenciaria.es/web/portal/Reeducacion/ProgramasEspecificos/mujeres.html

Programa Venezolano de Educación-Acción en Derechos Humanos. (2014). *Situación de los Derechos Humanos en Venezuela. Informe Anual Enero-Diciembre 2013*. Derechos de las personas privadas de libertad. Caracas, Venezuela. Pág. 415-432.

Pulido, M. P. (2010). Programs promoting reading in Spanish prisons. *IFLA Journal*, *36*(2), 131–137. doi:10.1177/0340035210369875

Rader, H. B. (1990). Information literacy: A revolution in the library. *Research Quarterly*, *31*(1), 25–29.

Redondo Illescas, S., & Garrido Genovés, V. (2013). *Principios de Criminología* (4th ed.). Valencia: Tirant lo Blanch.

Reisdorf, B. C., & Jewkes, Y. (2016). (B)Locked sites: Cases of Internet use in three British prisons. *Information Communication and Society*, *19*(6), 771–786. doi:10.1080/1369118X.2016.1153124

Republic Act No 10575. (n.d.). Retrieved from http://www.lawphil.net/statutes/repacts/ra2013/ra_10575_2013.html

Reyes, A., Bacani, C., Horch, D., Rienstra, D., & Walter, J. (2016). *World Economic Forum Annual Meeting 2016 Mastering the Fourth Industrial Revolution*. Geneva: World Economic Forum.

Ribbens, W., & Malliet, S. (2015). Exploring the Appeal of Digital Games to Male Prisoners. *Poetics*, *48*, 1–20.

Ríos Martín, J. C., & Cabrera Cabrera, P. J. (1998). *Mil voces presas*. Madrid: Universidad Pontificia de Comillas.

Roberto, J. (2010). Anos 1990-1999. As novas tecnologias. In Visão/Expresso (Ed.), *Os nossos anos* (Vol. 9). Lisboa: Planeta DeAgostini.

Roberts, J. V., & Hough, M. (Eds.). (2002). *Changing Attitudes to Punishment - public opinion, crime and justice*. Devon: Willan Publishing.

Rocha, D. G. S. (2010). *Utilização da Internet nos Estabelecimentos Prisionais Portugueses. Realidade ou Utopia?* Aveiro: Departamento de Comunicação e Arte da Universidade de Aveiro.

Rocha, D. G. S. (2016). *Desenvolvimento de Competências Infocomunicacionais em Contexto Prisional: Proposta de um Modelo de Formação para a Utilização da Internet no Contexto Prisional Português*. Universidade de Aveiro-Portugal.

Rocha, D. G. S., & da Silva, L. J. O. L. (2016). Competências e-infocomunicacionais em contexto prisional: Proposta de um modelo de formação. *Ciência da Informação*, *45*(2), 41–51. http://revista.ibict.br/ciinf/article/view/3800

Rocha, D. G. S., & Oliveira, L. (2014). Informação e comunicação em plataformas digitais: novos desafios para o sistema prisional português. In A. M. da Silva, B. Passarelli, & F. Ramos (Eds.), *e-Infocomunicação - Estratégias e aplicações* (pp. 169–200). São Paulo: Senac; doi:10.13140/RG.2.1.3628.4329

Rodriguez, Gil, & García. (1999). *Metodología de la Investigación Cualitativa* (2nd ed.). Ediciones Aljibe.

Rogers, E. M. (2010). *Diffusion of innovations* (4th ed.). New York: The Free Press.

Rogers, L., Hurry, J., Simonot, M., & Wilson, A. (2014). The aspirations and realities of prison education for under-25s in the London area. *London Review of Education*, *12*(2), 184–196. doi:10.18546/LRE.12.2.04

Rosen, W. (2012). *The Most Powerful Idea in the World: A Story of Steam, Industry and Invention*. Chicago: University of Chicago Press.

Rowlands, I. (1996). Understanding information policy: Concepts, framework and research tools. *Journal of Information Science*, *22*(1), 13–25. doi:10.1177/016555159602200102

Rowlands, I. (1998). Some compass bearing for information policy orienteering. *Aslib Proceedings*, *50*(8), 230–237. doi:10.1108/eb051501

RTL 2. (2016). *Berlin - Tag und Nacht*. Retrieved from http://www.rtl2.de/sendung/berlin-tag-und-nacht

Rubin, A. M. (1984). Ritualized and Instrumental Television Viewing. *Journal of Communication*, *34*(3), 67–77. doi:10.1111/j.1460-2466.1984.tb02174.x

Rudolph, J., Smith, P., & Argall, R. (1996). *The library literate*. Dubuque, IA: Kendall/Hunt.

Ruiz-Mercado, I., Masera, O., Zamora, H., & Smith, K. R. (2011). Adoption and sustained use of improved cookstoves. *Energy Policy*, *39*(12), 7557–7566. doi:10.1016/j.enpol.2011.03.028

Sackett, D. L. (2004). *Evidence Based medicine: How to practice and teach EBM*. London: Churchill Livingstone.

Sahara Reporters. (2017). *Fire Attack on Kuje Prison in Abuja*. Accessed online on 19/9/2017 from http://saharareporters.com/2017/07/21/fire-attack-kuje-prison-abuja

Sandoval, E. (1982). *Penología. Parte General*. Universidad Externado de Colombia.

Sansom, M. (2015, January 28). A digital future for prisons. *GovernmentNews*. Retrieved from https://governmentnews.com.au/2015/01/a-digital-future-for-prisons/

Santos, R. (1999). História das Telecomunicações em Portugal. *Biblioteca on-Line de Ciências Da Comunicação*, 1–11.

Sarkin, J. (2008). Prisons in Africa: An evaluation from a human rights perspective. *Sur. Revista Internacional de Direitos Humanos*, *5*(9), 22–51. doi:10.1590/S1806-64452008000200003

Scharager, J., & Armijo, I. (2001). *Metodología de la Investigación para las Ciencias Sociales* [Research Methodology for the Social Sciences] [CD-ROM]: Versión 1.0. Santiago: Escuela de Psicología, SECICO Pontificia Universidad Católica de Chile.

Schirmer, S. L. (2008). Education Behind Bars. *Current*, *11*(2), 1–128.

Scott, J. C. (2013). *A Dominação e a Arte da Resistência – discursos ocultos*. Lisboa: Letra Livre.

Sedgley, N. H., Scott, C. E., Williams, N. A., & Derrick, F. W. (2010). Prison's Dilemma: Do education and jobs programmes affect recidivism? *Economica*, *77*(307), 497–517. doi:10.1111/j.1468-0335.2008.00751.x

Segundo Pacto Europeo por la Igualdad de Género. (2011-2020). Retrieved October, 15, 2017 from http://eur-lex.europa.eu/LexUriServ/LexUriServ.do?uri=OJ:C:2011:155:0010:0013:ES:PDF

Sennett, R. (2006). *The New Culture of Capitalism*. New Haven, CT: Yale University Press.

Silva, A. M. (2010). Inclusão digital e literacia informacional em Ciência da Informação. *Revista Prisma. Com*, (7).

Simons, H. (2011). *El Estudio de caso: teoría y práctica*. Ediciones Morata, S.L.

Sobel, S. B. (1982). Difficulties Experienced by Women in Prison. *Psychology of Women Quarterly*, *7*(2), 107–118. doi:10.1111/j.1471-6402.1983.tb00823.x

Sollund, R. (2008). Tested Neutrality: Emotional Challenges in Qualitative Interviews on Homicide and Rape. *Journal of Scandinavian Studies in Criminology and Crime Prevention*, *9*(9), 181–201. doi:10.1080/14043850802450138

Statista. (2016a). *Number of monthly active Facebook users worldwide as of 2nd quarter 2016 (in millions)*. Retrieved from https://www.statista.com/statistics/264810/number-of-monthly-active-facebook-users-worldwide/

Statista. (2016b). *Anzahl der Gefangenen und Verwahrten in den Justizvollzugsanstalten in Deutschland nach Bundesländern am 31*. Retrieved from https://de.statista.com/statistik/daten/studie/72216/umfrage/gefangene-und-verwahrte-in-justizvollzugsanstalten-nach-bundeslaendern/

Statista. (2018). *Bevölkerung - Einwohnerzahl in Deutschland nach Geschlecht von 1995 bis 2016 (in 1.000)*. Retrieved from https://de.statista.com/statistik/daten/studie/161868/umfrage/entwicklung-der-gesamtbevoelkerung-nach-geschlecht-seit-1995/

Steiner, M., & Lestigni, V. (2016). Die Telio-Tarifparade! *Lichtblick*, *1*(366), 12–20.

Steurer, S. J., Smith, L., & Tracy, A. (2001). *OCE/CEA Three State Recidivism Study*. Retrieved from http://www.ceanational.org/PDFs/3StateFinal.pdf

Straßmeir, A. (2015). *Antwort über Knasttelefonie von Telio zu teuer*. Berlin: Senatsverwaltung für Justiz und Verbraucherschutz.

Strauss & Corbin. (2002). *Bases de la Investigación Cualitativa. Técnicas y Procedimientos para Desarrollar la Teoría Fundamentada*. Editorial Universidad de Antioquía.

Strauss, A. R., & Corbin, J. M. (2002). *Bases de la investigación cualitativa: Técnicas y procedimientos para desarrollar la teoría* [Basis of qualitative research: Techniques and procedures to develop the theory]. Medellín, Colombia: Universidad de Antioquía.

Sulé, A. (2005). Serveis de dinamització cultural. In *Les biblioteques de presó a Catalunya*. Doctoral dissertation. Retrieved from http://tdx.cat/handle/10803/2901

Sulé, A. (2006, June). Recomanacions de serveis bibliotecaris per a interns. *BiD: textos universitaris de biblioteconomia i documentació*, no. 16. Retrieved from http://bid.ub.edu/16sule.htm

Telio. (2016). *Telio. Innovative Technologien für den Vollzug*. Retrieved from http://www.tel.io/de/

The Condition of Philippine Prison and Jails. (n.d.). Retrieved from http://www.preda.org/media/research-documents/the-condition-of-philippine-prisons-and-jails/

The Nation. (2017a). *How Ikoyi prison inmates fared in UTME*. Accessed online on 19/9/2017 http://thenationonlineng.net/ikoyi-prison-inmates-fared-utme/

The Nation. (2017b). *322 prisons inmates registered for WASSCE*. Accessed online on 19/9/2017 from http://thenationonlineng.net/322-prisons-inmates-registered-for-wassce/

The Nigerian Expression. (2017). *22 inmates in Jos register for examination*. Accessed online on 19/9/2017 from http://thenigerianexpression.com/2017/08/12/22-inmates-in-jos-register-for-examination/

Therborn, G. (2006). Meaning, Mechanisms, Patterns and Forces: an Introduction. In G. Therborn (Ed.), *Inequalities of the World – New Theoretical Frameworks, Multiple empirical approaches* (pp. 1–58). London: Verso.

Tighe, S. (2016, April 22). Prisoners allowed access to adult films and internet. *BBC News*. Retrieved from http://www.bbc.com/news/world-europe-36067653

Tocino Hernández, C. M. (2014). Internet en la cárcel. In *Sistema penitenciario y nuevas tecnologías* (pp. 29–43). Valladolid: Lex Artis.

Travis, J., Solomon, A. L., & Waul, S. (2001). *From prison to home – The dimensions and consequences of prisoner re-entry*. Retrieved from https://www.urban.org/research/publication/prison-home-dimensions-and-consequences-prisoner-reentry/view/full_report

Tronbacke, B. (2010). *Guidelines for easy-to-read materials.* Revision by Misako Nomura, Gyda Skat Nielsen and Bror Tronbacke on behalf of the IFLA/Library Services to People with Special Needs Section. The Hague: International Federation of Library Associations and Institutions. Retrieved from http://ifla.org/files/assets/hq/publications/professional-report/120.pdf

Tselios, V., McCann, P., & van Dijk, J. (2017). Understanding the gap between reality and expectation: Local social engagement and ethnic concentration. *Urban Studies (Edinburgh, Scotland), 54*(11), 2592–2612. doi:10.1177/0042098016650395

Tselios, V., Noback, I., Dijk, J., & McCann, P. (2015). Integration of immigrants, bridging social capital, ethnicity, and locality. *Journal of Regional Science, 55*(3), 416–441. doi:10.1111/jors.12160

Tsend-Ayush, G. (2017). The Impact of Information and Communication Technologies on Prison Institutions. *Hadmernok, 12*(1), 278–289.

Tyler, J. H., & Kling, J. R. (2002). *What is the Value of a Prison GED?* Unpublished, Brown University. Retrieved from http://users.nber.org/~kling/PrisonGED.pdf

Tynan, D. (2016, October 3). Online behind bars: if internet access is a human right, should prisoners have it? *The Guardian.* Retrieved from https://www.theguardian.com/us-news/2016/oct/03/prison-internet-access-tablets-edovo-jpay

Uche, I. B., Uche, O. A., Ezumah, N. N., Ebue, M. O., Okafor, A. E., & Ezegbe, B. N. (2015). Effectiveness of Rehabilitation Programmes in the Nigerian Prisons: A Study of Perception of Inmates in Enugu Prison. *Mediterranean Journal of Social Sciences, 6*(S2), 164-170.

Ugwumba, N. C. F., & Usang, E. E. (2014). The challenges of rehabilitation and reintegration of ex-convicts from Nigerian prisons. *Journal of Science, Engineering and Technology, 3*(2), 59–64.

Unión Europea Decisión N° 1720/2006/CE del Parlamento Europeo y del Consejo de 15 de noviembre de 2006, por la que se establece un programa de acción en el ámbito del aprendizaje permanente. Diario Oficial de la Unión Europea, 24/11/2006. (n.d.). Retrieved October, 15, 2017 from http://europa.eu/legislation_summaries/education_training_youth/general_framework/c11082_es .htm

Unión Europea. (1997). *Tratado de Ámsterdam.* Retrieved October, 15, 2017 from http://www.europarl.europa.eu/topics/treaty/pdf/amst-es.pdf

United Nations General Assembly. (2011). *Report of the Special Rapporteur on the promotion and protection of the right to freedom of opinion and expression.* Human Rights Council of the General Assembly of the United Nations. Retrieved from http://www2.ohchr.org/english/bodies/hrcouncil/docs/17session/A.HRC.17.27_en.pdf

United Nations Office on Drugs and Crime. (2015). *The United Nations Standard Minimum Rules for the Treatment of Prisoners (the Nelson Mandela Rules): An updated blueprint for prison management in the 21st century.* Accessed on 20/09/2017 from https://www.unodc.org/documents/justice-and-prison-reform/Brochure_on_the_UN_SMRs.pdf

United Nations. (1990). *UN basic principle for treatment of prison inmates* (Resolution 45/III). UN.

Valente, T. W., & Rogers, E. M. (1995). The origins and development of the diffusion of innovations paradigm as an example of scientific growth. *Science Communication*, *16*(3), 242–273. doi:10.1177/1075547095016003002 PMID:12319357

Van Voorhis, P., Lee Browning, S., Simon, M., & Gordon, J. (1997). The Meaning of Punishment: Inmates' Orientation to the Prison Experience. *The Prison Journal*, *77*(2), 135–167. doi:10.1177/0032855597077002003

Vandebosch, H. (2001). Media Use as an Adaptation or Coping Tool in Prison. *Communications*, *4*(26), 371–387.

Vanguard. (2017a). *22 inmates of Jos prison adult education scheme register for examination.* Accessed online on 19/9/2017 from https://www.vanguardngr.com/2017/08/22-inmates-jos-prison-adult-education-scheme-register-examination/

Vanguard. (2017b). *Kaduna Prison trains 60 inmates in tailoring, ICT.* Accessed online on 19/9/2017 https://www.dailytrust.com.ng/news/general/kaduna-prison-trains-60-inmates-in-tailoring-ict/180008.html

Vieira, J. (2001). Crónica em imagens 1990-2000. In J. Vieira (Ed.), *Portugal Século XX* (Vol. 10). Lisboa: Círculo de Leitores;

Villagra, C. (2008). Reinserción: Lecciones para una Política Pública. *Revista Debates Penitenciarios, 6*, 3-18.

Vogel, B. (2009). *The Prison Library Primer. A Program for the Twenty-First Century*. London: The Scarecrow Press.

Vogel, B. (2009). *The Prison Library Primer: A Program for the Twenty-First Century*. Plymouth: Scarecrow Press, Inc.

Wacquant, L. (2016, October). *The puzzling return of prisons in the 21st Century*. Paper presented at the meeting of Ordem dos Advogados, Lisboa, Portugal.

Wacquant, L. (2000). *As Prisões da Miséria*. Oeiras: Celta.

Wacquant, L. (2001). Moralisme et panoptisme punitif - La chasse aux délinquants sexuels aux États-Unis. *Sociologie et Sociétés*, *33*, 139–157.

Walker, R. (1983). La realización de estudios de casos en Educación. Ética, teoría y procedimientos. In W. Dockrell & D. Hamilton (Eds.), *Nuevas reflexiones sobre la investigación educativa* (pp. 48–82). Madrid: Narcea.

Wall, D. S. (2017). Crime, security and information communication technologies: The changing cybersecurity threat landscape and its implications for regulation and policing. In R. Brownsword, E. Scotford, & K. Yeung (Eds.), *The Oxford Handbook of Law, Regulation and Technology* (pp. 1076–23). Oxford University Press. doi:10.2139srn.3005872

Walmsley, R. (2015). *World Female Imprisonment List* (3rd ed.). London: Institute for Criminal Policy Research.

Walmsley, R. (2016). *World Prison Population List* (11th ed.). London: Institute for Criminal Policy Research.

Walsham, G. (2012). Are we making a better world with ICTs? Reflections on a future agenda for the IS field. *Journal of Information Technology*, *27*(2), 87–93. doi:10.1057/jit.2012.4

Ware, N. C., Hopper, K., Tugenberg, T., Dickey, B., & Fisher, D. (2008). A theory of social integration as quality of life. *Psychiatric Services (Washington, D.C.)*, *59*(1), 27–33. doi:10.1176/ps.2008.59.1.27 PMID:18182536

Warschauer, M. (2003). *Technology and Social inclusion: Rethinking the digital divide*. Cambridge, MA: MIT Press.

Warschauer, M. (2004). *Technology and social inclusion: Rethinking the digital divide*. Cambridge, MA: MIT Press.

Warschauer, M. (2006). *Tecnologia e inclusão social: a exclusão digital em debate*. São Paulo: Editora Senac.

Weber, M. (2005). *Protestant Ethic and the Spirit of Capitalism*. London: Routledge.

Webster, C. A., Caputi, P., Perreault, M., Doan, R., Doutis, P., & Weaver, R. G. (2013). Elementary classroom teachers' adoption of physical activity promotion in the context of a statewide policy: An innovation diffusion and socio-ecologic perspective. *Journal of Teaching in Physical Education*, *32*(4), 419–440. doi:10.1123/jtpe.32.4.419

Weinrath, M. (2016). *Behind the walls. Inmates and Correctional Officers on the State of Canadian Prisons*. Vancouver: UBC Press.

Weissman, M., Cregor, M., Gainsborough, J., Kief, N., Leone, P., & Sullivan, E. (2008). *The right to education in the juvenile and criminal justice systems in the United States. Dignity in Schools Campaign*. Retrieved from https://www.aclu.org/files/images/asset_upload_file164_38663.pdf

Wexler, H. K., Melnick, G., Lowe, L., & Peters, J. (1999). Three-year Reincarceration Outcomes for In-prison Therapeutic Community and Aftercare in California. *The Prison Journal*, *79*(3), 321–336. doi:10.1177/0032885599079003003

Wexler, J., Pyle, N., Flower, A., Williams, J. L., & Cole, H. (2014). A Synthesis of Academic Interventions for Incarcerated Adolescents. *Review of Educational Research*, *84*(1), 3–46. doi:10.3102/0034654313499410

Widmann, M. (2015). *Neues von der Anstalt*. Retrieved from http://www.zeit.de/2015/40/hamburg-gefaengnis-hahnoefersand

Williams, N. (n.d.). 1974/1984. In *Cronologia Enciclopédica do Mundo Moderno* (Vol. 8). Lisboa: Círculo de Leitores;

Woodiwiss, M. (1988). *Crime, Crusades and Corruption - Prohibitions in the United States, 1900-1987*. London: Piter Publisher.

Woodiwiss, M. (2001). *Organized Crime and American Power: A History*. Toronto: University of Toronto Press.

World Prison Brief Data. (2017). *Nigeria*. Accessed on 14/09/2017 from http://www.prisonstudies.org/country/nigeria

Yagüe, C. (2012). Políticas de Género y prisión en España. In Condenadas desigualdad: sistema de indicadores de discriminación penitenciaria. Icaria editorial.

Yuan, E. (2011). New Consumption across multiple Media Platforms. *Information Communication and Society*, *14*(7), 998–1016. doi:10.1080/1369118X.2010.549235

Zgoba, K. M., Haugebrook, S., & Jenkins, K. (2008). The influence of GED obtainment on inmate release outcome. *Criminal Justice and Behavior*, *35*(3), 375–387. doi:10.1177/0093854807311853

Zimbardo, P. (2007). *The Lucifer Effect: understanding how good people turn evil*. Random House.

Zino, J., & Martín, E. (2012, March). La utilización de las narrativas digitales como factor de empoderamiento en el ámbito penitenciario. *International Conference Digital Storytelling*. Retrieved from http://roderic.uv.es/handle/10550/25600

Zwischenbericht des Senats. (2016). *Gemeinsamer Zwischenbericht zum Ausbau der Kooperation auf dem Gebiet des Strafvollzuges*. Hamburg: Author.

About the Contributors

Lídia Oliveira has a degree in Philosophy from the University of Coimbra (1990), a Master's degree in Educational Technology from the University of Aveiro, in partnership with the University of Valenciennes (France) and Mons (Belgium) (1995), and a PhD in Sciences and Technologies of Communication from the University of Aveiro (2002). She has been a professor in the Department of Communication and Art (http://www.ua.pt) at the University of Aveiro since 1995 until the present. Her main scientific interest is in cyberculture studies and social network analysis. Her areas of interest are: Science and Technologies of Communication, ICT and Education, Multimedia, Social Network Analysis, Cyberculture Studies, Sociology of Communication, Information Systems, Digital Libraries, Time Studies, Science Communication, Communication in the Scientific Community (theoretical and empirical studies). She has published both nationally and internationally in peer review journals, book chapters and, conferences proceedings.

* * *

Janet Aver Adikpo is a Ph.D candidate at the Faculty of Communication and Media Studies, Eastern Mediterranean University, Famagusta, Cyprus.

Ignacio Aguaded-Gómez is Professor of Education and Communication at the University of Huelva. He is president of the Comunicar Group, a veteran collective in Spain in "Media Literacy". Director of the Research Group "Agora" within the Andalusian Research Plan (HUM-648), Editor of the scientific journal JCR/Scopus "Comunicar", Director of the International Master's Degree in Communication and Education (UNIA/UHU) and UHU coordinator of the Inter-University Programme of Doctorate in Communication (US, UMA, UCA, UHU).

Mª Antonia Agúndez Soriano (Madrid, Spain, 1961). Doctor of Documentation (2016). Qualification "CUM LAUDE" extraordinary prize. In 2011 he participated in several seminars, within the framework of the activities carried out by the research group ALFINBRASIL. From 2011 to 2017 he participated in several Hispano-Brazilian Research, Documentation and Society seminars. In 2012 and 2016 she participated as a table moderator in the I and II Interuniversity Seminar of students of ALFIN of the UCM and the University of Brasilia. In 2017 he gave a conference on social inclusion of women prisoners and information literacy. Currently Professor-Doctor in the University College of Financial Studies and library assistant in the same center. His research focuses on information literacy and social inclusion.

Paloma Contreras-Pulido is Journalist and Social Educator. PhD in educommunication from the University of Huelva. Professor at the University of Huelva in "Media, social control and critical consciousness" which belongs to degree of Social Education and Professor to degree of Primary Education (TIC in Primary Education). Professor in several official Masters as "Audiovisual Communication and Education"; Máster "Radio" in Radio Television Española and "Journalism" in Francisco de Vitoria University. Nowadays teaches for "Interuniversity Doctorate in Communication". Is member of Comunicar Group and Scientific Reviewer of Journal Comunicar. Member of Alfamed (Euro-American InterUniversity Network for Research on Media Literacy for Citizenship).

Aurora Cuevas Cerveró has a PhD Library and Information Science. Post-doctorate at the University of Brasilia. Degree in Philosophy and Education Sciences. Professor and researcher at the Complutense University of Madrid. Co-director of the international information literacy research group, University of Brasilia, in which 25 researchers from Ibero-American universities participate. Research lines: Information literacy, social inclusion, digital inclusion, library and society, reading, educational libraries, and citizenship.

António Dores, PhD, Professor of Sociology and fellow researcher at Instituto Universitário de Lisboa (ISCTE-IUL). Born in 1956, he is founder member of Human Rights NGO concerning prison issues, built by inmates in Portugal, since 1997 till 2016, ACED http://iscte.pt/~apad/ACED. He wrote several book, and coauthor Prisons in Europe; Vozes contra o silêncio – movimentos sociais nas prisões portuguesas, and Segredos das Prisões, books about prisons.

Carmen Rocío Fernández Díaz is a Doctor in Law, Masters in Criminal Law and Criminal Policy and Expert in Criminality and Publich Security. Lecturer and researcher in Criminal Law and Criminology in the Univesity of Malaga (Spain) and in the International University of Andalucia (UNIA). Co-director of the Master's degree in Private Detective of the Andalusian Interuniversity Institute of Criminology. She has several national and international scientific publications related with her research lines, which are: socioeconomic delinquency, cybercrime, penitentiary law and sex crimes. She has done research stays at renowned international institutions such as the University of Modena (Italy), the Max Planck Institute for International and Foreign Criminal Law (Germany) and the University of Suffolk (Boston, USA) and she has also participated in numerous scientific conferences in Spain and abroad. She was awarded with the first prize of the XVII edition (2018) of the legal articles contest "García Goyena" of the UNED and second prize Dorado Montero, in the 2011 edition, of the University of Salamanca. She is also performing currently legal advice tasks for the European Commission as an expert for Spain.

Leandra Carolina Flor is a PhD candidate in Development Communication at the Universtiy of the Philippines Los Baños, and currently doing her dissertation. She has worked in Lao People's Democratic Republic as Communication Specialist for various international aid agencies and project areas such as FAO and UNICEF. She also worked in Singapore as a research associate with Nanyang Technological University. Her latest stint was a UN Volunteer posting for a Governance project under UNDP and the Government of Lao PDR.

Jorge Franganillo is Professor of Library and Information Science at the University of Barcelona. PhD in Information and Communication. Member of the Research Center on Information, Communication and Culture. Participating in a number of research projects as a member of several research teams and teaching innovation groups.

Ana Melro has a Ph.D. in Information and Communication in Digital Platforms, from University of Aveiro and University of Porto (2013). A master degree in Sociology and a degree in Sociology (2004), from University of Minho.

Peter Iorper Ugondo lectures mass communication and journalism at the Department of Mass Communication, Kwarafa University, Wukari, Taraba State, Nigeria.

Bettina Zbinden is a researcher and journalist born in Switzerland in the year 1990. She completed her Bachelor's degree in Media Studies and Cultural Anthropology at the University of Basel, Switzerland. She took part in the Erasmus Mundus Master's program in Media, Journalism and Globalization, where she received a joint Master's degree at the University of Aarhus, Denmark and the University of Hamburg, Germany. Her master thesis was dedicated to the social relationships and the media use of female prisoners in Germany.

Index

www.ingramcontent.com/pod-product-compliance
Ingram Content Group UK Ltd.
Pitfield, Milton Keynes, MK11 3LW, UK
UKHW050947290926
15470UKWH00005B/1692

9 781522 559757